Exam AZ-100 Study & Lab Guide
Microsoft Azure Infrastructure and Deployment

Harinder Kohli

This edition has been published by arrangement with **Kindle Direct Publishing**.

ISBN
ISBN: 9781794486423

Edition: 1st Edition, January 2019

You never know what you can do till you try
William Cobbett

Contents at a Glance

Contents

Backup scenarios with Azure Backup
Architecture of Azure Backup using Azure Backup Agent
Architecture of Azure Backup using System Center Data Protection Manager
Architecture of Azure Backup using Azure Backup Server
Azure IaaS VM Backup
Backup Reports

Azure AD Introduction
Default Azure AD Domain
Azure AD Basic & Premium License upgrade options
Azure AD Users
Azure AD Groups
Custom Domains
Self Service Password Reset (SSPR)
Azure AD Join
Azure AD Conditional Access
Azure AD Identity Protection
Managing Multiple Azure AD Directories

Azure AD Hybrid Identity options with AD Connect
Components of AD Connect
Requirements for deploying AD Connect Server
AD Connect with Federation with ADFS option
Seamless Single Sign-on
Password Writeback

Azure Subscription
Subscription Usage & Quota
Cost or Spend Analysis
Monitor Azure Spend and Create Billing Alarms using Budgets
Identify unused or underutilized Resources and Optimize Azure Cost
Implementing IT Governance using Azure Policy
Assign Administrative Permissions using Azure AD Directory Role
Assigning Administrative Permissions using Role Based Access Control

Lab Exercises

Chapter 1 Virtual Networks
1. Create Resource Group HKPortal using Azure Portal
2. Create Virtual Network using Portal
3. Create additional Subnet (DB-Subnet 10.1.2.0/24)
4. Create additional Subnet (DMZ-Subnet 10.1.3.0/24)
5. Create Gateway Subnet 10.1.5.0/24
6. Create Virtual Network representing On-Premises Network
7. Create Gateway Subnet 192.168.3.0/24
8. Create Virtual Network VNETPortal2
9. Create Virtual Network VNETPortal3
10. Create Dynamic Public IP
11. Changing Dynamic Public IP to Static IP
12. Create NSG and add inbound http and RDP allow rule
13. Associate Network Security Group (NSG) with Subnet
14. DNS Zone, DNS Records and Delegation to Azure DNS
15. Connecting Virtual Networks using S2S VPN
16. Peering between VNETs VNETPortal & VNETPortal2
17. Peering between VNETs VNETPortal & VNETPortal3
18. Routing Traffic between 2 Subnets to pass through another Subnet using UDR

Chapter 2 Implementing Virtual Networks with CLI & PS
19. Create Resource Group HKCLI using Azure CLI
20. Create Resource Group HKPS using Azure PowerShell
21. Create Virtual Network VNETCLI using Azure CLI
22. Create Virtual Network VNETPS using Azure PowerShell

Deploy and Manage Virtual Machines (VMs)
23. Create Availability Set (AS) using Azure Portal
24. Create Windows Virtual Machine using Azure Portal
25. Log on to Windows VM with RDP
26. Install IIS and Access default Website
27. Connecting to Default IIS website on wvmportal VM
28. Add Data Disk
29. Initialize the Data Disk
30. Create and Add Network Interface to VM wvmportal
31. Create Snapshot of VM wvmportal OS Hard Disk
32. Create Windows VM representing On-Premises AD DS
33. Enable AD DS Role in Virtual Machine OnPremAD

34. Create Linux VM
35. Connecting to Linux VM
36. Update Linux VM & Install NGINX Web Server
37. Create Custom Image of Azure VM
38. Deploy VM from Custom image
39. Demonstrating various VM Extensions available
40. Demonstrating Custom Script Extension using Azure Portal
41. Resizing VM
42. Virtual Machine Auto-Shutdown
43. Reset Password
44. Redeploy

Chapter 4 Deploy Virtual Machines with CLI and PS
45. Create Windows Server 2016 VM using Azure CLI
46. Create Windows Server 2016 VM using Azure PowerShell

Chapter 5 Deploy Virtual Machines Scale Sets (VMSS)
47. Deploying VMSS
48. Connecting to Instances in VMSS
49. Enabling Autoscaling

Chapter 6 Implement and Manage Storage Accounts
50. Create GPv2 Standard Storage Account using Portal
51. Create GPv2 Premium Storage Account
52. Demonstrating Storage Account sastdportal functionalities
53. Demonstrating Storage Account Security
54. Setting up Virtual Network Service Endpoints
55. Connect to Azure Storage using Azure Account Credentials
56. Get Storage Account sastdportal Access Keys
57. Connect to Storage Account sastdportal using Access key
58. Generate Shared Access Signature of Storage Account
59. Connect to Storage Account using Shared Access Signature

Chapter 7 Storage Accounts with CLI and PS
60. Create Storage Account Using CLI
61. Create Storage Account Using PowerShell

Chapter 8 Implement and Manage Storage
62. Create Blob Storage Container and upload a File
63. Blob Storage Tiering
64. Create Blob Storage Container using Storage Explorer

65. Creating and using File Share
66. Deploying Azure File Sync in 4 Steps
67. Demonstrating Export Job Creation
68. Demonstrating Data Box Order through Azure Portal
69. Implementing Azure CDN using Azure Portal
70. Enabling or Disabling Compression
71. Changing Optimization type
72. Changing Caching Rules
73. Allow or Block CDN in Specific Countries

Chapter 9 Implement Storage with CLI and PowerShell
74. Create Blob Storage Container using Azure CLI
75. Create Blob Storage Container using PowerShell

Chapter 10 Implement Azure Backup
76. Create Recovery Services Vault
77. Backup Files & Folder using Azure Backup Agent
78. Azure VM-level backup
79. Restoring Azure VM-level backup
80. Create Custom Backup Policy
81. Associating Custom Policy with VM wvmportal Backup Job

Chapter 11 Implementing and Managing Azure AD
82. Exploring Dashboard of Default Azure AD
83. Activating Premium P2 Free Trial Licenses
84. Create User (User1 with Global Administrator Role)
85. Create User (User2 with Limited Administrator Role)
86. Create User (User3 with Directory Role User)
87. Exploring Dashboard of User
88. Checking User3 Access level
89. Create Group and add users manually
90. Assigning Azure AD Premium P2 License to Users
91. Create Test Group and add users
92. Add Custom Domain
93. Create TXT record in Domain Name Registrar
94. Verify the Custom Domain in Azure AD
95. Change Azure AD Login names to custom domain for User2
96. Enabling SSPR for Cloud Users (User2 & User3)
97. Setup SSPR Authentications for User3
98. Test SSPR for User3

Chapter 14 Azure Resource Groups, Tags and Locks

134.   Create Resource Group HKTest
135.   Applying Azure Policy at Resource Group Level
136.   Test the Allowed storage accounts SKU Policy
137.   Move resources to new resource group
138.   Create Tag with name Mktg for VM wvmportal
139.   Create Tag with name Mktg for VM wvmportal OS Disk
140.   Find Cost of Resources Associated with Mktg
141.   Create CanNotDelete Lock on VM wvmportal
142.   Test the Lock

Chapter 15 Analyzing & Monitoring Azure Resources

143.   Accessing & Exploring Monitor Dashboard
144.   Accessing Activity Log from a Monitor Dashboard
145.   Accessing Activity Log from a Resource Dashboard
146.   Creating Alert on Activity Log
147.   Accessing Diagnostic Log from the Monitor Dashboard
148.   Enabling Diagnostic Logs for Recovery Services Vault
149.   Enabling Guest OS Diagnostic Logs in VM wvmportal
150.   Virtual Machine Percentage CPU Metrics
151.   Storage Account Used Capacity Metrics
152.   Accessing Metric from Resource (VM) Dashboard
153.   Create Action Group
154.   Create an alert on Metric (Percentage CPU)
155.   Accessing Alert from Resource (VM) Dashboard
156.   Monitoring IIS Web Server with Log Analytics
157.   Connect VM OnPremAD to Log Analytics
158.   Installing Management Agent (AD Heath Check)
159.   Installing Microsoft Monitoring Agent in On-Premises VM
160.   Checking Advisor Recommendations
161.   Checking Service Health Events
162.   Configuring Alerts for Service Health Events

Chapter 16 Azure Automation

163.   Create Automation Account
164.   Desired State Configuration (DSC) using Azure Automation
165.   PowerShell DSC Extension
166.   Enabling Update Management and Add Azure VM
167.   Scheduling Update Deployment
168.   Enabling Inventory Management and Add VM wvmportal
169.   Checking Change Tracking for VM wvmportal

Introduction

Exam AZ-100: Microsoft Azure Infrastructure and Deployment is targeted towards Azure Administrators who can implement and Administer Hybrid Cloud Solutions using Azure Services. AZ-100 Exam focuses on Infrastructure Topics such as Virtual Servers, Networks, Storage, Azure Active Directory, Azure CDN, Hybrid Solutions, Subscription Management, Monitoring and Azure Automation Solutions.

One of the key success points to pass the exam is to work with Azure portal and practice configuring various Azure services.

Exam AZ-100 Study & lab Guide helps you prepare for AZ-100 Exam. It contains Topic lessons & Lab Exercises. Students will create a Hybrid Topology as they progress through Chapter labs.

The twin focus of this book is to get your fundamental on Azure Services on strong footing and to prepare you to implement and Administer Azure Cloud solutions through hands on Lab Exercises.

Best of Luck for AZ-100 Exam.

I would be pleased to hear your feedback and thoughts on the book. Please comment on Amazon or mail to: harinder-kohli@outlook.com.

Harinder Kohli

Contact Author

Email: harinder-kohli@outlook.com
Linkedin: www.linkedin.com/in/harinderkohli
Azure Blog @ https://mykloud.wordpress.com

Download TOC, Topologies and Sample Chapter from Box.com

https://app.box.com/s/dxprgdapyigrdwq14ieabmzyefsmppuv

Errata & Updates

Information about Book Errata & Updates will be published at following link
@ Box.com.
https://app.box.com/s/w6us8dkpl0oezwrs2xezirwmn5aacslc

Topologies

Main Topology

We will create 4 Virtual Networks – VNETPortal, VNETOnPrem, VNETPortal2 & VNETPortal3 as shown below.

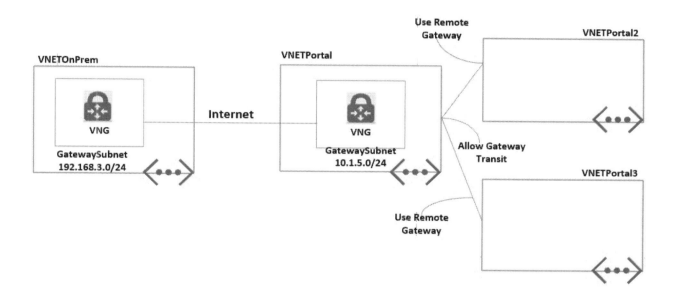

Virtual Network **VNETOnPrem** will represent on-premises Datacentre.

We will connect VNETPortal and VNETOnPrem using Virtual Network Gateway and S2S VPN over Internet connectivity.

We will connect VNETPortal to VNETPortal2 & VNETPortal3 using Virtual Network Peering. The peering connectivity will be over Azure Backbone Network.

VNETPortal Topology

Virtual Network VNETPortal will be our main Virtual Networks for all labs in all the Chapters.

We will create below Topology using Virtual Network VNETPortal. It will have Four Subnets – Web-Subnet, DB-Subnet, DMZ-Subnet and GatewaySubnet. DMZ-Subnet and GatewaySubnet are not shown because of space constraint.

Students will create the topology as they progress through Chapter Labs.

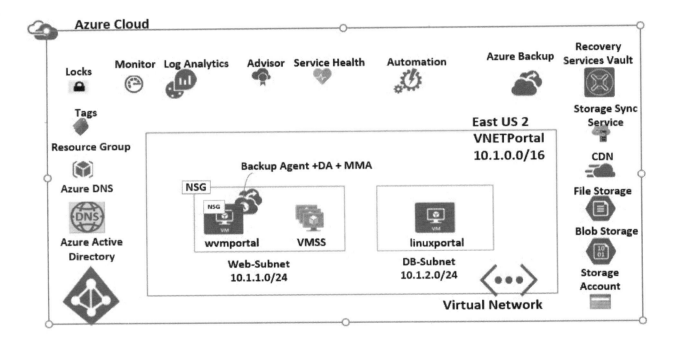

Virtual Machine wvmportal will be our main VM for all the Labs in the book.

Most of the Resources in this topology were created in Resource Group HKPortal. Azure Portal was used to create resources in this topology.

VNETOnPrem Topology

Virtual Network **VNETOnPrem** will represent on-premises Datacentre.

We will create below Topology using Virtual Network VNETOnPrem. It will have two Subnets – OnPrem-Subnet and GatewaySubnet.

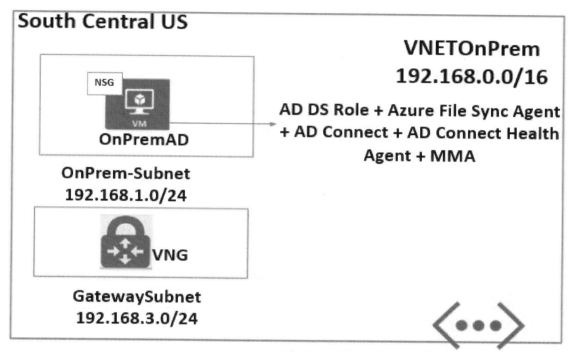

Virtual Machine OnPremAD will be created in Virtual Network VNETOnPrem. Following will be installed or enabled on Virtual Machine OnPremAD.

Active Directory Domain services (AD DS) role
Azure File Sync Agent
Azure AD Connect
AD Connect Health Agent
Microsoft Monitoring Agent (MMA)

Resources in this topology were created in Resource Group OnPrem.
Azure Portal was used to create resources in this topology.

Lab Exercises using Azure CLI and PowerShell

Labs in Chapter 2, 4, 7 & 9 are done using Azure CLI and PowerShell. I used Azure CLI and Azure PowerShell Installed on my desktop.

Readers are requested to go through **Chapter 18 Installing Azure PowerShell Module & Azure CLI** before proceeding with labs using Azure CLI and PowerShell.

All Lab resources using Azure CLI were created in Resource Group HKCLI and Virtual Network VNETCLI.
All Lab resources using Azure PowerShell were created in Resource Group HKPS and Virtual Network VNETPS.

I did these labs separately from Lab exercises using Azure Portal. Readers can proceed as per their comfort factor with Azure CLI and PowerShell.

Lab Requirements & Tricks

Browser Requirements for Lab Exercises

You will require 3 Browsers for completing Lab Activities. I used following Browser options for completing lab activities.

1. **Chrome Browser** was my main Browser. I used it with Subscription User. This was the user with which I signed for Azure Subscription.
2. **Firefox Browser** was used with users created in Azure AD.
3. **TOR Browser** was used to simulate suspicious locations or IP Addresses. This was used in Conditional Access and Identity Protection Labs.

Custom Domain Requirement for Lab Exercises

I used domain **mykloud.in**. This was used in 2 Exercises – Azure DNS and Add Custom Domain in Azure AD. I purchased it for around USD 9.

Subscription type used

I started with Free Trial Subscription and after 1 Month converted it to Pay as you go Subscription. In lab Exercises you will find both free trial Subscription and Pay as you go Subscription. Both are actually same Subscription.

How to Save Azure Credits

1. Stop the Virtual Machine in Azure Portal if you are not using it. This will save you lot of money.
2. Remember Log Analytics and Diagnostic logs (Compute) consume lot of credits. Do these Exercises in the end.

How to go to Resource Dashboard

In lab Exercises I will just tell you to go resource dashboard but will not explain how to go. Read below on how to go to Resource Dashboard.

How to go to Resource Dashboard: Preferred Approach

In Azure Portal click the resource type in left pane. For Example if you have to go Virtual Machine or Storage Account or Resource Group Dashboard click the Virtual Machines or Storage Account or Resource Group in left pane and select your Resource in Right pane.

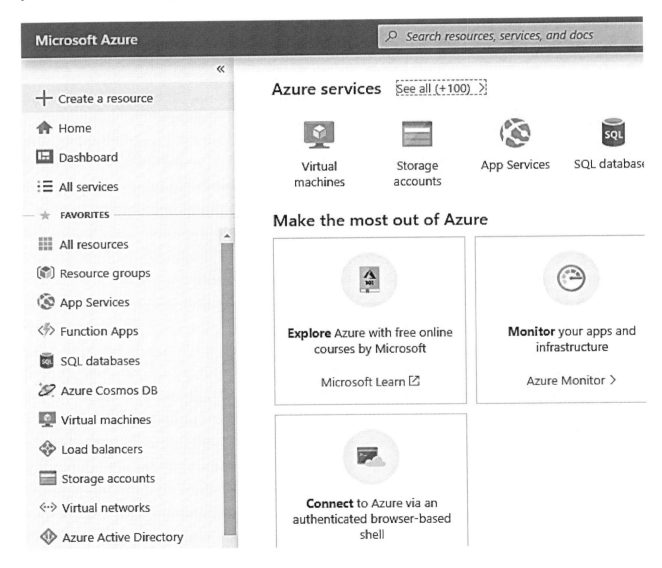

How to go to Resource Dashboard: Option 2

You will not find certain Resources like Azure Automation or Azure DNS etc in left pane in Azure Portal. Click All Resources in left pane. This will show all Resources which you have created till now. Click your resource to go to dashboard.

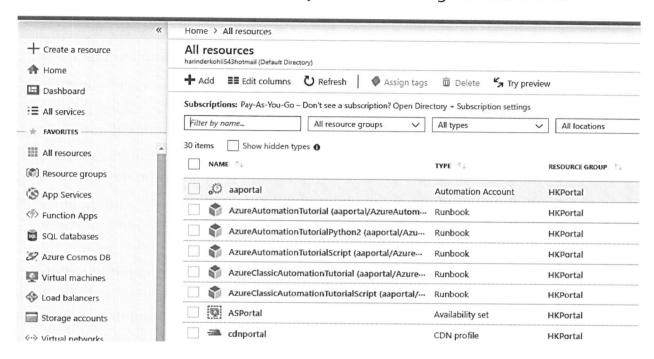

How to go to Resource Dashboard: Option 3

In Azure Portal Click All Services in left pane> In right pane select your resource type. This will open pane for that Resource type. Select your resource to go to its dashboard.

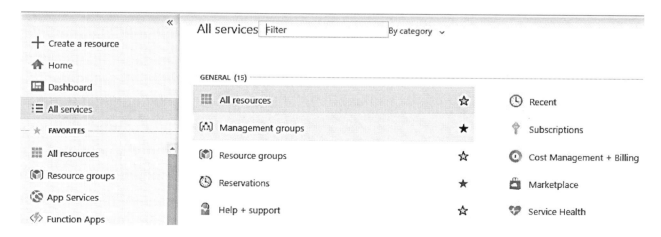

Chapter 1 Virtual Networks

This Chapter covers following Topic Lessons

- Virtual Networks
- Public IP Addresses in Azure
- Private IP Addresses
- Network Security Groups
- Azure DNS
- Virtual Network Gateway
- Virtual Networks Peering
- Routing within VNET using System Route
- Routing within VNET using User Defined Route (UDR)

This Chapter covers following Lab Exercises

- Create Resource Group HKPortal using Azure Portal
- Create Virtual Network using Portal
- Create additional Subnet (DB-Subnet 10.1.2.0/24)
- Create additional Subnet (DMZ-Subnet 10.1.3.0/24)
- Create Gateway Subnet 10.1.5.0/24
- Create Virtual Network representing On-Premises Network
- Create Gateway Subnet 192.168.3.0/24
- Create Virtual Network VNETPortal2
- Create Virtual Network VNETPortal3
- Create Dynamic Public IP
- Changing Dynamic Public IP to Static IP
- Create NSG and add inbound http and RDP allow rule
- Associate Network Security Group (NSG) with Subnet
- DNS Zone, DNS Records and Delegation to Azure DNS
- Connecting Virtual Networks using S2S VPN
- Peering between VNETs VNETPortal & VNETPortal2
- Peering between VNETs VNETPortal & VNETPortal3
- Routing Traffic between 2 Subnets to pass through another Subnet using UDR

Chapter Topology

In this chapter we will create 4 Virtual Networks – VNETPortal, VNETOnPrem, VNETPortal2 & VNETPortal3. VNETPortal will be our main Virtual Network for all labs in all the Chapters. In some labs we will also use VNETOnPrem.

In This Chapter we will create below Topology using Virtual Network VNETPortal. We will create 4 Subnets. We will add Azure DNS & Resource Group to the topology. Default Azure AD is created when you sign for Azure subscription.

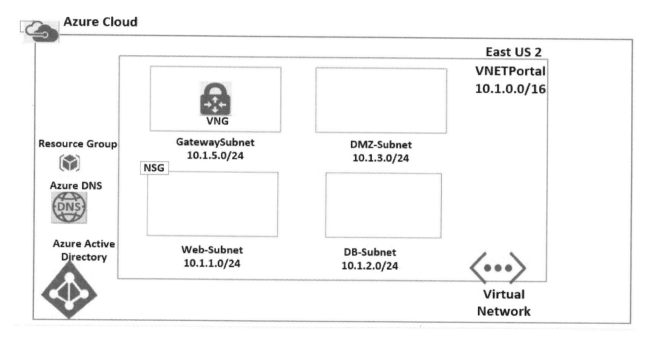

Figure below shows Topology for Virtual Network VNETOnPrem. We will create 2 Subnet. There was lack of space in above figure so I am showing it separately.

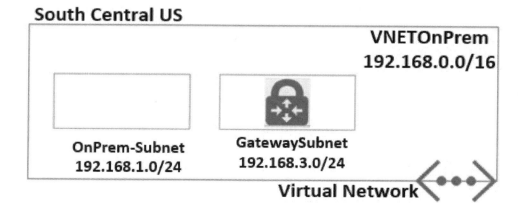

Following Topology will be used in Virtual Network gateway and VNET Peering Labs.

In Exercise 15 we will connect VNETPortal and VNETOnPrem using Virtual Network Gateway and S2S VPN over Internet connectivity.

In Exercise 16 we will do peering between VNETPortal and VNETPortal2.
In Exercise 17 we will do peering between VNETPortal and VNETPortal3.
The peering connectivity will be over Azure Backbone Network.

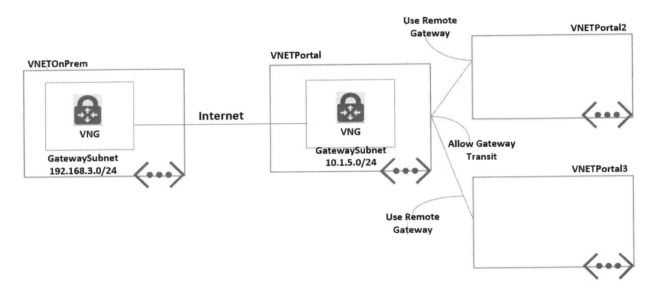

Virtual Networks (VNET)

An Azure virtual network (VNET) is Virtual Data Centre in the cloud. Virtual Network is further segmented into subnets. Access to the subnets can be controlled using Network Security groups. Virtual Machines are created in Subnets.

End customers create Virtual Networks. End customers define the IP address blocks, security policies, and route tables within this network.

Figure below shows virtual network KNET1 with 2 subnets – Web-Subnet and DB-Subnet. There are 3 virtual machines in these subnets.
End customer has defined Network address of 192.168.0.0/16 for virtual network KNET1, 192.168.1.0/24 for Web-Subnet and 192.168.2.0/24 for DB-Subnet.

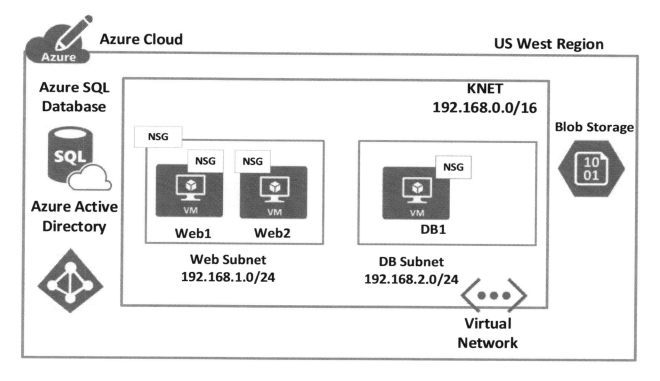

Virtual Network is created by the customer. Resources within Virtual Network are created and managed by end customers. Whereas Resources outside of VNET (Azure SQL, Azure AD etc) are Azure Managed Resources with Public IPs. Azure Managed Resources are not only accessed by VMs in VNET but are also accessed through internet.

Virtual Network Subnets

VNET is divided into subnets. Subnets are assigned IP addresses by subneting VNET network address space. Access to the subnet can be controlled through Network Security groups (NSG). User defined route (UDR) tables can also be assigned to subnets. Virtual Machines are created in Subnets.

Default Communication within and between Virtual Network Subnets

1. All VM to VM traffic within subnet or between subnets is allowed.
2. VM to internet traffic is allowed.
3. Azure Load balancer to VM is allowed.
4. Inbound internet to VM is blocked.

Note: Default rules can be overridden by new rules you create using NSG.

Private Address Range for Virtual Networks

You can use following class A, Class B and Class C address range for virtual networks.

10.0.0.0/8
172.16.0.0/12
192.168.0.0/16

Once the IP address range is decided, we can then divide this range into subnets. Virtual Machines NICs in the subnet are assigned private IP addresses via Azure DHCP from the subnet network address range.

There are 5 Reserved addresses within the subnet: Within a virtual network subnet, the protocol reserves the first and last IP addresses of a subnet: a host ID of all 0s is used for the network address, and a host ID of all 1s is used for broadcast. In addition, Azure reserves the first three IP addresses in each subnet (binary 01, 10, and 11 in the host ID portion of the IP address) for internal purposes.

Exercise 1: Create Resource Group HKPortal using Azure Portal

1. In Azure Portal click Resource Groups in left pane> All Resource Groups pane opens> Click +Add> Create Resource Group blade opens>Enter HKPortal for name and Select East US 2 as location and click create.

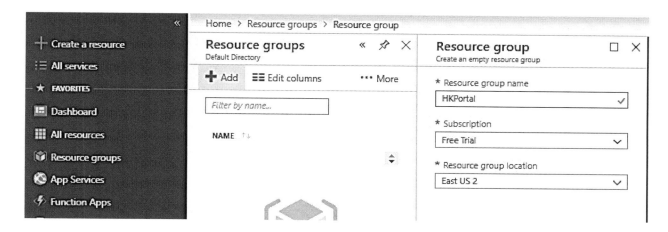

Figure below show dashboard of Resource Group HK Portal.

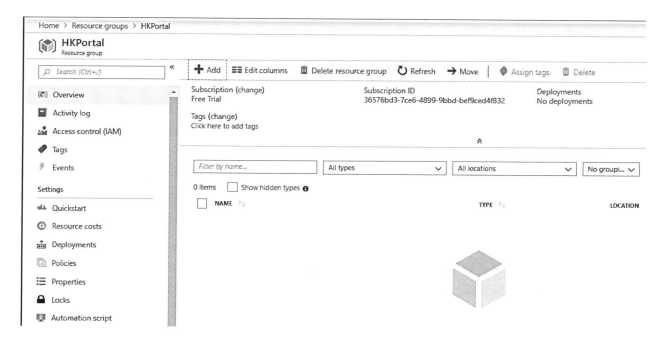

Note: Resource Groups will be discussed extensively in Chapter 14.

Exercise 2: Create Virtual Network using Portal

In this exercise we will create Virtual Network "VNETPortal" in Resource Group HKPortal using 10.1.0.0/16 address space in East US 2 Location. We will name Default Subnet as Web-Subnet with address 10.1.1.0/24.

1. In Azure Portal Click +Create a Resource in left pane> Networking> Virtual Networks> Create Virtual Network blade opens> Enter VNETPortal for name, Select HKPortal in Resource Group Box and Select East US 2 in location Box and click create.

Note: Rest select all values as default- DDoS Protection Basic, Service endpoints disabled and Firewall disabled. You need to scroll down to see these options.

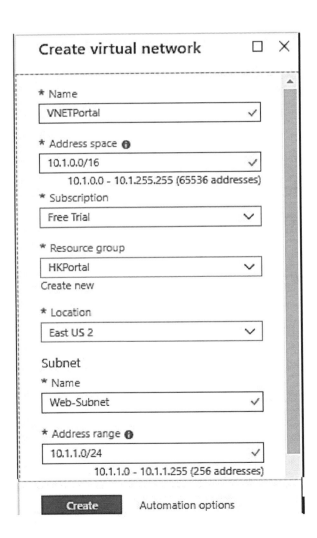

Exercise 3: Create additional Subnet (DB-Subnet 10.1.2.0/24)

1. In Azure Portal Click Virtual Network in Left Pane>Select Virtual Network VNETPortal>Virtual Network Dashboard opens as shown below.

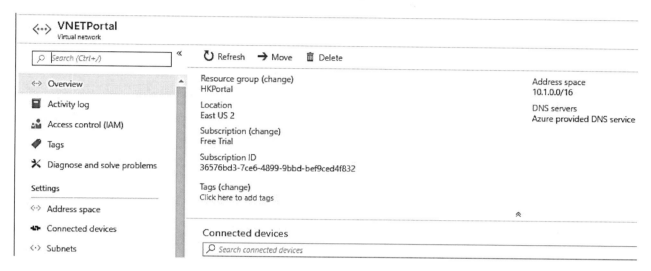

2. Click Subnets in left pane>Subnet blade opens as shown below.

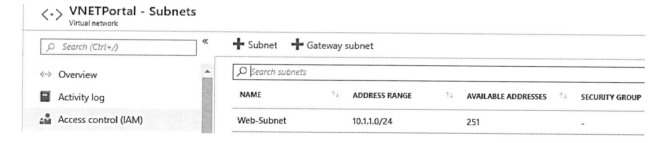

3. Click + Subnet>Add Subnet blade opens>Enter DB-Subnet in name and Address Range as 10.1.2.0/24. Select none for NSG, Route table & 0 for Service Endpoints>Click Ok.

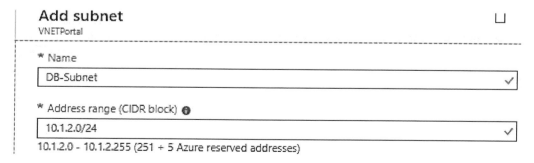

Exercise 4: Create additional Subnet (DMZ-Subnet 10.1.3.0/24)

1. In Virtual Network HKPortal Dashboard Click Subnets in left pane> Subnet blade opens as shown below.

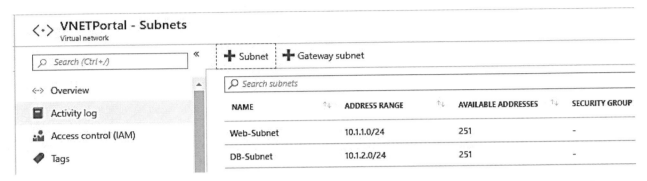

2. Click + Subnet>Add Subnet blade opens>Enter DMZ-Subnet in name and Address Range as 10.1.3.0/24. Select none for NSG, Route table & 0 for Service Endpoints>Click Ok.

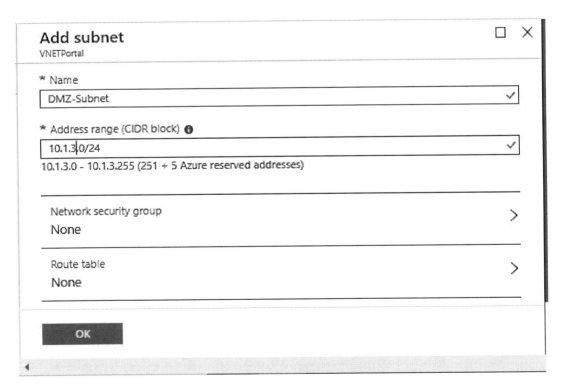

Note: Note + Gateway subnet in Right pane. Gateway Subnet is used for running Virtual Network Gateway. We will use it in next lab.

Exercise 5: Create Gateway Subnet 10.1.5.0/24

In This Exercise we will create Gateway Subnet in Virtual Network VNETPortal. Gateway Subnet will be used in Virtual Network Gateway Exercise 15. VNG will be created in GatewaySubnet.

1. In Virtual Network HKPortal Dashboard Click Subnets in left pane> Subnet blade opens in Right pane> Click + **Gateway subnet** in right pane>Add Subnet blade opens>**Note that subnet name is Pre-filled**> Enter Address Range as 10.1.5.0/24. Select none for Route table & 0 for Service Endpoints>Click Ok.

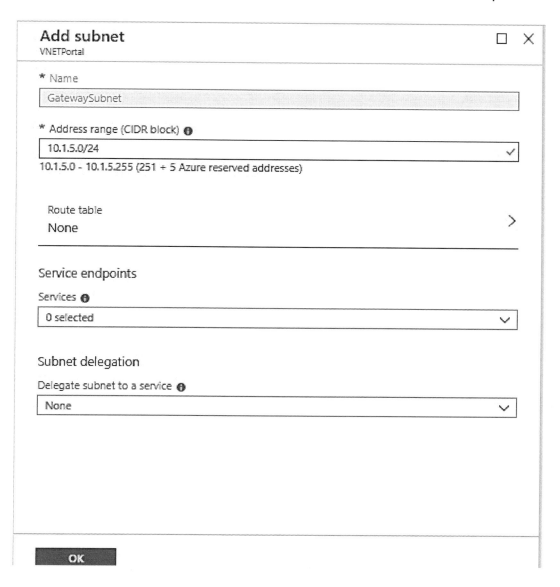

Exercise 6: Create Virtual Network representing On-Premises Network

In this exercise we will create Virtual Network "**VNETOnPrem**" in South Central US Location using. 192.168.0.0/16 address space. We will name Default Subnet as **OnPrem-Subnet** with address 192.168.1.0/16. We will also create Resource Group **OnPrem.**
This Virtual Network will act as on-premises datacentre for our topology.

1. In Azure Portal Click +Create a Resource in left pane> Networking> Virtual Networks> Create Virtual Network blade opens> Enter **VNETOnPrem** for name, Create Resource Group **OnPrem**, Select South Central US in location Box, Rename Default Subnet as **OnPrem-Subnet** and click create.

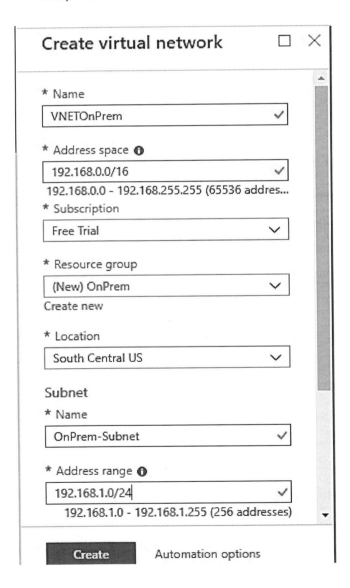

2. Figure below shows the Dashboard of Virtual Network VNETOnPrem.

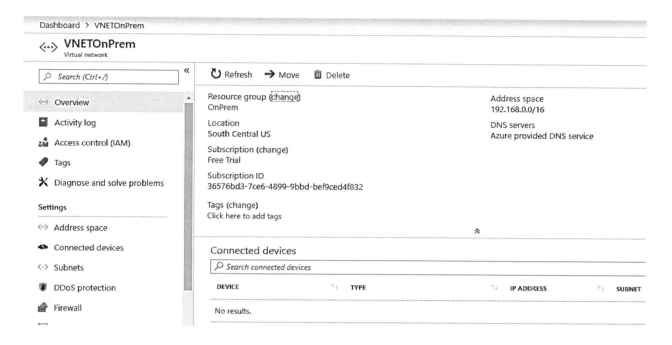

Exercise 7: Create Gateway Subnet 192.168.3.0/24

In This Exercise we will create Gateway Subnet in Virtual Network VNETOnPrem. Gateway Subnet will be used in Virtual Network gateway Exercise 15.

1. In Virtual Network VNETOnPrem Dashboard Click Subnets in left pane> Subnet blade opens in Right pane> Click + **Gateway subnet** in right pane>Add Subnet blade opens>Note that name is Pre-filled> Enter Address Range as 192.168.3.0/24. Select none for Route table & 0 for Service Endpoints>Click Ok.

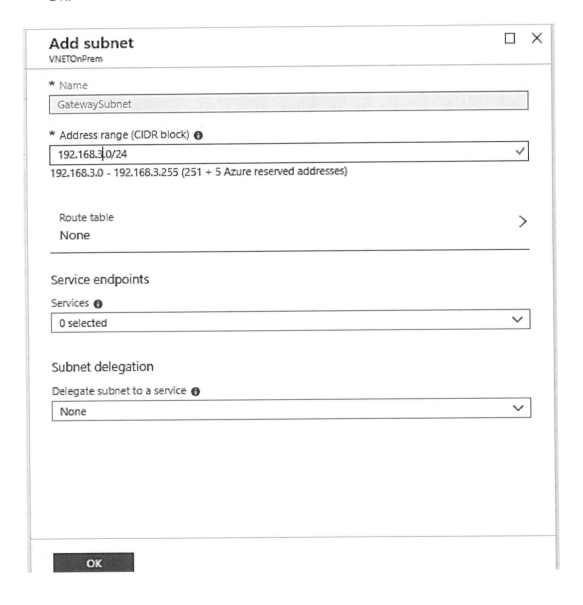

Exercise 8: Create Virtual Network VNETPortal2

In this exercise we will create Virtual Network "**VNETPortal2**" in Resource Group HKPortal using 10.7.0.0/16 address space. The Default Subnet Address will be changed to 10.7.1.0/24. **This Virtual Network will be used in Peering Lab Exercise 16.**

1. In Azure Portal Click +Create a Resource in left pane> Networking> Virtual Networks> Create Virtual Network blade opens> Enter VNETPortal2 for name, Select HKPortal in Resource Group Box and Select East US 2 in location Box and click create.

Note: Rest select all values as default values.

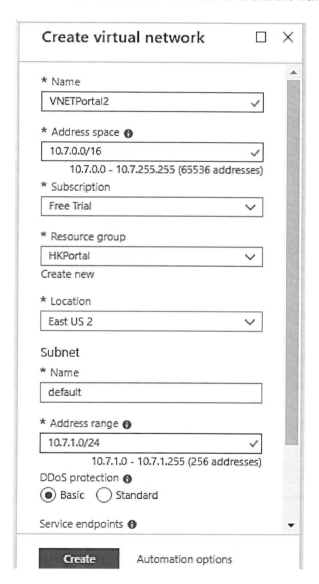

Exercise 9: Create Virtual Network VNETPortal3

In this exercise we will create Virtual Network "**VNETPortal3**" in Resource Group HKPortal using 10.8.0.0/16 address space. The Default Subnet Address will be changed to 10.8.1.0/24. **This Virtual Network will be used in Peering Lab Exercise 17.**

1. In Azure Portal Click +Create a Resource in left pane> Networking> Virtual Networks> Create Virtual Network blade opens> Enter VNETPortal2 for name, Select HKPortal in Resource Group Box and Select East US 2 in location Box and click create.

Note: Rest select all values as default values.

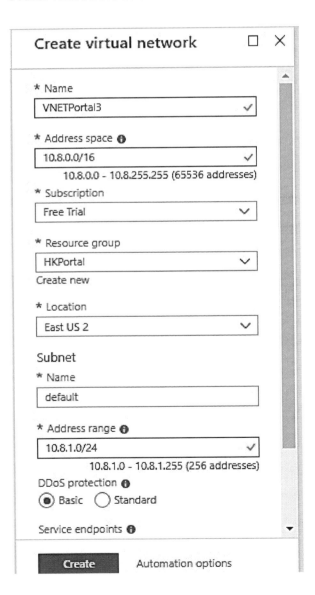

Public IP Addresses in Azure

Public IP addresses allow Azure resources to communicate with Internet and to Azure public-facing services such as Azure Redis Cache, Azure Event Hubs, SQL databases, and Azure storage etc.

Public IP Address Allocation Methods

Dynamic Public IP: IP address is **not** allocated at the time of its creation. Instead, the Dynamic public IP address is allocated when you start or create the associated resource (like a VM or load balancer).
The IP address is released when you stop or delete the resource. This causes the IP address to change when you stop and start a resource.

Static Public IP: IP address for the associated resource remains the same when start or stop the resource.
In this case an IP address is assigned immediately. It is released only when you delete the resource or change its allocation method to dynamic.

You can associate a public IP address resource with following resources:

VMs | Internet-facing load balancers | VPN gateways | Application gateways

Azure Resource	Dynamic	Static
Virtual Machine	Yes	Yes
Internet-facing load balancers	Yes	Yes
VPN gateways	Yes	No
Application gateways	Yes	No

Static Public IP Use Case

Static Public IP addresses are often used for web servers that require SSL connections in which the SSL certificate is linked to an IP address.

Types of Public IP Addresses (Basic & Standard)

Basic IP Address Features

1. Assigned with the static or dynamic allocation method.
2. Network security groups are recommended but optional for restricting inbound or outbound traffic.
3. Assigned to Azure resource such as network interfaces, VPN Gateways, Application Gateways, and Internet-facing load balancers.
4. Can be assigned to a specific zone. Not zone redundant.

Standard IP Address Features

1. Assigned with the static allocation method only.
2. Are secure by default and closed to inbound traffic. You must explicit whitelist allowed inbound traffic with a network security group.
3. Assigned to network interfaces or public standard load balancers.
4. Zone redundant by default.

Default DNS hostname resolution for Resources with Public IP

Resources with Public IP have Fully Qualified Domain Name in the format **resourcename.location.cloudapp.azure.com.**
For Example, if you create a public IP resource with **test** as a resource name in the **West US** Azure location, the fully qualified domain name (FQDN) **test.westus.cloudapp.azure.com** resolves to the public IP address of the resource.

DNS hostname resolution for Resources using Custom Domain options

If you want use your own domain name (Test.com) with Azure Resource with Public IP, you have 2 options depending upon IP Address allocation method.
Dynamic IP: Use cname record to point to Azure resource FQDN.
Static IP: You can either use A record name to point to Azure resource Public IP or use cname record to point Azure Resource FQDN.

Private IP Addresses

Private IP addresses allow Azure resources to communicate with other resources in a virtual network or an on-premises network through a VPN gateway or ExpressRoute circuit, without using an Internet-reachable IP address.

Private IP address is associated with following types of Azure resources:

1. VMs
2. Internal load balancers (ILBs)
3. Application gateways

Private IP Addresses are assigned from the subnet address range in which the resource is created. Private IP Address can be Static or Dynamic. Private IP Address is created during resource creation time.

Private Dynamic IP Address: Azure assigns the next available unassigned or unreserved IP address in the subnet's address range. Once assigned, dynamic IP addresses are only released if a network interface is deleted, assigned to a different subnet within the same virtual network, or the allocation method is changed to static, and a different IP address is specified.
Dynamic is the default allocation method.

Private Static IP Address: You select and assign any unassigned or unreserved IP address in the subnet's address range. Static addresses are only released if a network interface is deleted. Static Private IP addresses are often used with DNS or Domain Controller VMs.

Internal DNS hostname resolution for virtual machines with Private IP using Azure Managed DNS Servers

When you create a virtual machine, a mapping for the hostname to its private IP address is added to the Azure-managed DNS servers by default.
These DNS servers provide name resolution for virtual machines that reside within the same virtual network. To resolve host names of virtual machines in different virtual networks, you must use a custom DNS server.

Exercise 10: Create Dynamic Public IP

In this Exercise we will create Dynamic Public IP in Resource Group HKPortal. We will use this IP with Virtual Machine wvmportal in Compute Chapter.

1. In Azure Portal Click All Services in left pane>Scroll down and Under Networking Click Public IP Addresses>Public IP Addresses Dashboard opens>Click +Add>Create Public IP Address blade opens> Enter DPIPPortal in name box, Select Basic SKU, Select IP address as Dynamic, Give a unique DNS name dpipportal, select RG HKPortal and Location EastUS2> Click create.

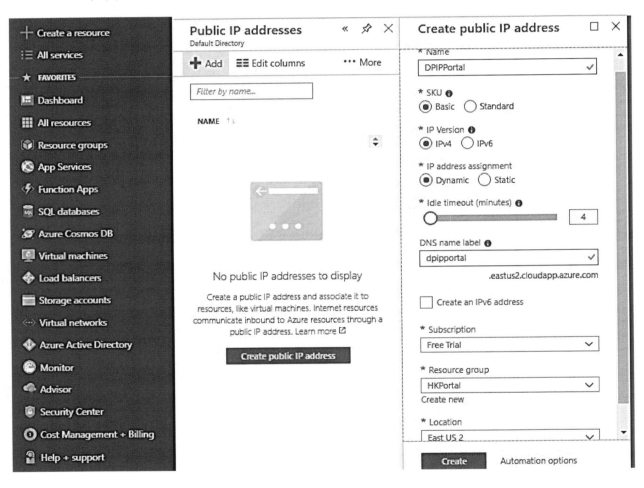

Note 1: Private IP is associated with Network Interface card and can be created only during resource creation time. Private IP Address cannot be created independently.
Note 2: You can create Public IP either through Azure Portal separately or create during Resource creation time.

Figure below shows Dynamic Public IP "DPIPPortal" Dashboard.

Note that no address is assigned. Dynamic public IP address is allocated when you start or create the associated resource (like a VM or load balancer).

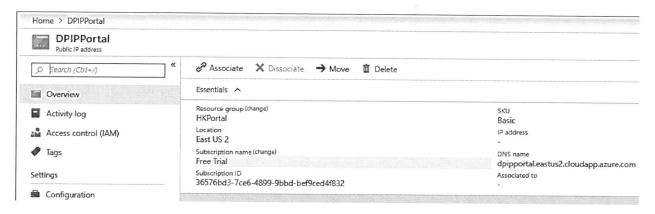

Exercise 11: Changing Dynamic Public IP to Static IP

In Public IP "**DPIPPortal**" Dashboard Click Configuration in left pane>Select Static and click save.

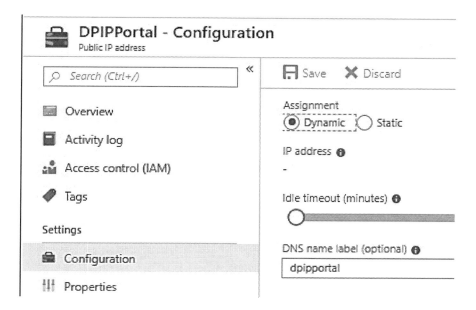

Network Security Groups

Network Security Group (NSG) is a Virtual Firewall. NSGs control **inbound** and **outbound** access to network interfaces (NICs) and subnets. Each NSG contains one or more rules specifying whether or not traffic is approved or denied based on source IP address, source port, destination IP address, destination port and protocol.

NSGs can be associated with subnets and network interfaces of Virtual Machines within that subnet. When a NSG is associated with a subnet, the ACL rules apply to all the VM instances in that subnet. In addition, traffic to an individual VM can be further restricted by associating a NSG directly to that VM NIC.

Figure below Shows VNET with 2 Subnets. Virtual Machine in Web-Subnet is protected by 2 Levels of NSG – NSG at Subnet level and NSG at Virtual Machine Network Interface level. Whereas Virtual Machine in DB-Subnet is protected by one level of NSG applied at Virtual Machine Network Interface Level.

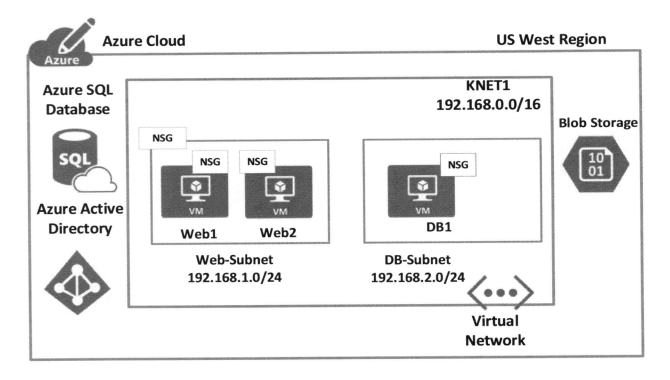

Default NSG rules

NSGs contain a set of default rules. The default rules cannot be deleted, but because they are assigned the lowest priority, they can be overridden by creating new rules with higher priority. **Higher the Number Lower the priority.**

Inbound default rules

Name	Priority	Source IP	Src Port	Dest IP	Dest Port	Protocol	Access
ALLOW VNET INBOUND	65000	VIRTUAL_NETWORK	*	VIRTUAL_NETWORK	*	*	Allow
ALLOW AZURE LOAD BALANCER INBOUND	65001	AZURE_LOADBALANCER	*	*	*	*	Allow
DENY ALL INBOUND	65500	*	*	*	*	*	Deny

Outbound default rules

Name	Priority	Source IP	Src Port	Dest IP	Dest Port	Protocol	Access
ALLOW VNET OUTBOUND	65000	VIRTUAL_NETWORK	*	VIRTUAL_NETWORK	*	*	Allow
ALLOW INTERNET OUTBOUND	65001	*	*	Internet	*	*	Allow
DENY ALL OUTBOUND	65500	*	*	*	*	*	Deny

- * Represent all addresses, Ports & Protocols.

We can infer following from the above default rules:

1. All VM to VM traffic within subnet or between subnets is allowed.
2. VM to internet traffic is allowed.
3. Azure Load balancer to VM is allowed.
4. Inbound internet to VM is blocked.
5. Default rules can be overridden by creating new rules with higher priority.

NSG Design Rules

1. By Default there is no NSG assigned to a subnet. But you have option of adding NSG during subnet creation or after subnet is created. To assign a NSG to a subnet you need to first create NSG.
2. Associating NSG to subnet is recommended and not compulsory.
3. You can apply only one NSG to a subnet or a VM NIC. But same NSG can be applied to multiple resources.
4. Deploy each tier of your workload into different subnet and then apply NSG to the subnets.
5. When implementing a subnet for a VPN gateway, or ExpressRoute circuit, do not apply an NSG to that subnet. If you do so, your cross-VNet or cross-premises connectivity will not work.
6. **Each NSG rules has a priority. Higher the priority number, lower the priority. You can override default NSG by creating new NSG rules with higher priority than default rules.**

Service Tags for identification of category of IP Addresses in NSG Rules

Service tags are system-provided identifiers to address a category of IP addresses. Service tags are used in the **source address prefix** and **destination address prefix** properties of any NSG rule.

1. **VirtualNetwork**: This default tag denotes virtual network address space assigned to Azure Virtual Network.
2. **AzureLoadBalancer**: This default tag denotes Azure's Infrastructure load balancer. This will translate to an Azure datacenter IP where Azure's health probes originate.
3. **Internet**: This default tag denotes the IP address space that is outside the virtual network and reachable by public Internet. This range includes Azure owned public IP space as well.
4. **AzureTrafficManager**: This tag denotes the IP address space for the Azure Traffic Manager probe IPs.
5. **Storage**: This tag denotes the IP address space for the Azure Storage service. If you specify *Storage* for the value, traffic is allowed or denied to storage. If you only want to allow access to storage in a specific region, you can specify the region.
6. **Sql**: This tag denotes the address prefixes of the Azure SQL Database and Azure SQL Data Warehouse services. If you specify *Sql* for the value, traffic is allowed or denied to Sql.
7. **AzureCosmosDB** (Resource Manager only): This tag denotes the address prefixes of the Azure Cosmos Database service. If you specify AzureCosmosDB for the value, traffic is allowed or denied to AzureCosmosDB.
8. **AzureKeyVault** (Resource Manager only): This tag denotes the address prefixes of the Azure KeyVault service. If you specify *AzureKeyVault* for the value, traffic is allowed or denied to AzureKeyVault.

Effective NSG Permissions or Rules

NSG can be applied at Subnet or VM NIC level or both Subnet and VM NIC.

Let's take an example to check what's the effective traffic reaching Virtual Machine when NSG is applied at both Subnet and VM NIC level. We have 2 VMs (App-Prod & App-Test) created in App Subnet as shown in below figure.

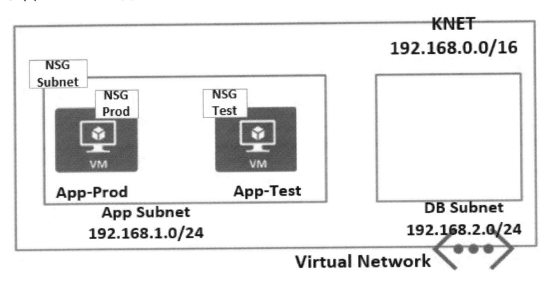

NSGSubnet has 3 inbound allow rules - http, https & RDP.
NSGProd has 2 inbound allow rules - https & RDP.
NSGTest has 2 inbound allow rules - http & RDP.

Effective traffic entering the subnet is http, https & RDP. NSG Subnet blocks any other traffic apart from http, https & RDP.
Effective traffic entering VM App-prod is https & RDP. NSG Prod blocks http traffic.
Effective traffic entering VM App-Test is http & RDP. NSG Prod blocks https traffic.

Exercise 12: Create NSG and add inbound http and RDP allow rule

In this Exercise we will create Network Security Group **portalnsg** in resource group HKPortal and in US East 2 Location. We will add inbound http and RDP allow rule in hknsg1. This rule will allow http and RDP traffic to windows server **VM wvmportal in web-subnet**. Windows VM will be created in compute chapter. In Next exercise we will associate this rule with Web-Subnet in Virtual Network VNETPortal.

1. In Azure Portal Click + Create a resource>Networking>Network Security Group>Create Network Security Group opens> Enter a name, Select resource group HKPortal and Click create.

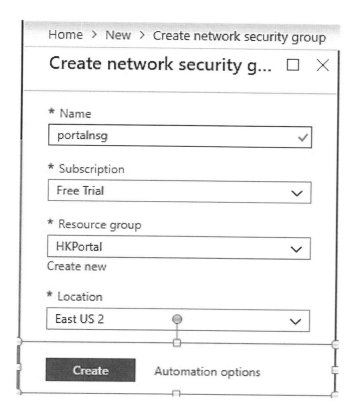

2. Network Security Group Dashboard shown below shows default inbound and outbound security rules of Network Security Group portalnsg.

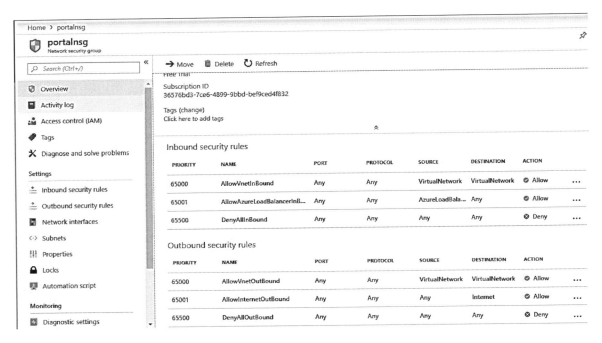

Note on Inbound Rules

Note 1: In inbound security rules, all inbound traffic is set to deny (Rule number 3) except for VNET to VNET and Azure Load Balancer to Any.

Note 2: Best Practice is to create a new inbound rule and allow traffic which is needed. Do not make this rule allow for all the traffic.

Note 3: Override Default inbound rule by creating new rule with higher priority or lower number than the default inbound rule.

Note 4: In next step we will allow inbound RDP and http traffic to windows server VM in web-subnet. Windows Server VM will be created in compute chapter.

Note on Outbound Rules

Note 1: Internet outbound is allowed.

3. **Add inbound RDP rule**: In NSG dashboard click inbound security rules in left pane>In Right pane click +Add>Add inbound security rule blade opens> Enter RDP port 3389 in destination port range> Assign Priority of 100>Give a name to the rule and click Add.

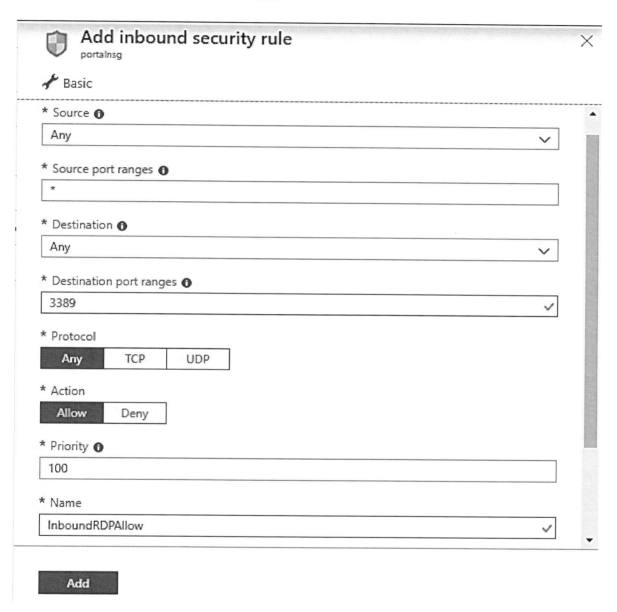

Note: Readers are advised to click the Source and destination drop boxes to see the options.

4. **Add inbound allow http rule**: Similarly add allow http rule. Enter http port 80 in destination port range> Assign Priority of 110>Give a name to the rule and click Add.

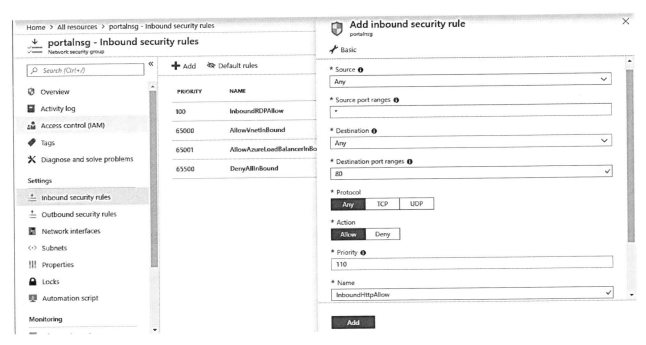

5. Figure below shows inbound rules with 2 new rules added.

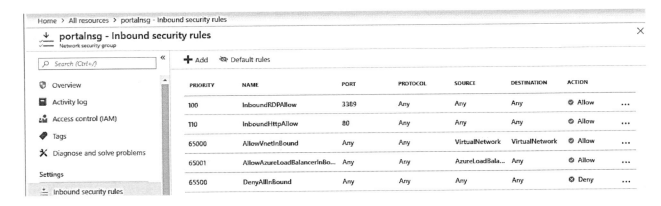

Exercise 13: Associate Network Security Group (NSG) with Subnet

In this exercise we will associate NSG created in previous exercise with Web-Subnet in Virtual Network VNETPortal.

1. In NSG Dashboard click Subnets in left pane.

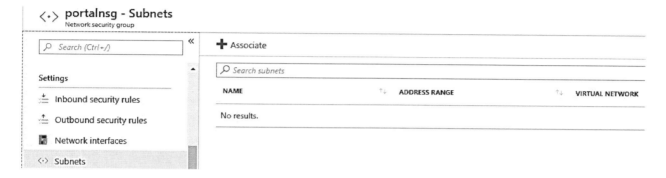

2. In right pane click +Associate > Associate Subnet blade opens> In Associate Subnet Blade select Virtual Network "VNETPortal" & Subnet "Web-Subnet" and click ok.

3. Figure below shows Web-Subnet in Virtual Network VNETPortal associated with NSG.

Name Resolution with Azure DNS

Before going into Azure DNS let's discuss about DNS. DNS or Domain Name System translates domain name to IP Address. The process of DNS resolution involves converting a hostname such as www.test.com into IP address such as 192.168.10.1. When a user wants to access www.test.com, a translation occurs between test.com and the IP address assigned to End user Server. This whole translation involves Global infrastructure of DNS Servers including top level name servers, root servers and Authoritative name server for that particular domain etc.

Azure DNS is a managed hosting service which provides Global infrastructure of name servers to translate Domain Name to IP Address. Azure DNS is a hosting service for DNS domains (Containing DNS Records of a Domain), providing name resolution using Microsoft Azure infrastructure.

Design Nugget: You can't use Azure DNS to buy a domain name.

Features and Benefits of Azure DNS

Availability: DNS domains in Azure DNS are hosted on Azure's global network of DNS name servers which can withstand Datacentre or a Region failure.
Performance: Azure DNS uses anycast networking so that each DNS query is answered by the closest DNS server available to user. This provides fast performance.
Ease of use: You can manage your DNS records using the same credentials, APIs, tools, and billing as your other Azure services. You can use Azure portal, Cli or PowerShell to manage Azure DNS.
Security: Azure DNS can be secured using RBAC & Resource locking. You can use Activity logs to monitor user actions and for troubleshooting.
DNS Record types: Azure DNS supports all common DNS record types including A, AAAA, CAA, CNAME, MX, NS, PTR, SOA, SRV, and TXT records.

Solution Components of Azure DNS

DNS Zones
DNS Records
Delegation to Azure DNS Name Servers from Domain Registrar of your domain.

Working in Brief

Using Azure DNS create DNS Zone. DNS Zone creates 4 Name Servers for Your Domain. In DNS Zone, Add DNS records (A, CNAME or MX) pointing to your resource. In domain registrar where you have registered you domain, add Azure DNS Name servers which will delegate DNS Name resolution to Azure DNS Name servers for your domain.

DNS Zones & Records

A DNS zone is used to host the DNS records for a particular domain. DNS record for your domain is created inside this DNS zone. For example, the domain 'contoso.com' may contain several DNS records, such as 'mail.contoso.com' (MX record for a mail server) and 'www.contoso.com' (A record for a web site).

DNS Records

DNS records are mapping files that tell the DNS server which IP address each domain is associated with, and how to handle requests sent to each domain. Each DNS record has a name and a type. Azure DNS supports all common DNS record types including A, AAAA, CAA, CNAME, MX, NS, PTR, SOA, SRV, and TXT.

A Record: An A record points a domain or subdomain to an IP address.
MX Record: A MX record specifies a mail server responsible for accepting email messages on behalf of a recipient's domain.
CNAME or Alias Record: A CNAME Record points one domain or subdomain to another domain. For Example when you create Azure VM it is assigned a domain name in the form pipportal.eastus2.cloudapp.azure.com. Using CNAME records you can use www.test.com to point to pipportal.eastus2.cloudapp.azure.com.
NS Record: NS record set contains the names of the Azure DNS name servers assigned to the zone. The NS record is set at the zone apex and is created automatically with each DNS zone, and is deleted automatically when the zone is deleted
SOA Record: A start of authority (SOA) record is information stored in a domain name system (DNS) zone about that zone and about other DNS records. Each zone contains a single SOA record. The SOA record stores information about the name of the server that supplied the data for the zone; the administrator of the zone; the current version of the data file; the number of seconds a secondary

name server should wait before checking for updates; the number of seconds a secondary name server should wait before retrying a failed zone transfer; the maximum number of seconds that a secondary name server can use data before it must either be refreshed or expire; and a default number of seconds for the time-to-live file on resource records.

Time to Live (TTL)
TTL specifies how long each record is cached by clients before being re-queried.

Exercise 14: DNS Zone, DNS Records and Delegation to Azure DNS

For this exercise we will use **mykloud.in** domain which is registered with Domain Registrar Go Daddy. We will Create DNS Zone and Add DNS Record (www.mykloud.in) pointing to VM wvmportal IP Address. We will then delegate DNS Resolution for myKloud.in domain to Azure DNS Name servers. <u>Do this Exercise after you have done Exercise 24 in Chapter 3 where VM wvmportal was created.</u>

Step 1 Create DNS Zone

1. In Azure Portal Click + Create a resource>In Search Box Type DNS Zone and press Enter>In search Result you can see DNS Zone by Microsoft.

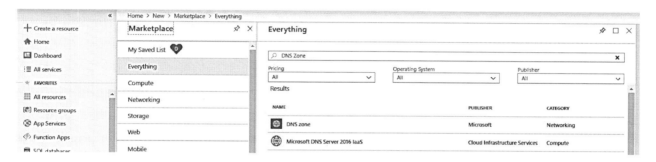

2. Click DNS Zone in search Result>DNS Zone Blade opens>Click Create.

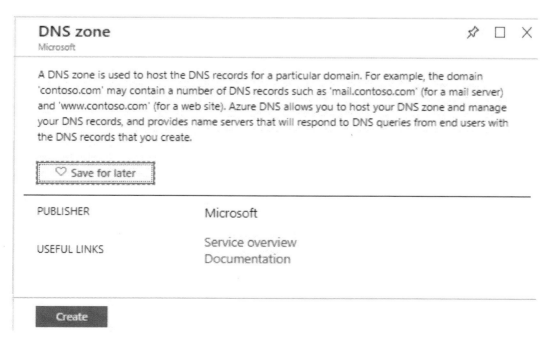

3. Create DNS Zone Blade opens>Enter your Domain name **mykloud.in**>Select Resource Group HK Portal and click

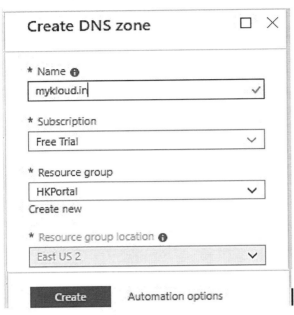

4. Figure below shows DNS Zone Dashboard. There are 4 Name Servers- ns1, ns2, ns3 & ns4. The SOA is ns1.

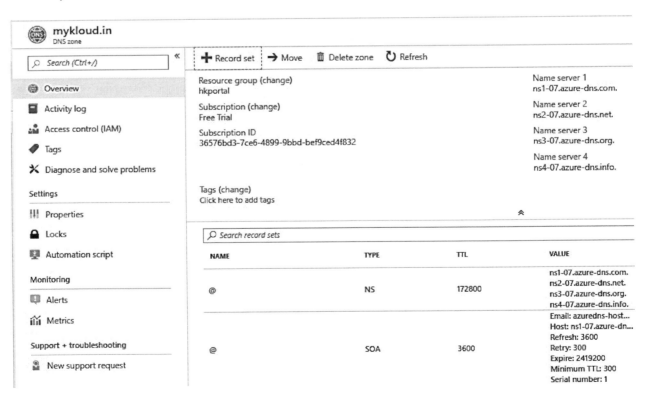

Step 2 Create DNS Records

In DNS Zone dashboard click +Record Set>Add Record Set Blade opens>Enter www, Select Record type A and Enter IP Address of VM wvmportal and click OK.

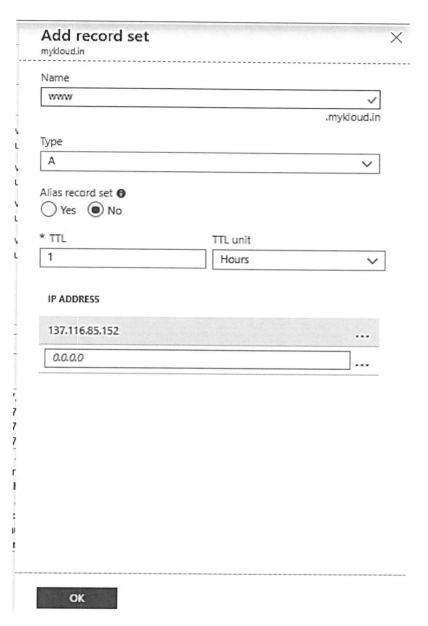

Note 1: If you want to use VM wvmportal DNS name instead of IP Address then use Alias Record Set.

Step 3 Add Azure DNS Name Servers in Go Daddy Portal for delegation

1. Copy the Name servers from DNS Zone Dashboard.
2. Go to Go Daddy DNS Management page>Scroll down and you can see Name Servers for mykloud.in

3. Click change>Select Custom from dropdown box>Click Add Name Server two Times to make space for 4 Name Servers>Add the Azure DNS Name Servers copied from DNS Zone dashboard>Click save> You can see Azure DNS Name servers in Go Daddy DNS Management responsible for domain mykloud.in

Nameservers

Last updated 01-01-0001 00:00 AM

Using custom nameservers

Nameserver

ns1-07.azure-dns.com

ns2-07.azure-dns.net

ns3-07.azure-dns.org

ns4-07.azure-dns.info

With this step Azure DNS servers become Authoritative Name Servers for domain mykloud.in

Step 4: Test the name resolution

1. From DNS zone dashboard copy the name of Azure DNS name server and run following nslookup command.

The domain name **www.mykloud.in** resolves to **137.116.85.152** which is the IP address of VM wvmportal. The result verifies that name resolution is working correctly using Azure DNS Name Servers.

2. Open Browser and enter www.mykloud.in. You can see the VM wvmportal default website opens. Do this step after 15-20 Minutes as it takes time to propagate DNS changes.

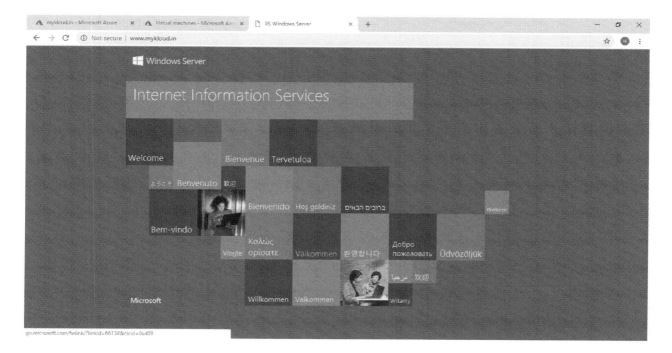

Virtual Network Connectivity using Virtual Network Gateway

You can connect Virtual Network to on-premises Datacenter through virtual network gateway located in GatewaySubnet using either Internet VPN (P2S or S2S VPN) or ExpressRoute Private WAN connectivity.

For Internet VPN you deploy virtual network gateway of type VPN. For Private WAN connectivity you deploy virtual network gateway of type ExpressRoute.

Figure below shows Virtual Network Connected to on-premises Datacenter.

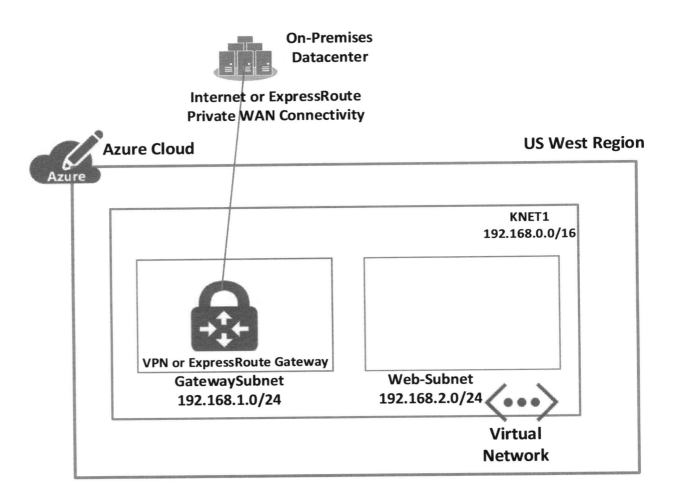

Every Azure VPN gateway consists of two instances in an active-standby or active-active configuration.

VNET External Connectivity over internet

You can connect Virtual Network (VNET) to your on-premises networks over public internet using Azure VPN Gateway. A VPN gateway is a type of virtual network gateway that sends encrypted traffic across a public connection. The connectivity uses the industry-standard protocols Internet Protocol Security (IPsec) and Internet Key Exchange (IKE).

VPN gateway connects VNET to on-premises network using Site to Site VPN (S2S) or Point to Site VPN (P2S). S2S VPN uses **VPN device** on-premises. P2S VPN uses **VPN client software** on client computers in on premises infrastructure.

VPN Gateway is created in GatewaySubnet. A GatewaySubnet is created in Azure Virtual Network (VNET).

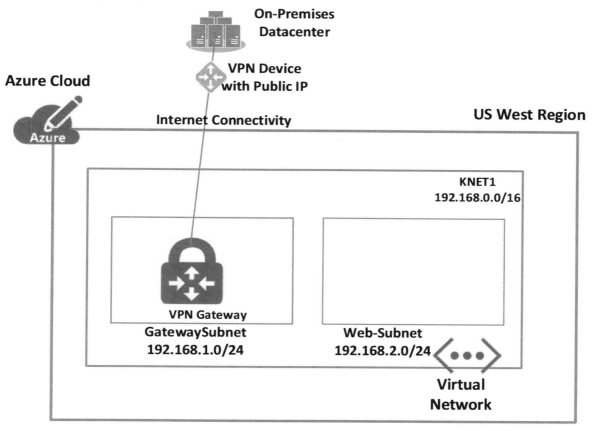

Every Azure VPN gateway consists of two instances in an active-standby configuration.

VPN Type

VPN gateway supports following 2 type of VPN. VPN Types are selected when you are creating Virtual Network gateway of type VPN.

PolicyBased: PolicyBased VPNs were previously called static routing gateways. Policy-based VPNs encrypt and direct packets through IPsec tunnels based on the IPsec policies configured with the combinations of address prefixes between your on-premises network and the Azure VNet.

1. PolicyBased VPNs can **only** be used on the Basic gateway SKU.
2. You can have only 1 tunnel when using a PolicyBased VPN.
3. You can only use PolicyBased VPNs for S2S connections.
4. PolicyBased VPN does not support Point to Site VPN (P2S).

RouteBased: RouteBased VPNs were previously called dynamic routing gateways. RouteBased VPNs use "routes" in the IP forwarding or routing table to direct packets into their corresponding tunnel interfaces. The tunnel interfaces then encrypt or decrypt the packets in and out of the tunnels.

Table below shows comparison between Route-Based and Policy Based VPN.

Features	Route-Based	Policy-Based
Point-to-Site (P2S)	Supported	Not Supported
Site-to-Site (S2S)	Supported	Supported
S2S VNet-to-VNet	Supported	Not Supported
S2S Multi-Site	Supported	Not Supported
S2S and ExpressRoute coexist	Supported	Not Supported
Max IPSec Tunnels	128	1
Authentication	Pre-shared key for S2S connectivity, Certificates for P2S connectivity	Pre-shared key
Gateway SKU	Basic, VpnGw1, VpnGw1, VpnGw1	Basic

VPN Gateway Editions

VPN gateway comes in following 4 Editions or SKUs.

Features	Basic Gateway	VpnGw1	VpnGw2	VpnGw3
Gateway throughput	100 Mbps	650 Mbps	1 Gbps	1.25 Gbps
Gateway max IPsec tunnels for Route Based VPN	10	30	30	30
Gateway max IPsec tunnels for Policy Based VPN	1	NA	NA	NA
Max P2S connections	128	128	128	128
Active-Active S2S VPN	No	Yes	Yes	Yes
BGP support	No	Yes	Yes	Yes
Route-Based VPN	Yes	Yes	Yes	Yes
Policy-Based VPN	Yes	No	No	No

VPN Gateway SKUs Use cases

Workloads	SKUs
Production & critical workloads	VpnGw1, VpnGw2, VpnGw3
Dev-test or proof of concept	Basic

Site to Site VPN (S2S)

A Site-to-Site (S2S) VPN gateway connects Virtual Network (VNET) to on premises infrastructure over IPsec/IKE VPN tunnel. This type of connection requires a VPN device located on-premises that has public IP address assigned to it and is not located behind a NAT.

Site to Site VPN can also be used to connect VNET to VNET.

Figure below shows VNET to on-premises connectivity. A VPN Device is required on-premises with Public IP (Not shown in below Figure).

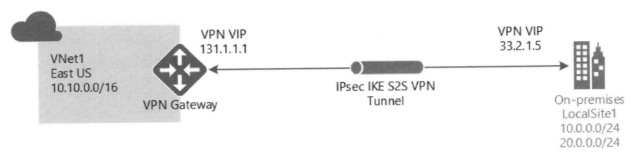

Figure below Shows VNET to on-premises Connectivity (Multisite).

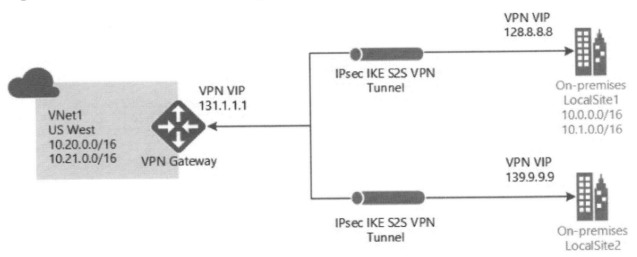

Figure below shows VNET to VNET connectivity.

Design Nuggets for S2S VPN

1. VPN Gateway is created in GatewaySubnet (Not shown above).
2. By default VPN gateway consists of two instances in an active-standby configuration.
3. On-Premises require a VPN device with Public IP (Not shown above).
4. On premises addresses should not overlap with VNET addresses.
5. **S2S VPN only supports pre shared key as Authentication.**
6. Public IP is dynamically assigned. Static IP is not supported for VPN Gateway.
7. Do not assign Network Security Group (NSG) to GatewaySubnet.

Point to Site VPN (P2S)

A Point-to-Site (P2S) VPN gateway creates a secure connection between virtual network and on-premises using VPN client software installed on individual client computers. P2S is a VPN connection over SSTP (Secure Socket Tunneling Protocol). P2S connections do not require a VPN device or a public-facing IP address to work.

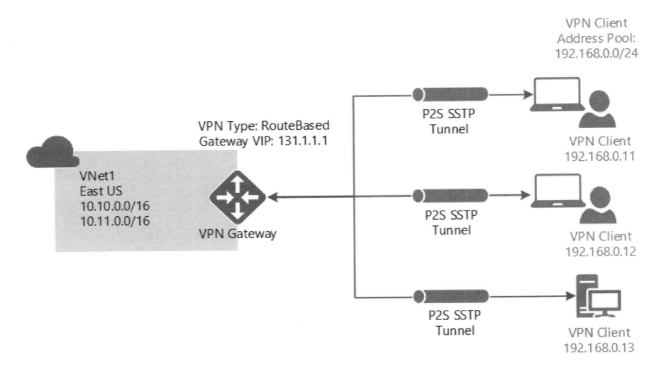

Design Nuggets P2S VPN

1. VPN Gateway is created in GatewaySubnet (Not shown above).
2. By default VPN gateway consists of two instances in an active-standby configuration.
3. On premises addresses should not overlap with VNET addresses.
4. **P2S VPN uses certificates as Authentication for client connections**.
5. Public IP is dynamically assigned. Static IP is not supported for VPN Gateway.
6. Do not assign Network Security Group (NSG) to GatewaySubnet.

Exercise 15: Connecting Virtual Networks using S2S VPN

In this exercise we will Connect Virtual Networks VNETPortal & VNETOnPrem using Virtual Network Gateway (VNG). Refer to topology on page 26.

Step 1 Create Virtual Network Gateway in Virtual Network VNETPortal

Create a resource>Networking>Virtual Network gateway> Create virtual network gateway blade opens>Select gateway type as VPN, VPN type as route based, Click and Select Virtual Network VNETPortal, Select Create new Public IP with Basic SKU and Select Location EASTUS2 (Not Shown in Figure)>Click create.

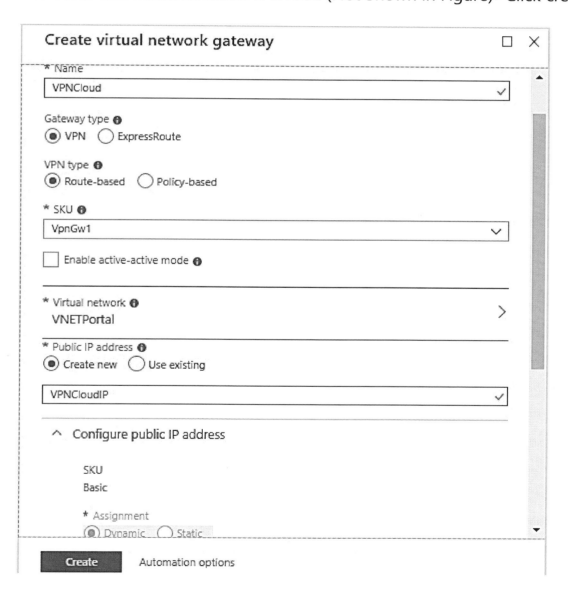

Figure below shows Dashboard of Virtual Network gateway VPNCloud.

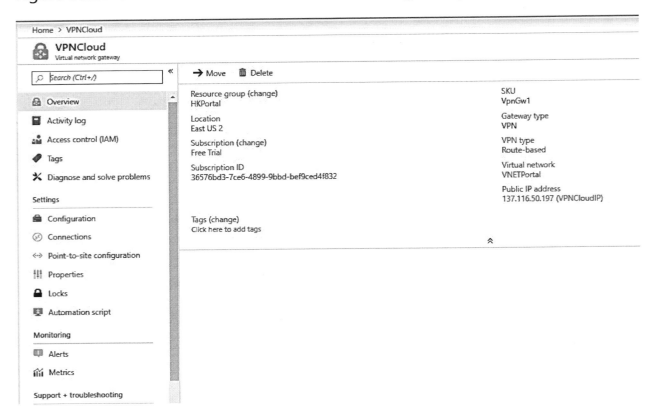

Step 2 Create Virtual Network Gateway in Virtual Network VNETOnPrem

Create a resource>Networking>Virtual Network gateway> Create virtual network gateway blade opens>Select gateway type as VPN, VPN type as route based, Click and Select Virtual Network VNETPortal, Select Create new Public IP with Basic SKU and Select Location South Central US (Not Shown in Figure)>Click create.

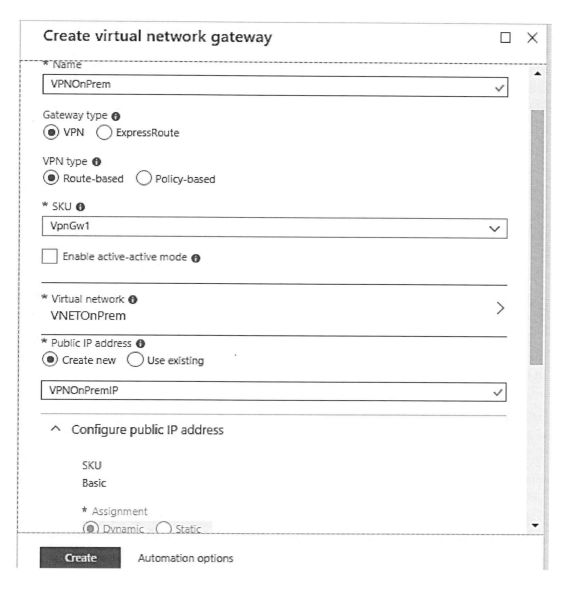

Figure below shows Dashboard of Virtual Network Gateway VPNOnPrem

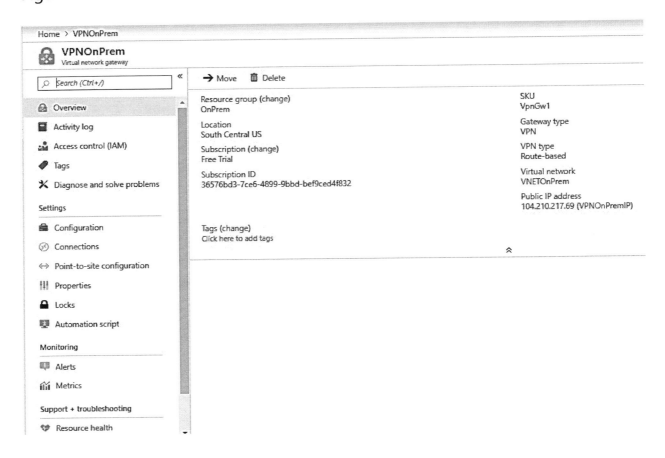

Step 3 Create Virtual Network VNETPortal Gateway Connection

Go to Virtual Network gateway VPNCloud Dashboard>Click Connections in left pane> In Right pane Click +Add> Add Connection Blade opens> First VNG should be VPNCloud, Second VNG should be VPNOnPrem, Enter a shared key 123xyz> Click Ok.

Note: Shared key must be same on both sides.

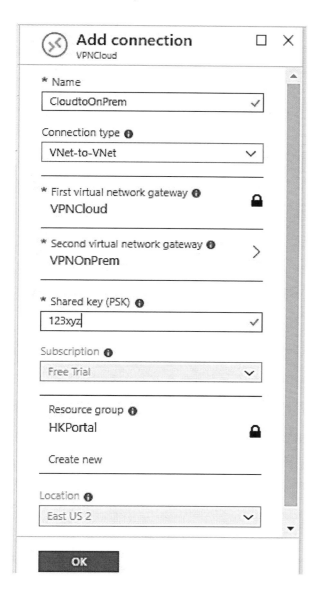

Step 4 Create Virtual Network VNETOnPrem Gateway Connection

Go to Virtual Network gateway VPNOnPrem Dashboard>Click Connections in left pane> In Right pane Click +Add> Add Connection Blade opens> First VNG should be VPNOnPrem, Second VNG should be VPNCloud, Enter a shared key 123xyz> Click Ok.
Note: Shared key must be same on both sides.

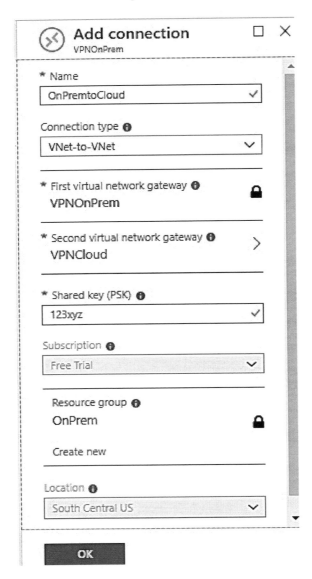

Step 5 Checking the Connections Created and flow of Data

Do this exercise after 5 minutes of previous exercise.

1. Go to either Virtual Network Gateway VPNCloud or VPNOnPrem Dashboard> Click Connections in left pane> It will show both the connection with status Connected. If not then wait till it shows. If required refresh the screen with F5.

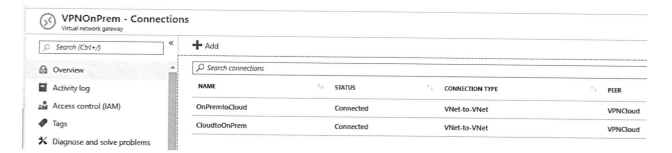

2. Click on one of the Connection and you can see Data in and Data out.

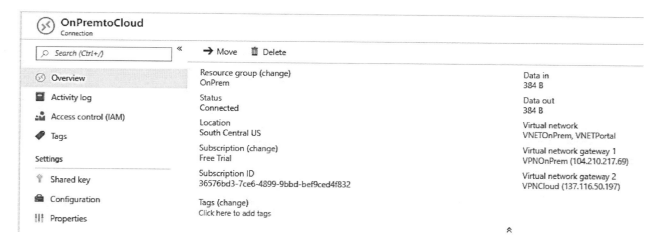

Virtual Networks Peering

Virtual network (VNET) peering connects two VNETs in the same region or different region through the Azure backbone network. Once peered, the two VNETs appear as one for connectivity purposes. Virtual machines (VM) in the peered VNETs can communicate with each other directly by using private IP addresses.

You no longer have to configure Site-to-Site (S2S) VPN between Virtual Networks using Virtual Network gateway. The disadvantage of this option is that connectivity between VNET is over the internet backbone.

Figure Below shows VNET peering between 2 Virtual Networks (VNET1 & VNET2). VMs in both VNETs can now communicate with each other using their Private IPs.

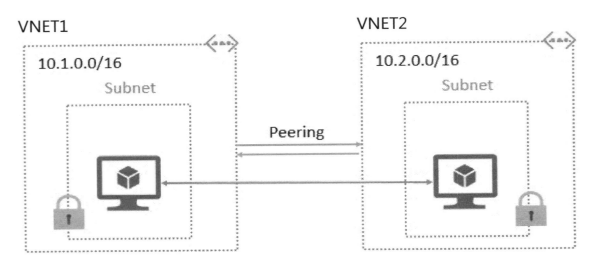

Advantages of VNET Peering

1. VNET-VNET connectivity happens over a low-latency, high-bandwidth connection instead of internet in the case S2S VPN.

2. You no longer have to configure Site-to-Site (S2S) VPN between Virtual Networks using Virtual Network gateway. This results in operational simplicity as Installing and Configuring VPN Gateway is a complex operation. Installation of VPN Gateway takes around 45 Minutes.

Pre-requisite for VNET-VNET Connectivity

1. The peered VNETs must have non-overlapping IP address spaces.

Features of VNET Peering

1. You can peer across VNETs in the same region or different regions.
2. You can globally peer across subscriptions.
3. Traffic across peered links is completely private and stays on the Microsoft Backbone Network.

Note 1: You pay for Data charges for inbound and outbound traffic
Note 2: You pay more data charges for inbound and outbound traffic when VNETs are in different regions.

Gateway Transit and Remote Gateways

A Virtual Network can connect to on-premises Network even if it does not have its own Virtual Network Gateway. It can use the Gateway of Peered Network.

You must Enable **Use Remote gateways** option in Virtual Network for Virtual Network to use Virtual Network Gateway of Peered Virtual Network.

You must Enable **Allow Transit gateway** option in Virtual Network for Virtual Network to provide its Virtual Network Gateway to other Peered Virtual Networks.

Figure below shows VNETPortal and VNETOnPrem are connected through Virtual Network Gateway over Internet Connectivity. By enabling Use Remote Gateway option in VNETPortal2, VNETPortal2 can use Gateway of VNETPortal. You also need to enable Allow Gateway Transit on VNETPortal.

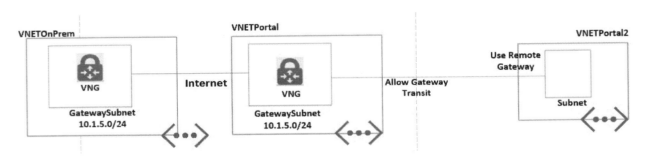

In Exercise 16 we will create Peering between VNETPortal and VNETPortal2.
In Exercise 17 we will create Peering between VNETPortal and VNETPortal3.

In Next 2 Exercises we will allow VNETPortal2 and VNETPortal3 to connect to on-premises Network represented by VNETOnPrem using Virtual Network Gateway Located in VNETPortal.
For this during peering we will enable **Allow Gateway Transit** on VNETPortal and will enable **Use Remote Gateways** on VNETPortal2 and VNETPortal3.

Exercise 16: Peering between VNETs VNETPortal & VNETPortal2

In this exercise we will do peering between Virtual Networks VNETPortal & VNETPortal2. Refer to figure on page 26.

1. Go to VNETPortal Dashboard>Click Peering in left pane> In Right Pane Click +Add > Add Peering blade opens > Select VNETPortal2 in Virtual Network> Select **Allow Gateway Transit**> click ok.

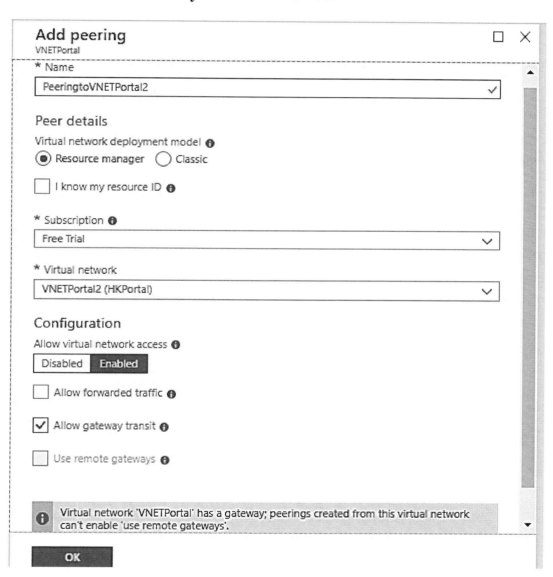

Note: Check Allow Gateway Transit will allow VNETPortal2 to use Virtual Network Gateway Configured on VNETPortal. In Exercise 15 we configured Virtual Network Gateway on VNETPortal.

2. Go to VNETPortal2 Dashboard>Click Peering in left pane> In Right Pane Click +Add > Add Peering blade opens > Select VNETPortal in Virtual Network> Select **Use Remote Gateway**> click ok.

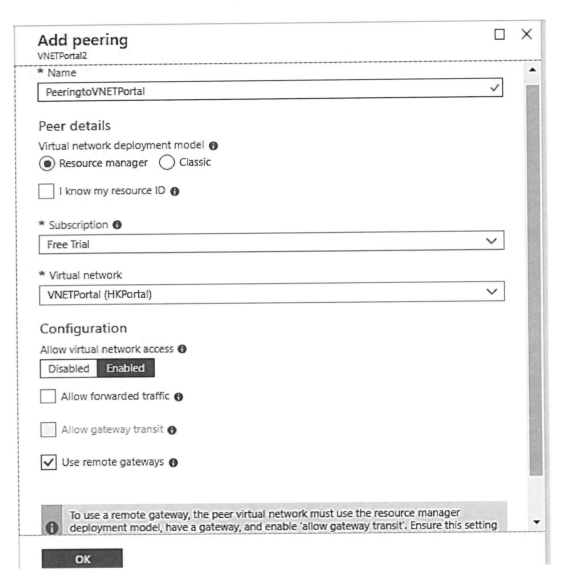

Note: Check Use Remote Gateways will allow VNETPortal2 to use Virtual Network Gateway Configured on VNETPortal. In Exercise 15 we configured Virtual Network Gateway on VNETPortal.

3. The 2 VNETs are now peered and connected. You can check the peering status by clicking peering in Virtual Network dashboard. Figure below shows VNETPortal Dashboard with Peering selected in left pane.

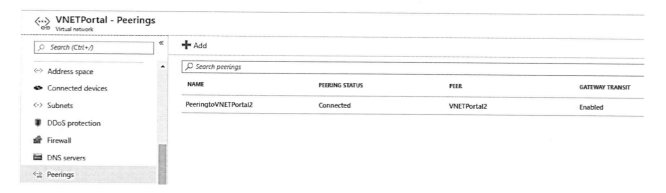

4. Figure below shows VNETPortal2 Dashboard with Peering selected in left pane.

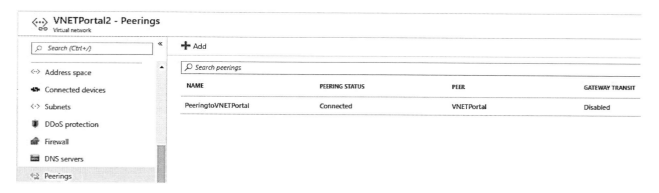

You can see in above configuration how easily VNET peering was done in just 2 steps. Secondly there was no complex configuration to be completed as we do in S2S VPN using Virtual Network gateway.

Exercise 17: Peering between VNETs VNETPortal & VNETPortal3

In this exercise we will do peering between Virtual Networks VNETPortal & VNETPortal3. Refer to figure on page 26.

1. Go to VNETPortal Dashboard>Click Peering in left pane> In Right Pane Click +Add > Add Peering blade opens > Select VNETPortal3 in Virtual Network> Select Allow Gateway Transit> click ok.

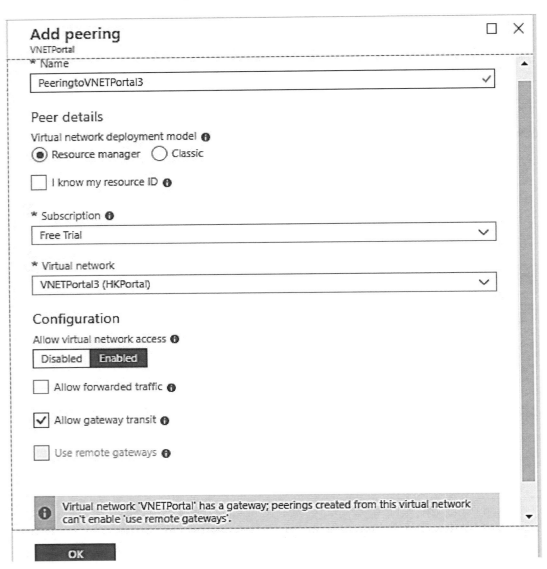

2. Go to VNETPortal3 Dashboard>Click Peering in left pane> In Right Pane Click +Add > Add Peering blade opens > Select VNETPortal in Virtual Network> Select Use Remote Gateway> click ok.

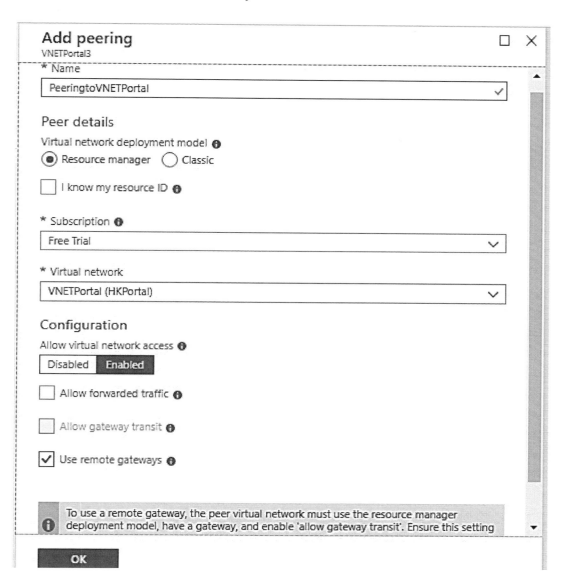

3. The 2 VNETs are now peered and connected. You can check the peering status by clicking peering in Virtual Network dashboard. Figure below shows VNETPortal Dashboard with Peering selected in left pane.

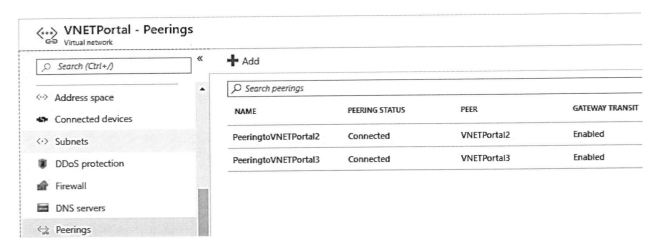

4. Figure below shows VNETPortal3 Dashboard with Peering selected in left pane.

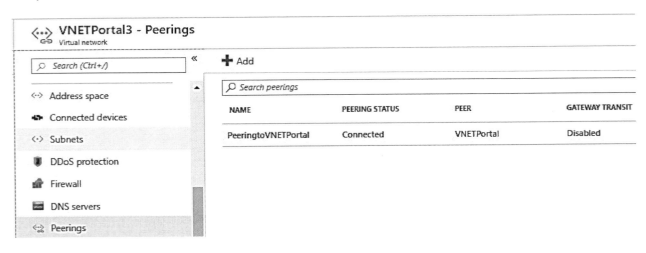

Routing within VNET using System Route

Azure automatically creates Default system routes and assigns the routes to each subnet in a virtual network. You can't create system routes, nor can you remove system routes, but you can override some system routes with Custom Routes which can be User Defined Routes (UDR) or BGP Routes or both.

For Example Virtual machines (VMs) in virtual networks can communicate with each other and to the public internet, automatically. You do not need to specify a gateway, even though the VMs are in different subnets.

This happens because every subnet created in a virtual network is automatically associated with a system routes that contains the following system route rules:

- **Local VNET Rule**: This rule is automatically created for every subnet in a virtual network. It specifies that there is a direct link between the VMs in the VNET and there is no intermediate next hop.
- **Internet Rule**: This rule handles all traffic destined to the public Internet (address prefix 0.0.0.0/0) and uses the infrastructure internet gateway as the next hop for all traffic destined to the Internet.
- **On-premises Rule**: This rule applies to all traffic destined to the on-premises address range and uses VPN gateway as the next hop destination.

Azure automatically creates the following default system routes for each subnet:

Source	Address Prefix	Next Hop Type
Default	Unique to the virtual network	Virtual network
Default	0.0.0.0/0	Internet
Default	10.0.0.0/8	None
Default	172.16.0.0/12	None
Default	192.168.0.0/16	None
Default	100.64.0.0/10	None

Traffic routed to the **None** next hop type is dropped, rather than routed outside the subnet. But for these Addresses (10.0.0.0/8, 172.16.0.0/12, 192.168.0.0/16, 100.64.0.0/10) Azure automatically changes the next hop type for the route from None to **Virtual network** (Local VNET Rule).

Optional Default System Routes

Azure creates default system routes for each subnet, and adds additional optional default routes to specific subnets, or every subnet, when you enable specific Azure capabilities.

Source	Address Prefix	Next Hop Type	Subnet within VNET that route is added to
Default	Unique to the virtual network	VNET peering	All
Virtual network gateway	Prefixes advertised from on-premises via BGP or configured in the local network gateway	Virtual Network Gateway	All
Default	Multiple	VirtualNetworkServiceEndpoint	Only the subnet a service endpoint is enabled for.

System routes control the flow of communication in the following scenarios:

- From within the same subnet.
- From a subnet to another within a VNET.
- From VMs to the Internet.
- From a VNET to another VNET through a VPN gateway.
- From a VNET to another VNET through VNET Peering.
- From a VNET to your on-premises network through a VPN gateway.
- From a Subnet to Azure Services through VirtualNetworkServiceEndpoint.

Figure Below shows Default System Route associated with Subnets.

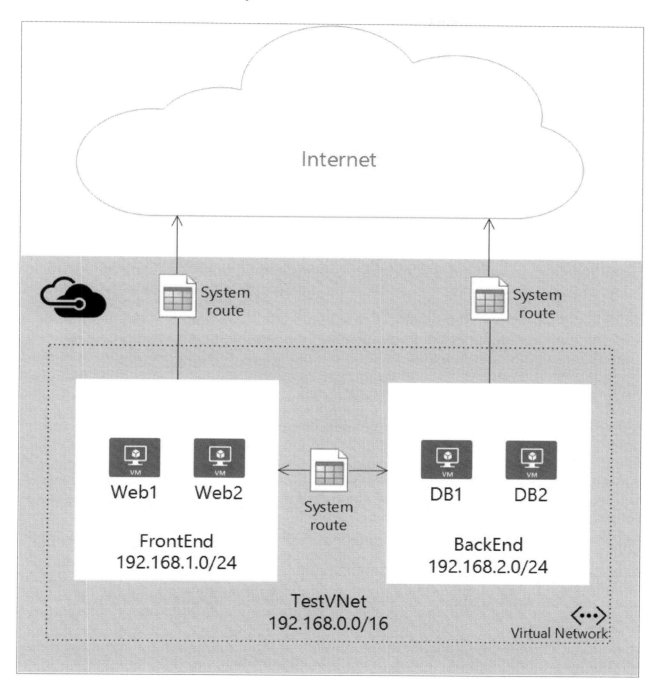

Routing within VNET using User Defined Route (UDR)

With user-defined routes you not only override Azure's default system routes but can also add additional routes to a subnet's route table.

With User Defined routes, Virtual Machine traffic in a Subnet goes through a **Network virtual appliance (NVA)** located in another subnet. This is done by creating Route table (Consisting User Defined Routes) and associating Route Table with the Subnets where traffic originates and terminates.

With UDR, NVA VM acts the gateway for other VMs in your virtual network.

In Figure below a Custom route table consisting of UDR is created and Associated with Web-Subnet and DB-Subnet. Traffic from Web-Subnet to DB-subnet and Vice versa goes through network virtual appliance (NVA) located in DMZ subnet **as UDR Route is preferred over Default System Route.**

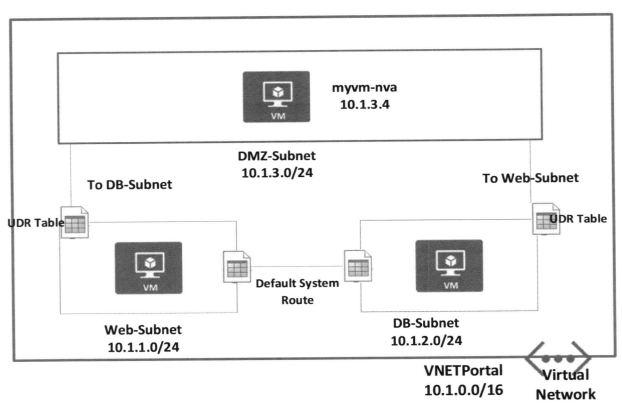

Network virtual appliance (NVA) VM: NVA VM is a Windows Server VM with Private IP and with IP forwarding enabled on Network Interface of the VM.

How Azure selects a route

Subnets rely on Default system routes until a route table is associated to the subnet. Once an association exists, routing is done based on Longest Prefix Match (LPM) among both user defined routes and system routes. If multiple routes contain the same address prefix, Azure selects the route type, based on the following priority:

1. User defined route.
2. BGP route (when ExpressRoute is used).
3. System route.

Route Table

A route table is a collection of individual routes used to decide where to forward packets based on the destination IP address. Route table is associated with Subnet. A route consists of the following:

Address prefix: The destination address in CIDR format.
Next hop type: Next hop type can be Virtual Network, Virtual Network gateway, Internet, virtual appliance (NVA) or none.
Next hop Address: It is the Address of the Virtual Appliance VM. Next hop values are only allowed in routes where the next hop type is *Virtual Appliance*.

IP Forwarding

To allow Virtual Machine (NVA) to receive traffic addressed to other destinations, enable IP Forwarding for the NVA VM.

Design Nugget UDR

Design Nugget 1: User defined routes are only applied to traffic leaving a subnet. You cannot create routes to specify how traffic comes into a subnet.
Design Nugget 2: The appliance you are forwarding traffic to cannot be in the same subnet where the traffic originates. Always create a separate subnet for your appliances.
Design Nugget 3: Each subnet can be associated with one or zero route table apart from system routes. But the same route table can be associated to one or more subnets. All VMs in a subnet use the route table associated to that subnet.

Exercise 18: Routing Traffic between 2 Subnets to pass through another Subnet using UDR

For this Demonstration Exercise we will create user-defined routes to route traffic between Web-Subnet and DB-Subnet to pass-through a network virtual appliance located in DMZ-Subnet as shown in figure below. For this Demonstration lab we will use Virtual Network **VNETPortal** created in Exercise 2.

Note: Readers are requested to attempt this Exercise at the end of the book otherwise by mistake you can break the topology.

Pre-Req for this Exercise

Windows Server 2016 NVA VM (myvm-nva) is created in DMZ-Subnet with Private IP 10.1.3.4 only. You can do this Exercise even If you have not created NVA VM. If you have not deployed NVA VM then just skip step 1.

Solution

Figure below shows the architecture of the solution.

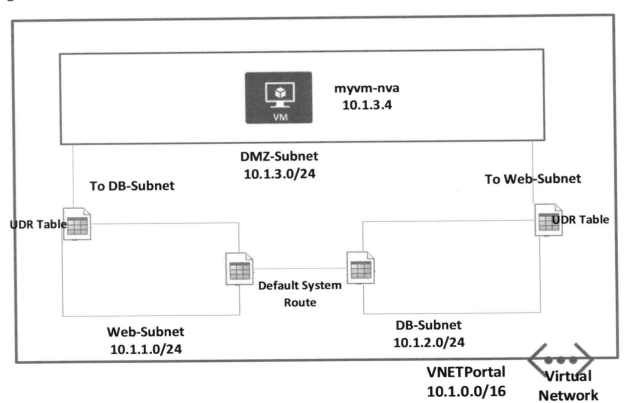

Step 1: To allow NVA Virtual Machine in DMZ subnet to receive traffic addressed to other destinations, enable IP Forwarding for the NVA VM.

Enable IP Forwarding in NVA Virtual Machine in DMZ subnet: Go to NVA VM Dashboard> Click Networking under settings> In Right pane click Private Network Interface attached to NVA VM>Network Interface Dashboard opens>Click IP Configuration in left Pane>In Right Pane Click Enabled.

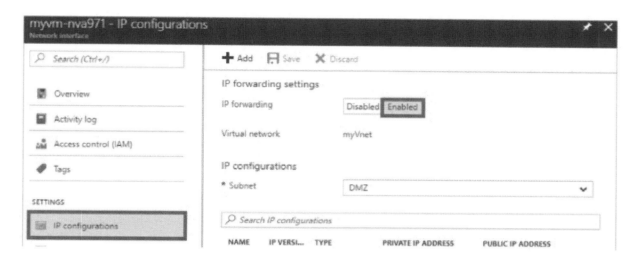

Step 2 Create Route Table (To be associated with Web-Subnet): Click + Create a Resource> Networking> Route Table> Create Route Table Blade opens>Enter name ToDBSubnet, Select Resource Group HKPortal and click create.

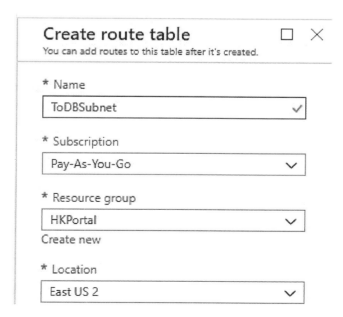

Figure below shows Dashboard of Route Table **ToDBSubnet.**

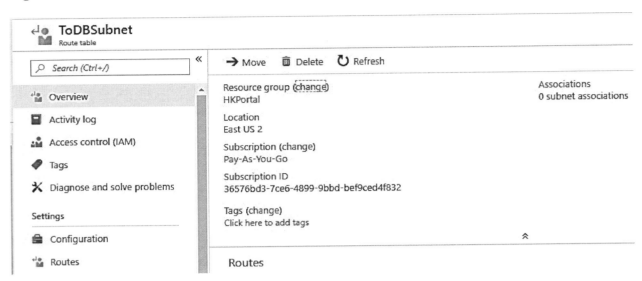

Step 3 Add a route in Route Table (ToDBSubnet): Go to ToDBSubnet Route table Dashboard> Click Routes in left Pane>Click +Add> Add Route Blade opens > Enter following information and click ok.
Route name: RouteToDBSubnet.
Address Prefix: Network Address of DB-Subnet 10.1.2.0/24.
Next Hop type: Select Virtual Appliance from Drop Down box.
Next Hop Address: IP Address of NVA VM (myvm-nva) 10.1.3.4.

Step 4 Associate Route Table (ToDBSubnet) with Web-Subnet: Go to Route Table ToDBSubnet Dashboard>click Subnets in left pane>In Right pane click + Associate>Associate Subnet Blade opens>Click Virtual Network and select VNETPortal>Click Subnet and select Web-Subnet>Click Ok.

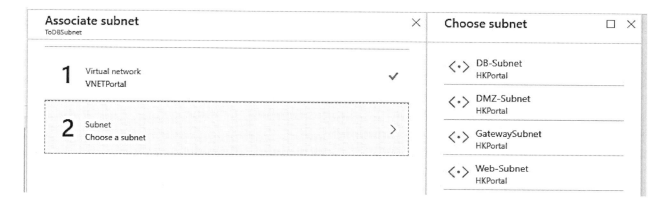

Figure below shows Route Table Dashboard. It has one Route and is associated with Web-Subnet.

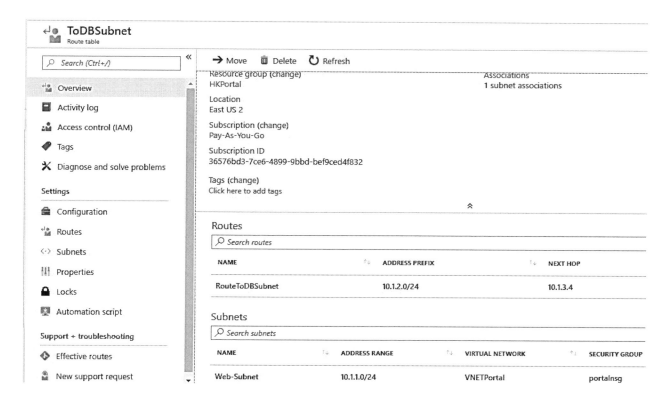

Step 5: **Create Route Table (To be associated with DB-Subnet)**: Click + Create a Resource> Networking> Route Table> Create Route Table Blade opens>Enter name ToWebSubnet, Select Resource Group HKPortal and click create.

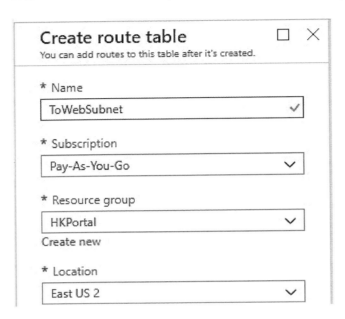

Step 6 Add a route in Route Table (ToWebSubnet): Go to ToWebSubnet Route table Dashboard> Click Routes in left Pane>Click +Add> Add Route Blade opens > Enter following information and click ok.

Route name: RouteToWebSubnet.

Address Prefix: Network Address of Web-Subnet 10.1.1.0/24.

Next Hop type: Select Virtual Appliance from Drop Down box.

Next Hop Address: IP Address of NVA VM (myvm-nva) 10.1.3.4.

Step 7 Associate Route Table (ToWebSubnet) with DB-Subnet: Go to Route Table ToWebSubnet Dashboard>click Subnets in left pane>In Right pane click + Associate>Associate Subnet Blade opens>Click Virtual Network and select VNETPortal>Click Subnet and select DB-Subnet>Click Ok.

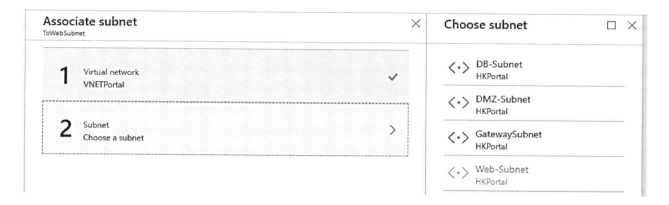

Figure below shows the Dashboard of Route Table ToWebSubnet. It has one Route and is associated with DB-Subnet.

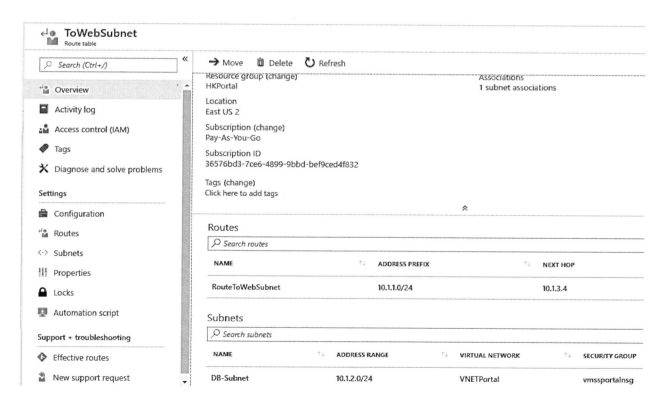

Result 1 of above actions: We have both default route and User defined Route associated with Web-Subnet & DB-Subnet.

Result 2 of above actions: Network traffic between Web-Subnet and DB- Subnets flows through the network virtual appliance (NVA). Though system route specify that Traffic can flow directly between Web and DB subnet but Traffic flows through NVA **as UDR is preferred.**

Chapter 2 Implementing Virtual Networks with CLI & PS

This Chapter covers following Lab Exercises

- Create Resource Group HKCLI using Azure CLI
- Create Resource Group HKPS using Azure PowerShell
- Create Virtual Network VNETCLI using Azure CLI
- Create Virtual Network VNETPS using Azure PowerShell

Exercise 19: Create Resource Group HKCLI using Azure CLI

You can either use Azure CLI on your desktop or use Cloud shell. For this lab use Azure CLI installed on our desktop. See Chapter 18 on how to use Azure CLI.

1. Open windows CMD on your desktop where Azure CLI is installed>Enter Command **az login**> This will open a browser. Select Account and Enter subscription credentials.

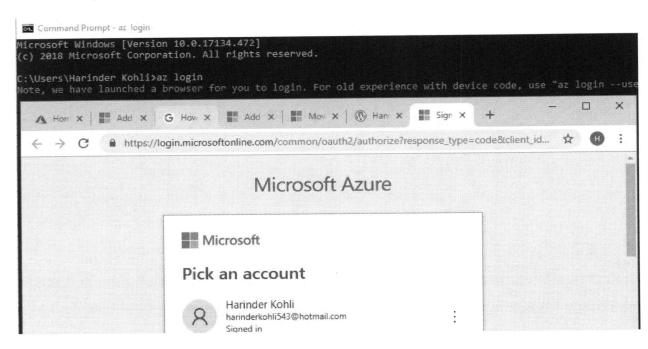

2. After you have successfully authenticated to Azure through Browser, The CMD window will now show Azure login information as shown below.

Create Resource Group using az group command

az group create --name HKCLI --location eastus2

```
Command Prompt

C:\Users\Harinder Kohli>az group create --name HKCLI --location eastus2
{
  "id": "/subscriptions/36576bd3-7ce6-4899-9bbd-bef9ced4f832/resourceGroups/HKCLI",
  "location": "eastus2",
  "managedBy": null,
  "name": "HKCLI",
  "properties": {
    "provisioningState": "Succeeded"
  },
  "tags": null
}

C:\Users\Harinder Kohli>
```

Check the Resource Group created

az group show --name HKCLI or

az group show --resource-group HKCLI

```
Command Prompt

C:\Users\Harinder Kohli>az group show --name HKCLI
{
  "id": "/subscriptions/36576bd3-7ce6-4899-9bbd-bef9ced4f832/resourceGroups/HKCLI",
  "location": "eastus2",
  "managedBy": null,
  "name": "HKCLI",
  "properties": {
    "provisioningState": "Succeeded"
  },
  "tags": null
}

C:\Users\Harinder Kohli>
```

Deleting Resource Group

az group delete --name HKCLI --yes

Note: Don't run above command as we need to create resources in the group.

Exercise 20: Create Resource Group HKPS using Azure PowerShell

Note: you can either install and use Azure PowerShell Module on your desktop or use Cloud shell. Refer to chapter 18 for Installing and using Azure PowerShell.

Open PowerShell on your desktop and login using Connect-AzureRmAccount.

```
PS C:\Users\Harinder Kohli> Connect-AzureRmAccount


Account          : harinderkohli543@outlook.com
SubscriptionName : Pay-As-You-Go
SubscriptionId   : 7593a7e7-0d4e-493a-922e-c433ef24df3b
TenantId         : 9dc252df-4ca2-40e7-9f9c-e2d717846ca4
Environment      : AzureCloud
```

Create Resource Group
New-AzureRmResourceGroup –Name HKPS –Location eastus2

```
PS C:\Users\Harinder Kohli> New-AzureRmResourceGroup -Name HKPS -Location eastus2

Confirm
Provided resource group already exists. Are you sure you want to update it?
[Y] Yes  [N] No  [S] Suspend  [?] Help (default is "Y"): Y


ResourceGroupName : HKPS
Location          : eastus2
ProvisioningState : Succeeded
Tags              :
ResourceId        : /subscriptions/7593a7e7-0d4e-493a-922e-c433ef24df3b/resourceGroups/HKPS
```

Check the Resource Group HKPS created
Get-AzureRMResourceGroup
Get-AzureRmResourceGroup –Name HKPS

```
PS C:\Users\Harinder Kohli> Get-AzureRmResourceGroup -Name HKPS


ResourceGroupName : HKPS
Location          : eastus2
ProvisioningState : Succeeded
Tags              :
ResourceId        : /subscriptions/7593a7e7-0d4e-493a-922e-c433ef24df3b/resourceGroups/HKPS
```

Deleting Resource Group
Remove-AzureRmResourceGroup –Name HKPS –Force
Note: Don't run above command as we need to create resources in the group.

Exercise 21: Create Virtual Network VNETCLI using Azure CLI

In this exercise we will create Virtual Network "VNETCLI" in Resource Group HKCLI using 10.2.0.0/16 address space in East US 2 Location. We will also create Subnet with name Web-Subnet with address 10.2.1.0/24.

Open cmd and enter **az login** command for Authenticating to Subscription.

Create Virtual Network using az network vnet command
az network vnet create --name VNETCLI --address-prefix 10.2.0.0/16 --resource-group HKCLI --subnet-name Web-Subnet --address-prefix 10.2.1.0/24

Check the Virtual Network created
az network vnet show --name VNETCLI --resource-group HKCLI

Delete Virtual Network
az network vnet delete --name VNETCLI --resource-group HKCLI
Note: Don't run above command as we need to create resources in the VNET.

Exercise 22: Create Virtual Network VNETPS using Azure PowerShell

In this exercise we will create Virtual Network "VNETPS" in Resource Group HKPS using 10.3.0.0/16 address space in East US 2 Location. We will also create Subnet with name Web-Subnet with address 10.3.1.0/24.

Open PowerShell on your desktop and login using Connect-AzureRmAccount.

Create Subnet name Web-Subnet
$subnet = New-AzureRmVirtualNetworkSubnetConfig –Name Web-Subnet -AddressPrefix 10.3.1.0/24

Create Virtual Network
New-AzureRmVirtualNetwork –Name VNETPS –ResourceGroupName HKPS –Location eastus2 –AddressPrefix 10.3.0.0/16 –Subnet $subnet

```
PS C:\Users\Harinder Kohli> New-AzureRmVirtualNetwork -Name VNETPS -ResourceGroupName HKPS -Location eastus2
-AddressPrefix 10.3.0.0/16 -Subnet $subnet
WARNING: Breaking changes in the cmdlet 'New-AzureRmVirtualNetwork' :
WARNING:    - "The output type 'Microsoft.Azure.Commands.Network.Models.PSVirtualNetwork' is changing"
 - The following properties in the output type are being deprecated :
 'EnableVmProtection'

Confirm
Are you sure you want to overwrite resource 'VNETPS'
[Y] Yes  [N] No  [S] Suspend  [?] Help (default is "Y"): Y

ResourceGroupName Name    Location ProvisioningState EnableDdosProtection EnableVmProtection
----------------- ----    -------- ----------------- -------------------- ------------------
HKPS              VNETPS  eastus2  Succeeded         False                False
```

Check the Virtual Network created
Get-AzureRmVirtualNetwork –Name VNETPS –ResourceGroupName HKPS

```
PS C:\Users\Harinder Kohli> Get-AzureRmVirtualNetwork -Name VNETPS -ResourceGroupName HKPS
WARNING: Breaking changes in the cmdlet 'Get-AzureRmVirtualNetwork' :
WARNING:    - "The output type 'Microsoft.Azure.Commands.Network.Models.PSVirtualNetwork' is changing"
 - The following properties in the output type are being deprecated :
 'EnableVmProtection'


ResourceGroupName Name    Location ProvisioningState EnableDdosProtection EnableVmProtection
----------------- ----    -------- ----------------- -------------------- ------------------
HKPS              VNETPS  eastus2  Succeeded         False                False
```

Delete Virtual Network
Remove-AzureRmVirtualNetwork –Name VNETPS –ResourceGroupName HKPS
Note: Don't run above command as we need to create resources in the VNET.

Chapter 3 Deploy and Manage Virtual Machines (VMs)

This Chapter covers following Topic Lessons

- Azure Virtual Machine
- Azure Virtual Machine Storage
- Azure Virtual Machine Networking
- Virtual Machine Security using Network Security Group (NSG)
- VM High Availability using Availability Set (AS)
- VM High Availability using Availability Zones and Load Balancers
- Virtual Machine Snapshot
- Linux VM in Azure
- Images
- Azure Virtual Machine Agent
- Virtual Machine Extensions
- Custom Script Extension
- Manage VM Sizes
- VM Auto-Shutdown
- Reset Password
- Redeploy VM
- VM Backup & Restore
- Moving Virtual Machines
- VM Alerts, Metrics & Diagnostic Settings
- VM Update, Inventory, Change & Configuration Management
- PowerShell DSC Extension
- ARM Template

This Chapter covers following Lab Exercises

- Create Availability Set (AS) using Azure Portal
- Create Windows Virtual Machine using Azure Portal
- Log on to Windows VM with RDP
- Install IIS and Access default Website
- Connecting to Default IIS website on wvmportal VM
- Add Data Disk
- Initialize the Data Disk
- Create and Add Network Interface to VM wvmportal

- Create Snapshot of VM wvmportal OS Hard Disk
- Create Windows VM representing On-Premises AD DS
- Enable AD DS Role in Virtual Machine OnPremAD
- Create Linux VM
- Connecting to Linux VM
- Update Linux VM & Install NGINX Web Server
- Create Custom Image of Azure VM
- Deploy VM from Custom image
- Demonstrating various VM Extensions available
- Demonstrating Custom Script Extension using Azure Portal
- Resizing VM
- Virtual Machine Auto-Shutdown
- Reset Password

Chapter Topology

In this chapter we will add Virtual Machines **wvmportal and linuxportal** to the topology. These VMs will be created in Web-Subnet and DB-Subnet respectively in Virtual Network VNETPortal.

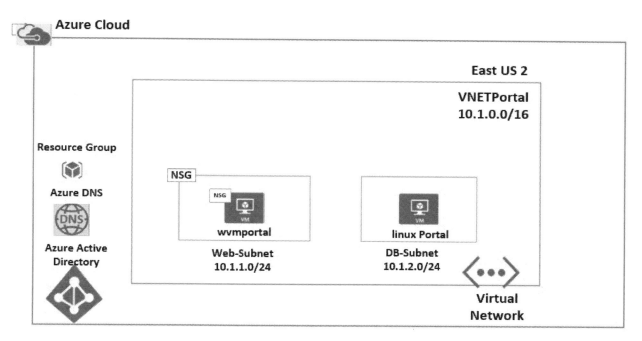

We will add Virtual Machine **OnPremAD** in Virtual Network VNETOnPrem. We will also install Active Directory Domain Services (AD DS) role in VM OnPremAD.

South Central US

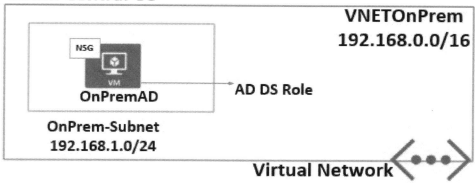

Note 1: This diagram is shown separately as there is space constrained in top diagram.

Note 2: I am not showing GatewaySubnet and DMZ-Subnet as they are no longer being used for the rest of the Chapters.

Azure Virtual Machine (VM)

Azure Virtual Machine is on-demand resizable computing resource in the cloud that can be used to host variety of applications. Azure Virtual Machine runs on a Hyper-V host which also runs other Virtual Machines.

You can scale up by using bigger size Virtual Machine or scale out using additional instance of the virtual machine and then Load Balancing them.

Azure VM can be Windows or Linux based.

Virtual Machine (VM) Sizes

Virtual Machines are available in various sizes and categorized under series. Under each series various virtual machine sizes are available with options for memory, CPU family, Number of CPU cores, Standard or Premium Storage, Number of Data Disks, Number of NIC's and Temporary Storage.

Various Virtual Machine Series are available either with Standard Storage or both Standard & Premium Storage.

Virtual Machines with standard storage are available under A-series, Av2-series, D-series, Dv2-series, Dv3, F-series, G-Series, H-series and N-series. These VMs use magnetic HDD to host a virtual machine disks (OS and Data Disk). Temporary storage is on SSD except for A series which are on magnetic HDD.

Virtual Machines with premium Storage are available under DS-series, DSv2-series, DSv3, ESv3, FS-series, GS-series etc. These VMs can use solid-state drives (SSDs) or HDD to host a virtual machine disks (OS and Data Disk) and also provide a local SSD disk cache. Temporary storage is on SSD.

Note: Virtual Machines with letter **s** in its size designation support both Standard Storage and Premium Storage.

Virtual Machines Series

Virtual Machines series in Azure can be categorized under General purpose, Compute optimized, Memory optimized, Storage Optimized, GPU and High Performance Compute.

Type	Series	Description
General purpose	DSv3, Dv3, DSv2, Dv2, DS, D, Av2, A0-4 Basic, A0-A7 Standard	Balanced CPU-to-memory ratio. Ideal for testing and development, General Purpose Production workloads, small to medium databases, and low to medium traffic web servers.
Compute optimized	Fs, F, Fv2 & FSv2	High CPU-to-memory ratio. Good for medium traffic web servers, network appliances, batch processes, and application servers.
Memory optimized	ESv3, Ev3, M, GS, G, DSv2, Dv2, DS & D	High memory-to-core ratio. Great for relational database servers, medium to large caches, and in-memory analytics.
Storage optimized	Ls	High disk throughput and IO. Ideal for Big Data, SQL, and NoSQL databases.
GPU	NC, NCv2, NCv3, NV & ND	Specialized virtual machines targeted for heavy graphic rendering and video editing. Available with single or multiple GPUs.
High performance compute	H, A8-11	High Performance Computing VMs are good for high performance & parallel computing workloads such as financial risk modeling, seismic and reservoir simulation, molecular modeling and genomic research.

Note 1: D, DS and A0-A7 Standard are being phased out.
Note 2: Virtual Machines with letter **s** in its size designation support both Standard Storage and Premium Storage.
Note 3: Dv2 & DSv2 machines are included in both General Purpose & Memory. General Purpose includes following sizes: D1v2, D2v2, D3v2, D4v2 and D5v2. Memory Optimised includes following: D11v2, D12v2, D13v2, D14v2 & D15v2.
Note 4: Microsoft recommends that to get the best performance for price, use the latest generation VMs where possible.

Low Priority VMs

Low Priority VMs are available at lower cost than normal VMs and are allocated from surplus or spare Azure compute capacity.

The advantage of Low Priority VM is that it reduce the costs of running workloads or allow much more work to be performed at a greater scale for the same cost.

The disadvantage of Low Priority VM is that Azure can take back Low priority VMs when spare compute capacity decreases.

Low Priority VMs are currently available for Azure Batch and Virtual Machine Scale Set (VMSS).

Virtual Machine Storage

Storage for Virtual Machines is provided by Virtual Machine Disks. Azure Virtual Machine Disks (OS & Data) are stored in Page Blob and are accessed over the network.

You can also mount Azure File shares to Virtual Machine disks for additional Storage. File shares will be further discussed in Storage chapter.

Figure bellows shows Storage options for Azure Virtual Machines.

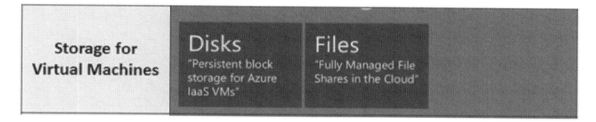

Figure below shows OS and Data Disks are stored in Azure Blob (Page) Storage and are accessed over the network. Temporary disk is located on the physical host where the virtual machine is running.

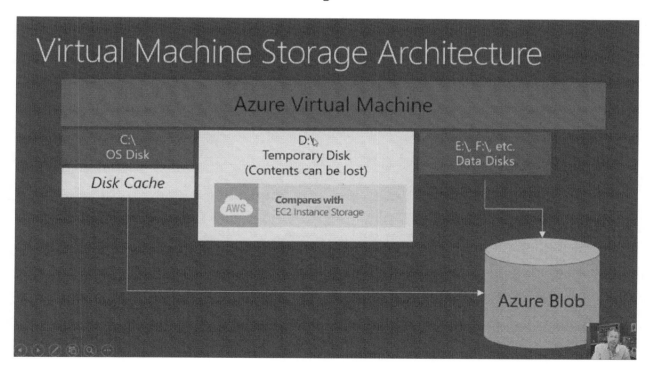

Virtual Machine Storage Disk Types

Azure Virtual Machine Disks are stored in Page Blob storage. Page Blob storage can use Standard Storage or Premium Storage. Standard Storage is backed by Magnetic HDD and Premium Storage is backed by SSD.

Azure Virtual Machines have minimum of 2 disks: OS Disk and Temporary Disk. You can also attach additional Data Disks. Number of Data Disks depend upon the series and the size of the VM choosen.

Virtual Machine Disks (OS and Data disk) are accessed over the network. Temporary disk is located on the physical host where the virtual machine is running. Virtual machines use virtual hard disks (VHDs) to store their operating system (OS) and data. Virtual Machine disks (VHDs) are stored in page blobs.

Operating System Disks

Every virtual machine has one **network attached** operating system disk and is **accessed over the network**. It's labeled as the C: drive. This disk has a maximum capacity of 4095 gigabytes (GB). Data is persisted in the event virtual machine is rebooted, started or stopped. It is registered as SATA Drive.

Temporary Disk

The temporary disk is automatically created on physical host where virtual machine is running. The temporary disk is labeled as the D: drive and it is used for storing page or swap files. Data is lost in the event virtual machine is rebooted or stopped. The size of the temporary disk is based on the size of the VM.

Data Disk

A data disk is a VHD that's network attached to a virtual machine to store application data and is **accessed over the network**. The size of the virtual machine determines how many data disks you can attach to it. Data is persisted in the event virtual machine is rebooted, started or stopped. Data disks are registered as SCSI drives and are labelled with a letter that you choose.

Managed and Unmanaged Disk

Azure Virtual Machine disk types (OS & Data Disk) can be Unmanaged or Managed.

Disks are associated with storage accounts. Maximum IOPS of storage account is 20000 IOPS. We have to make sure that IOPS of all disks in the storage account should not exceed 20000 IOPS otherwise throttling happens.

Unmanaged Disks

With unmanaged disks we have to create and specify the storage account when we create unmanaged disk. We have to make sure that the combined IOPS of disks in the storage account do not exceed 20000 IOPS. We have to also plan number of storage accounts needed to accommodate our disks.

Managed Disks

Managed Disk option takes care of storage account creation and management and also ensures that users do not have to worry about 20000 IOPS limit in the storage account.

Managed Disks allow you to create up to 10,000 VM **disks** in a subscription.

When using availability set (AS) managed disk option ensures that disks of VMs in AS are isolated from each other to avoid SPOF.

The advantage of Managed Disk option is that it eliminates the operational overhead of planning, creating and managing Storage Accounts.

MS recommends that Managed Disk option to be used for all new VMs and convert previously created unmanaged disks to managed disks to take advantage of new features in managed disks.

Note: Unmanaged or Managed OS Disk is chosen during Virtual Machine creation.

Comparing Managed & Unmanaged Disks

	Managed Disks	**Unmanaged Disk**
Replication	LRS	LRS, GRS & RA-GRS
Pricing	Standard Storage: Per Disk Premium Storage: Per Disk	Standard Storage: Per GB Premium Storage: Per Disk
Storage Account Selection	Automatic	Manual
RBAC	Disk Level	Storage Account Level
Tags	Disk Level	Storage Account Level
Locks	Disk Level	Storage Account Level

Virtual Machine Disk Performance Tiers

There are **three** Performance tiers for virtual machine disk storage – Standard Storage, Premium SSD Storage & Standard SSD Storage. Virtual Machines disks are stored in Page Blobs. Page blobs can be created under General Purpose Standard Storage account or General purpose premium Storage account.

Standard Storage

With Standard Storage, OS and Data disks are stored in page blob backed by Magnetic HDD. You can use standard storage disks for Dev/Test scenarios and less critical workloads.

Standard Storage disks can be created in 2 ways – Unmanaged disks or Managed Disks. With Unmanaged disk you need to create storage account. Whereas Managed Disk option takes care of storage account creation.

Standard Unmanaged disk limits

VM Tier	Basic Tier	Standard Tier
Max Disk size	4095 GB	4095 GB
Max 8 KB IOPS per disk	300	500
Max throughput per disk	60 MB/s	60 MB/s

Maximum Disk Size in Standard Unmanaged disk is 4095 GB. You pay only for the capacity used. It is therefore recommended you create the disk with Max size as you are paying only for the capacity used.

Standard Managed Disk Limits

Standard Managed Disk Type	S4	S6	S10	S20	S30	S40	S50
Disk Size (GB)	32	64	128	512	1024	2048	4095
Max IOPS per disk	500	500	500	500	500	500	500
Max throughput per disk	60 MB/s	60 MB/s	60 MB/s	60 MB/s	60 MB/s	60 MB/s	60 MB/s

Premium SSD Storage

Premium Storage disks are backed by solid-state drives (SSDs). With Premium Storage, OS and Data disks are stored in page blob backed by SSD.

Azure Premium Storage delivers high-performance, low-latency disk support for virtual machines (VMs) with input/output (I/O)-intensive workloads. You can use Premium storage disks for I/O intensive and mission-critical production applications.

Requirements for Premium Storage

1. You can use Premium Storage disks only with VMs that are compatible with Premium Storage Disks. Premium Storage supports DS-series, DSv2-series, DSv3 Series, GS-series, Ls-series, and Fs-series, ESv3 VMs etc only.

2. You will require Premium storage account to create Premium Storage Disks. A premium storage account supports only locally redundant storage (LRS) as the replication option. Locally redundant storage keeps three copies of the data within a single region.

Features of Virtual Machines (DS-series, DSv2-series, DSv3, ESv3GS-series, Ls-series, and Fs-series, M etc) backed by Premium Storage

1. **Virtual Machine OS Disk:** Premium Storage VM can use either a premium or a standard operating system disk.

2. **Virtual Machine Data Disk:** Premium Storage VM can use both Premium and Standard Storage Disks.

3. **Cache:** VMs with Premium Storage have a unique caching capability for high levels of throughput and latency. The caching capability exceeds underlying premium storage disk performance. You can set the disk caching policy on premium storage disks to **ReadOnly**, **ReadWrite**, or **None**. The default disk caching policy is **Read Only** for all premium data disks and **ReadWrite** for operating system disks.

Note: Premium Storage is supported in Virtual Machines with letter **s** in its size designation.

VM scale limits and performance: Premium Storage-supported VMs have scale limits and performance specifications for IOPS, bandwidth, and the number of disks that can be attached per VM.

For example, a STANDARD_DS1 VM has a dedicated bandwidth of 32 MB/s for premium storage disk traffic. A P10 premium storage disk can provide a bandwidth of 100 MB/s. If a P10 premium storage disk is attached to this VM, it can only go up to 32 MB/s. It cannot use the maximum 100 MB/s that the P10 disk can provide.

Premium Storage disk Sizes and limits (Unmanaged)

Premium storage disk type	P10	P20	P30	P40	P50
Disk Size (GB)	128	512	1024	2048	4095
Max Throughput per Disk	100 MB/s	150 MB/s	200 MB/s	250 MB/s	250 MB/s
Max IOPS per Disk	500 IOPS	2300 IOPS	5000 IOPS	7500 IOPS	7500 IOPS

Premium Storage Managed disk Sizes and limits

Premium storage disk type	P4	P6	P10	P20	P30	P40	P50
Disk Size (GB)	32	64	128	512	1024	2048	4095
Max Throughput per Disk	25 MB/s	50 MB/s	100 MB/s	150 MB/s	200 MB/s	250 MB/s	250 MB/s
Max IOPS per Disk	120 IOPS	240 IOPS	500 IOPS	2300 IOPS	5000 IOPS	7500 IOPS	7500 IOPS

Standard SSD Storage

Standard SSD Storage disks are backed by solid-state drives (SSDs). With Standard SSD Storage, OS and Data disks are stored in page blob backed by SSD.

Standard SSD Storage comes in Managed Disk option only.

Standard SSD Managed Disk is a low-cost SSD offering and are optimized for test and entry-level production workloads requiring consistent latency. Standard SSD Managed Disks can also be used for big data workloads that require high throughput.

Standard SSD Managed Disks deliver lower latency compared to Standard HDDs, while improving reliability and scalability for your applications, and are available with all Azure VM sizes. Standard SSD Managed Disks can be easily upgraded to Premium SSD Managed Disks for more demanding and latency-sensitive enterprise workloads.

Standard SSD Managed Storage disk Sizes and limits

	E10	E15	E20	E30	E40	E50	E60
Disk Size (GB)	128 GB	256 GB	512 GB	1 TB	2 TB	4 TB	8 TB
Max Throughput	60 MB/s	60 MB/s	60 MB/s	60 MB/s	60 MB/s	60 MB/s	300 MB/s
Max IOPS per Disk	500	500	500	500	500	500	1300

Virtual Machine Networking

Azure Virtual Machines are created in Virtual Networks. An Azure virtual network (VNET) is Virtual Datacenter in the cloud. You can further segment virtual network (VNET) into subnets. Access to the subnets can be controlled using Network Security groups. You can define the IP address blocks, security policies, and route tables within this network.

In the below diagram you have Virtual Network KNET1 with network address 192.168.0.0/16 divided into two Subnets- Web-Subnet1 and DB-Subnet1 with network addresses 192.168.1.0/24 and 192.168.2.0/24 respectively.

These Network Addresses are defined by the user and not by Azure Cloud.

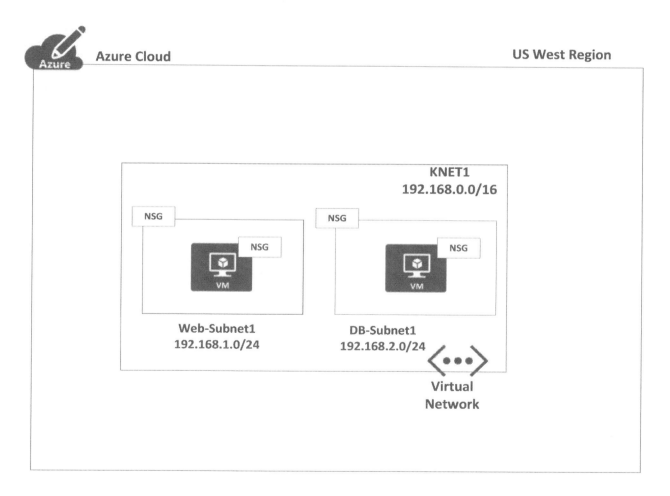

Azure Virtual Machines private address is derived from subnet address. In the above figure Virtual Machines in Web-Subnet1 will get **private address** of 192.168.1.x/24 and Virtual Machines in DB-Subnet1 will get private address of 192.168.2.x/24. Private IP Address is used for communication within a Virtual Network, your on-premises network and the Internet (with NAT).

You can use following class A, Class B and Class C address range for virtual networks.

10.0.0.0/8
172.16.0.0/12
192.168.0.0/16

Once the IP address range is decided, we can then divide this range into subnets. Azure Virtual Machines private address is derived from subnet address.

VM Private IP Address can be dynamic or Static. The default allocation is dynamic. You can assign static private IP address to VM from VM Subnet address range.

Virtual Machine Public address is assigned by Azure. Public Address can be Static or Dynamic. Dynamic Public IP will change every time you stop or reboot your Virtual Machine. To ensure the IP address for the VM remains the same, set the allocation method to static.
Public IP address is used for communication with internet and Public facing Azure resources which are not part of Virtual Network.

Virtual Machine Security using Network Security Group (NSG)

Network Security Group (NSG) acts as a Firewall. Network Security Group (NSG) contains a list of rules that allow or deny network traffic to VM NICs or subnets or both.

NSGs can be associated with subnets and/or individual VM NICs connected to a subnet. When an NSG is associated with a subnet, the rules apply to all the VMs in that subnet. In addition, traffic to an individual VM NIC can be restricted by associating an NSG directly to a VM NIC.

NSGs contain rules that specify whether the traffic is approved or denied. Each rule is based on a source IP address, a source port, a destination IP address, and a destination port. Based on whether the traffic matches this combination, it either is allowed or denied.

Figure below shows Web1 & Web2 VMs are protected by 2 levels of Firewall. One at VM NIC level and other at Subnet Level. Whereas DB1 VM is protected at VM NIC level only.

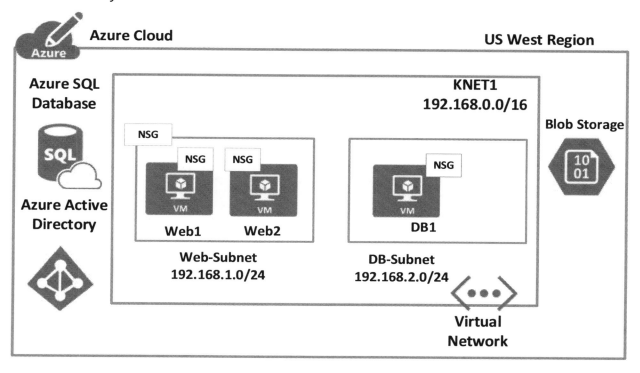

Note: NSG was discussed in Implementing Virtual Networks chapter.

VM High Availability using Availability Set (AS)

Availability Set (AS) Provides high Availability against hardware failure in Azure Cloud by eliminating single point of failure. Availability Set (AS) in itself is not a full high availability solution. **To provide application HA, Availability Set (AS) has to be combined with Azure Load Balancer.**

Before going into details of Availability Set, let's discuss why we need it in first place. Consider a scenario where there are 2 applications and each application is running 2 instances - Application A (VMA-1 & VMA-2) & Application B (VMB-1 & VMB-2). Application Instances are load balanced.

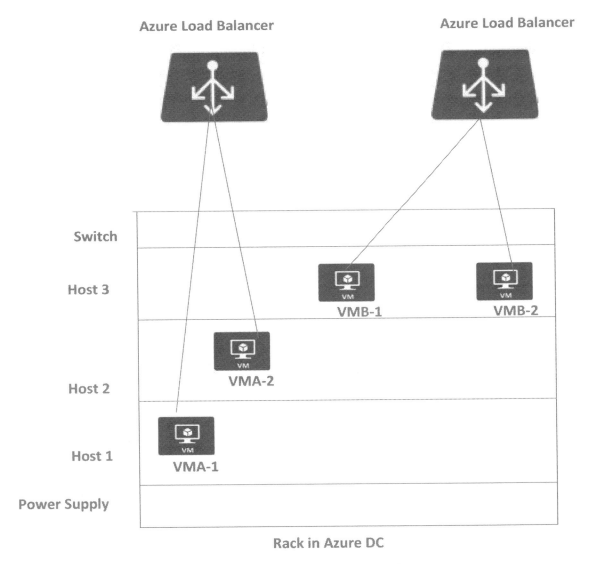

Note: Load Balancing will be discussed in AZ 101 Guide.

Application A has 2 single point of failure – Power Supply & TOR Switch.
Application B has 3 single point of failure - Host, Power Supply & TOR Switch.

With Availability Set we can eliminate above single point of failures.
By creating an **Availability Set** and adding virtual machines to the Availability Set, Azure will ensure that the virtual machines in the set get distributed across the physical hosts, Network switch & Rack that run them in such a way that a hardware failure will not bring down all the machines in the set.
Each virtual machine in the Availability Set is assigned an update domain and a fault domain by Azure.

An **Update Domain (UD)** is used to determine the sets of virtual machines and the underlying hardware that can be rebooted together. For each Availability Set created, five Update Domains will be created by default, but can be changed. You can configure Maximum of 20 Update Domains. When Microsoft is updating physical host it will reboot only one update domains at a time.

Fault domains (FD) define the group of virtual machines that share a common power source and network switch. For each Availability Set, two Fault Domains will be created by default, but can be changed. You can configure Maximum of 3 Fault Domains.

Design Nuggets

1. Update Domains helps with Planned Maintenance events like host reboot by Azure.
2. Fault Domain helps with unplanned Maintenance events like hardware (Host, TOR Switch or Rack Power Supply) failure.
3. Configure each application tier into separate availability sets.
4. Assign different storage accounts to virtual machines in the availability set. If there is an outage in the storage account it will not affect all the virtual machines in the set.
5. Use Azure Load Balancer to distribute traffic to virtual machines in the Availability Set. If there is a Hardware failure (Host, TOR Switch, Rack Power Supply) then it will not affect traffic to other virtual machines in the Availability Set.

VM High Availability using Availability Zones and Load Balancers

Azure Availability Zone protects your applications and data from Complete Location breakdown or Datacenter wide outage which affects the entire Azure Data Center.

With Azure Availability Zones (AZ), **Azure Region will have 3 or more physically separate Data Centre's within Metro distance connected by High Speed Fibre Optic cables.** This distance can be 500M, 1 KM, 5 KM or 10 KM etc. The important point here is that Availability Zones (AZ) will not be sharing any infrastructure like Networking, Grid Power Supply and Cooling etc. The figure below shows three Availability Zones in a Region connected by High speed Fibre Optic Cables. These AZs are separate Azure Data Centers.

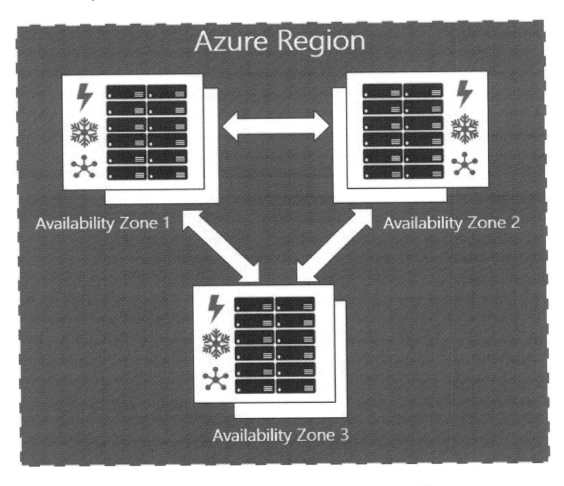

Note: Load Balancing will be discussed in AZ 101 Guide.

Azure services that support Availability Zones fall into two categories:
Zonal services – you pin the resource to a specific zone (for example, virtual machines, managed disks, IP addresses).
Zone-redundant services – platform replicates automatically across zones (for example, zone-redundant storage, SQL Database).

STEP BY STEP PROVIDING HIGH AVAILABILITY TO LOAD BALANCED WEB 1, WEB2 & WEB3 VIRTUAL SERVERS USING AZURE AVAILABILITY ZONES

1. Virtual Network & Subnet created will span Availability Zone 1 (AZ1), Availability Zone 2 (AZ2) and Availability Zone 3 (AZ3) in the region.
2. Create Web1 VM with Managed disk in Subnet1 in AZ1.
3. Create Web2 VM with Managed disk in Subnet1 in AZ2.
4. Create Web3 VM with Managed disk in Subnet1 in AZ3.
5. Use Azure Standard Load Balancer (Zone Redundant) with Standard IP (Zone Redundant) to Load Balance Traffic to Web1, Web2 & Web3 Virtual Server.

Figure below shows Azure Standard Load Balancer providing cross-zone Load Balancing to 3 VMs located in AZ1, AZ2 and AZ3 respectively.

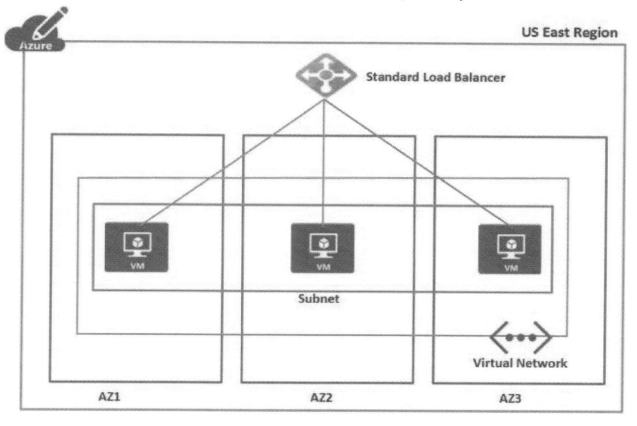

Azure Services that support Availability Zones

Azure Availability Zones preview supports following Azure Services:

Windows Virtual Machine
Linux Virtual Machine
Zonal Virtual Machine Scale Sets
Managed Disks
Load Balancer
Public IP address
Zone-redundant storage
SQL Database

Important Note: Availability Zones (AZ) are currently in Preview in many regions. AZ is not currently part of AZ 100 Exam topics.

Exercise 23: Create Availability Set (AS) using Azure Portal

1. In Azure Portal click All Services in left pane>Under Compute section Click Availability Sets> Availability Sets Dashboard opens>Click +Add>Create Availability Set Blade opens>Enter ASPortal in name box, Select HKPortal in Resource Group and rest select all defaults and click create.

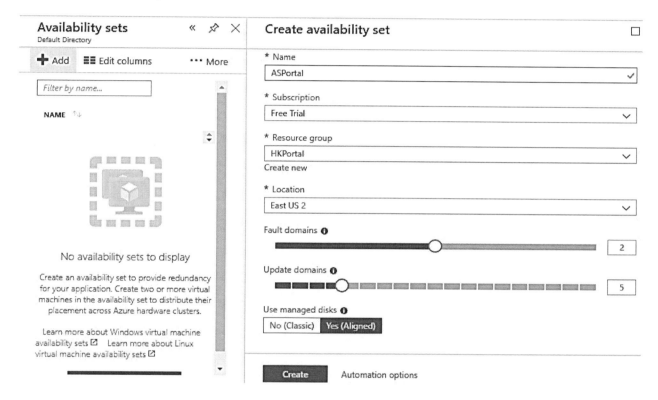

Note 1: AS is off use when you are using 2 or more VMs in the set. Single VM in an AS does not provide any benefit.

Note 2: We will use above AS with Windows VM in next exercise. It will not provide any High Availability benefit as we are using a single VM. The exercise is to show how to create AS and add VM to it.

Exercise 24: Create Windows Virtual Machine using Azure Portal

In this exercise we will create Windows Server 2016 VM in Virtual Network VNETPortal and in Resource Group HKPortal. We will use Managed disk option, select AS created in Exercise 23 and Select Public IP created in Exercise 10.

1. In Azure Portal Click Create a Resource> Compute> Windows Server 2016 Datacenter> Create Virtual Machine Blade opens>Select Resource Group HKPortal, Region East US 2 and Availability Set ASPortal> Click Disks.

   Note 1: Enter the admin name and password. Not shown below.
   Note 2: select none for inbound port option. Not shown below. We will select under networking.

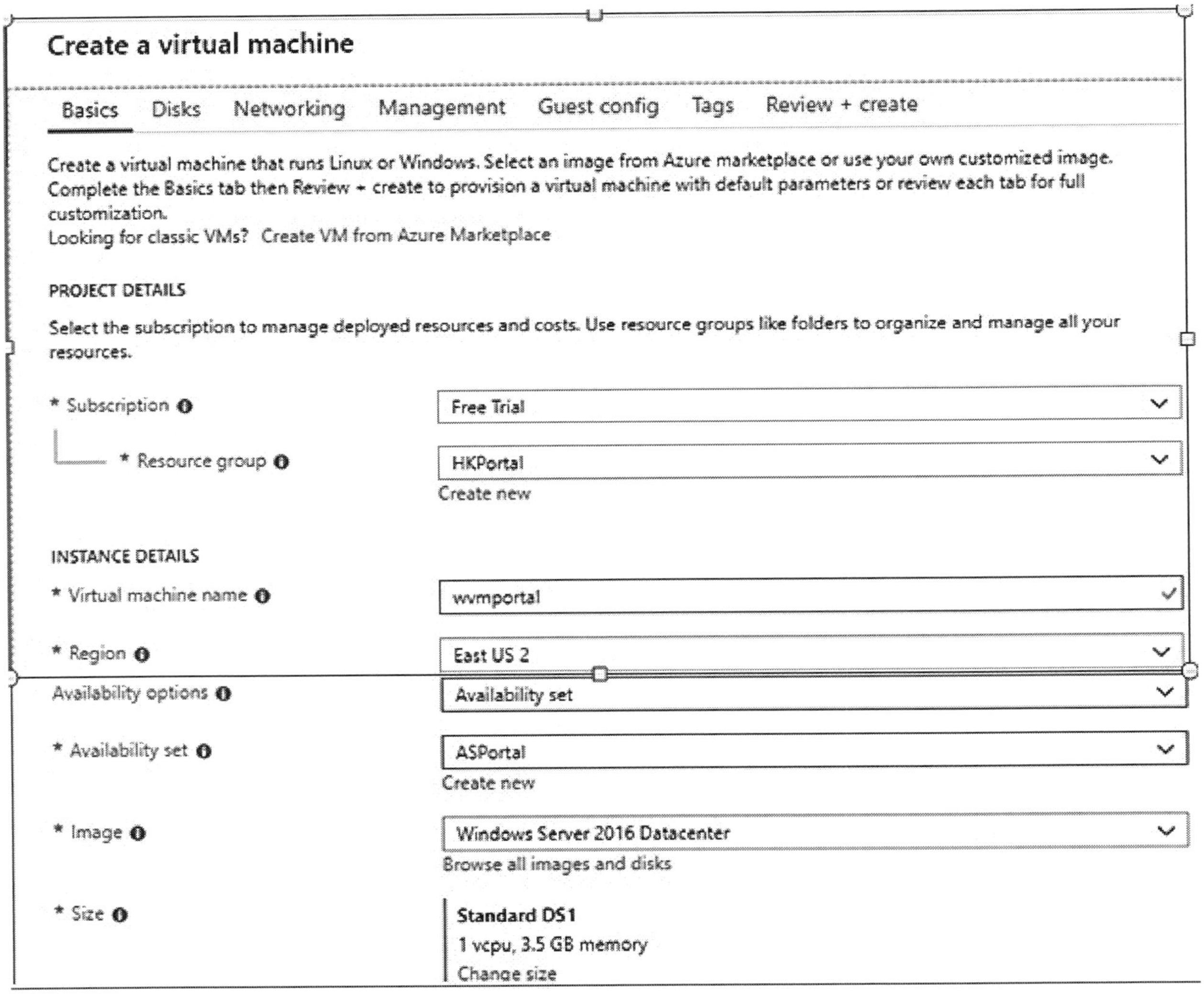

Create a virtual machine

Basics	Disks	Networking	Management	Guest config	Tags	Review + create

Create a virtual machine that runs Linux or Windows. Select an image from Azure marketplace or use your own customized image. Complete the Basics tab then Review + create to provision a virtual machine with default parameters or review each tab for full customization.
Looking for classic VMs? Create VM from Azure Marketplace

PROJECT DETAILS

Select the subscription to manage deployed resources and costs. Use resource groups like folders to organize and manage all your resources.

* Subscription ❶	Free Trial ⌄
* Resource group ❶	HKPortal ⌄
	Create new

INSTANCE DETAILS

* Virtual machine name ❶	wvmportal ✓
* Region ❶	East US 2 ⌄
Availability options ❶	Availability set ⌄
* Availability set ❶	ASPortal ⌄
	Create new
* Image ❶	Windows Server 2016 Datacenter ⌄
	Browse all images and disks
* Size ❶	**Standard DS1**
	1 vcpu, 3.5 GB memory
	Change size

2. Disk Screen opens>Select your HDD Option>Use yes for managed disk and click Next: Networking.

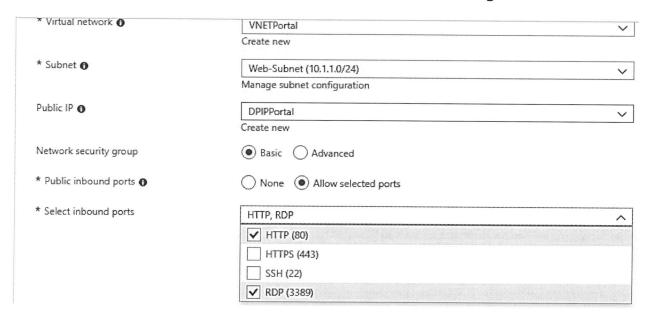

| Basics | Disks | Networking | Management | Guest config | Tags | Review + create |

Azure VMs have one operating system disk and a temporary disk for short-term storage. You can attach additional data disks. The size of the VM determines the type of storage you can use and the number of data disks allowed. Learn more

DISK OPTIONS

* OS disk type ❶

Standard HDD ⌄

The selected VM size supports premium disks. We recommend Premium SSD for high IOPS workloads. Virtual machines with Premium SSD disks qualify for the 99.9% connectivity SLA.

DATA DISKS

You can add and configure additional data disks for your virtual machine or attach existing disks. This VM also comes with a temporary disk.

| LUN | NAME | SIZE (GIB) | DISK TYPE | HOST CACHING |

Create and attach a new disk   Attach an existing disk

∧ ADVANCED

Use managed disks ❶   ○ No ● Yes

Review + create   Previous   Next : Networking >

3. Networking Screen opens> Select VNETPortal, Web-Subnet and DPIPPortal from dropdown boxes> Select Basic in NSG>select allow selected ports and select RDP and HTTP> Select off for AN> Click Next: Management.

* Virtual network ❶	VNETPortal ⌄
	Create new
* Subnet ❶	Web-Subnet (10.1.1.0/24) ⌄
	Manage subnet configuration
Public IP ❶	DPIPPortal ⌄
	Create new
Network security group	● Basic ○ Advanced
* Public inbound ports ❶	○ None ● Allow selected ports
* Select inbound ports	HTTP, RDP ∧

☑ HTTP (80)
☐ HTTPS (443)
☐ SSH (22)
☑ RDP (3389)

4. Select all default values in Management Screen> Click Guest Config.

Basics	Disks	Networking	Management	Guest config	Tags	Review + create

Configure monitoring and management options for your VM.

MONITORING

Boot diagnostics ❶   ◉ On   ○ Off

OS guest diagnostics ❶   ○ On   ◉ Off

* Diagnostics storage account ❶   (new) hkportaldiag
                                      Create new

IDENTITY

System assigned managed identity ❶   ○ On   ◉ Off

AUTO-SHUTDOWN

Enable auto-shutdown ❶   ○ On   ◉ Off

BACKUP

Enable backup ❶   ○ On   ◉ Off

5. Select all default values in Guest Config Screen>Click Tags.

Basics	Disks	Networking	Management	Guest config	Tags	Review + create

Add additional configuration, agents, scripts or applications via virtual machine extensions or cloud-init.

EXTENSIONS

Extensions provide post-deployment configuration and automation.

Extensions ❶   Select an extension to install

6. Select all default values in Tags>Click Review +Create.

7. In Review+Create Screen click create after validation is passed.

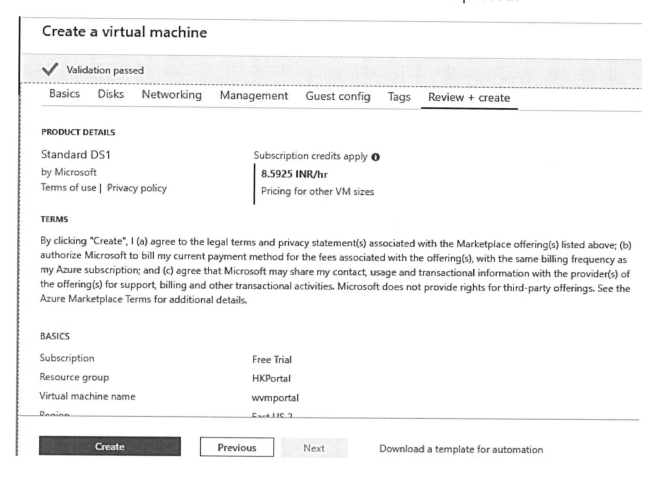

Note 1: In disk screen if you select no for use managed disk option then you need to specify the storage account or use a system created storage account.

Note 2: In Network Security Group under Networking you have the option to select advanced. With advanced option you can assign pre-created NSG. Exercise 12 shows how to create NSG.

8. Figure below shows the dashboard of wvmportal Virtual Machine. DNS name of the Virtual Machine is based on name of Public IP created in Exercise 10.

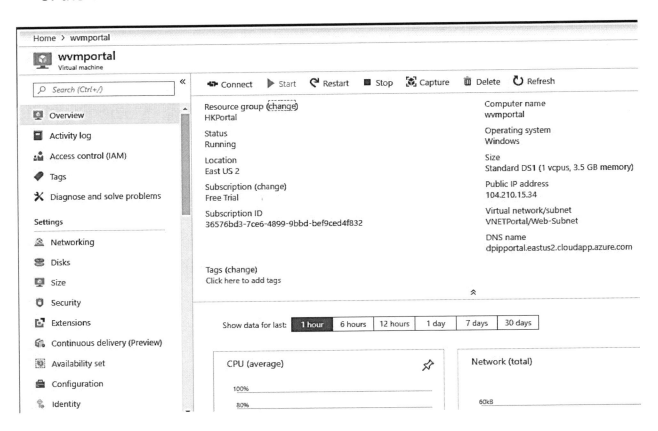

9. Readers are advised to go through all options in left pane of Virtual Machine dashboard.

Exercise 25: Log on to Windows VM with RDP

1. From the VM wvmportal dashboard click **connect** in top pane and download the RDP file on your desktop. Under IP address you have option to download RDP file based on DNS name or on Public IP. Best option is to choose on DNS.

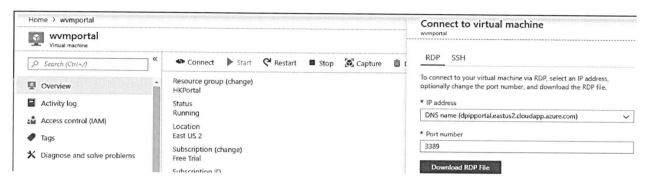

2. Click the downloaded RDP file on your desktop>Click Connect>Credential box for connecting to VM will Pop up on your desktop. Enter the admin name and password you entered during VM creation and click ok.

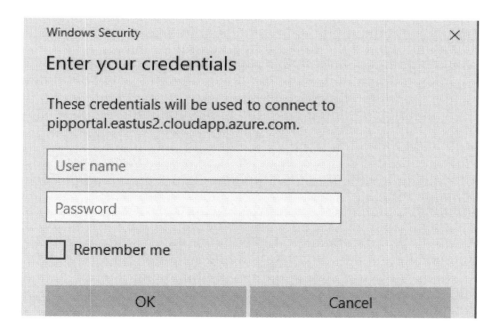

Note 1: If you Stop or restart the VM the Dynamic Public IP will change. When connecting to VM with RDP change the IP in the RDP box if VM IP is changed or download RDP with DNS name option.

3. Figure below shows the screen of Windows VM with Server Manager open.

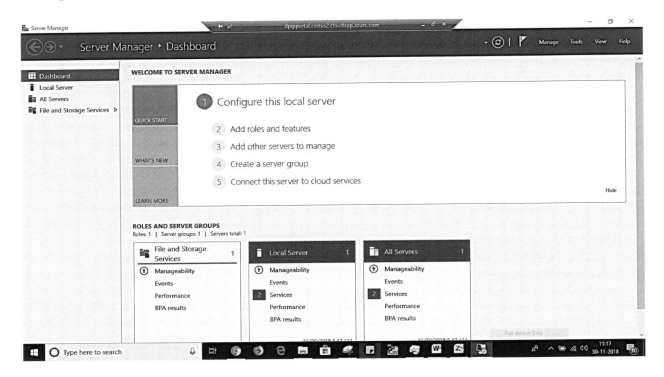

Exercise 26: Install IIS and Access default Website

1. Connect to wvmportal VM using RDP.
2. Open server Manager> Click add roles and features>Next.

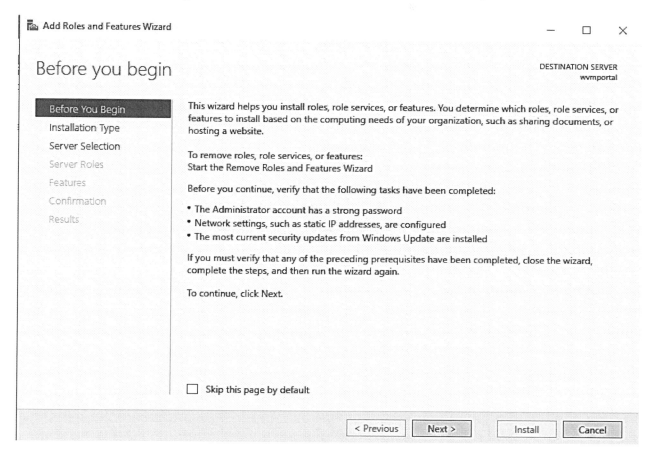

3. In the Add Roles and Features Wizard, on the Installation Type page, choose Role-based or feature-based installation, and then click Next.
4. Select wvmportal VM from the server pool and click Next.
5. On the Server Roles page, select Web Server (IIS).
6. In the pop-up about adding features needed for IIS, make sure that Include management tools is selected and then click Add Features. When the pop-up closes, click Next in the wizard.
7. next, next, next, next.
8. Install.
9. It will take around 1 minute to install the IIS. After Installation is complete click close.

Exercise 27: Connecting to Default IIS website on wvmportal VM

1. Go to wvmportal VM dashboard. Note down VM IP address or DNS name.
2. Open a browser and type: http://dpipportal.eastus2.cloudapp.azure.com/ or http://104.210.15.34

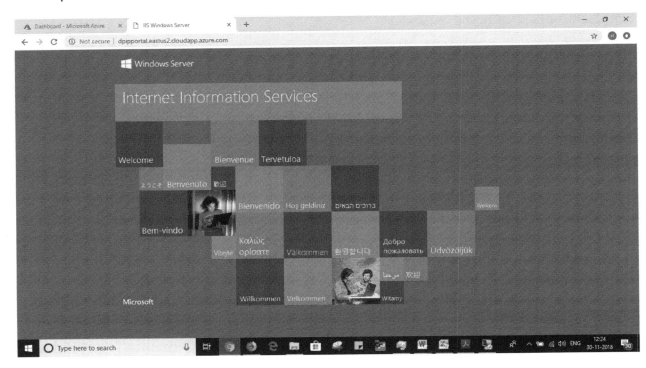

Exercise 28: Add Data Disk

1. Go to wvmportal VM dashboard> Click Disks in left pane.

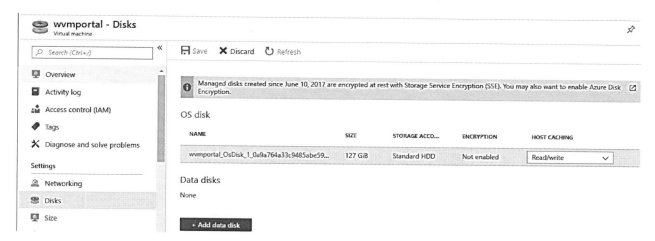

2. Click +Add data disk> Add disk pane opens under Data disks>Enter 1 as LUN value> Select **create disk** under Name Dailog Box (Not shown in the figure).

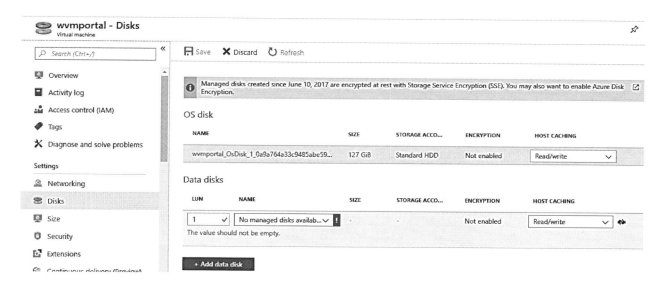

3. When you select create disk under name dialog box> Create Managed Disk Blade opens> Enter name, Resource group as HKPortal (Not shown) and select Type and size as per your requirement>Click create.

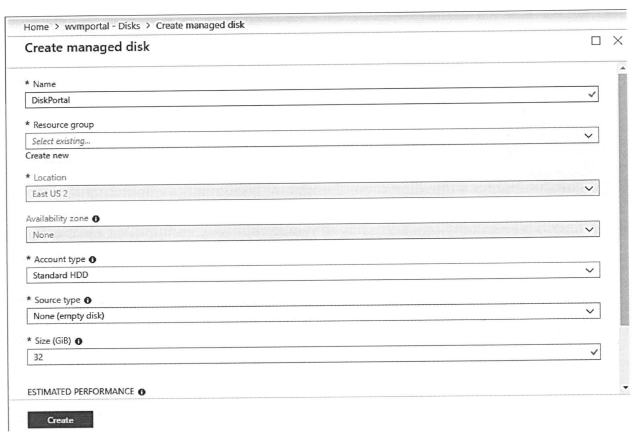

4. Click save in Disk Dashboard. You can see disk added.

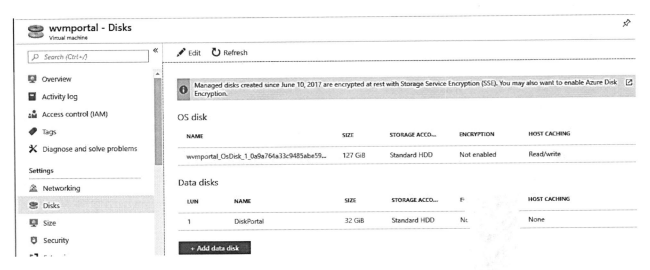

Exercise 29: Initialize the Data Disk

1. Connect to KWeb1 VM using RDP.
2. Open Server Manager. In the left pane> click File and Storage Services.
3. Click Disks. The Disks section lists the disks. The Disk 0 is the operating system Disk. Disk 1 is the temporary disk. Disk 2 is the Data Disk. The Data disk you just added will list the Partition as Unknown.

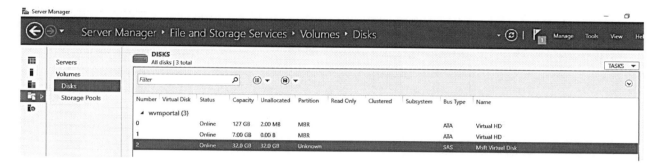

4. The Data disk you just added will list the Partition as Unknown. Right-click the data disk and select Initialize. Once complete, the Partition will be listed as GPT.

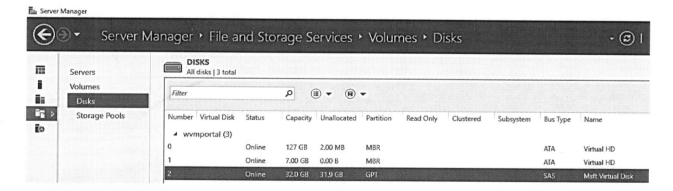

Exercise 30: Create and Add Network Interface to VM wvmportal

1. In vm wvmportal dashboard click Networking in left pane> Click Attach network Interface in right pane>You are provided with 2 options - either create a new interface or select an existing interface from drop down box.

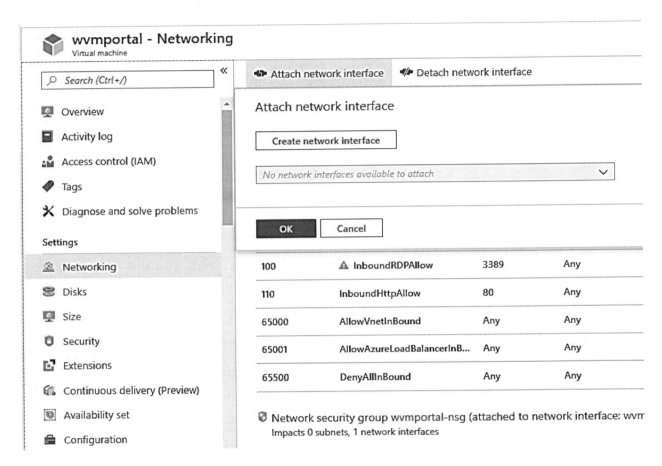

2. In this exercise we will create a network interface. Click Create network interface> Create network interface blade opens>Enter a name, Select Web-Subnet and Resource Group HKPortal>Click create.

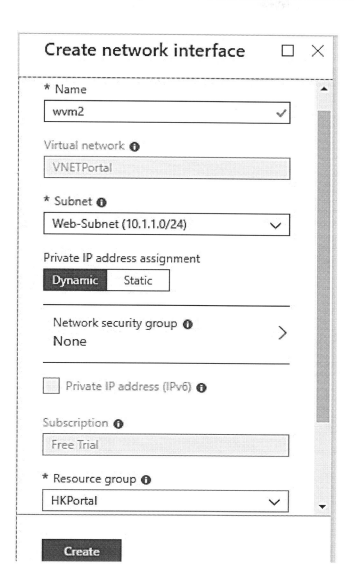

Virtual Machine Snapshot

A snapshot is a full, read-only copy of a VM virtual hard drive (VHD). You can take a snapshot of an OS or data disk VHD to use as a backup, or to troubleshoot virtual machine (VM) issues.

You can also use snapshot to create new Virtual Machine.

Exercise 31: Create Snapshot of VM wvmportal OS Hard Disk

1. Click All resources in left pane> All resources dashboard opens>Click wvmportal_OsDisk_1_xxxxxxx> wvmportal_OsDisk_1_xxxxxxx dashboard opens>

2. Click +Create Snapshot> Create snapshot blade opens> Give a name, Select HKPortal Resource group and select Account type and click create.

Exercise 32: Create Windows VM representing On-Premises AD DS

In this exercise we will create Windows Server 2016 VM in Virtual Network VNETOnPrem, Resource Group OnPrem and Location US South Central. Virtual Network VNETOnPrem & Resource group OnPrem were created in Exercise 6. <u>This VM will represent on-premises Active Directory Domain Services (AD DS).</u>

1. In Azure Portal Click Create a Resource> Compute> Windows Server 2016 Datacenter> Create Virtual Machine pane opens>Select Resource Group **OnPrem**>Select Region **South Central US**>Enter Username and password>Check Allow Selected Ports and Select Http, Https & RDP>Rest keep all Default Value default for Disk and Networking>Click Review +Create

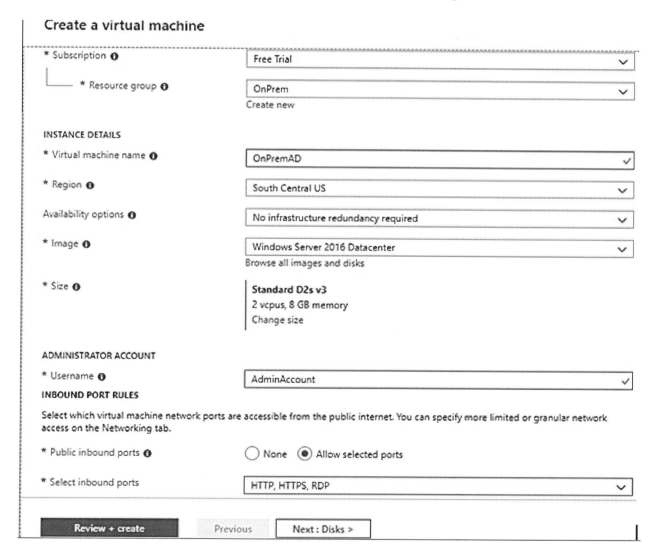

2. After Validation is passed click create.

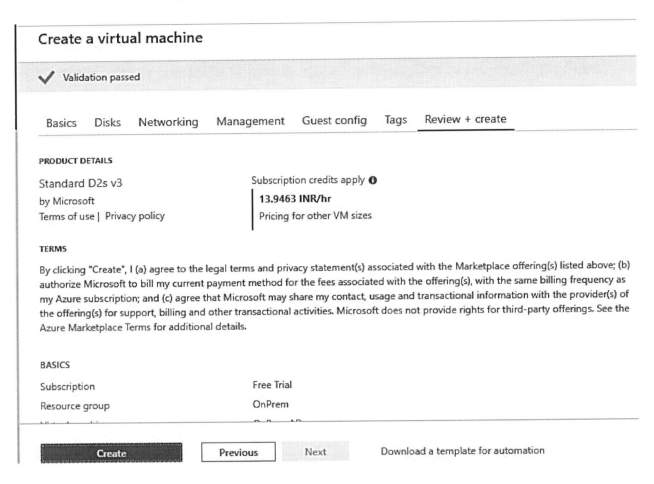

Note 1: Check in the Networking Screen that Virtual Network VNETOnPrem is selected.

Note 2: You must select Resource group **OnPrem** and Region **South Central US.**

Note 3: Keep all values default in Disk and Networking.

Note 4: This VM will be used in Azure File Sync and Azure AD Connect Labs.

Note 5: After VM is created and configured stop the VM. Start VM in Azure Sync and Azure AD Connect Lab.

3. Figure below shows VM dashboard.

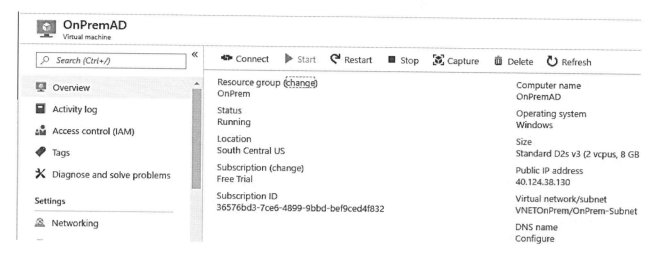

4. In Right pane under DNS click configure> Configure the DNS name of the VM. In this I entered onpremad.>Click save.

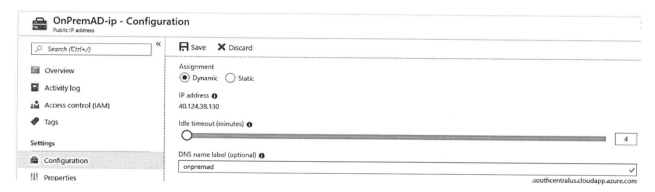

5. From Virtual Machine dashboard click connect and download RDP File based on DNS Address.

Exercise 33: Enable AD DS Role in Virtual Machine OnPremAD

In this exercise we will enable Active Directory Domain services (AD DS) role in Virtual Machine OnPremAD created in previous Exercise.

1. RDP to VM OnPremAD.
2. Open server Manager> Click add roles and features>Next.
3. In the Add Roles and Features Wizard, on the Installation Type page, choose Role-based or feature-based installation, and then click Next.
4. Select OnPremAD VM from the server pool and click Next.
5. On the Server Roles page, select Active Directory Domain Services.
6. In the pop-up about adding features, make sure that Include management tools is selected and then click Add Features. When the pop-up closes, click Next in the wizard.

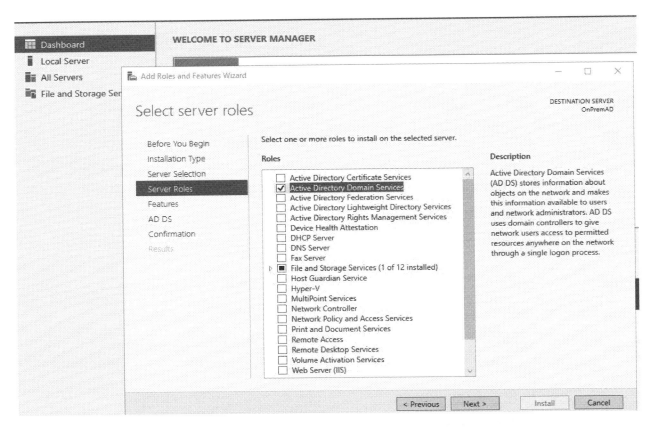

7. Next, Next. In the Confirmation select checkbox for Restart and click Install.
8. It will take around 2-3 minute to install the AD DS. After Installation is complete click close.

9. In the Server Manager click the Flag icon with Yellow triangle> dropdown box opens. In the dropdown box click the link **Promote this server to a domain controller.**

10. Active Directory Domain Services Configuration wizard opens>Select Add a New Forest> Enter a Domain name. I entered **AZX0X.local**>Click Next.

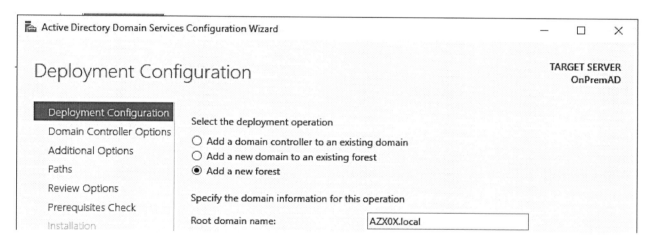

11. Enter the Directory Services Restore mode password >Click next 4 or 5 times.
12. In Prerequisites Check click Install. After Installation Server will automatically restart and RDP windows will close automatically.
13. After 3-4 Minutes RDP to windows VM again. You can see AD DS role.

14. **Install Azure PowerShell Module**. Open PowerShell in VM OnPremAD>Change directory to WINDOWS/system32 and run following commands.
Install-Module -Name AzureRM

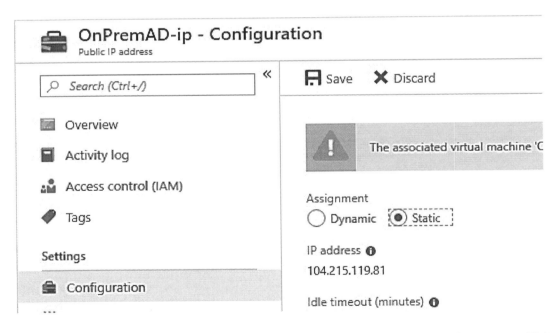

15. **Change Dynamic IP to Static IP.** In VM OnPremAD dashboard click the IP Address link under Public IP Address>IP Address dashboard opens> click configuration in left pane>Select Radio Button for Static and click save> In VM dashboard click restart>Download RDP file again.

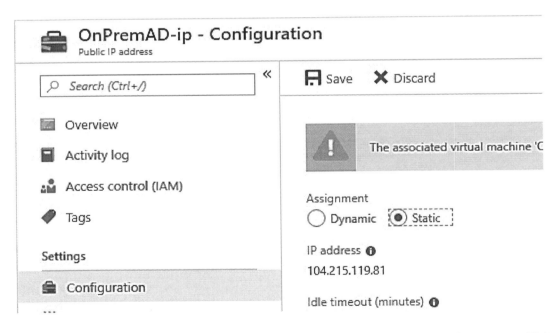

Note: Go to VM dashboard and click Stop in Right pane. This VM will be used in Azure File Sync and Azure AD Connect Labs. If we don't stop it will continuously incur charges and might finish the credit in case you are using trial account.

Linux VM in Azure

Linux is fully supported in Azure with images available from multiple vendors including Red Hat, Suse, Ubuntu, Debian, Free BSD and CoreOS etc.

Connecting to Linux VM

You can connect and log on to Linux VM with **SSH Keys** or **Password.**

Passwords over SSH connections are vulnerable to brute-force attacks or guessing of passwords.

MS recommends connecting to a Linux VM using a public-private key-pair known as SSH keys. Azure currently supports SSH protocol 2 (SSH-2) RSA public-private key pairs with a minimum length of 2048 bits.

The **public key** is placed on your Azure Linux VM.
The **private key** is place on your local system and is used by an SSH client to verify your identity when you connect to your Linux VM. Do not share the private key.

You can generate Public-Private key pair on your windows system using ssh-keygen command or a GUI tool like PuTTYgen.

For the next lab we will be using password option.

Exercise 34: Create Linux VM

In this exercise we will create Ubuntu Server VM in **DB-Subnet** of Virtual Network VNETPortal and in Resource Group HKPortal. We will use Unmanaged disk option using Storage Account sastdportal. **Attempt this Disk Exercise after you have completed Exercise 50 in Storage Accounts chapter 6.**

1. In Azure Portal Click Create a Resource> Compute> Ubuntu server 18.04 LTS> Create Virtual Machine Blade opens>Select Resource Group HKPortal, Region East US 2, Enter Username and Password and select none for inbound ports.

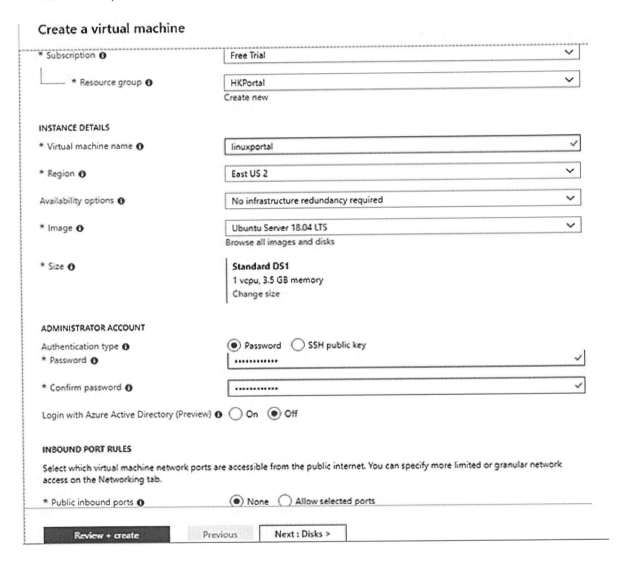

2. Click Next:Disks in bottom pane or Disks in Top pane> Disk pane opens>Select Standard HDD>Click Advanced and select No for Managed disk option>Select Storage Account sastdportal.

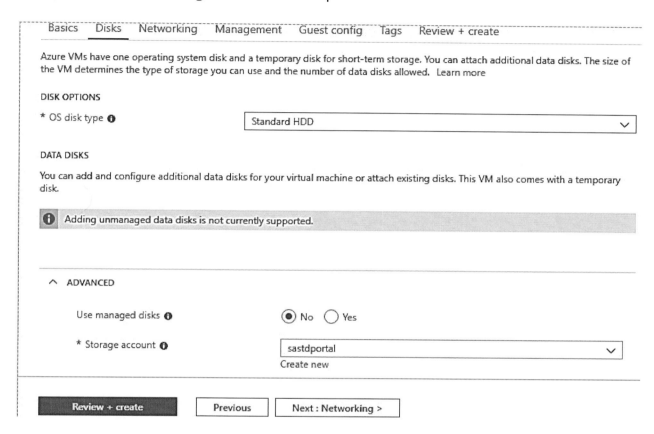

3. Click Next:Networking>Networking pane opens> Select VNETPortal and **DB-Subnet** from drop down box>Dynamic Public is automatically created, >Select None for NSG.

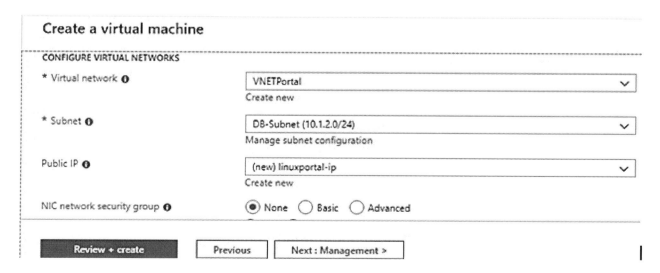

4. Click Review + Create> After Validation is passed Click create.

5. Figure below dashboard of Ubuntu VM.

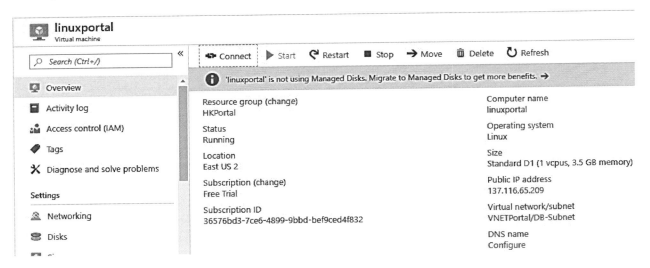

6. To Configure DNS name click Configure in Right pane under DNS>Public IP Address pane opens> Enter a name. In this case I entered linuxportal>click save.

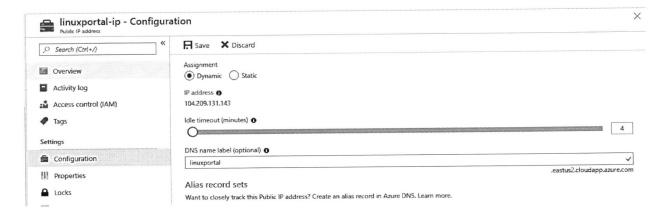

Note 1: In this we selected none for Network security Group on VM NIC.
Note 2: Secondly VM was installed in DB-Subnet which didn't have any NSG. In real world there will be NSG on both VM NIC and Subnet.

Exercise 35: Connecting to Linux VM

For this exercise I downloaded and installed Putty client.

1. Open putty Client and enter Linux VM IP or DNS name and select SSH.

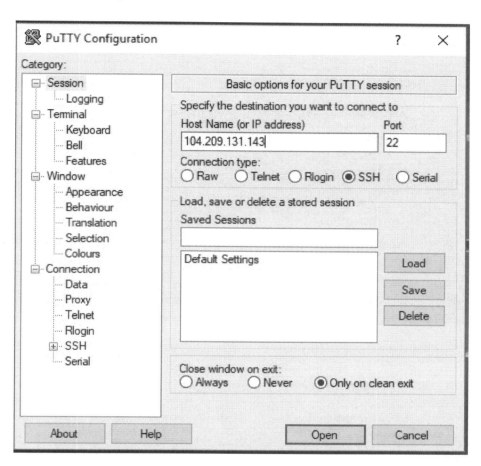

2. Click open and Putty client connects to Linux VM> Enter Username and password you entered during VM creation>Press Enter> You are now connected to Linux VM.

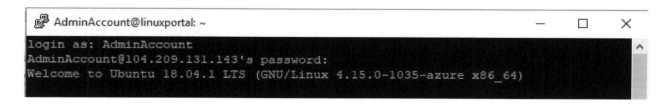

Exercise 36: Update Linux VM & Install NGINX Web Server

1. **Elevate Permission to root user**> sudo su.

```
root@linuxportal: /home/AdminAccount                    —    □    ×
AdminAccount@linuxportal:~$ sudo su
root@linuxportal:/home/AdminAccount#
```

2. **Update Ubuntu Linux Machine**> apt-get –y update.

```
root@linuxportal: /home/AdminAccount                    —    □    ×
AdminAccount@linuxportal:~$ sudo su
root@linuxportal:/home/AdminAccount# apt-get -y update
Hit:1 http://azure.archive.ubuntu.com/ubuntu bionic InRelease
Get:2 http://azure.archive.ubuntu.com/ubuntu bionic-updates InRelease [88.7 kB]
Get:3 http://azure.archive.ubuntu.com/ubuntu bionic-backports InRelease [74.6 kB
]
Get:4 http://security.ubuntu.com/ubuntu bionic-security InRelease [83.2 kB]
Get:5 http://azure.archive.ubuntu.com/ubuntu bionic/restricted Sources [5324 B]
Get:6 http://azure.archive.ubuntu.com/ubuntu bionic/main Sources [829 kB]
Get:7 http://azure.archive.ubuntu.com/ubuntu bionic/multiverse Sources [181 kB]
Get:8 http://azure.archive.ubuntu.com/ubuntu bionic/universe Sources [9051 kB]
Get:9 http://azure.archive.ubuntu.com/ubuntu bionic-updates/restricted Sources [
2064 B]
```

3. **Install Nginx Web Server**> apt-get –y install nginx

```
root@linuxportal: /home/AdminAccount                    —    □    ×
root@linuxportal:/home/AdminAccount# clear
root@linuxportal:/home/AdminAccount# apt-get -y install nginx
Reading package lists... Done
Building dependency tree
Reading state information... Done
The following additional packages will be installed:
  fontconfig-config fonts-dejavu-core libfontconfig1 libgd3 libjbig0
  libjpeg-turbo8 libjpeg8 libnginx-mod-http-geoip
  libnginx-mod-http-image-filter libnginx-mod-http-xslt-filter
  libnginx-mod-mail libnginx-mod-stream libtiff5 libwebp6 libxpm4 nginx-common
  nginx-core
Suggested packages:
  libgd-tools fcgiwrap nginx-doc ssl-cert
```

Note: We also used clear command to clear the screen. This is optional.

4. **Access the default NGINX Website**> open browser and enter VM IP address or DNS name> Default website opens.

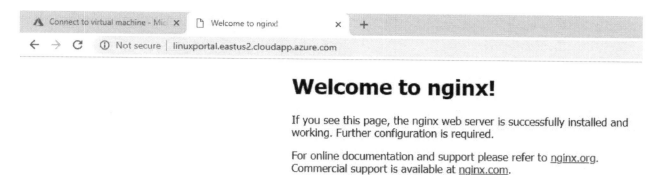

5. **Delete the VM, Public IP and Network Interface** as we no longer need it.

Images

Images are VHD files that contains syspreped version of Windows VM. Sysprep removes all your personal account and security information, and then prepares the machine to be used as an image. Image contains all the information necessary for creating a VM.

Why Custom Image

Many Organization's have a requirement that their VMs should have certain dot net version or IIS Server installed or a Monitoring Agent installed. Instead of installing feature in each VM, just install the required feature in one VM and create image of the VM. Then deploy your VMs with the image.

Custom Image Deployment

To create a custom image start by installing required features in the Virtual Machine, Sysprep the VM and thirdly create image from the Syspreped VM.

Custom Image Advantages

Custom image reduces the administrative overhead of deploying VMs.

Exercise 37: Create Custom Image of Azure VM

Step 1 Deploy Windows Server 2016 VM in Web-Subnet in Virtual Network VNETPortal and Resource Group HKPortal > Make sure that Web-Subnet, VNETPortal and inbound ports http, https and RDP are selected during VM creation. **Follow the exact procedure shown in exercise 24.** Figure below shows the dashboard of VM cimageportal.

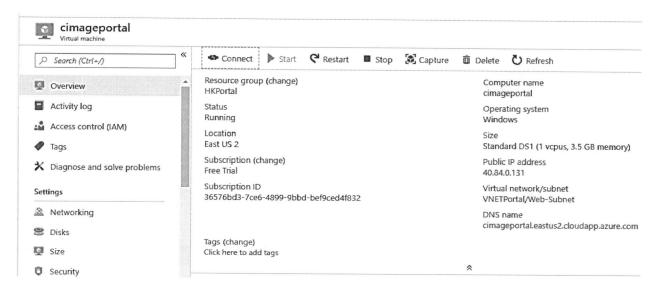

Step 2 Configure the DNS name> In VM dashboard click configure under DNS name> Public IP address opens>enter a name and click save.

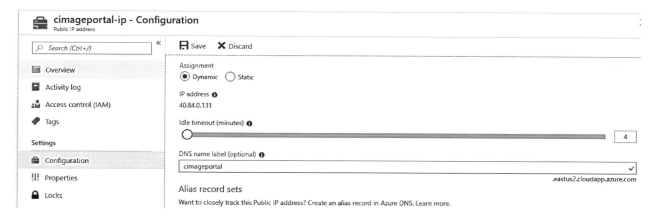

Step 3 Download RDP file from VM dashboard & Install IIS Role>RDP to VM>The Procedure to **Download RDP file & install IIS** was shown in Exercise 25 & 26.

Step 4: **Generalize the Windows VM using Sysprep**.

Sysprep removes all your personal account and security information, and then prepares the machine to be used as an image.

1. RDP to VM>open Command Prompt and enter following command to change directory> **cd %windir%/system32/sysprep**

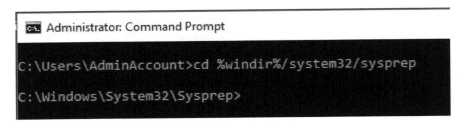

2. **Run sysprep.exe**> System Preparation Tool Box opens>In the System Preparation Tool dialog box, select Enter System Out-of-Box Experience (OOBE) and select the Generalize check box and For Shutdown Options select Shutdown and click OK.

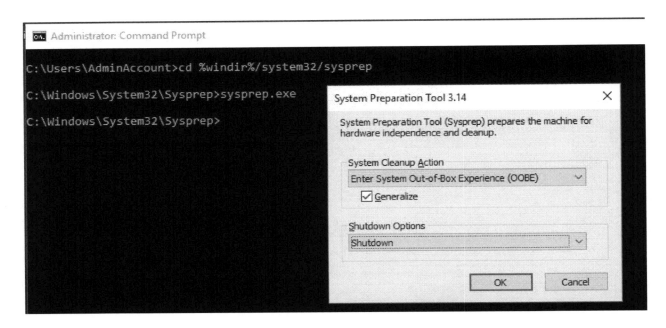

3. After Sysprep operation is complete RDP automatically closes.

Note: You can capture image of VM only when it is in stop state.

Step 5: Capture the image from the VM cimageportal Dashboard

Go to VM cimageportal dashboard which was syspreped in step 4>Click capture in top pane>Create image Dailog box opens as shown below> Select Resource group HKPortal, Check Automatically delete this VM> click create. It will take couple of minutes to complete the image creation process.

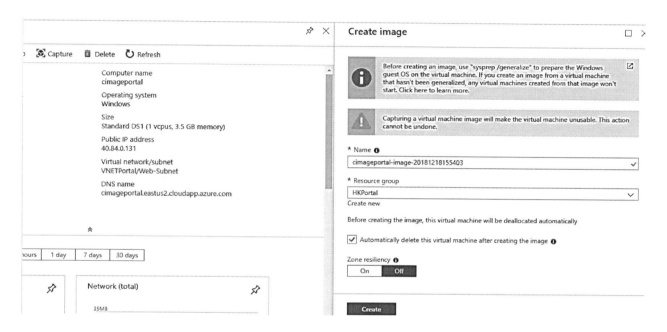

Step 4: Check the image In Azure Portal

In Azure Portal click All Services in left pane> Under Compute option Click images> Images dashboard opens as shown below with the image created.

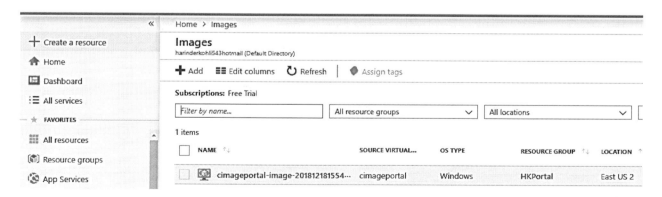

Note 1: we will use this image to deploy a VM in next exercise.
Note 2: In Exercise 47 we will use this image to deploy VM Scale Set (VMSS).

Exercise 38: Deploy VM from Custom image created in EX 37

1. In Azure Portal click All Services in left pane> Under Compute option Click images> Al Images pane opens >Click the image cimageportal-image- xxx >Image Dashboard opens.

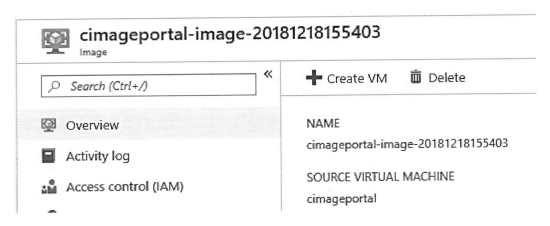

2. In the image Dashboard>Click Create VM>Create Virtual Machine dialog box opens>Enter information as per your requirement.

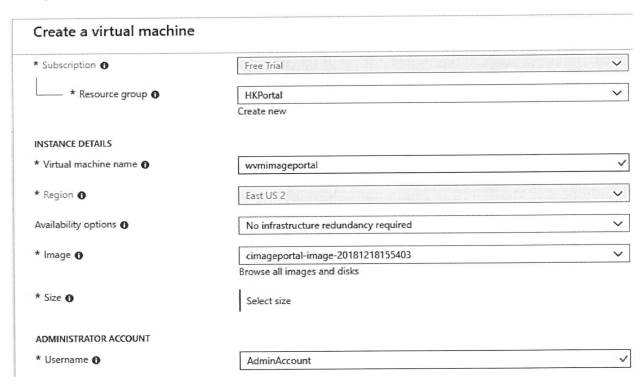

Rest steps are same as shown in exercise 24. Access the default website. Delete the VM, OS Disk. Public IP and NIC after it is created.

Azure Virtual Machine Agent

The Microsoft Azure Virtual Machine Agent (VM Agent) is a secure, lightweight process that manages virtual machine (VM) interaction with the Azure Fabric Controller. The Primary role of Azure VM Agent is to enable and execute Azure virtual machine extensions.

VM Extensions enable post-deployment configuration of VM, such as installing and configuring software. VM extensions also enable recovery features such as resetting the administrative password of a VM. Without the Azure VM Agent, VM extensions cannot be run.

Installing the VM Agent

The Azure VM Agent is installed by default on any Windows VM deployed from an Azure Marketplace image.

Manual Installation of VM Agent: Manual installation is required when you deploy a Virtual Machine with a custom VM image. The Windows VM agent can be manually installed with a Windows installer package. Download the Windows installer package from go.microsoft.com/fwlink/?LinkID=394789

Checking for VM Agent using "Get-AzureRmVM" PowerShell Command

Get-AzureRmVM -ResourceGroupName myrg -Name myVM

```
OSProfile              :
  ComputerName         : myVM
  AdminUsername        : myUserName
  WindowsConfiguration :
    ProvisionVMAgent     : True
    EnableAutomaticUpdates : True
```

To get properties of all VMs running in resource group use following command:
Get-AzureRmVM -ResourceGroupName myrg

To get properties of all VMs running in Subscription use following command:
Get-AzureRmVM

Manually Checking for VM Agent

Log on to Azure VM and open Task Manager and click details tab. Look for a process name **WindowsAzureGuestAgent.exe**. The presence of this process indicates that the VM agent is installed.

Figure below shows Task Manager of wvmportal VM. It shows **WindowsAzureGuestAgent.exe**.

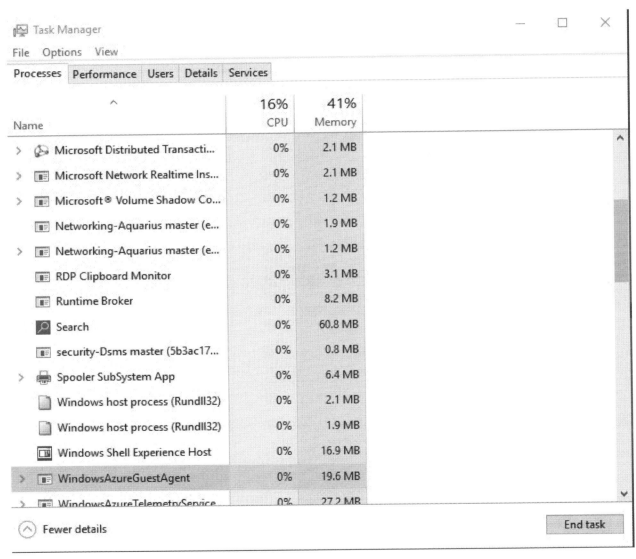

Virtual Machine Extensions

Azure virtual machine (VM) extensions are small applications that provide post-deployment configuration and automation tasks on Azure VMs. For example, if a virtual machine requires software installation, anti-virus protection, or to run a script inside of it, a VM extension can be used.

Types of Virtual Machines Extensions

1. VM Extensions provided by Microsoft. Example of VM Extension provided by Microsoft include Microsoft Monitoring Agent VM extension for monitoring VMs.
2. Third Party VM Extensions provided by companies like Symantec, Qualys, Rapid7 & HPE etc. Examples of third part VM Extensions include VM vulnerability tool from Qualys, Rapid7, HPE or Anti Virus products from Symantec & TrendMicro etc.
3. Custom Script Extensions written by customers themselves.

Note: Extensions can be added to Azure Virtual Machine during installation time or post installation.

Exercise 39: Demonstrating various VM Extensions available

Go to VM wvmportal dashboard>Click Extension in left pane>In Right pane click + Add> Add Extension blade opens> click an Extension. In this case I clicked Kaspersky Agent Extension> In Right pane Kaspersky Security agent opens.

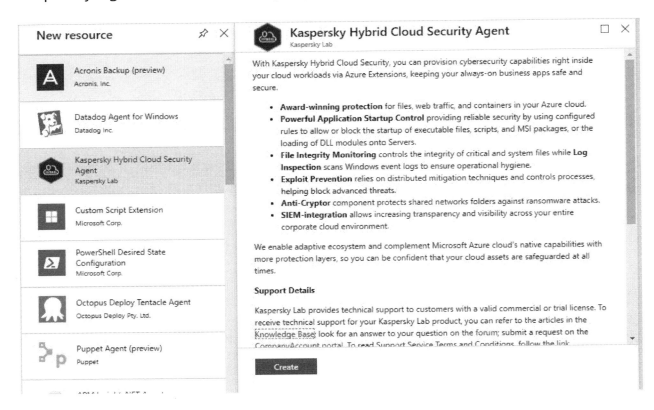

Custom Script Extension

Custom Script Extension is a tool that can be used to automatically launch and execute VM customization tasks. Custom Scripts are written by customers themselves.

The Custom Script Extension downloads and executes scripts on Azure Virtual Machines. Scripts can be downloaded from Azure storage or GitHub, or provided to the Azure portal at extension run time.

Custom Script Extension extension is useful for post deployment configuration, software installation, or any other VM configuration/management task.

Custom Script Installation Methods

Azure Templates
Azure CLI using az vm extension set command.
Azure PowerShell using Set-AzureRmVMExtension command.
Azure Portal

Exercise 40: Demonstrating Custom Script Extension using Azure Portal

1. Go to VM wvmportal dashboard>Click Extension in left pane>In Right pane click + Add> Add Extension blade opens>Select Custom Script Extension> Custom Script Extension blade opens in right pane.

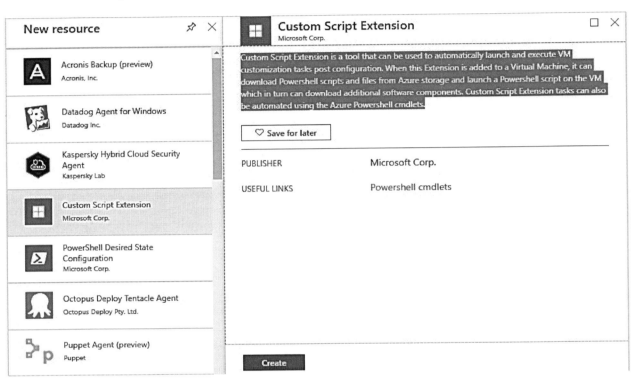

2. In right pane click create> Install Extension Blade opens>Click folder and upload file for executing on VM wvmportal.

Manage VM Sizes

You can resize Azure VM to give it more/less CPU cores and RAM.

You can resize VM within same series to a larger VM or a smaller VM.
You can resize VM between different series (From D series to E Series). In this case resizing depends upon whether resize is to same hardware or different hardware families.

The typical impact to resizing a VM is a restart which can take up to five minutes for the resizing operation to complete.
If you are resizing VM's onto new hardware which is in an Availability Set (AS), then all the VMs need to be powered off for the resizing operation to begin.
If you are resizing to a VM onto new hardware (e.g. change in chipset), then the VM will need to be powered off first before the resize operation can begin.

Exercise41: Resizing VM

In this exercise we will just show how to resize a VM but will not implement it.

1. Go to VM wvmportal Dashboard>Click Size in left pane>Select size of new VM and click Resize.

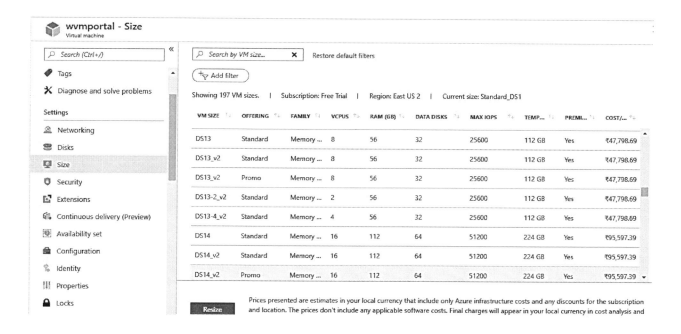

VM Auto-Shutdown

With VM Auto-Shutdown feature you can control VM cost.

Let's say that you don't require VMs to operate after office hours (After 5.30 PM). You can enable VM Auto shutdown to shut down VM @ 5.30 PM.

This feature will not enable auto start-up. You need to start-up the VM manually.

Note: Auto Start-up & Auto-Stop VMs will be discussed in Azure Automation chapter.

Exercise 42: Virtual Machine Auto-Shutdown

Go to VM wvmportal Dashboard>Click Auto-Shutdown in left pane>In Right pane click On to enable Auto-Shutdown> Enter the Required time as per your requirement>Click save.

If you require notification when VM is about to be shutdown you can enable Notification. You have 2 options for notification – Webhook URL and Email.

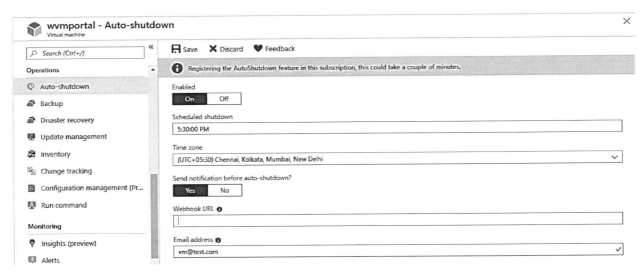

Reset Password

If you have forgotten the administrator password of Azure Virtual machine you can reset it from Azure Portal.

Exercise 43: Reset Password

Go to VM wvmportal Dashboard> Click Reset Password in left pane>In right pane select reset password button, enter username, password and click update.

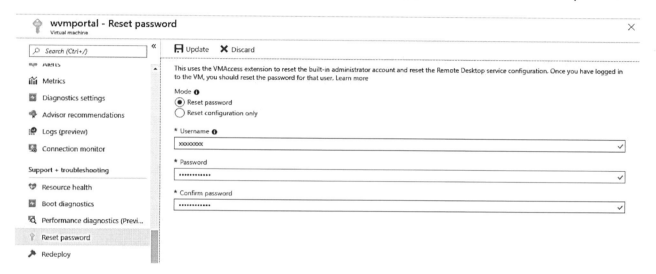

Redeploy VM

With Redeploy options you can migrate Azure VM to a new Azure host. During redeployment VM will be restarted and you will lose any data on the temporary drive. While the redeployment is in progress, the VM will be unavailable.

Exercise 44: Redeploy

Go to VM wvmportal dashboard> Click Redeploy in left pane>In right pane click Redeploy. Your VM will be migrated to new host.

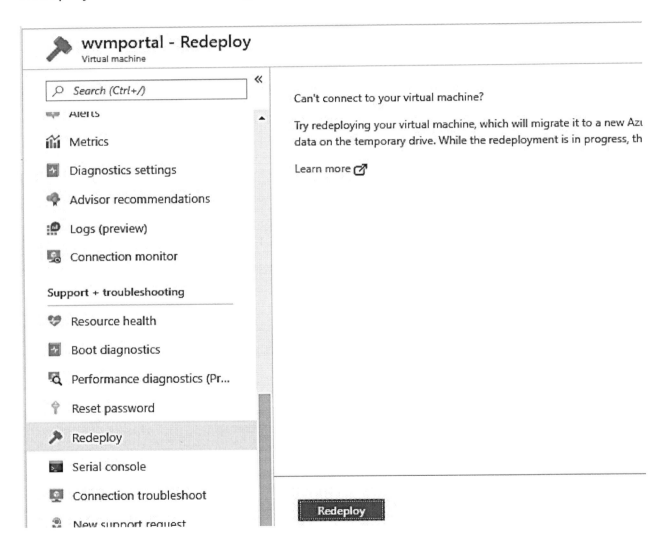

VM Backup & Restore

Chapter 8 Implement Azure Backup

Moving Virtual Machines

Chapter 14 Azure Resource Groups, Tags and Locks

VM Alerts, Metrics & Diagnostic Settings

Chapter 15 Analyzing & Monitoring Azure Resources

VM Update, Inventory, Change & Configuration Management

Chapter 16 Azure Automation

PowerShell DSC Extension

Chapter 16 Azure Automation

ARM Template

Chapter 17 Azure Resource Manager (ARM) Tempalate

Chapter 4 Deploy Virtual Machines with CLI and PS

This Chapter covers following Lab Exercises

- Create Windows Server 2016 VM using Azure CLI
- Create Windows Server 2016 VM using Azure PowerShell

Exercise 45: Create Windows Server 2016 VM using Azure CLI

In this lab we will create Windows Server 2016 VM in Resource Group HKCLI and Subnet Web-Subnet in Virtual Network VNETCLI. HKCLI Resource Group was created in Chapter 2, Exercise 19. Virtual Network VNETCLI was created in Chapter 2, Exercise 21.

Get the URNAlias name of the image
az vm image list

Above command is not shown in below diagram as I scrolled to locate the Windows Server 2016 image. You can see urnAlias name is **Win2016Datacenter**

```
Command Prompt
 {
    "offer": "WindowsServer",
    "publisher": "MicrosoftWindowsServer",
    "sku": "2019-Datacenter",
    "urn": "MicrosoftWindowsServer:WindowsServer:2019-Datacenter:latest",
    "urnAlias": "Win2019Datacenter",
    "version": "latest"
 },
 {
    "offer": "WindowsServer",
    "publisher": "MicrosoftWindowsServer",
    "sku": "2016-Datacenter",
    "urn": "MicrosoftWindowsServer:WindowsServer:2016-Datacenter:latest",
    "urnAlias": "Win2016Datacenter",
    "version": "latest"
 },
```

Get the name of VM Size
az vm list-sizes –location eastus2

```
C:\Users\Harinder Kohli>az vm list-sizes --location eastus2
[
 {
    "maxDataDiskCount": 1,
    "memoryInMb": 768,
    "name": "Standard_A0",
    "numberOfCores": 1,
    "osDiskSizeInMb": 1047552,
    "resourceDiskSizeInMb": 20480
```

For this lab I selected size **Standard_D2_v2** (You need to scroll down to see it).

Create Virtual Machine using az vm command

az vm create --name VMCLI --vnet-name VNETCLI --subnet Web-Subnet
--resource-group HKCLI --image Win2016Datacenter --size Standard_D2_v2 --
admin-username AdminAccount --admin-password Aadmin@12345

```
C:\WINDOWS\system32>az vm create --name VMCLI --vnet-name VNETCLI --subnet Web-Subnet --resource-group HKCLI
--image Win2016Datacenter --size Standard_D2_v2 --admin-username AdminAccount --admin-password Aadmin@12345
{
  "fqdns": "",
  "id": "/subscriptions/36576bd3-7ce6-4899-9bbd-bef9ced4f832/resourceGroups/HKCLI/providers/Microsoft.Compute
/virtualMachines/VMCLI",
  "location": "eastus2",
  "macAddress": "00-0D-3A-04-C7-ED",
  "powerState": "VM running",
  "privateIpAddress": "10.2.1.4",
  "publicIpAddress": "40.84.20.119",
  "resourceGroup": "HKCLI",
  "zones": ""
}
```

Check the Virtual Machine created
az vm show --name VMCLI --resource-group HKCLI

```
C:\WINDOWS\system32>az vm show --name VMCLI --resource-group HKCLI
{
  "additionalCapabilities": null,
  "availabilitySet": null,
  "diagnosticsProfile": null,
  "hardwareProfile": {
    "vmSize": "Standard_D2_v2"
  },
  "id": "/subscriptions/36576bd3-7ce6-4899-9bbd-bef9ced4f832/resourceGroups/HKCLI/providers/Microsoft.Compute
/virtualMachines/VMCLI"
```

Delete Virtual Machine
az vm delete --name VMCLI --resource-group HKCLI

```
C:\WINDOWS\system32>az vm delete --name VMCLI --resource-group HKCLI
Are you sure you want to perform this operation? (y/n): y

C:\WINDOWS\system32>az vm show --name VMCLI --resource-group HKCLI
The Resource 'Microsoft.Compute/virtualMachines/VMCLI' under resource group 'HKCLI' was not found.

C:\WINDOWS\system32>
```

Note 1: I checked up if VM is deleted or not by using **az vm show** command.
Note 2: Make sure to delete the VM otherwise it will incur charges.

Checking VM in Portal

Go VM VMCLI Dashboard>You can see it was created in Virtual Network VNETCLI. The size is Standard D2 v2.

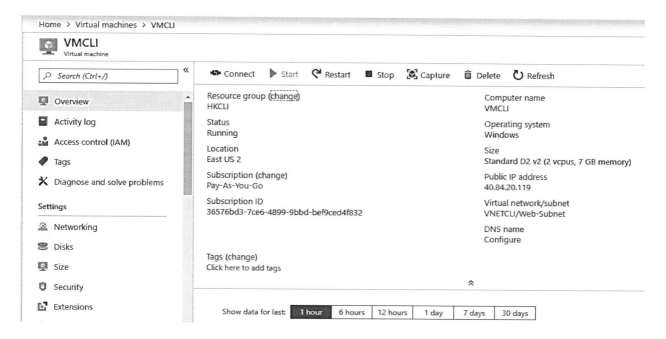

Exercise 46: Create Windows Server 2016 VM using Azure PowerShell

In this lab we will create Windows Server 2016 VM in Resource Group HKPS and
Virtual Network VNETPS. HKPS Resource Group was created in Chapter 2,
Exercise 20. Virtual Network VNETPS was created in Chapter 2, Exercise 22.

Get the SKU, Offer & Publisher Name of the image
Get-AzureRmVMImageSku -Location EastUS2 -PublisherName MicrosoftWindowsServer
-Offer WindowsServer

```
PS C:\Users\Harinder Kohli> Get-AzureRmVMImageSku -Location EastUS2 -PublisherName MicrosoftWindowsServer  -Offer WindowsServer

Skus                                           Offer          PublisherName           Location  Id
----                                           -----          -------------           --------  --
2008-R2-SP1                                    WindowsServer  MicrosoftWindowsServer  eastus2   /Subscriptio...
2008-R2-SP1-smalldisk                          WindowsServer  MicrosoftWindowsServer  eastus2   /Subscriptio...
2008-R2-SP1-zhcn                               WindowsServer  MicrosoftWindowsServer  eastus2   /Subscriptio...
2012-Datacenter                                WindowsServer  MicrosoftWindowsServer  eastus2   /Subscriptio...
2012-Datacenter-smalldisk                      WindowsServer  MicrosoftWindowsServer  eastus2   /Subscriptio...
2012-Datacenter-zhcn                           WindowsServer  MicrosoftWindowsServer  eastus2   /Subscriptio...
2012-R2-Datacenter                             WindowsServer  MicrosoftWindowsServer  eastus2   /Subscriptio...
2012-R2-Datacenter-smalldisk                   WindowsServer  MicrosoftWindowsServer  eastus2   /Subscriptio...
2012-R2-Datacenter-zhcn                        WindowsServer  MicrosoftWindowsServer  eastus2   /Subscriptio...
2016-Datacenter                                WindowsServer  MicrosoftWindowsServer  eastus2   /Subscriptio...
2016-Datacenter-Server-Core                    WindowsServer  MicrosoftWindowsServer  eastus2   /Subscriptio...
2016-Datacenter-Server-Core-smalldisk          WindowsServer  MicrosoftWindowsServer  eastus2   /Subscriptio...
2016-Datacenter-smalldisk                      WindowsServer  MicrosoftWindowsServer  eastus2   /Subscriptio...
2016-Datacenter-with-Containers                WindowsServer  MicrosoftWindowsServer  eastus2   /Subscriptio...
2016-Datacenter-with-RDSH                      WindowsServer  MicrosoftWindowsServer  eastus2   /Subscriptio...
2016-Datacenter-zhcn                           WindowsServer  MicrosoftWindowsServer  eastus2   /Subscriptio...
2019-Datacenter                                WindowsServer  MicrosoftWindowsServer  eastus2   /Subscriptio...
2019-Datacenter-Core                           WindowsServer  MicrosoftWindowsServer  eastus2   /Subscriptio...
2019-Datacenter-Core-smalldisk                 WindowsServer  MicrosoftWindowsServer  eastus2   /Subscriptio...
2019-Datacenter-Core-with-Containers           WindowsServer  MicrosoftWindowsServer  eastus2   /Subscriptio...
2019-Datacenter-Core-with-Containers-smalldisk WindowsServer  MicrosoftWindowsServer  eastus2   /Subscriptio...
2019-Datacenter-smalldisk                      WindowsServer  MicrosoftWindowsServer  eastus2   /Subscriptio...
2019-Datacenter-with-Containers                WindowsServer  MicrosoftWindowsServer  eastus2   /Subscriptio...
2019-Datacenter-with-Containers-smalldisk      WindowsServer  MicrosoftWindowsServer  eastus2   /Subscriptio...
2019-Datacenter-zhcn                           WindowsServer  MicrosoftWindowsServer  eastus2   /Subscriptio...
```

Get the name of VM Size
Get-AzureRmVMSize -Location EastUS2

```
PS C:\Users\Harinder Kohli> Get-AzureRmVMSize -Location EastUS2

Name           NumberOfCores  MemoryInMB  MaxDataDiskCount  OSDiskSizeInMB  ResourceDiskSizeInMB
----           -------------  ----------  ----------------  --------------  --------------------
Standard_A0                1         768                 1         1047552                 20480
Standard_A1                1        1792                 2         1047552                 71680
Standard_A2                2        3584                 4         1047552                138240
Standard_A3                4        7168                 8         1047552                291840
Standard_A5                2       14336                 4         1047552                138240
Standard_A4                8       14336                16         1047552                619520
Standard_A6                4       28672                 8         1047552                291840
Standard_A7                8       57344                16         1047552                619520
Basic_A0                   1         768                 1         1047552                 20480
Basic_A1                   1        1792                 2         1047552                 40960
Basic_A2                   2        3584                 4         1047552                 61440
Basic_A3                   4        7168                 8         1047552                122880
Basic_A4                   8       14336                16         1047552                245760
Standard_D1_v2             1        3584                 4         1047552                 51200
Standard_D2_v2             2        7168                 8         1047552                102400
```

174

Create Virtual Machine

New-AzureRmVm -ResourceGroupName HKPS -Name VMPS -Location EastUS2 -VirtualNetworkName VNETPS -SubnetName Web-Subnet –ImageName MicrosoftWindowsServer:WindowsServer:2016-Datacenter:Latest

```
PS C:\Users\Harinder Kohli> New-AzureRmVm -ResourceGroupName HKPS -Name VMPS -Location EastUS2 -VirtualNetworkName
 VNETPS -SubnetName Web-Subnet -ImageName MicrosoftWindowsServer:WindowsServer:2016-Datacenter:Latest

cmdlet New-AzureRmVM at command pipeline position 1
Supply values for the following parameters:
Credential


ResourceGroupName       : HKPS
Id                      : /subscriptions/7593a7e7-0d4e-493a-922e-c433ef24df3b/resourceGroups/HKPS/providers/Micro
soft.Compute/virtualMachines/VMPS
VmId                    : c2fd537f-c8eb-4542-8b0c-4cd54e65749b
Name                    : VMPS
Type                    : Microsoft.Compute/virtualMachines
Location                : eastus2
Tags                    : {}
HardwareProfile         : {VmSize}
NetworkProfile          : {NetworkInterfaces}
OSProfile               : {ComputerName, AdminUsername, WindowsConfiguration, Secrets, AllowExtensionOperations}
ProvisioningState       : Succeeded
StorageProfile          : {ImageReference, OsDisk, DataDisks}
FullyQualifiedDomainName : vmps-6bbd13.EastUS2.cloudapp.azure.com
```

Check the Virtual Machine created

Get-AzureRmVm –Name VMPS –ResourceGroupName HKPS

```
PS C:\Users\Harinder Kohli> Get-AzureRmVm -Name VMPS -ResourceGroupName HKPS
PS C:\Users\Harinder Kohli>

ResourceGroupName : HKPS
Id                : /subscriptions/7593a7e7-0d4e-493a-922e-c433ef24df3b/resourceGroups/HKPS/providers/Microsoft.C
ompute/virtualMachines/VMPS
VmId              : c2fd537f-c8eb-4542-8b0c-4cd54e65749b
Name              : VMPS
Type              : Microsoft.Compute/virtualMachines
Location          : eastus2
Tags              : {}
HardwareProfile   : {VmSize}
NetworkProfile    : {NetworkInterfaces}
OSProfile         : {ComputerName, AdminUsername, WindowsConfiguration, Secrets, AllowExtensionOperations}
ProvisioningState : Succeeded
StorageProfile    : {ImageReference, OsDisk, DataDisks}
```

Delete Virtual Machine

Remove-AzureRmVm –Name VMPS –ResourceGroupName HKPS

```
PS C:\Users\Harinder Kohli> Remove-AzureRmVm -Name VMPS -ResourceGroupName HKPS

Virtual machine removal operation
This cmdlet will remove the specified virtual machine. Do you want to continue?
[Y] Yes  [N] No  [S] Suspend  [?] Help (default is "Y"): Y


OperationId : 00a9b657-b441-49f4-9d79-0d8fca8559b2
Status      : Succeeded
StartTime   : 22-12-2018 17:07:51
EndTime     : 22-12-2018 17:08:38
```

Chapter 5 Deploy Virtual Machines Scale Sets (VMSS)

This Chapter covers following Topic Lessons

- Virtual Machine Scale Set (VMSS)
- Virtual Machine Scale Set (VMSS) Architecture
- Autoscaling with VMSS

This Chapter covers following Lab Exercises

- Deploying VMSS
- Connecting to Instances in VMSS
- Enabling Autoscaling

Chapter Topology

In this chapter we will add Virtual Machines Scale Set (VMSS) to the topology. VMSS will be created in Web-Subnet of Virtual Network VNETPortal.

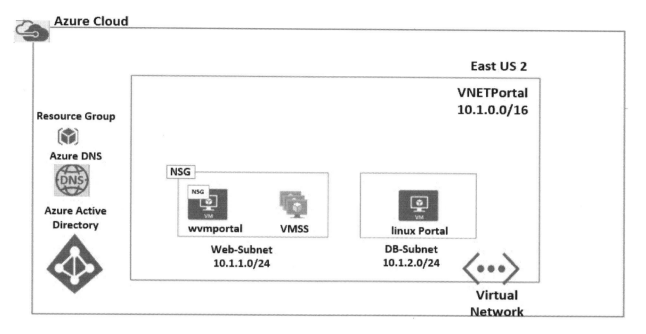

Virtual Machine Scale Sets (VMSS)

Virtual Machine Scale Sets creates scalable & high available Virtual Machine infrastructure by deploying and managing identical VMs as a set in a single Subnet of Virtual Network. An Azure Load Balancer or Azure Application Gateway is also deployed along with set of identical VMs.

Scale sets provide high availability to your applications, and allow you to centrally manage, configure, and update a large number of VMs. With virtual machine scale sets, you can build large-scale services for areas such as compute, big data, and container workloads.

VMs in the scale set are managed as a unit. All VMs in the scale set are identical and are either Windows VM or Linux VMs. All VMs are of same size and series.

VMSS supports Azure Windows and Linux images and Custom images.

Optionally by enabling Autoscaling on VMSS, Virtual Machines instances in the set can be added or removed automatically.

Features of Virtual Machine Scale Sets

Identical VMs deployed as a set.
Easy to create and manage multiple VMs.
Provides high availability and application resiliency.
Allows your application to automatically scale as resource demand changes.
Works at large-scale.

VM-specific features not available in Scale Set

1. You can snapshot an individual VM but not a VM in a scale set.
2. You can capture an image from an individual VM but not from a VM in a scale set.
3. You can migrate an individual VM from native disks to managed disks, but you cannot do this for VMs in a scale set.

Virtual Machine Scale Set (VMSS) Architecture

Virtual Machine Scale Set (VMSS) deploys set of Identical VMs in a single subnet of a Virtual Network. Figure below shows Architecture of Virtual Machine Scale Set (VMSS) deployed in single subnet with Single Placement group.

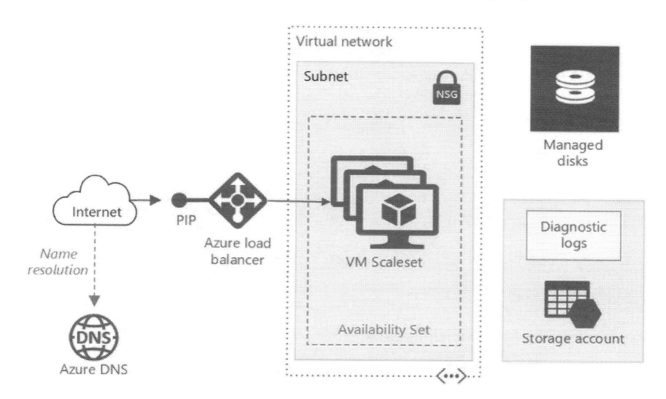

Set of identical VMs are deployed in the Single Subnet of Virtual Network.
You can select Existing or create new Virtual Network with **Single Subnet** during VM Scale set deployment.
Azure Load Balancer or Application Gateway with Public IP is created during VMSS deployment.
Placement group is availability set with five fault domains and five update domains and support up to 100 VMs. Placement group is automatically created by VMSS. Additional Placement groups will be automatically created by VMSS if you are deploying more than 100 instances.
Storage: VMSS can use managed disks or unmanaged disks for Virtual Machine storage. Managed disks are required to create more than 100 Virtual Machines. Unmanaged disks are limited to 100 VMs and single Placement Group.

Autoscaling with VMSS

With Autoscaling, Virtual Machines can be added (scale-out) or removed (scale-in) automatically from Virtual Machine Scale Set (VMSS) based on rules configured for metrics (CPU utilization, Memory utilization, Storage Queue etc.).

During Autoscaling the application continues to run without interruption as new resources are provisioned. When the provisioning process is complete, the solution is deployed on these additional resources. If demand drops, the additional resources can be shut down cleanly and de-allocated automatically.

How to Enable Autoscaling in VMSS

You can enable Autoscaling during VMSS creation or after the creation from VMSS dashboard or Azure Monitor Dashboard. If enabled during VMSS creation then only CPU metrics can be used for Autoscaling. Autoscaling can be based on schedule or on metric condition. **Metrics can be derived locally from VMSS or externally from Azure Resources such Service Bus, Storage Queue etc.**

Autoscaling Metrics

Autoscaling is enabled by configuring rules on Metrics or on Schedule. VMSS supports following types of metrics for configuring Autoscaling rules:

Host level Metrics: Host level metrics such as % CPU Utilization, Disk Read/write, Network in/out traffic at Network interface etc are emitted by Virtual Machines by default.

Guest OS level Metrics: You need to enable Guest OS diagnostics to use OS level metrics. OS level metrics are Operating system performance counters. Performance metrics are collected from inside of each VM instance and are streamed to an Azure storage account. VMSS can configure Autoscaling rules based on Guest OS level metrics,.

Application Insights: Application insights provide performance data for application running on VM.

Azure Resources: Azure resources such as Azure Storage queue can be used as a metric for configuring Autoscaling rules. For Example you can configure Autoscaling rule which scale-out by 2 instances when Storage Queue length is greater than 5.

Autoscaling Working

When threshold for a metric is reached scale-out or scale-in happens. For Example a rule configured for CPU utilization states that if CPU utilization crosses 80% then scale-out by 2 instances and if CPU utilization drops below 30% then scale-in by one instance.

All thresholds are calculated at an instance level (Average of all instances in VMSS). For example scale- out by 2 instance when average CPU > 80%, means scale-out happens when the average CPU across all instances is greater than 80%.

VIRTUAL MACHINE SCALE SET (VMSS) MAXIMUMS

1. Maximum Number of VMs in a scale set when using Azure Platform images is 1000.
2. Maximum Number of VMs in a scale set when using Custom VM images is 300.
3. To have more than 100 VMs in the scale set you need to use Managed Disks for VM storage.
4. A scale set configured with unmanaged disks for VM storage is limited to 100 VMs.

DESIGN NUGGETS

Design Nugget: If Multiple Rules are configured then *scale-out* happens if any rule is met and *scale-in* happens when all rules are met.

Design Nuggets: You can only attach data disks to a scale set that has been created with Azure Managed Disks.

Design Nuggets: If you are not using managed disks, we recommend no more than 20 VMs per storage account with overprovisioning enabled and no more than 40 VMs with overprovisioning disabled.

Exercise 47: Deploying VMSS

In Azure Portal click +Create a Resource> In search box type virtual machine scale set and click enter>In the result click Virtual Machine Scale set>Click create>Create Virtual Machine Scale set blade opens>Enter a name> For OS image click Browse all images>Select an image blade opens>Click My Items>**Select the image we created in Exercise 37**> Select RG HKPortal>Enter username and password>Autoscale Disabled>Select Load Balancer> For Virtual Network Select VNET Portal and Subnet DB-Subnet>Click create.

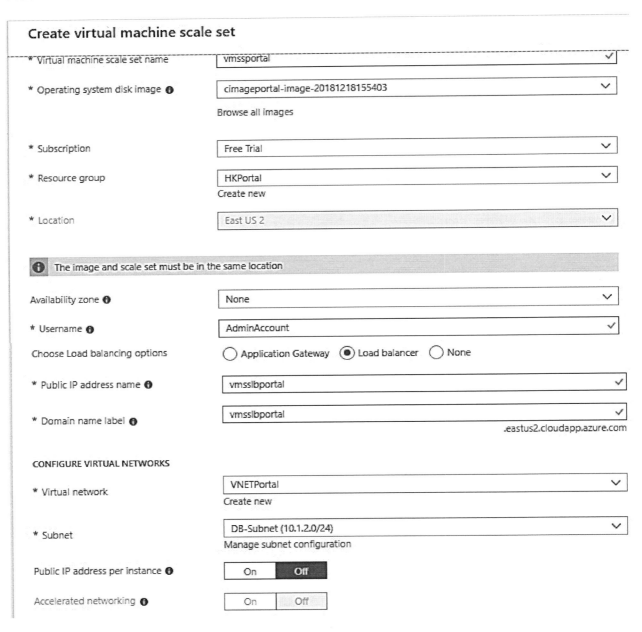

Note: If you have not done image exercise you can choose any Windows image.

Figure below shows the Dashboard of VMSS

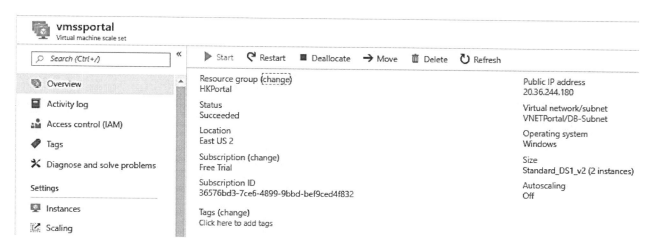

In a browser enter Load Balancer Public IP shown in VMSS dashboard. Default website opens. Public IP is 20.36.244.180.

Note: Using Custom Image is the best way to deploy VMSS. Create a VM and Install Applications, add Disks or NIC etc. Create Image of it. In this way you need not go and install apps on individual Instances.

Exercise 48: Connecting to Instances in VMSS

When you create a scale set in the portal, a load balancer is created. Based on Public IP of Load Balancer, Network Address Translation (NAT) rules are used to distribute traffic to the scale set instances.

1. Click All Resources in left pane>Select HKPortal in Resource Group and in type select Load Balancer> You can see Load Balancer vmssportallb. Alternatively in All Resources just scroll down and select vmssportallb.

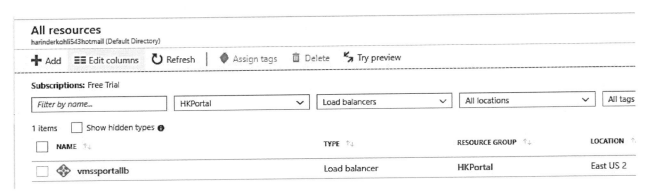

2. Click Load Balancer **vmssportallb** in All Resources pane>Load Balancer pane opens>Click Inbound NAT Rules in left pane> In right pane you can Instances IP address which is same for both instances but TCP Port for Instances are 50001 & 50002 respectively.

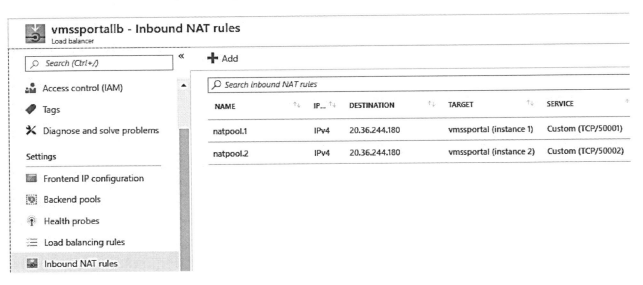

3. To connect to Instances using RDP use IP address appended with TCP Port.
    For Instance 1 connect to RDP using 20.36.244.180:50001
    For Instance 2 connect to RDP using 20.36.244.180:50002

4. Open RDP Application on your PC and enter 20.36.244.180:50001 and click
    Connect> Enter username and password you entered during VMSS creation.

5. RDP session is opened for Instance 1. Server Manager is already opened.

Exercise 49: Enabling Autoscaling

1. Click Scaling in VMSS dashboard>Scaling blade opens in right pane.

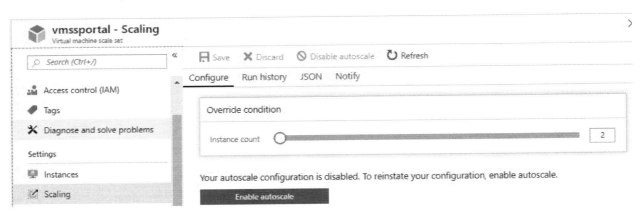

2. Click Enable Autoscale in right pane> Scale Condition Blade opens> we will edit the default scale condition Rule>In Instance limits Enter 3 in Maximum. Note + **Add a Rule Link**. We will use this to create Scale out and Scale in Rule.

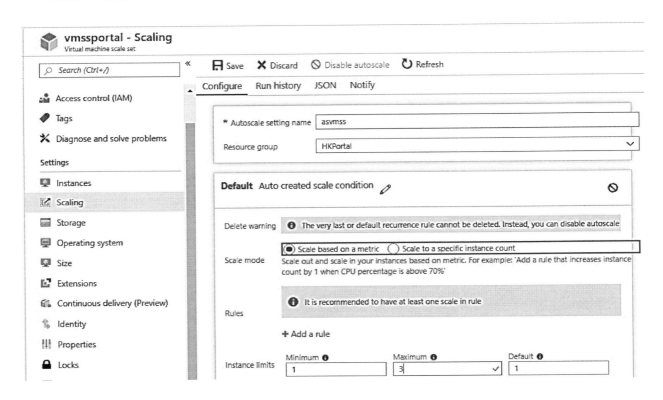

Create Scale Out Rule: In Scale condition pane Click + Add a rule >Scale rule opens in right pane. Note the metrics sources. Metric Sources can be VMSS or External Sources such as Storage queue or Service Bus Queue etc. For Metric we will select % CPU> In operation Box select **Increase count by**> Rest select all default values and click Add

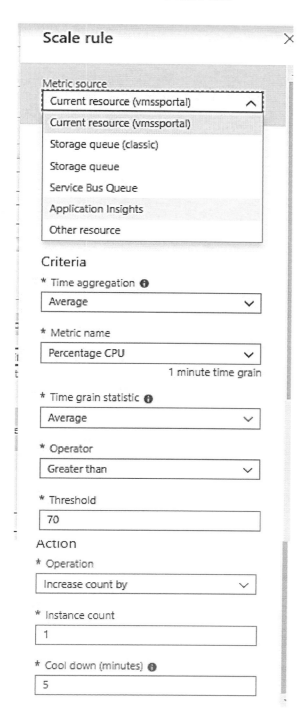

3. **Create Scale in Rule**: In Scale condition pane Click + Add a rule >Scale rule opens in right pane. For Metric we will select % CPU> Select 30% in Threshold> In operation Box select **decrease count by**>Rest select all default values and click Add> click Save.

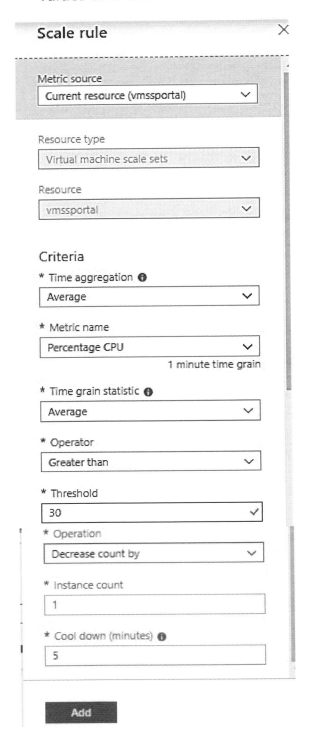

4. In scaling pane you can see the Scale in and scale out rules created.

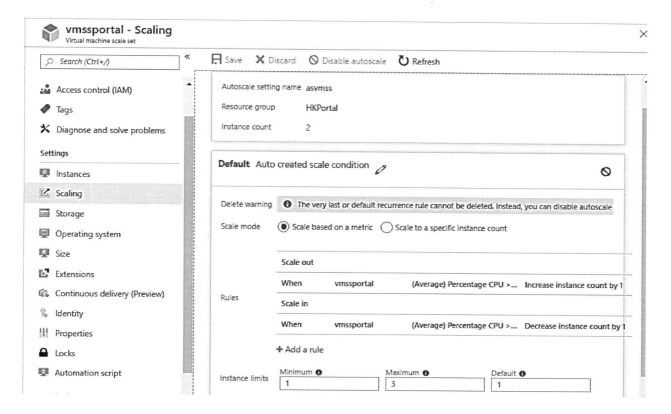

Note: Delete the VMSS, Load Balancers & Public IP as we longer need it.

Chapter 6 Implement and Manage Storage Accounts

This Chapter covers following Topic Lessons

- Storage Accounts
- Storage Account Types
- Azure Storage Account Replication
- Storage Account endpoints
- Object Endpoints
- Securing Storage Account using Azure VNET Service Endpoints
- Azure Storage Explorer
- Options to Connect to Azure Storage using Storage Explorer
- Download Storage Explorer
- Accessing Azure Storage Accounts using Azure Account Credentials
- Accessing Azure Storage Account using Storage Account Access Keys
- Accessing Storage Account using Shared Access Signature
- Accessing Storage Account using Azure Active Directory (Preview)

This Chapter covers following Lab Exercises

- Create GPv2 Standard Storage Account using Portal
- Create GPv2 Premium Storage Account
- Demonstrating Storage Account sastdportal functionalities
- Demonstrating Storage Account Security
- Setting up Virtual Network Service Endpoints
- Connect to Azure Storage using Azure Account Credentials
- Get Storage Account sastdportal Access Keys
- Connect to Storage Account sastdportal using Access key
- Generate Shared Access Signature of Storage Account
- Connect to Storage Account using Shared Access Signature

Chapter Topology

In this chapter we will add Azure Storage Account to the topology. We will create two Storage Accounts - GPv2 Standard Storage Account & GPv2 Premium Storage Account.

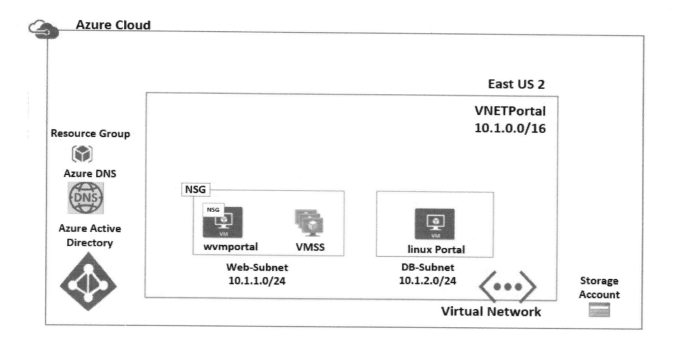

Storage Accounts

An Azure storage account provides a unique namespace to store and access your Azure Storage data objects.

Azure Storage (Blob, Table, Queue and Files) is created under Storage Accounts. Storage Account is prerequisite for creating Azure Storage.

The image below shows the dashboard of General Purpose Storage Account. From here you will create Blob, File, table or Queue Storage.

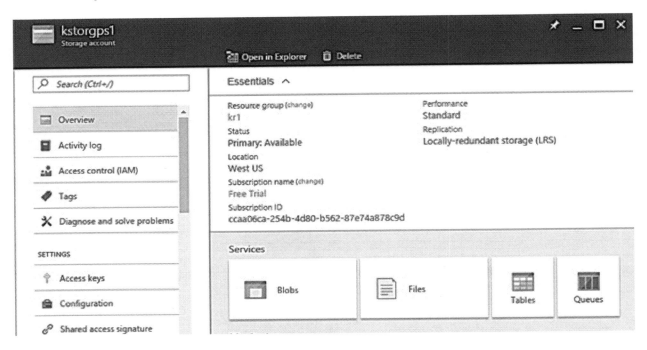

Figure below shows components of Blob, Table, Queue and File Storage.

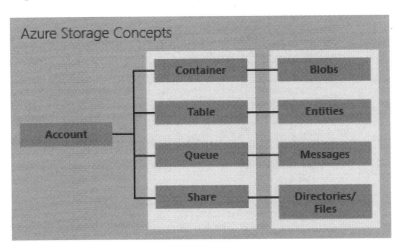

Storage Account Types

There are three types of storage accounts - General-purpose v2 (GPv2) Storage Account, General-purpose v1 (GPv1) Storage Account & Blob Storage Account.

General-purpose v2 (GPv2) Storage Account

General-purpose v2 (GPv2) storage accounts support storage services including blobs, files, queues, and tables. It supports all latest features for storage services.

For block blobs in a GPv2 storage account, you can choose between hot and cool storage tiers at the account level, or hot, cool, and archive tiers at the blob level.

General-purpose v1 (GPv1) Storage Account

General-purpose v1 (GPv1) storage account supports storage services including blobs, files, queues, and tables. It does not support latest features for storage services. It does not support blob storage tiering.

Blob Storage Account

Blob Storage accounts are specialized for storing blob data and support choosing an access tier – Hot or cool at account level.
Blob storage accounts support only block and append blobs and not page blobs.

Storage Account Performance Tiers

1. A **standard storage performance tier** allows you to create Blobs, Tables, Queues, Files and Azure virtual machine disks.
   It is backed by magnetic disk HDD.
   Supports GPv1, GPv2 and Blob Storage Account.

2. A **premium storage performance tier** allows you to create Blobs and Azure virtual machine disks.
   It is backed by SSD.
   Supports GPv1 & GPv2 Storage Account. Supports LRS replication only.

   Note: Premier storage performance tier now also supports and Azure File Storage (Preview). It is in Preview as of writing.

Comparing Storage Accounts

Description	GPv2	GPv1	Blob Storage Account
Storage Type Supported	Blob, File, Table and Queue	Blob, File, Table and Queue	Blob (block and append blob)
Types of Blob supported	page, block and append blob	page, block and append blob	block and append blob
Disk Type	HDD & SSD	HDD & SSD	HDD
Replication Options (Standard Storage	LRS, ZRS, GRS and RA-GRS	LRS, GRS and RA-GRS	LRS, GRS, RA-GRS
Replication Options (Premium Storage)	LRS	LRS	NA
Can be used for Virtual Machine Disks	Yes through page blobs	Yes through page blobs	No
Blob Storage Tiering	Yes	No	Yes
Use Case	It has wide and large use cases including VM disk.	It has wide and large use cases including VM disk.	Object Storage and Archiving

Azure Storage Account Replication

The data in the Microsoft Azure storage account is always replicated to ensure high availability. Replication copies data, either within the same Data Centre, or to a second Data Centre, depending on the replication option chosen. Azure Storage Accounts offer 4 Replication options – LRS, ZRS, GRS, RA-GRS.

Comparing Storage Account Replication Options

Features	LRS	ZRS	GRS	RA-GRS
Data is replicated across multiple datacenters.	No	Yes	Yes	Yes
Data can be read from a secondary location as well as the primary location.	No	No	No	Yes
Data Availability if Node becomes unavailable within Data Center	Yes	Yes	Yes	Yes
Data Availability if Data Center goes down	No	Yes	Yes	Yes
Data Availability if there is Region wide outage	No	No	Yes	Yes
SLA	11 9's	12 9's	16 9's	16 9's
Storage Account Supported	GPv1, GPv2, Blob	GPv2	GPv1, GPv2, Blob	GPv1, GPv2, Blob

Locally redundant storage (LRS)

Locally redundant storage (LRS) replicates your data three times in a datacenter in the region in which you created your storage account. A write request returns successfully only once it has been written to all three replicas. The three replicas each reside in separate fault domains and upgrade domains within one storage scale unit.

LRS is the lowest cost option. LRS can protect your data from underlying storage node failure but not from Data Centre wide outage.

Use Case for Locally Redundant Storage

LRS can be used in cases where applications are restricted to replicating data only within a country due to data governance requirements.

Storage Accounts Supported: GPv2, GPv1 and Blob Storage Account.

Zone-redundant storage (ZRS)

ZRS replicates your data synchronously across three availability zones. ZRS enables customers to read and write data even if a single zone is unavailable or unrecoverable. Inserts and updates to data are made synchronously and are strongly consistent.

ZRS provides durability for storage objects of at least 99.9999999999% (12 9's) over a given year. Consider ZRS for scenarios like transactional applications where downtime is not acceptable.

ZRS provides higher durability than LRS. Data stored in ZRS is durable even if the primary Datacentre is unavailable or unrecoverable.

ZRS will not protect your data against a regional disaster where multiple zones are permanently affected. For protection against regional disasters, Microsoft recommends using Geo-redundant storage (GRS): Cross-regional replication for Azure Storage.

Storage Accounts Supported: GPv2.

Geo Redundant Storage (GRS)

Geo-redundant storage (GRS) replicates your data to a secondary region that is hundreds of miles away from the primary region.

With GRS, data is first replicated 3 times within the primary region and then asynchronously replicated to the secondary region, where it is also replicated three times.
With GRS, data is durable even in the case of a complete regional outage or a disaster in which the primary region is not recoverable.

When you create a storage account, you select the primary region for the account. The secondary region is determined based on the primary region, and cannot be changed.

Storage Accounts Supported: GPv2, GPv1 and Blob Storage Account.

Read-access geo-redundant storage (RA-GRS)

Read-access geo-redundant storage (RA-GRS) not only replicates your data to a secondary region but also provides read-only access to the data in the secondary location.

With RA-GRS, data is first replicated 3 times within the primary region and then asynchronously replicated to the secondary region, where it is also replicated three times.

With RA-GRS, data is durable even in the case of a complete regional outage or a disaster in which the primary region is not recoverable.

When you create a storage account, you select the primary region for the account. The secondary region is determined based on the primary region, and cannot be changed.

Storage Accounts Supported: GPv2, GPv1 and Blob Storage Account.

Storage Account endpoints

Every object that you store in Azure Storage has a unique URL address. The storage account name forms the subdomain of that address. The combination of subdomain and domain name, which is specific to each service, forms an ***endpoint*** for your storage account.

For example, if your storage account is named ***mystorageaccount***, then the **default endpoints for your storage account** are:

Blob service: http://*mystorageaccount*.blob.core.windows.net
Table service: http://*mystorageaccount*.table.core.windows.net
Queue service: http://*mystorageaccount*.queue.core.windows.net
File service: http://mystorageaccount.file.core.windows.net

Object Endpoints

The URL for accessing an object in a storage account is built by appending the object's location in the storage account to the endpoint. For example, a blob address might have this format:
http://mystorageaccount.blob.core.windows.net/mycontainer/myblob.

You can also configure a custom domain name to use with your storage account.

Storage Account Design Nuggets

1. Storage Account name must be unique within Azure.
2. Read-access geo-redundant storage (RA-GRS) is the default replication option when you create a storage account.

Exercise 50: Create GPv2 Standard Storage Account using Portal

In this exercise we will create Standard GPv2 Storage Account with name sastdportal in resource group HKPortal and in location US East 2.

1. In Azure Portal Click +Create a Resource in left pane>Storage> Storage Accounts> Create Storage Account Blade opens> Select Resource Group **HKPortal**> Give a unique name to storage Account **sastdportal**> Select location East US 2>Performance standard>Account Type as GPv2>Replication RA-GRS> Access Tier Hot> Rest keep as default> Click Next: Advanced

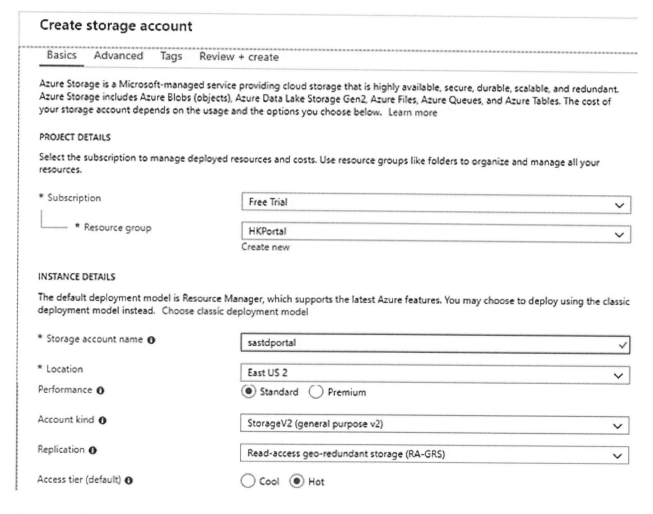

Note 1: Storage Account name has to be unique within Azure.
Note 2: You can choose between Standard or premium (SSD) performance Tier.
Note 3: Note Access Tier option. This is not available with GPv1 Account.

2. In Advanced screen just go through options. Keep everything at default and click Review +create.

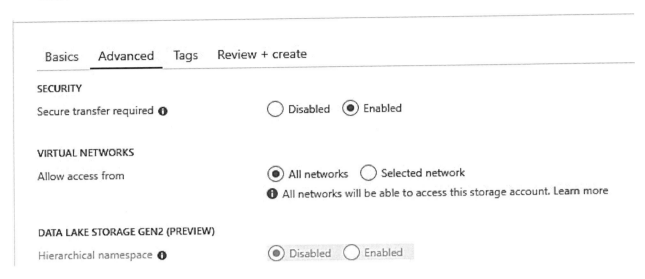

3. After validation is passed click create.
4. Figure below shows the dashboard of Storage Account. From here you can create Blob, file, table or queue Storage.

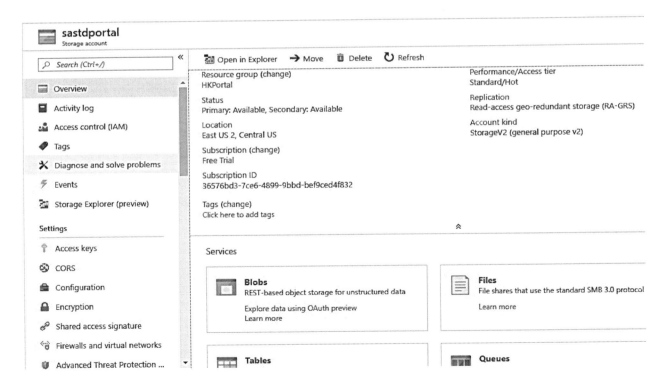

Exercise 51: Create GPv2 Premium Storage Account

In this exercise we will create Standard GPv2 Storage Account with name **sapremportal** in resource group **HKPortal** and in location US East 2.

1. In Azure Portal Click Storage Accounts in left pane> Storage Accounts Dashboard opens> Click + Add> Create Storage Account Blade opens> Select Resource Group **HKPortal**> Give a unique name to storage Account **sapremportal**> Select location East US 2>Performance Premium>Account Type as GPv2>Replication LRS> Rest keep as default> Click Review +create>After Validation is passed click create.

Create storage account

Basics   Advanced   Tags   Review + create

Azure Storage is a Microsoft-managed service providing cloud storage that is highly available, secure, durable, scalable, and redundant. Azure Storage includes Azure Blobs (objects), Azure Data Lake Storage Gen2, Azure Files, Azure Queues, and Azure Tables. The cost of your storage account depends on the usage and the options you choose below. Learn more

PROJECT DETAILS

Select the subscription to manage deployed resources and costs. Use resource groups like folders to organize and manage all your resources.

* Subscription — Free Trial

* Resource group — HKPortal
Create new

INSTANCE DETAILS

The default deployment model is Resource Manager, which supports the latest Azure features. You may choose to deploy using the classic deployment model instead. Choose classic deployment model

* Storage account name — sapremportal

* Location — East US 2

Performance — ( ) Standard (•) Premium

Account kind — StorageV2 (general purpose v2)

Replication — Locally-redundant storage (LRS)

Accounts with the selected kind, replication and performance type only support page blobs. Block blobs, append blobs, file shares, tables, and queues will not be available.

2. Figure below shows the dashboard of Storage Account.

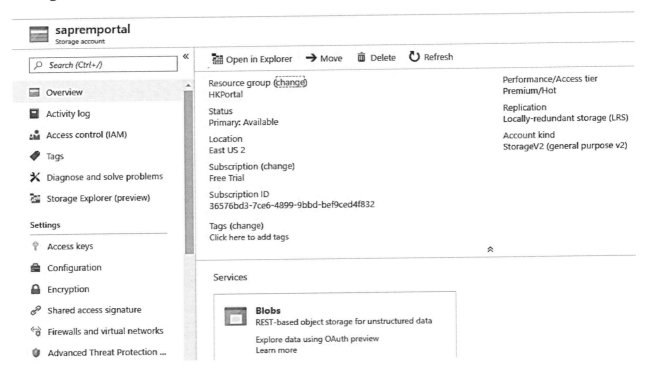

With Premium Account only Blob Storage option is there. This only supports Page Blobs. Recall that Page Blobs are used for Virtual Machine Disks.

Note: Premier storage performance tier now also supports and Azure File Storage (Preview). It is in Preview as of writing.

Exercise 52: Demonstrating Storage Account sastdportal functionalities

1. Figure below shows dashboard of the GPv2 Storage Account **sastdportal**. From here you can create Blob, file, table or queue Storage.

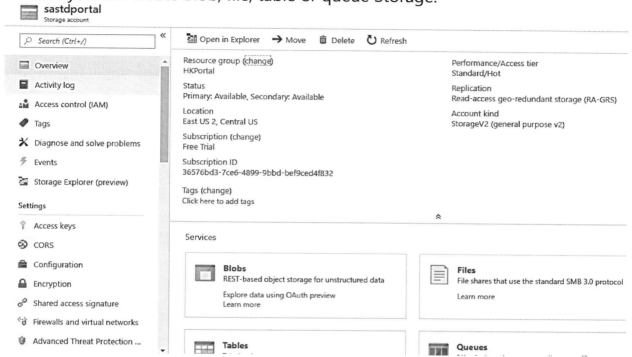

2. **Change configuration of storage account**: Click configuration in left pane. From here you can change Access tier and Replication option.

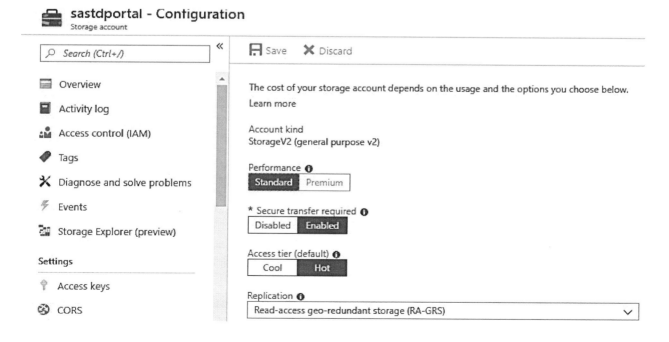

Exercise 53: Demonstrating Storage Account Security

Storage Account Security with RBAC: By default owner can access the Storage Account. You can delegate the Storage Account administration using Role Based Access control (RBAC). You can assign role of an owner, contributor, reader, Backup operator etc depending upon your requirement.

Go to sastdportal Dashboard>Click Access Control (IAM) in left pane>+ Add Role assignment>Add role assignment blade opens> Select the role and the user.

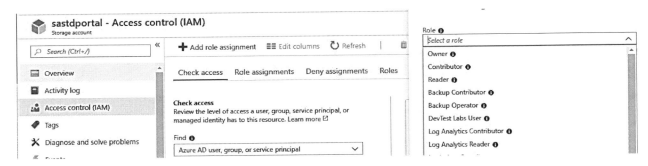

Storage Account Security with Storage Service Encryption (SSE): By default SSE protects your data at Rest using MS managed keys. You can use your own to keys to encryption storage data. Click encryption in left pane.

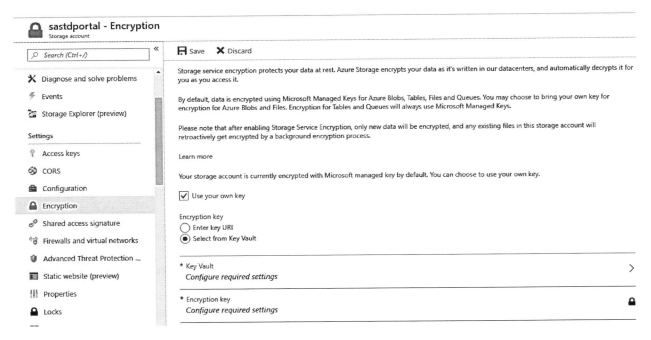

Note: Readers are advised to go through options in left pane.

Storage Account Security using Azure Virtual Network Service Endpoints: By default owner can access storage account from internet. This is a security loophole. Using **Firewall and Virtual Network** option you can limit access to Storage account from Virtual Network only. You also have the option of allowing Storage account access from internet from particular IP address only.

Click Firewall and Virtual Networks in left pane>Click Add existing Virtual Network>Select your Virtual Network.

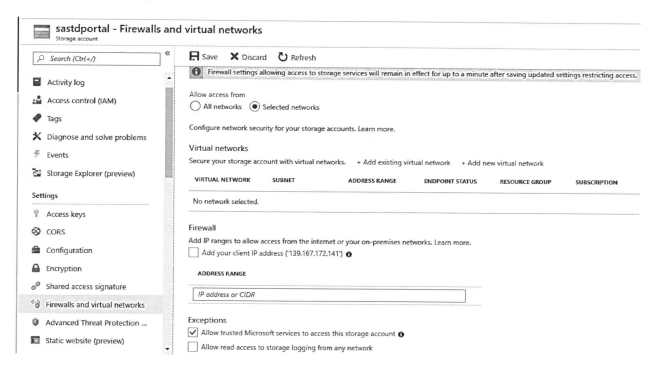

In Next section we will discuss in detail about Azure Virtual Network Service Endpoints.

Network Access to Storage Account using VNET Service Endpoints

Azure Managed Resources such as Azure Storage can be accessed from outside Azure and by VMs in Virtual Network over internet connection.

With Azure Virtual Network Service Endpoints, traffic between Azure Virtual Network and Azure Managed Resources such as Storage Accounts remains on the Microsoft Azure backbone network and not on Public Internet.

Virtual Network Service Endpoint Architecture

Figure below shows the Architecture of VNET Service Endpoints. Resources in Virtual Network are accessing Azure Storage over Microsoft backbone network.

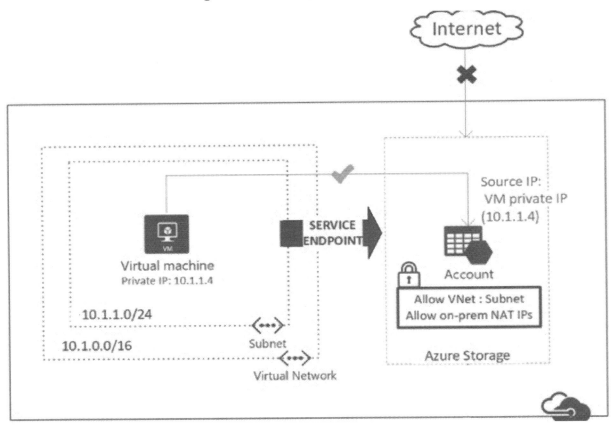

WHY WE NEED AZURE VIRTUAL NETWORK ENDPOINTS

Azures Managed Resources such as Azure Storage and Azure SQL have Internet facing IP addresses. Because of security reasons many customers prefer that their Azure Managed Services not be exposed directly to the Internet.

WORKING OF VNET SERVICE ENDPOINTS

Virtual Network Service Endpoints are created in Virtual Network and are attached to Subnets. They extend Azure Virtual Network private address space to Azure Managed services. You can also restrict Azure resources to only be accessed from your VNET and not via the Internet. You also have the option to allow access from internet or from particular IP range only.

Exercise 54: Setting up Virtual Network Service Endpoints

In this Exercise we will create VNET Service Endpoints for Azure Storage Account sastdportal. After setting up Service Endpoint and blocking access of Azure Storage Account from internet we will check whether we can still open Blob Container hk410 or File share Dashboard.
We will then access Blob Container Dashboard using Internet Explorer from Azure VM wvmportal located in Web-Subnet in Virtual Network VNETPortal.

Note for the Readers: Attempt this exercise after you have completed Exercises in Storage chapter 7. In Storage chapter we created Container hk410 in Storage Account sastdportal.

Step 1: Create VNET Service Endpoints for Azure Storage Account sastdportal

Go to Storage Account sastdportal dashboard>Click Firewalls and Virtual Networks in left pane>Click selected Networks Radio Button in right pane>click +Add Existing Virtual Network> Add Networks blade opens>Select VNETPortal> Select Web-Subnet from dropdown box>Click Enable>Click Add>Click Save.

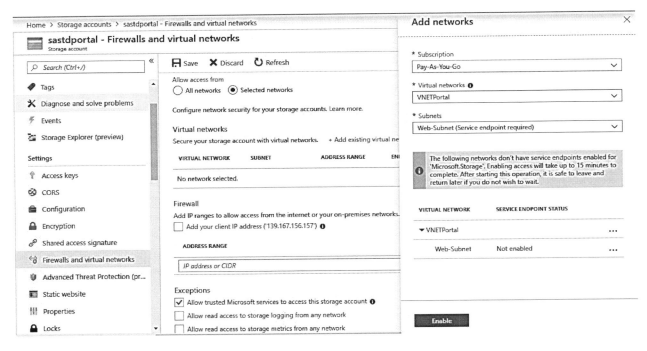

Note Firewall option: Here you can add IP address range which can access Azure storage from internet. You can select your Client IP Address also.

Step 2: Check whether you can access Blob Container Dashboard hk410.

Go to Storage Account sastdportal Dashboard>Click Blobs>All Container Dashboard opens>Click hk410> Access Denied because of VNET Service Endpoints which denies access to Storage account from Internet.

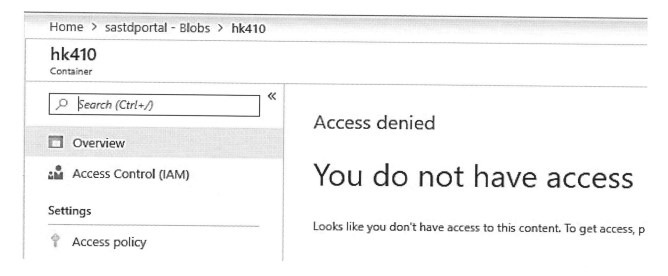

Step 3: Access Blob Container hk410 from Virtual Machine wvmportal

RDP to Virtual Machine wvmportal>open internet explorer and log on Azure Portal>Go to Storage Account sastdportal Dashboard>Click Blobs>Click container hk410>hk410 dashboard opens.

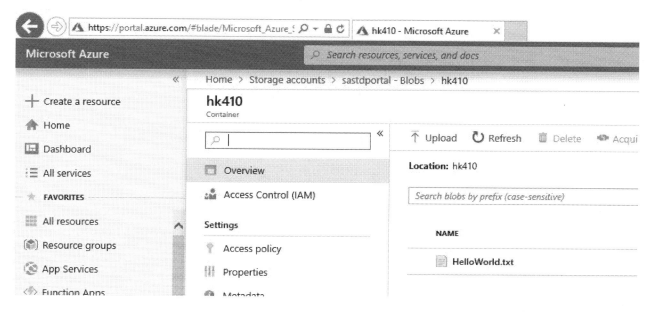

Step 4: Enable back Storage Account access from all Networks

In Storage Network sastdportal Dashboard click Firewall and Virtual Networks in left pane>Select the radio button All Networks>Click save.

Note: We need access to Storage Account from internet for other exercises.

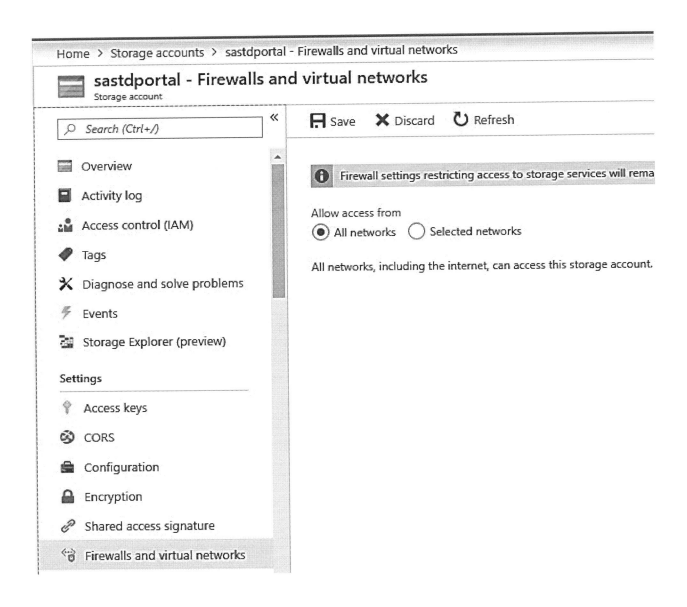

Azure Storage Explorer

Microsoft Azure Storage Explorer is a standalone app (available on Windows, Mac & Linux) that allows you to easily work with Azure Storage data.

Using Storage Explorer you can Upload, download and manage blobs, files, queues, tables and Cosmos DB entities. Storage Explorer also provides easy access to manage your virtual machine disks.

Figure below shows Dashboard of Storage Explorer Application running on Windows Desktop.

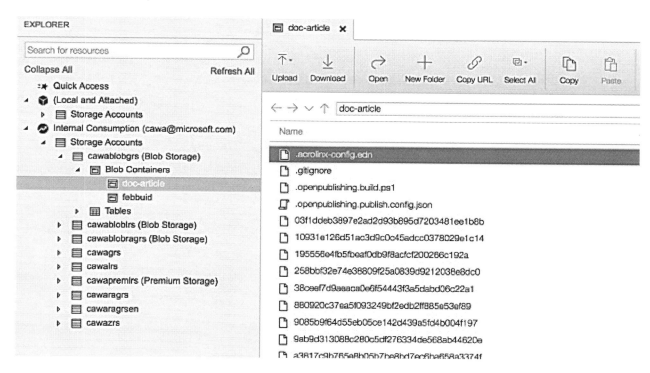

Options to Connect to Azure Storage using Storage Explorer

Azure Account Subscription credentials
Storage Account Name and Key
Use a Shared Access Signature URI
Use a Connection String

Download Storage Explorer

https://go.microsoft.com/fwlink/?LinkId=708343&cIcid=0x4009

Accessing Azure Storage Accounts using Azure Account Credentials

By using Azure Subscription Account credentials with Azure Storage Explorer you get full access to **all Storage Accounts** in Azure Subscription.

Exercise 55: Connect to Azure Storage using Azure Account Credentials

1. Open Storage Explorer app on your desktop>In left pane right click Storage Accounts and click connect to Azure Storage> A dialog Box will pop and will show 5 options to connect to Azure Storage.

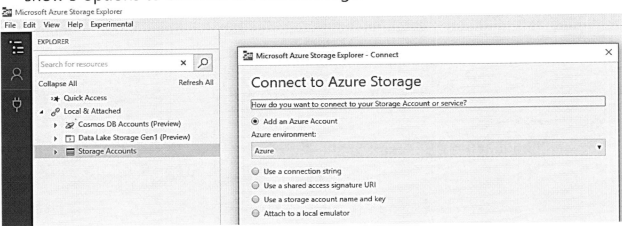

2. Select Add an Azure Account radio Button and click sign in box at the bottom of the Pop up dialog box>Sign-in to your account Blade will pop up. Enter your account credentials>click apply in Storage Explorer Dashboard. You can see all your storage Accounts (Created in Ex 50 & 51) in your subscription.

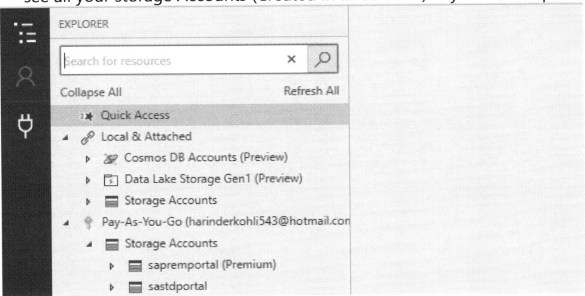

3. Enlarge the Storage Accounts and you can see the options available under each Storage Account. Storage Account sapremportal has only Blob Storage option as it is was created with Premium Performance Tier (SSD) whereas Storage Account sastdportal has Blob, File, table and Queue option as it was created with Standard Storage Performance tier (HDD).

I also enlarged Blob container under Storage account sastdportal and clicked vhds. In right pane you can see OS disk for Linux VM linuxportal which was created in Chapter 3, exercise 34.

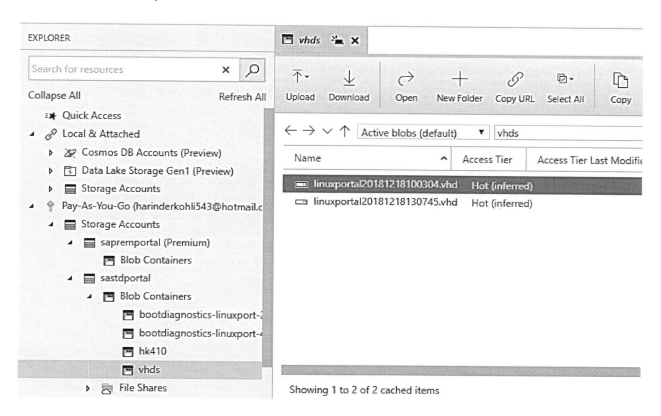

Note: Readers are advised to go through all the options here. Just Right click Blob Container and you can create a container. In next chapter we will show how to create a container and upload a file using Storage Explorer.

Accessing Azure Storage Account using Storage Account Access Keys

Using Azure Storage Explorer with Storage Account Access keys you get full access to that **particular** Storage Account only.

Anybody having access to Storage account key will have unlimited access to storage account.
Be careful not give account key to anybody as this will give them full access control to Storage Account.

Exercise 56: Get Storage Account sastdportal Access Keys

1. In Azure Portal go to Storage Account sastdportal dashboard>Click Access Keys in left pane> Copy Key 1 and paste in Notepad. We will use this to connect to storage Account using Storage Explorer.

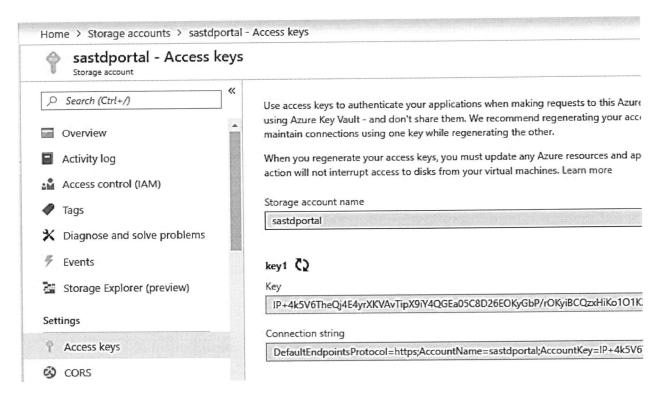

Exercise 57: Connect to Storage Account sastdportal using Access key

1. In Storage Explorer Dashboard right click Storage Accounts and click connect to Azure Storage> A dialog Box will pop and will show 5 options to connect to Azure Storage>Select use a Storage account name and key radio button.

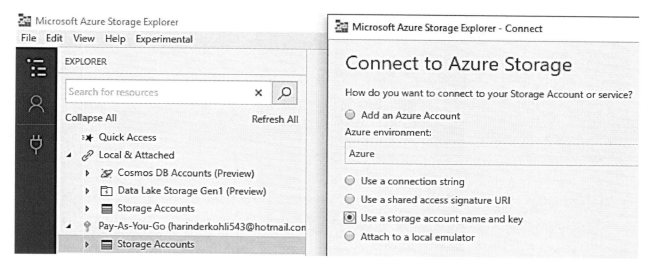

2. Select use a Storage account name and key radio button and click next button at bottom of the dialog box>Connect with Name and Key dialog box will pop up>Give a display name, enter Storage Account name sastdportal in Account name and paste the key you copied previous exercise and click next. (Hidekey)

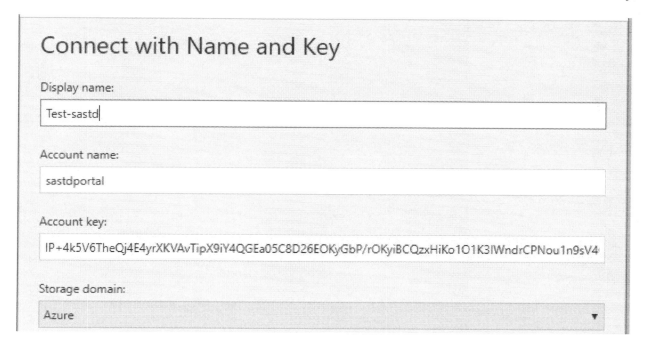

3. Connection summary box will pop up>Click connect.

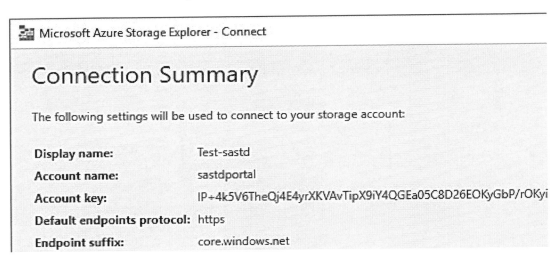

4. In Explorer Dashboard you can see Test-sastd. This name was given for storage Account sastdportal in step 3. Expand Test-sastd and it will show all the 4 options-Blob, File, Queues and tables>Expand Blob Containers.

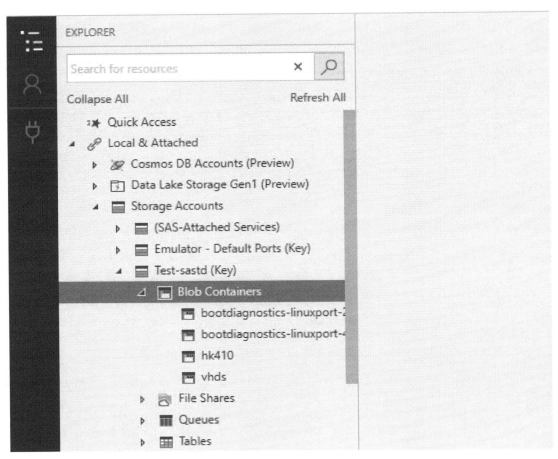

Accessing Storage Account using Shared Access Signature

Anybody having access to Storage account key will have unlimited access to storage account.

Shared access signature (SAS), provide delegated access to a resource in your storage account, without having to share your account access keys. SAS is a secure way to share your storage resources without compromising your account keys.

A shared access signature is a token that encapsulates all of the information needed to authorize a request to Azure Storage on the URL. You can specify the storage resource, the permissions granted, and the interval over which the permissions are valid as part of the shared access signature.

You can provide a shared access signature to clients who should not be trusted with your storage account key but whom you wish to delegate access to certain storage account resources. By distributing a shared access signature URI to these clients, you grant them access to a resource for a specified period of time.

SAS granular control features

1. You can specify interval over which the SAS is valid, including the start time and the expiry time.
2. You can specify permissions granted by the SAS. For example, a SAS on a blob might grant a user read and write permissions to that blob, but not delete permissions.
3. An optional IP address or range of IP addresses from which Azure Storage will accept the SAS
4. The protocol over which Azure Storage will accept the SAS. You can use this optional parameter to restrict access to clients using HTTPS.

Types of shared access signatures (SAS)

Service SAS delegates access to particular storage services: the Blob, Queue, Table, or File service.

An **Account-level SAS** can delegate access to multiple storage services (i.e. blob, file, queue, table).

Exercise 58: Generate Shared Access Signature of Storage Account

In this exercise we will generate Shared Access Signature (SAS) for Storage Account sastdportal for Blob service only.

1. In Azure Portal go to Storage Account sastdportal dashboard>Click Shared Access Signature in left pane>Select **Blob Service** only and rest select all default values>Click generate SAS and Connection String Box.

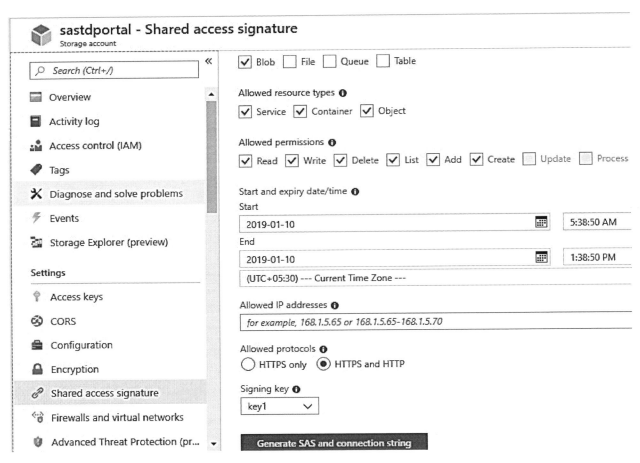

2. SAS will be generated and will be shown in bottom of the screen. Copy the Blob Service SAS URL.

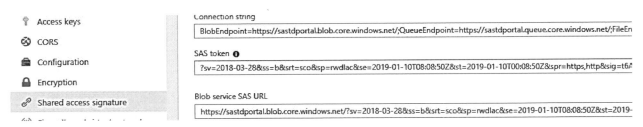

Exercise 59: Connect to Storage Account using Shared Access Signature

1. In Storage Explorer Dashboard right click Storage Accounts and click connect to Azure Storage> A dialog Box will pop and will show 5 options to connect to Azure Storage>Select use a Shared Access Signature URI radio button.

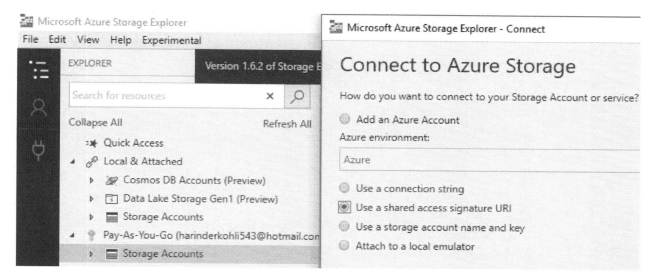

2. Select use a shared access signature URL and Click next> Attach with SAS URI Blade opens>Enter a Display name >Enter URL which was generated in previous exercise and click Next>In summary box click connect.

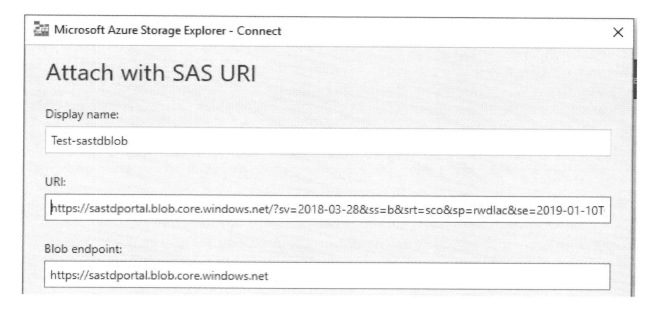

3. In Storage Explorer dashboard you can see Test-sastdblob under Storage Account. We only have access to Blob Service as we have generated SAS for Blob service in previous exercise.

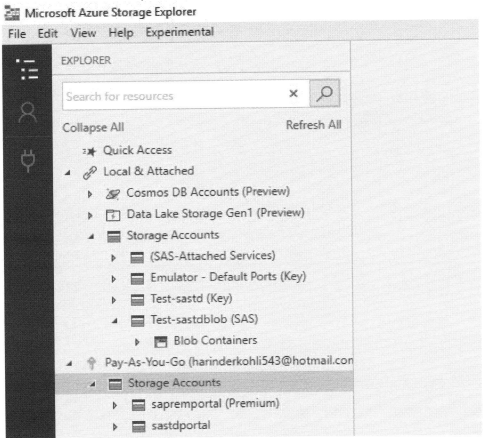

Inference from Above Figure

Test-sastd has all four services (Blob, File, Queue and Table) listed. This connection used the Storage Account sastdportal Access key.
Test-sastdblob has only Blob service listed. This connection used shared access signature. Shared access signature was generated for Storage Account sastdportal blob service only.
Pay-As-You-Go Subscription shows all the Storage Account created in the Subscription as we used Azure Subscription credentials for Connection.

Similarly you can connect your application to Azure Storage by adding Shared Access Signature (SAS) in your application code.

Accessing Storage Account using Azure Active Directory (Preview)

You can use Azure Active Directory (Azure AD) credentials to authenticate a user, group, or other identity for access to blob and queue data (preview). If authentication of an identity is successful, then Azure AD returns a token to use in authorizing the request to Azure Blob storage or Queue storage.

Note: Currently this feature is in preview and is not part of the exam and is not being discussed further.

Chapter 7 Storage Accounts with CLI and PS

This Chapter covers following Lab Exercises

- Create Storage Account Using CLI
- Create Storage Account Using PowerShell

Exercise 60: Create Storage Account Using CLI

In this exercise we will create GPv2 Storage Account "stdcli410" in Resource Group HKCLI in East US 2 Location. Resource Group HKCLI was created in Chapter 2, Exercise 19.

Connect to Azure using Azure CLI
Open command prompt (cmd) on your desktop and enter **az login** command for connecting and authenticating to Subscription.

Create Storage Account
az storage account create --name stdcli410 --resource-group HKCLI --location eastus2 --sku Standard_LRS --kind StorageV2

```
C:\WINDOWS\system32>az storage account create --name stdcli410 --resource-group HKCLI --location eastus2 --sku Standard_LRS --kind StorageV2
{
  "accessTier": "Hot",
  "creationTime": "2018-11-01T04:19:06.446222+00:00",
  "customDomain": null,
```

Check the Storage Account created
az storage account show --name stdcli410 or
az storage account show --name stdcli410 --resource-group HKCLI

```
C:\WINDOWS\system32>az storage account show --name stdcli410
{
  "accessTier": "Hot",
  "creationTime": "2018-11-01T04:19:06.446222+00:00",
  "customDomain": null,
  "enableHttpsTrafficOnly": false,
  "encryption": {
    "keySource": "Microsoft.Storage",
    "keyVaultProperties": null,
    "services": {
      "blob": {
        "enabled": true,
        "lastEnabledTime": "2018-11-01T04:19:06.539972+00:00"
```

Delete Storage Account
az storage account delete --name stdcli410
Note: Don't run above command.

Exercise 61: Create Storage Account Using PowerShell

In this exercise we will create GPv2 Storage Account "stdps410" in Resource Group HKPS in East US 2 Location. Resource Group HKCLI was created in Chapter 2, Exercise 20.

Connect to Azure using PowerShell
Open PowerShell command prompt on your desktop and login using Connect-AzureRmAccount.

Create Storage Account
New-AzureRmStorageAccount –ResourceGroupName HKPS –Name stdps410 – Location eastus2 –SkuName Standard_LRS –Kind StorageV2

Check the Storage Account created
Get-AzureRmStorageAccount –ResourceGroupName HKPS –Name stdps410

```
PS C:\Users\Harinder Kohli> Get-AzureRmStorageAccount -ResourceGroupName HKPS -Name stdps410

StorageAccountName ResourceGroupName Location SkuName     Kind     AccessTier CreationTime          Provisioni
------------------ ----------------- -------- -------     ----     ---------- ------------          ----------
stdps410           HKPS              eastus2  StandardLRS StorageV2 Hot        01-11-2018 02:26:54   Succeeded
```

Delete Storage Account
Remove-AzureRmStorageAccount –ResourceGroupName HKPS –Name stdps410
Note: Don't run above command.

Chapter 8 Implement and Manage Storage

This Chapter covers following Topic Lessons

- Azure Storage Introduction
- Blob Storage
- Azure File Storage
- Azure File Sync
- Import to Azure
- Export from Azure
- Azure Data Box
- Content Delivery Networks (CDN)

This Chapter covers following Lab Exercises

- Create Blob Storage Container and upload a File
- Blob Storage Tiering
- Create Blob Storage Container using Storage Explorer
- Creating and using File Share
- Deploying Azure File Sync in 4 Steps
- Demonstrating Export Job Creation
- Demonstrating Data Box Order through Azure Portal
- Implementing Azure CDN using Azure Portal
- Enabling or Disabling Compression
- Changing Optimization type
- Changing Caching Rules
- Allow or Block CDN in Specific Countries

Chapter Topology

In this chapter we will add Blob Storage, File Storage, Azure File Sync service & CDN to the Topology. We also demonstrate how to create Import/Export Service and Azure Data Box Ordering.

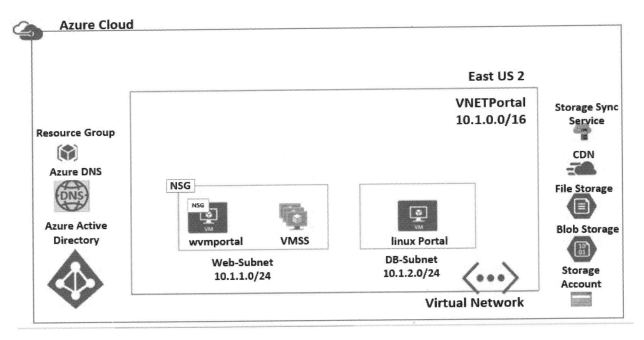

We will install Azure File Sync Agent on VM OnPremAD.

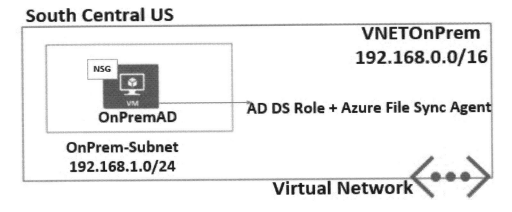

This diagram is shown separately as there is space constrained in top diagram.

Azure Storage Introduction

Azure Storage is the Managed cloud storage solution. Azure Storage is highly available and massively scalable. Azure provides five types of storage - Blob, Table, Queue, Files and Virtual Machine Disk storage (Page Blobs).

Azure Blobs: A massively scalable object store for unstructured data.
Azure Files: Managed file shares for cloud or on-premises deployments. File Storage provides shared storage for Azure/on-premises VMs using SMB protocol.
Azure Queues: A messaging store for reliable messaging between application components.
Azure Tables: A NoSQL store for schemaless storage of structured data.

Figure Below shows five types of Azure Storage Services.

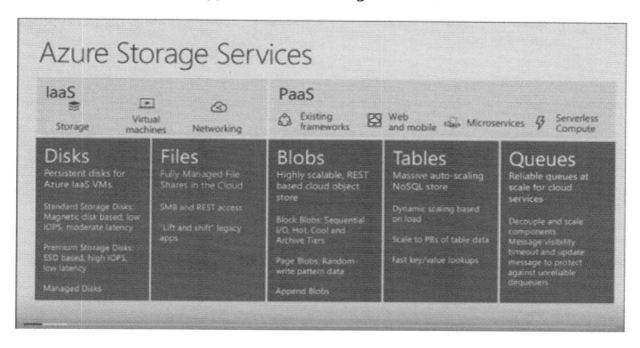

Comparing Different Azure Storage Services types

Azure Storage	Data Type
Blob	Unstructured
Table	Structured
Queue	Messaging
File	Shared Storage

Feature of Azure Storage

Durable and highly available: Redundancy ensures that your data is safe in the event of transient hardware failures. You can also opt to replicate data across datacenters or geographical regions for additional protection from local catastrophe or natural disaster. Data replicated in this way remains highly available in the event of an unexpected outage.

Secure: All data written to Azure Storage is encrypted by the service. Azure Storage provides you with fine-grained control over who has access to your data.

Scalable: Azure Storage is designed to be massively scalable to meet the data storage and performance needs of today's applications.

Managed: Microsoft Azure handles maintenance and any critical problems for you.

Accessible: Data in Azure Storage is accessible from anywhere in the world over HTTP or HTTPS. Microsoft provides SDKs for Azure Storage in a variety of languages -- .NET, Java, Node.js, Python, PHP, Ruby, Go, and others -- as well as a mature REST API. Azure Storage supports scription in Azure PowerShell or Azure CLI. And the Azure portal and Azure Storage Explorer offer easy visual solutions for working with your data.

Blob Storage

Azure Blob storage stores unstructured data in the cloud as objects/blobs. Azure Blob storage is massively scalable, highly redundant and secure **object storage** with a **URL/http based access** which allows it to be accessed within Azure or outside the Azure. Though Azure objects are regionally scoped you can access them from anywhere in the world.

Azure Blob Storage is **a Managed Service** that stores large amount of unstructured data in the cloud as objects/blobs. Blob storage can store any type of text or binary data, such as a document, media file, or application installer that can be accessed anywhere in the world via http or https.

Blob storage is also referred to as object storage.

Blobs are basically files like those that you store on your computer. They can be pictures, Excel files, HTML files, virtual hard disks (VHDs), log files & database backups etc. Blobs are stored in containers, which are similar to folders. Containers are created under Storage account.

You can access Blob storage from anywhere in the world using URLs, the REST interface, or one of the Azure SDK storage client libraries. Storage client libraries are available for multiple languages, including Node.js, Java, PHP, Ruby, Python, and .NET.

You can create Blob Storage using 3 ways – General Purpose Storage Account v1, General Purpose Storage Account v2 or Blob storage Account.

Common Use cases for Blob Object Storage

For users with large amounts of unstructured object data to store in the cloud, Blob storage offers a cost-effective and scalable solution. You can use Blob storage to store content such as:

- Serving images or documents directly to a browser.
- Storing files for distributed access.
- Streaming video and audio.
- Storing data for backup and restore, disaster recovery, and archiving.

Blob Storage Service Components

Blob Service contains 3 components.

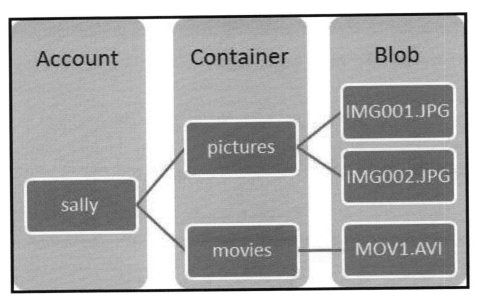

Storage Account

All access to Azure Storage is done through a storage account. This storage account can be a **General-purpose v1 & v2** or a **Blob storage account** which is specialized for storing objects/blobs.

Containers

Container is like a folder which store Blob Files. Container provides a grouping of a set of blobs. All blobs must be in a container. An account can contain an unlimited number of containers. A container can store an unlimited number of blobs. Container name must be lowercase.

Blob

A file of any type and size.
Azure Storage offers three types of blobs: block, page and append blobs.
Blob Storage tiering is available with GPv2 Account and Blob Storage Account.

Types of Blob Storage in Azure Cloud

Blob storage offers three types of blobs – Block Blobs, Page Blobs and Append Blobs.

Block blobs are optimized for storing cloud objects, streaming content and and are a good choice for storing documents, media files, backups etc. It is backed by HDD.

Append blobs are similar to block blobs, but are optimized for append operations. An append blob can be updated only by adding a new block to the end. Append blobs are a good choice for scenarios such as logging, where new data needs to be written only to the end of the blob. It is backed by magnetic HDD.

Page blobs are used for storing virtual machine disks (OS and Data Disks). Page Blob can use both HDD and SSD. Page Blob was covered in compute chapter. *Page blobs* can be up to 8 TB in size and are more efficient for frequent read/write operations.

Comparing 3 types of Blob Storage

Description	Block Blob	Append Blob	Page Blob
Storage Account Supported	General purpose v1 & v2 and Blob Storage Account	General purpose v1 & v2 and Blob Storage Account	General purpose – v1 & v2
Disk Type	**HDD**	**HDD**	**HDD & SSD**
Managed Disk Option	No	No	Yes
Can be used for Virtual Machine Disks	No	No	Yes
Use case	documents, media files, backups	logging	Virtual Machine Disks

In this chapter we will focus only on Block blobs and Append bobs as we already have covered Page Blobs in Azure Compute Chapter.

Azure Blob Storage Tiering: Hot, Cool & Archive Storage tiers

Azure Blob Storage tiering is available with General Purpose v2 Account and Blob Storage Account. General Purpose v1 Account does not offers Blob Storage Tiering. Microsoft Recommends using GPv2 instead of Blob Storage accounts for tiering.

General Purpose v2 Account & Blob storage accounts expose the **Access Tier** attribute, which allows you to specify the storage tier as **Hot** or **Cool**. **The Archive tier** is only available at the blob level and not at the storage account level.

Hot Storage Tier

The Azure **hot storage tier** is optimized for storing data that is frequently accessed at lower access cost but at higher storage cost.

Cool Storage Tier

The Azure **cool storage tier** is optimized for storing data that is infrequently accessed at lower storage cost but at higher access cost.

Archive Storage Tier

Archive storage tier is optimized for storing data that is rarely accessed and has the lowest storage cost and highest data retrieval costs compared to hot and cool storage. The archive tier can only be applied at the blob level.

Blob rehydration (Important Concept)

Data is offline in Archive Storage Tier. To read data in archive storage, you must first change the tier of the blob to hot or cool. This process is known as rehydration and can take up to 15 hours to complete.

If there is a change in the usage pattern of your data, you can also switch between these storage tiers at any time.

Data in hot storage tier has slightly higher availability (99.9%) than cool storage tier (99%). Availability is not applicable for Archive tier as data is offline.

Hot Tier use case

1. Data that is in active use or expected to be accessed frequently.
2. Data that is staged for processing and eventual migration to the cool storage tier.

Cold Tier Use case

1. Short-term backup and disaster recovery datasets.
2. Older media content not viewed frequently anymore but is expected to be available immediately when accessed.
3. Large data sets that need to be stored cost effectively while more data is being gathered for future processing.

Archive Tier Use case

1. Long-term backup, archival, and disaster recovery datasets.
2. Original (raw) data that must be preserved, even after it has been processed into final usable form.
3. Compliance and archival data that needs to be stored for a long time and is hardly ever accessed. (For example, Security camera footage, old X-Rays/MRIs for healthcare organizations, audio recordings, and transcripts of customer calls for financial services).

Comparison of the storage tiers

Features	Hot Storage Tier	Cool Storage Tier	Archive Tier
Availability	99.9%	99%	NA
Availability (RA-GRS reads)	99.99%	99.9%	NA
Usage charges	Higher storage costs, lower access and transaction costs	Lower storage costs, higher access and transaction costs	lowest storage cost and highest retrieval costs
Minimum Storage Duration	NA	30 days (GPv2 only)	180 days
Latency	Milliseconds	Milliseconds	<15 Hrs

Options to make blob data available to users

Private access: Owner of the Storage Account can access the Blob Data.
Anonymous access: You can make a container or its blobs publicly available for anonymous access.
Shared access signatures: Shared access signature (SAS), provide delegated access to a resource in your storage account, with permissions that you specify and for an interval that you specify without having to share your account access keys.

Anonymous read access to containers and blobs

By default, a container and any blobs within it may be accessed only by the owner of the storage account (Public Access level: Private). To give anonymous users read permissions to a container and its blobs, you can set the container & Blob permissions to allow full public access.

Container (anonymous read access for containers and blobs): Container and blob data can be read via anonymous request. Clients can enumerate blobs within the container via anonymous request, but cannot enumerate containers within the storage account.
Blob (anonymous read access for blobs only): Blob data within this container can be read via anonymous request, but container data is not available. Clients cannot enumerate blobs within the container via anonymous request.

Http access to Blob data using DNS names

By default the blob data in your storage account is accessible only to storage account owner because of Default **Private (no anonymous access)** Policy. Authenticating requests against Blob storage requires the account access key.

Using DNS names you can http access Blob endpoint if anonymous access is configured.

https://mystorageaccount.blob.core.windows.net/mycontainer/myblob

Here mystorageaccount is storage account name, mycontainer is container name and myblob is uploaded file name.

Controlling access to blob data using Shared access signatures (SAS)

Anybody having access to Storage account key will have unlimited access to storage account.

Shared access signature (SAS), provide delegated access to a resource in your storage account, without having to share your account access keys. SAS is a secure way to share your storage resources without compromising your account keys.

A shared access signature (SAS) is a URI that grants restricted access rights to Azure Storage resources. You can provide a shared access signature to clients who should not be trusted with your storage account key but whom you wish to delegate access to certain storage account resources. By distributing a shared access signature URI to these clients, you grant them access to a resource for a specified period of time.

SAS granular control features

1. The interval over which the SAS is valid, including the start time and the expiry time.
2. The permissions granted by the SAS. For example, a SAS on a blob might grant a user read and write permissions to that blob, but not delete permissions.
3. An optional IP address or range of IP addresses from which Azure Storage will accept the SAS.
4. The protocol over which Azure Storage will accept the SAS. You can use this optional parameter to restrict access to clients using HTTPS.

Types of shared access signatures (SAS)

Service SAS delegates access to a resource in just one of the storage services: the Blob, Queue, Table, or File service.

Account-level SAS can delegate access to multiple storage services (i.e. blob, file, queue, table).

Note: Exercise 58 & 59 shows how to create SAS and use it.

Exercise 62: Create Blob Storage Container and upload a File

In this exercise we will create Blob Storage Container hk410 in Storage Account sastdportal and in resource group HKPortal. Upload a file to the Blob Container and access it over internet. Change the permission to private and then access the file over internet.

1. Go to Storage Account sastdportal Dashboard > Click Blobs under services>Blob Dashboard opens> In Right pane click +container>Create New Container blade opens>Enter name **hk410** and select access level **Blob** and click ok.

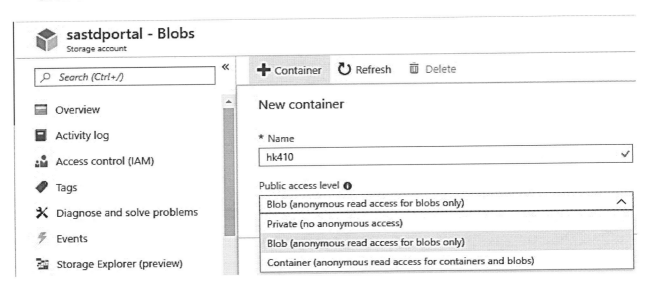

2. Container is created as shown below.

3. **Upload a file from your desktop**. I have created a helloworld.txt file on my desktop. I also added Hello World as content in the file.
Click the container hk410>Container hk410 dashboard opens>click upload>Upload blob blade opens>Click file button to upload HelloWorld.txt file from desktop>Rest keep all values as default>Click upload.

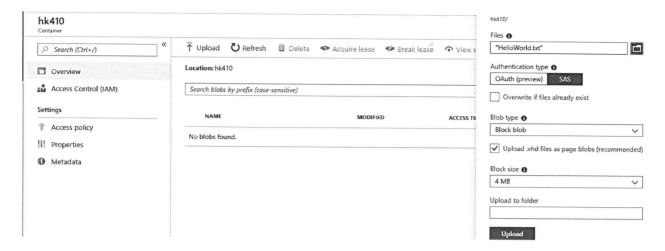

4. File is uploaded as shown below. I also clicked ... in extreme right to see the option available.

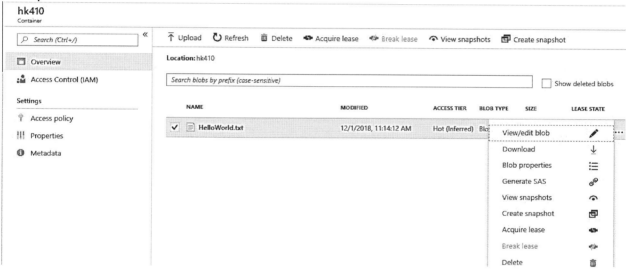

5. Double click HelloWorld.Txt in Container pane>Blob Dashboard opens>Copy the URL of the file.

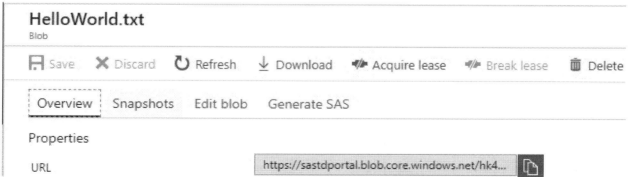

6. Open a browser and paste the URL copied in step 5. We were able to open the file as we had chosen Blob anonymous read permission.

Hello World.

7. **Change the permission to private**. In Blob dashboard select container hk410 and click ... and click access policy>Access Policy blade opens>Select private from drop down box and click **save** and close the Access Policy blade.

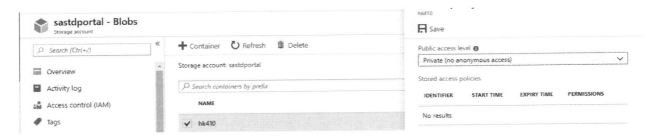

8. Open a browser and paste the URL copied in step 5. We were not able to open the file as we had chosen Private (no anonymous access) permission.

9. **Change the permission back to Blob** as we need it for other exercises.

Exercise 63: Blob Storage Tiering

In this exercise we will just demonstrate how to move Blob Object HelloWorld.txt from Hot Access tier to Cool or Archive Tier using Azure Portal. We will not actually move it.

1. Go to Blob Container hk410 dashboard>Click the HelloWorld.txt in right pane>Blob Properties pane open>Scroll down and under Access tier select cool or Archive tier.

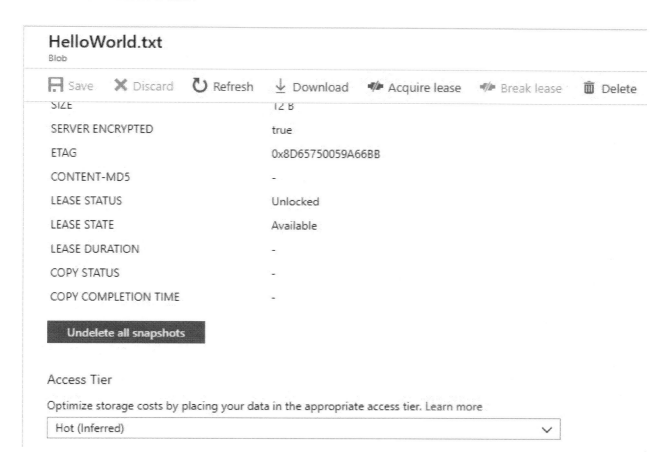

Exercise 64: Create Blob Storage Container using Storage Explorer

In this exercise we will create Blob Storage Container **test410** in Storage Account sastdportal. We will then upload a text file HelloWorld.txt to the Blob Container.

1. In Storage Explorer Dashboard enlarge Storage Account sastdportal under Pay you go subscription.

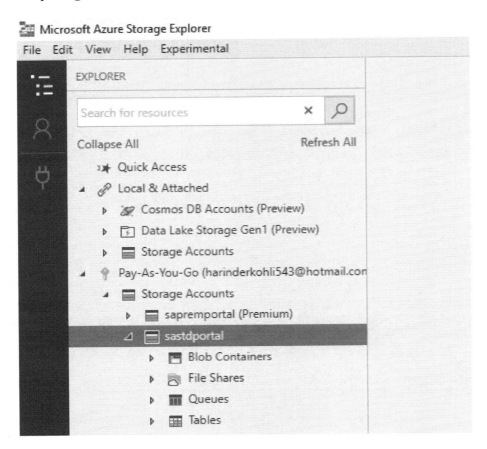

2. Right click Blob Containers under sastdportal and click create Blob container> In dialog box type test410. Container test410 is created as shown below with Private no anonymous access.

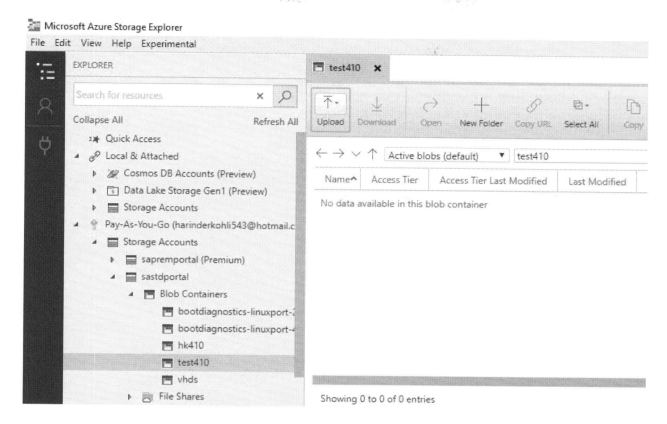

3. Create HelloWorld.txt file with contents Hello World on your desktop. Click upload in right pane and select upload files>Upload File Blade opens>Click ... and select HelloWorld.txt from your desktop>Click upload.

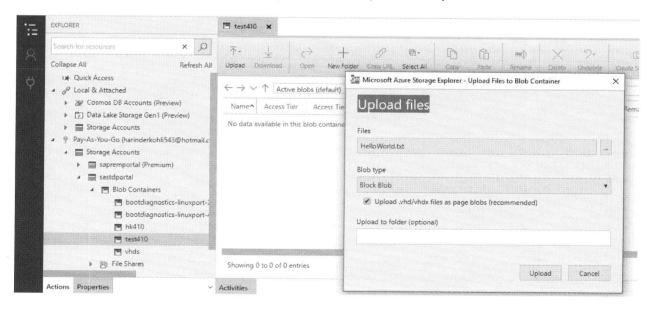

4. Figure below shows HelloWorld.txt file uploaded.

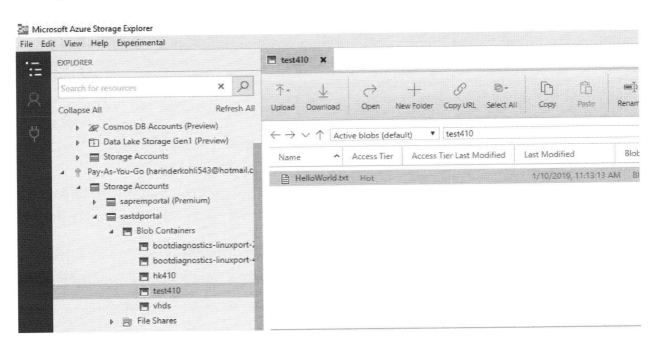

5. You can change the Public Access level by right clicking container test410 and click Set Public Access level>Public Access level blade opens. You can change access level as per your requirement.

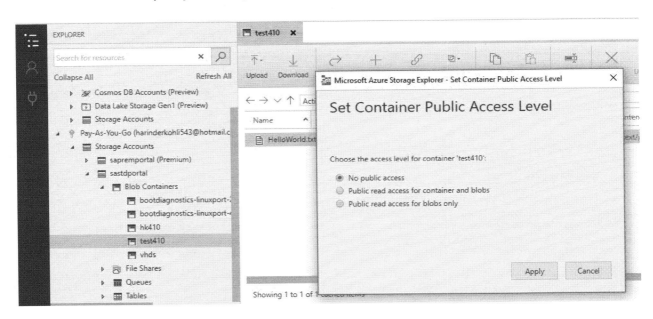

File Storage

Azure Files Storage offers fully managed file shares in the cloud that are accessible via the industry standard Server Message Block (SMB 3.0) protocol (also known as Common Internet File System or CIFS).
Azure File shares can be mounted concurrently by cloud or on-premises deployments of Windows, Mac OS, and Linux instances.

Figure below shows Multiple Virtual Machines accessing Azure File share.

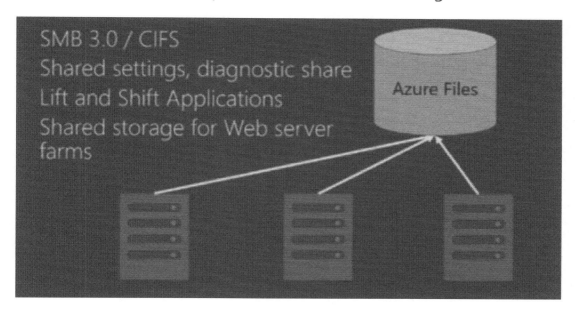

Azure File share Use case

1. Azure Files can be used to completely replace or supplement traditional on-premises file servers or NAS devices.
2. Developers can leverage their existing code and skills to migrate existing applications that rely on file shares to Azure quickly and without costly rewrites.
3. An Azure File share is a convenient place for cloud applications to write their logs, metrics, and crash dumps.
4. When developers or administrators are working on VMs in the cloud, they often need a set of tools or utilities. Copying such utilities and tools to each VM can be a time consuming exercise. By mounting an Azure File share locally on the VMs, a developer and administrator can quickly access their tools and utilities, no copying required.

File Service Architecture and components

Figure below shows the architecture of File share. File share is mounted as a drive on Virtual Machine and is accessed over the network.

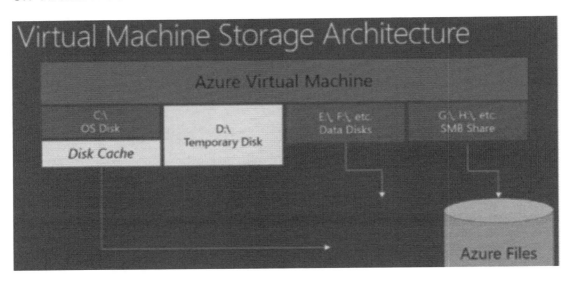

File Service contains 3 components: Storage Account, File Shares and Files.

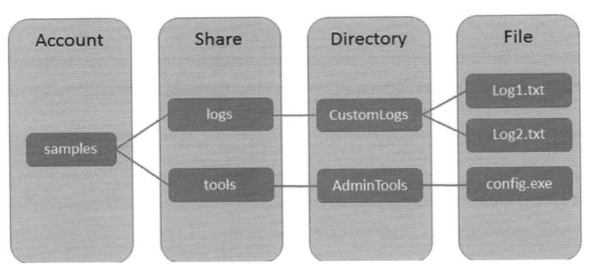

Storage Account: This storage account can be a **General-purpose v1 or v2 storage account.** It supports only Standard Storage for File service.
Share: Share stores the files. Azure File shares can be mounted and accessed concurrently by cloud or on-premises deployments of Windows, Linux, and macOS. A share can store an unlimited number of files.
Directory: Directory is optional. Directory is like a folder for files.
File: A file of any type with max size of 1 TB.

Exercise 65: Creating and using File Share

Creating and using File share is a 2 step process:
1. Create File Share and upload a file.
2. Mount the File share on a Server instance in cloud or on-Prem. In this Exercise we will mount file share on windows VM wvmportal created in Ex 24.

Creating File Share

1. Go to Storage Account sastdportal Dashboard>Click Files in right pane.

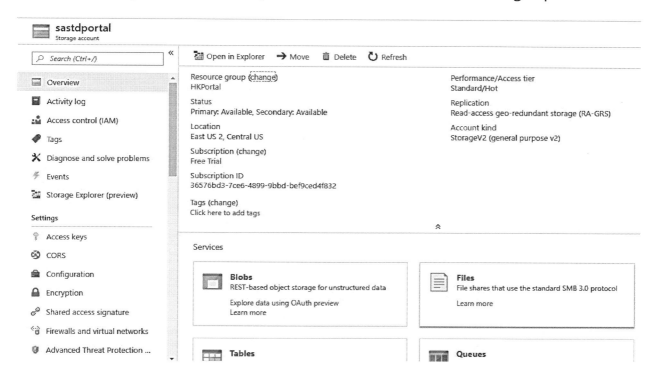

2. File Service dashboard opens>Click + File share> Create File share blade opens>Enter name **fsaz100** and Quota in 1 GB and click create.

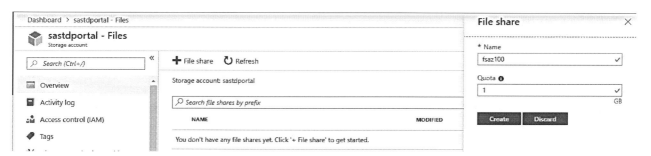

3. Click your Created File share in File service pane> Click upload in Middle pane> Upload File Blade open> Upload a file from your desktop and click upload.

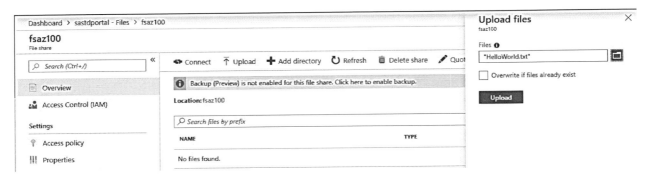

4. Click Connect in Middle pane>In connect pane copy net use Z command shown in the rectangular Box.

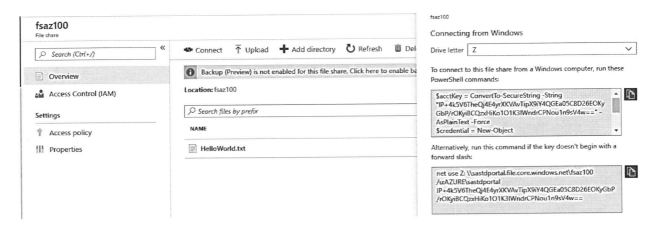

Open the notepad and copy the net use command as shown below.

net use Z: \\sastdportal.file.core.windows.net\fsaz100 /u:AZURE\sastdportal IP+4k5V6TheQj4E4yrXKVAvTipX9iY4QGEa05C8D26EOKyGbP/rOKyiBCQzxHiKo1O 1K3IWndrCPNou1n9sV4w==

5. Connect to Azure VM wvmportal using RDP> Go to Command Prompt and run the net use command copied in step 4. The command completed successfully.

6. Go to File Explorer in wvmportal>Click This PC> You can see the file share fsaz100 mounted.

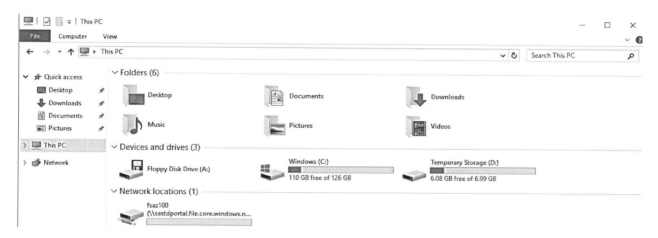

Azure File Sync Service

Azure File Sync enables synchronization or replication of file data between on-premises file servers and Azure Files shares while maintaining local access to your data. It's a 2 way synchronization.

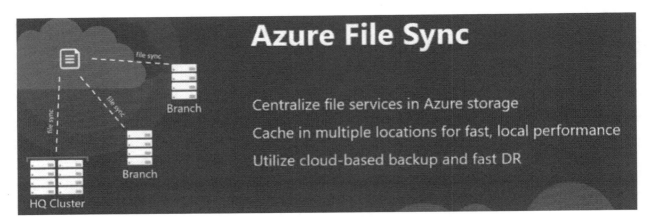

Benefits of Azure File Sync

1. By synchronizing on-premises File share data to Azure Share you can eliminate on-premises Backup and DR requirement. This reduces both cost and administrative overhead of managing Backup and DR.
2. With *Azure File Sync* you have the option to eliminate on-premises file server. User and On-premises application servers can access data in Azure File share.
3. With *Azure File Sync,* Branch office can access Head Office File share data in Azure File shares without requiring any complex set up to integrate Branch and HO File servers.

Azure File Sync Cloud Tiering Option

Cloud tiering is an optional feature of Azure File Sync in which infrequently used or accessed files greater than 64 KiB in size are moved or tiered to Azure File shares.

When a user opens a tiered file, Azure File Sync seamlessly recalls the file data from Azure Files without the user needing to know that the file is not stored locally on the system.

Components of Azure File Sync Solution

Azure Storage Sync Service

On-Premises Windows Server also known as Registered Server.

Azure File Sync Agent: Azure File Sync agent is installed on on-premises server which enables Windows Server to be synced with an Azure file share.

Server Endpoint: A server endpoint represents a specific location on a Windows or registered server, such as a folder on a server volume. Multiple server endpoints can exist on the same volume if their namespaces do not overlap (for example F:\sync1 and F:\sync2). You can configure cloud tiering policies individually for each server endpoint.

Cloud Endpoint: A cloud endpoint is an Azure file share. Azure file share can be a member of only one sync group. A cloud endpoint is a pointer to an Azure file share. All server endpoints will sync with a cloud endpoint, making the cloud endpoint the hub.

Sync Group: Sync Group has one cloud endpoint, which represents an Azure File share, and one or more server endpoints, which represents a path on a Windows Server. Endpoints within a sync group are kept in sync with each other.

Cloud tiering (optional): Cloud tiering is an optional feature of Azure File Sync in which infrequently used or accessed files greater than 64 KiB in size can be tiered to Azure Files. When a file is tiered, the Azure File Sync file system filter (StorageSync.sys) replaces the file locally with a pointer, or reparse point. The reparse point represents a URL to the file in Azure Files. A tiered file has the "offline" attribute set in NTFS so third-party applications can identify tiered files. When a user opens a tiered file, Azure File Sync seamlessly recalls the file data from Azure Files without the user needing to know that the file is not stored locally on the system.

Design Nugget: Storage Sync service should be in same region and Resource Group as Storage Account. The File Share should be in same Storage Account.

Exercise 66: Deploying Azure File Sync in 4 Steps

Pre- Requisite

1. Use Storage Account sastdportal created in Chapter 6, Exercise 50.
2. Use File Share fsaz100 created in Exercise 65.
3. For Registered Server Use VM OnPremAD created in Chapter 3, Exercise 32.

Step 1: Create File Sync Service

1. In Azure Portal Click create a Resource>Storage>Azure File Sync>Deploy
   Storage sync blade opens>Enter a name> Select **HKPortal** in Resource Group
   > Click create.

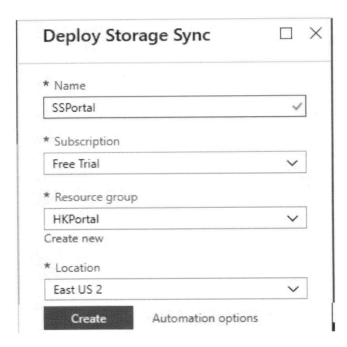

2. Figure below shows dashboard of Storage Sync Service.

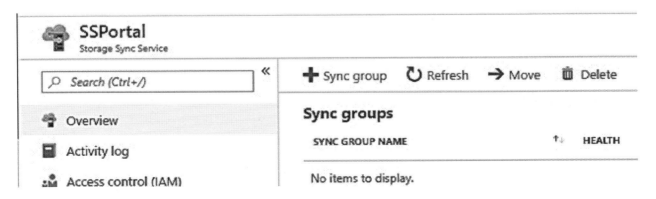

Step 2: Download, Install & Register Azure File Sync Agent on VM OnPremAD

1. RDP to Windows VM OnPremAD.
2. Open Internet explorer and Download Azure File Sync Agent for Windows Server 2016 from following link. Disable enhanced IE security settings.
   https://www.microsoft.com/en-us/download/details.aspx?id=57159
3. Click on Agent file to start the Installation. After Installation is complete Server Registration screen opens automatically.

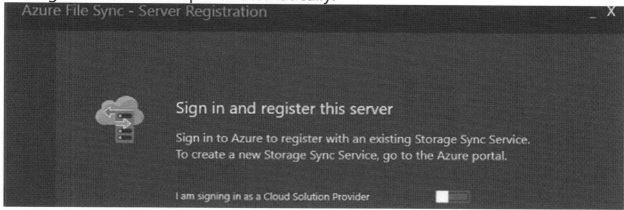

4. Click sign in and authentication box pops up> Enter your MS Account used for Subscription registration and following screen opens>Select your Subscription and Resource Group **HKPortal** and Storage Sync Service created in step 1.

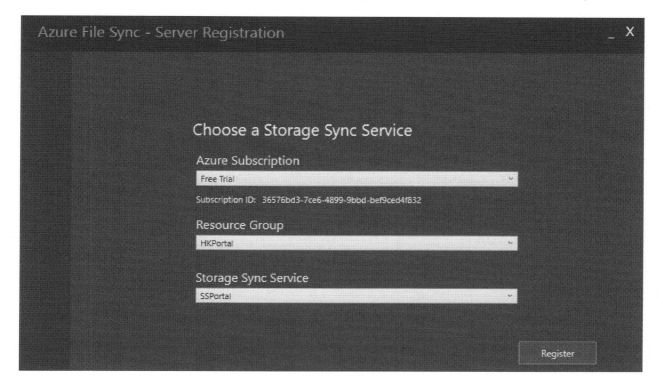

5. Click Register and authentication box pops up>Enter your Microsoft Account used for Subscription registration and password>Registration successful message pops up.

6. Go the Go Storage sync Service SSPortal created in step 1 Dashboard>Click Registered Servers in left pane>In right pane you can see VM OnPremAD was registered and is online.

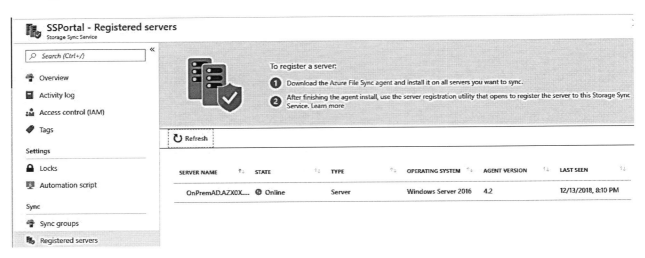

7. In Registered server VM OnPremAD I created a Folder **Public** under C Drive. In Public folder I created 2 text files – Test1 and Test2.

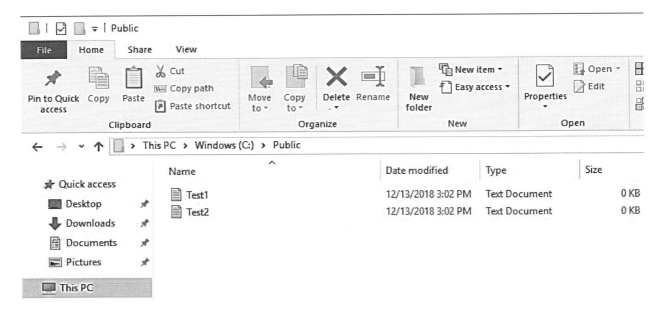

Step 3: Create a Sync group and add File share

In this we will add Storage Account sastdportal and File Share fsaz100. Storage Account sastdportal was created in exercise 100 and File share fsaz100 was created in exercise 200.

1. Go Storage sync Service SSPortal created in step 1 Dashboard>Click sync group in left pane>In Right pane click +Sync Group>Create Sync group blade opens> Select Storage account sastdportal created in exercise 50 and file share created in Exercise 65>click create.

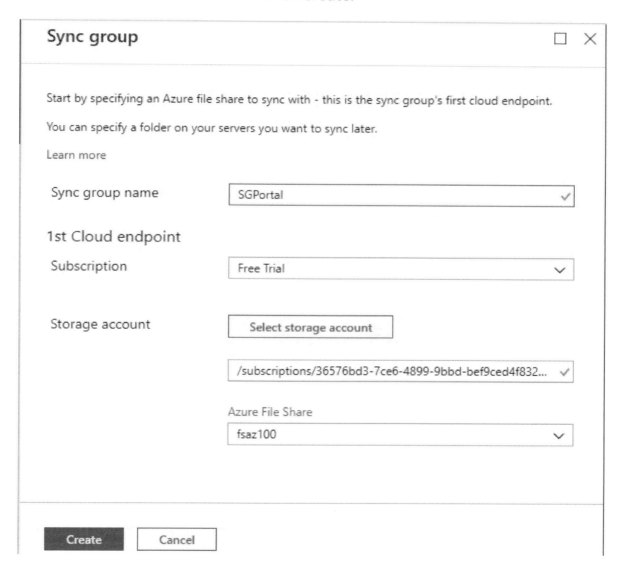

253

Step 4: Add Server Endpoint (Registered Server) to the sync Group

In this we will add VM OnPremAD on which we installed Azure File sync agent in step 2 to sync group. In Step 2 we also registered the VM with Storage sync service. VM OnPremAD was created in Chapter 3, Exercise 32.

1. Go Storage sync Service SSPortal created in step 1 Dashboard>You can see the sync group created in previous step.

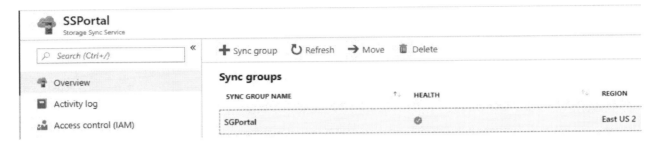

2. In right pane click the sync group SGPortal>Sync group pane opens>Click Add Server Endpoint>Add Server Endpoint blade opens>Select your registered server from drop down box> In path enter **C:\Public.** Public folder was created in Step 2>Click Enabled in Cloud Tiering> Click Create.

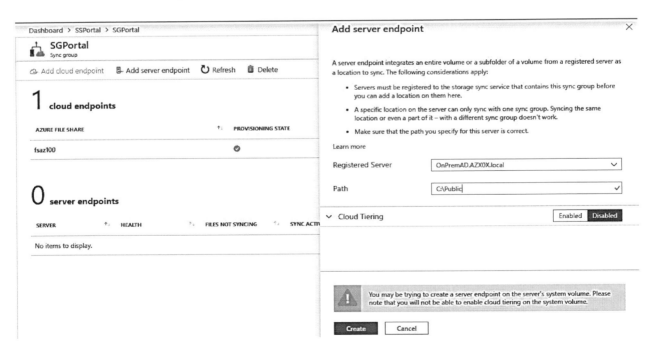

3. Sync Group pane now shows both Cloud Endpoint and Server endpoint. It will take 5-10 minutes for health status of Server Endpoint to get updated.

Step 5: Check whether Files from Public folder in Registered Server are synchronized to File share and vice versa or not.

1. In Azure Portal go to Storage Account sastsportal dashboard>Click Files in Right pane>Click the File share fsaz100>File share pane opens> You can see text files from Public Folder in Registered Server OnPremVM are synchronized to File Share fsaz100.

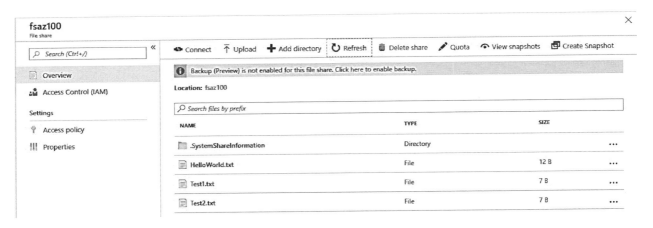

2. Go to Public Folder in registered server. HelloWorld from File share is synchronized to Public folder in Registered server.

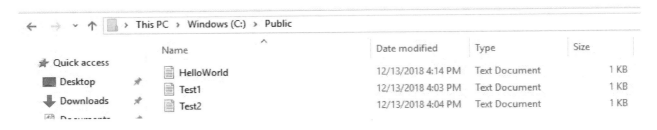

Note: After the exercise is completed stop the VM OnPremAD. We will now require this VM in Azure AD Connect lab.

Azure Import/Export service

Azure Import/Export service is used to securely **import/export** large amounts of data to Azure storage.

Azure Import service is used to import data to Azure Blob storage and Azure Files by shipping disk drives to an Azure Datacentre.
Azure Export service is used to export data from Azure Blob storage to disk drives and ship to your on-premises sites.

Important Point: In Azure Import/Export Service, Customer provides the Disks. Where as in Azure Data Box scenario the Disks are provided by Microsoft.

Azure Import/Export use cases

Consider using Azure Import/Export service when uploading or downloading data over the network is too slow, or getting additional network bandwidth is cost-prohibitive. Use this service in the following scenarios:

1. **Data migration to the cloud**: Move large amounts of data to Azure quickly and cost effectively.
2. **Content distribution**: Quickly send data to your customer sites.
3. **Backup**: Take backups of your on-premises data to store in Azure Storage.
4. **Data recovery**: Recover large amount of data stored in storage and have it delivered to your on-premises location.

Import/Export Service components

1. **Import/Export service**: This service available in Azure portal helps the user create and track data import (upload) and export (download) jobs.
2. **WAImportExport tool**: This is a command-line tool that does the following:
   Prepares your disk drives that are shipped for import.
   Facilitates copying your data to the drive.
   Encrypts the data on the drive with BitLocker.
   Generates the drive journal files used during import creation.
   Helps identify numbers of drives needed for export jobs.
3. **Disk Drives**: You can ship Solid-state drives (SSDs) or Hard disk drives (HDDs) to the Azure Datacentre. When creating an import job, you ship disk drives containing your data. When creating an export job, you ship empty drives.

Export from Azure Job

Azure Export service is used to transfer data from Azure Blob storage to disk drives and ship to your on-premises sites. When creating an export job, you ship empty drives to the Azure Datacentre. You can ship up to 10 disk drives per job.

Export Job Working in brief

1. Determine the data to be exported, number of drives you need, source blobs or container paths of your data in Blob storage.
2. Create an export job in your source storage account in Azure portal.
3. Specify source blobs or container paths for the data to be exported.
4. Provide the return address and carrier account number for shipping the drives back.
5. Ship the disk drives to the shipping address provided during job creation.
6. Update the delivery tracking number in the export job and submit the export job.
7. The drives are received and processed at the Azure Datacentre.
8. The drives are encrypted with BitLocker and the keys are available via the Azure portal.
9. The drives are shipped using your carrier account to the return address provided in the export job.

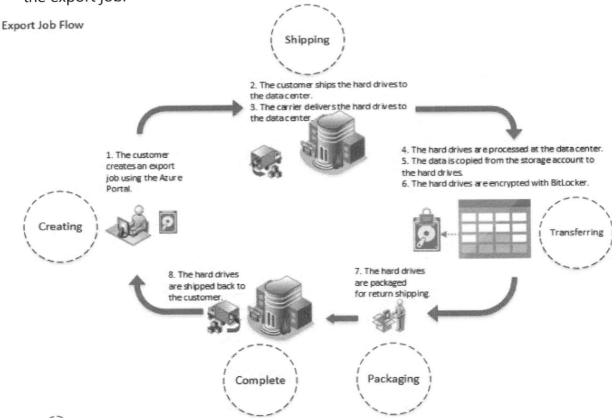

Export Job Flow

Import from Azure Job

Azure Import service is used to securely import large amounts of data to Azure Blob storage and Azure Files by shipping disk drives containing your data to an Azure Datacentre.

Import Job Working in brief

1. Determine data to be imported, number of drives you need, destination blob location for your data in Azure storage.
2. Use the WAImportExport tool to copy data to disk drives. Encrypt the disk drives with BitLocker.
3. Create an import job in your target storage account in Azure portal. Upload the drive journal files.
4. Provide the return address and carrier account number for shipping the drives back.
5. Ship the disk drives to the shipping address provided during job creation.
6. Update the delivery tracking number in the import details and submit the import job.
7. The drives are received and processed at the Azure Datacentre.
8. The drives are shipped using your carrier account to the return address provided in the import job. Figure below shows import job flow.

Exercise 67: Demonstrating Export Job Creation

In this exercise we will demonstrate how to create export job in Resource group HKPortal. We will export Blob file HelloWorld.txt. In Exercise 62 Helloworld.txt file was uploaded in container hk410 which is in Storage account sastdportal.

1. Click All Services in left pane>In Right pane All service blade opens>Scroll down to Storage section.

2. Click import/export jobs in storage section>Import/Export Jobs pane opens>click +Add>Create import/export job blade opens>Select export, enter a name and select HKPortal as resource group and click ok.

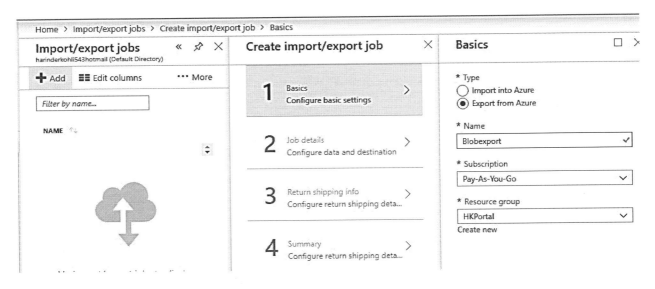

3. In Job detail pane select Storage Account sastdportal> Click Ok.

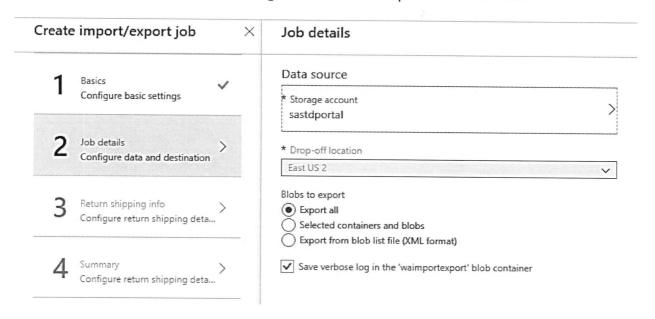

4. In return shipping information select your carrier, enter carrier account number and return address and click Ok.

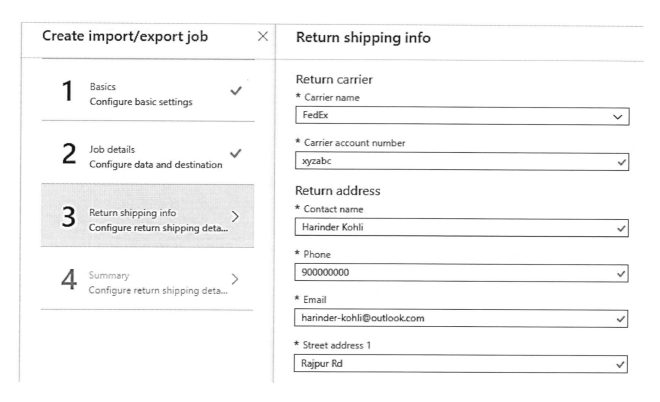

5. Summary pane will show you Export Job summary and MS Azure Datacenter address where you will ship your drives>Click Ok.

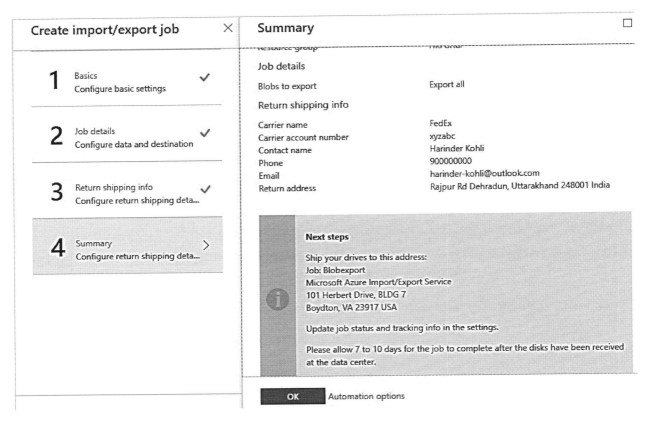

6. In Import/Export job pane you can see the job creation.

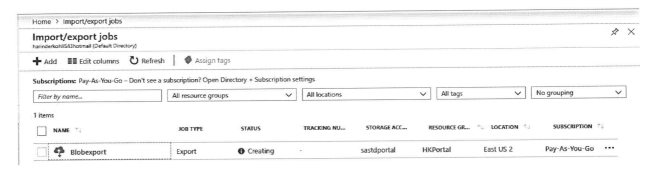

7. Ship the disk drives to Microsoft Azure Datacenter using the address provided in summary pane.

8. In Export job **Blobexport** dashboard update that drives are shipped. Some information is missing in the dashboard as I have not provided proper carrier account number.

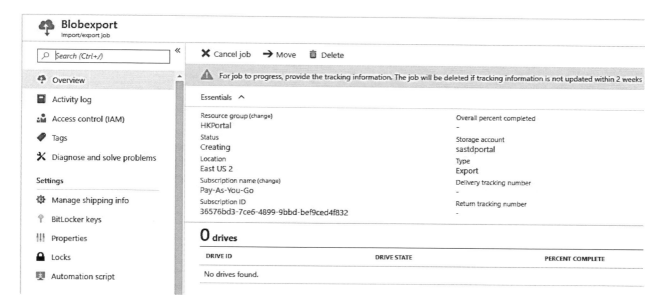

9. Once MS receives disk it will update the information in the dashboard. The disks are then shipped to you and the tracking number for the shipment is available on the portal.

10. You will receive the disk in encrypted format. You need to get the BitLocker keys to unlock the drives. Go to the export job dashboard and click BitLocker keys in left pane and copy the keys to unlock the drives.

Azure Data Box

Azure Data Box transfers on-premises data to Azure Cloud.

Azure Data Box is a Secure, Tamper proof and Ruggedised appliance as shown below. It is provided by Microsoft. Where as in Import/Export service, disks are provided by the customer.

Azure Data Box is used to transfer large amount of data which otherwise would have taken days, months or years to transfer using Internet or ExpressRoute connection.

Each storage device has a maximum usable storage capacity of 80 TB. Data Box can store a maximum of 500 million files.

Ordering, Setup & Working

Data Box is ordered to through Azure Portal.

Connect the Data Box to your existing Network. Assign an IP directly or through DHCP (Default). To access Web UI of Data box, connect a laptop to management port of Data Box and https://192.168.100.10. Sign in using the password generated from the Azure portal.

Load your data onto the Data Box using standard NAS protocols (SMB/CIFS). Your data is automatically protected using 256-AES encryption. The Data Box is returned to the Azure Data Centre to be uploaded to Azure. After data is uploaded the device is securely erased.

The entire process is tracked end-to-end by the Data Box service in the Azure portal.

Figure below shows the setup of Azure Data Box setup.

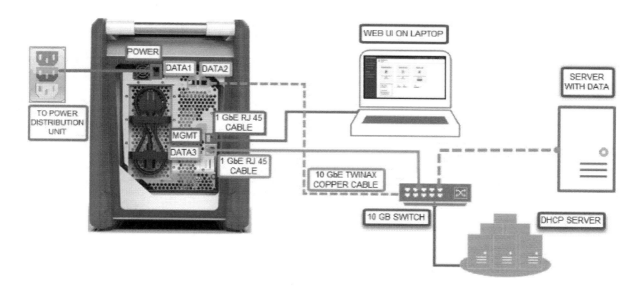

Azure Data Box Use Cases

Data Box is ideally suited to transfer data sizes larger than 40 TBs in scenarios with no to limited network connectivity. The data movement can be one-time, periodic, or an initial bulk data transfer followed by periodic transfers.

One time migration - when large amount of on-premises data is moved to Azure.

Initial bulk transfer - when an initial bulk transfer is done using Data Box followed by incremental transfers over the network. For example, backup solutions can use Data Box to move initial large backup to Azure. Once complete, the incremental data is transferred via network to Azure storage.

Periodic uploads - when large amount of data is generated periodically and needs to be moved to Azure. For example in energy exploration, where video content is generated on oil rigs and windmill farms.

Exercise 68: Demonstrating Data Box Order through Azure Portal

In Azure Portal click + Create a Resource>Storage>Azure Data Box>Select Your Azure Data Box Blade opens>Select your subscription>Transfer type>Source Country and Destination Azure region>Click Apply>Data Box options open> Select as per your requirement.

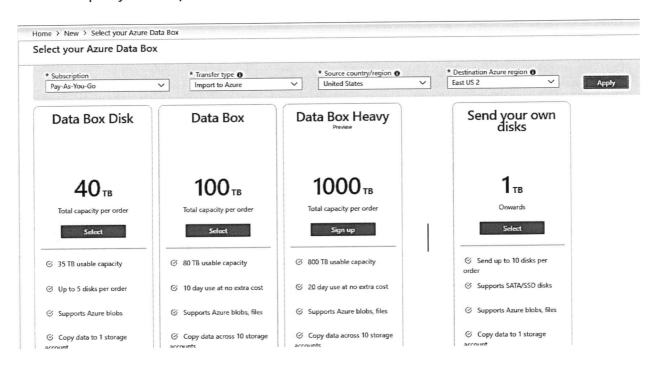

Azure Content Delivery Networks (CDN)

A content delivery network (CDN) is a distributed network of servers that deliver web content to users faster than the origin server. The Azure Content Delivery Network (CDN) caches web content from origin server at strategically placed locations to provide maximum throughput for delivering content to users.

Figure below shows Cached image being delivered to users by CDN server which is faster than the origin server.

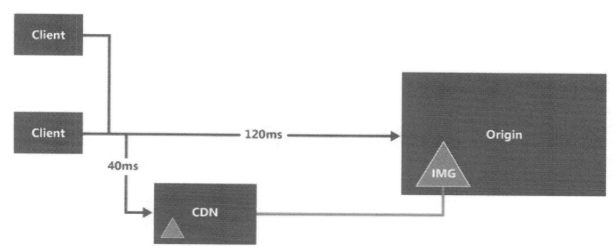

Use Cases

1. Azure CDNs are typically used to deliver static content such as images, style sheets, documents, client-side scripts, and HTML pages.
2. Streaming Video benefits from the low latency offered by CDN servers. Additionally Microsoft Azure Media Services (AMS) integrates with Azure CDN to deliver content directly to the CDN for further distribution.

Benefits of Azure CDN

1. CDN provides lower latency and faster delivery of content to users.
2. CDNs help to reduce load on a web application, because the application does not have to service requests for the content that is hosted in the CDN.
3. CDN helps to cope with peaks and surges in demand without requiring the application to scale, avoiding the consequent increased running costs.
4. Improved experience for users, especially those located far from the datacentre hosting the application.

Azure CDN Working

Figure below shows the working of Content Delivery Networks.

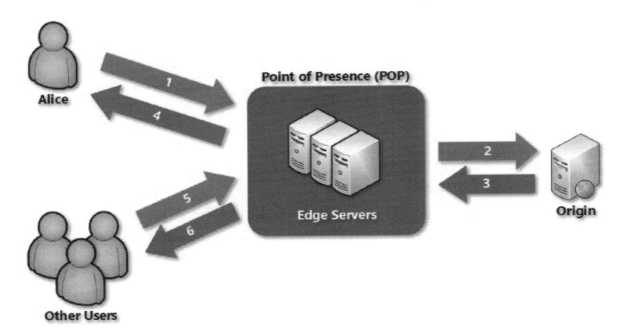

1. User Alice requests a file using URL (**<*endpoint name*>.azureedge.net**) in a browser. DNS routes the request to the CDN edge server Point-of-Presence (POP) location that is geographically closest to the user.

2. If the edge servers in the POP has file in their cache, it returns the file to the user Alice.

3. If the edge servers in the POP do not have the file in their cache, the edge server requests the file from the origin server. The origin server returns the file to the edge server, including optional HTTP headers describing the file's Time-to-Live (TTL). The edge server caches the file and returns the file to the user Alice. The file remains cached on the edge server until the TTL expires. If the origin didn't specify a TTL, the default TTL is seven days.

4. Additional users who request same file as user Alice and are geographically closest to the same POP will be get the file from Cache of the edge server instead of the origin server.

5. The above process results in a faster, more responsive user experience.

Azure CDN Architecture

Azure CDN Architecture consists of Origin Server, CDN Profile and CDN endpoints.

Origin Server

Origin server holds the web content which is cached by CDN Endpoints geographically closest to the user based on caching policy configured in CDN endpoint.

Origin Server type can be one of the following:

Storage
Web App
Cloud Service
Publically Accessible Web Server

CDN Profile

A CDN profile is a collection of CDN endpoints with the same pricing tier. CDN pricing is applied at the CDN profile level. Therefore, to use a mix of Azure CDN pricing tiers, you must create multiple CDN profiles.

CDN Endpoints

CDN Endpoint caches the web content from the origin server. It delivers cached content to end users faster than the origin server and is located geographically closest to the user. CDN Endpoints are distributed across the world.

The CDN Endpoint is exposed using the URL format **<endpoint name>.azureedge.net** by default, but custom domains can also be used.

A CDN Endpoint is an entity within a CDN Profile containing configuration information regarding caching behaviour and origin Server. Every CDN endpoint represents a specific configuration of content deliver behaviour and access.

Azure CDN Tiers

Azure CDN comes in Standard and Premium tiers. Azure CDN Standard Tier comes from Microsoft, Akamai and Verizon. Azure Premium Tier is from Verizon. Table below shows comparison between Standard and Premium Tiers.

	Standard MS	Standard Akamai	Standard Verizon	Premium Verizon
Performance Features and Optimizations				
Dynamic Site Acceleration (DSA)		✓	✓	✓
DSA - Adaptive Image Compression		✓		
DSA - Object Prefetch		✓		
Video streaming optimization	Note 1	✓	Note 1	Note 1
Large file optimization	Note 1	✓	Note 1	Note 1
Global Server Load balancing (GSLB)	✓	✓	✓	✓
Fast purge	✓	✓	✓	✓
Asset pre-loading			✓	✓
Cache/header settings (caching rules)		✓	✓	
Cache/header settings (rules engine)		✓		✓
Query string caching	✓	✓	✓	✓
IPv4/IPv6 dual-stack	✓	✓	✓	✓
HTTP/2 support	✓	✓	✓	✓
Security				
HTTPS support with CDN endpoint	✓	✓	✓	✓
Custom domain HTTPS	✓		✓	✓
Custom domain name support	✓	✓	✓	✓
Geo-filtering	✓	✓	✓	✓
Token authentication				✓
DDOS protection	✓	✓	✓	✓
Analytics and Reporting				
Azure diagnostic logs	✓	✓	✓	✓
Core reports from Verizon			✓	✓
Custom reports from Verizon				✓
Advanced HTTP reports				✓
Real-time stats				✓
Edge node performance				✓

Note 1: MS and Verizon support delivering large files and media directly via the general web delivery optimization.

Dynamic Site Acceleration (DSA) or Acceleration Data Transfer

Dynamic Site Acceleration (DSA), accelerates web content that is not cacheable such as shopping carts, search results, and other dynamic content.

Traditional CDN mainly uses caching to improve website and download performance. DSA accelerates delivery of dynamic content by optimising routing and networking between requester and content origin.

DSA configuration option can be selected during endpoint creation.

DSA Optimization Techniques

DSA speeds up delivery of dynamic assets using the following techniques:

Route optimization chooses the most optimal and the fastest path to the origin server.

TCP Optimizations: TCP connections take several requests back and forth in a handshake to establish a new connection. This results in delay in setting up the network connection.
Azure CDN solves this problem by optimizing in following three areas:
Eliminating slow start
Leveraging persistent connections
Tuning TCP packet parameters (Akamai only)

Object Prefetch (Akamai only): *Prefetch* is a technique to retrieve images and scripts embedded in the HTML page while the HTML is served to the browser, and before the browser even makes these object requests. When the client makes the requests for the linked assets, the CDN edge server already has the requested objects and can serve them immediately without a round trip to the origin.

Adaptive Image Compression (Akamai only): End users experience slower network speeds from time to time. In these scenarios, it is more beneficial for the user to receive smaller images in their webpage more quickly rather than waiting a long time for full resolution images. This feature automatically monitors network quality, and employs standard JPEG compression methods when network speeds are slower to improve delivery time.

Exercise 69: Implementing Azure CDN using Azure Portal

Implementing Azure CDN is a 2 step process – Create CDN profile and Add CDN endpoints to the profile.

In this exercise CDN Profile will be created in Resource Group HKPortal.
We will add VM wvmportal to CDN endpoint. CDN endpoint will cache default website on VM wvmportal. VM wvmportal was created in Exercise 24.

Create CDN Profile: In Azure portal click create a resource>Web > CDN> Create CDN profile blade opens>Enter name, select resource group as HKPortal, select pricing tier and click create. We have the option to add CDN endpoint but we will add later.

Note: In Next Exercise readers are advised to see options available in **optimized for** Dropdown box.

Fig below shows CDN Profile Dashboard.

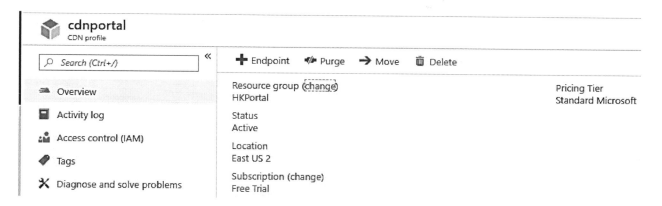

ADD CDN Endpoint: In CDN Profile dashboard click +Endpoint>Add an Endpoint Blade opens>Enter a name, Select Custom origin and in Origin hostname enter DNS name of VM wvmportal>Select HTTP as protocol.

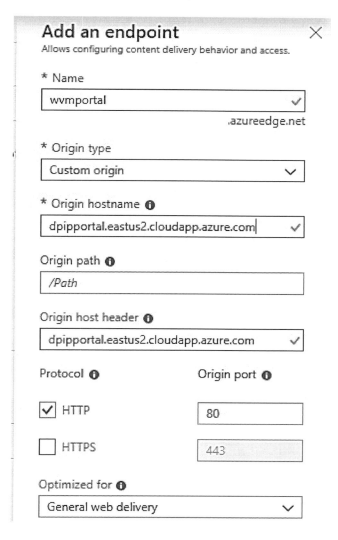

Figure below dashboard of CDN Endpoint wvmportal.

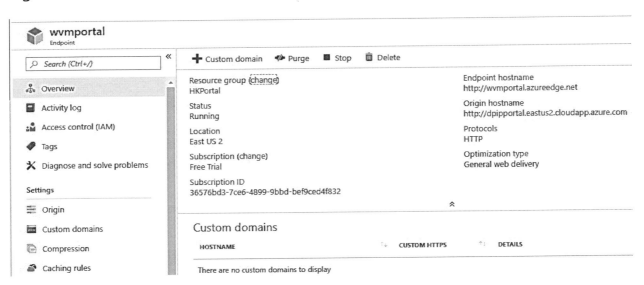

Access default website of wvmportal VM using CDN endpoint address: From CDN Endpoint Dashboard copy the Endpoint address- http://wvmportal.azureedge.net. Open a browser and paste the CDN Endpoint address. The default website opens.

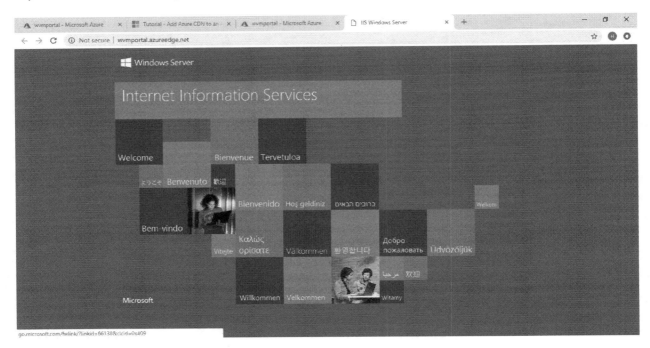

Virtual Machine wvmportal default site is located in US East 2 region. I am accessing the default site from India using CDN endpoint address. The CDN endpoint in Indian region will cache the default website. Next access of the website will happen through CDN endpoint.

CDN Endpoint Compression Functionality

Compression is used to reduce the bandwidth used to deliver and receive an object. By enabling compression directly on the CDN edge servers, CDN compresses the files and serves them to end users.

Compression is enabled by default.

Note that files are only compressed on the fly by the CDN if it is served from CDN cache. Compressed by the origin can still be delivered compressed to the client without being cached.

Exercise 70: Enabling or Disabling Compression

In CDN Endpoint Dashboard Click Compression in left pane> Compression pane opens>Click On or Off to Enable or Disable Compression.

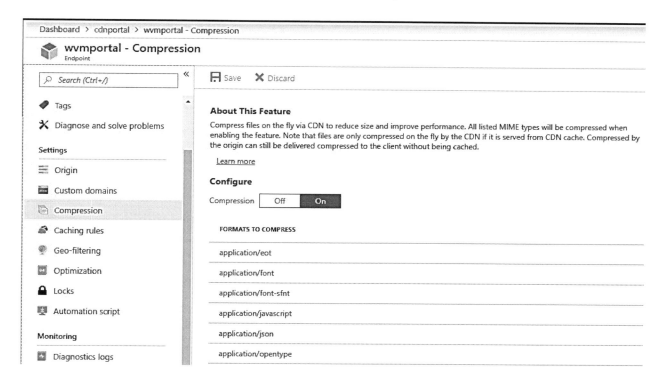

CDN Endpoint Optimization Functionality

Azure Content Delivery Network (CDN) can optimize the delivery experience based on the type of content you have. The content can be a website, a live stream, a video, or a large file for download. When you create a CDN endpoint, you specify optimization type. Your choice determines which optimization is applied to the content delivered from the CDN endpoint.

Optimization Types

General Web Delivery: It is designed for general web content optimization, such as webpages and web applications. This optimization also can be used for file and video downloads.

General media streaming: It is designed for live streaming and video-on-demand streaming. Media streaming is time-sensitive, because packets that arrive late on the client can cause a degraded viewing experience. Media streaming optimization reduces the latency of media content delivery and provides a smooth streaming experience for users.

Video-on-demand Streaming: Video-on-demand media streaming optimization improves video-on-demand streaming content. It reduces the latency of media content delivery and provides a smooth streaming experience for users.

Large File Download: This optimizes large file download (Files larger than 10 MB). If your average files sizes are consistently larger than 10 MB, it might be more efficient to create a separate endpoint for large files.

Dynamic site acceleration (DSA): DSA use optimization techniques such as route, network and TCP optimization to improve the latency and performance of dynamic content or non-cacheable content.

Note: Azure CDN Standard from Microsoft, Azure CDN Standard from Verizon, and Azure CDN Premium from Verizon, use the general web delivery optimization type to deliver general streaming media content, Video-on-demand media streaming and large File download.

Azure CDN optimization supported by various providers

Optimization	MS	Verizon	Akamai
General web Delivery	✓	✓	✓
General media streaming			✓
Video-on-demand media streaming			✓
Large file download (larger than 10 MB)			✓
Dynamic site acceleration		✓	✓

Important Note: MS & Verizon support Media Streaming, Video on demand streaming and large file download using the general web delivery optimization.

Exercise 71: Changing Optimization type

Go to CDN endpoint Dashboard>Click Optimization in left pane> Select optimized type from the drop down box>Click Save.

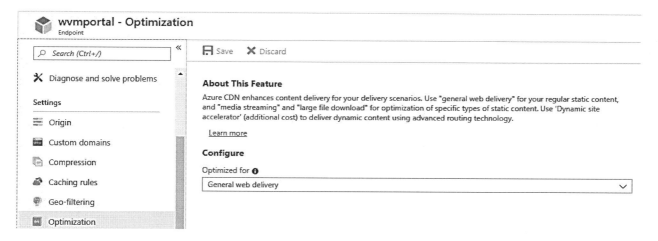

CDN Endpoint Caching Rules Functionality

Caching Rules Control how CDN caches your content including deciding caching duration and how unique query strings are handled.

Default Caching behaviour

The following table describes the default caching behaviour for the Azure CDN products and their optimizations.

	MS	Verizon	Verizon DSA	Akamai	Akamai DSA	Akamai Large File Download	Akamai VOD Streaming
Honor Origin	Yes	Yes	No	Yes	No	Yes	Yes
Cache Duration	2	7	None	7	None	1 day	1 Year

Honor origin: Specifies whether to honor the supported cache-directive headers if they exist in the HTTP response from the origin server.
CDN cache duration: Specifies the amount of time for which a resource is cached on the Azure CDN. If **Honor origin** is Yes and the HTTP response from the origin server includes the cache-directive header **Expires** or **Cache-Control: max-age**, Azure CDN uses the duration value specified by the header instead.

Control Azure CDN Caching behaviour with Query Strings

Before going into Caching behaviour with query Strings lets discuss what is Query String.

In a web request with a query string, the query string is that portion of the request that occurs after a question mark (?). A query string can contain one or more key-value pairs, in which the field name and its value are separated by an equals sign (=). Each key-value pair is separated by an ampersand (&). For example, http://www.contoso.com/content.mov?field1=value1&field2=value2.

With Azure Content Delivery Network (CDN), you can control how files are cached for a web request that contains a query string. Following Three query string modes are available:

Ignore query strings: This is default mode. In this mode, the CDN point-of-presence (POP) node passes the query strings from the requestor to the origin server on the first request and caches the asset. All subsequent requests for the asset that are served from the POP, until the cached asset expires.

Bypass caching for query strings: In this mode requests with query strings are not cached at the CDN POP node. The POP node retrieves the asset directly from the origin server and passes it to the requestor with each request.

Cache every unique URL: In this mode, each request with a unique URL, including the query string, is treated as a unique asset with its own cache.

You can Change query string caching settings for standard CDN profiles from Caching rules options in CDN Endpoint Dashboard.

Exercise 72: Demonstrating Changing Caching Rules

In CDN Endpoint Dashboard click Caching Rules in left pane> In right pane select the Query String caching option from Drop down box>Click save.

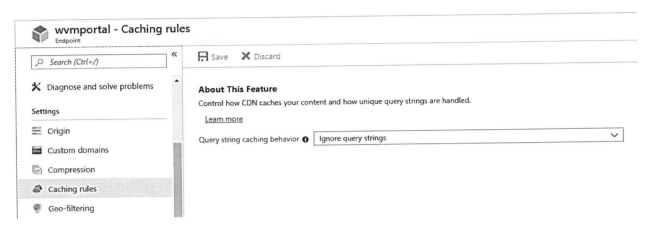

Geo-Filtering

By creating geo-filtering rules you can **block** or **allow** CDN content in the selected countries.

Exercise 73: Demonstrating Allow or Block CDN in Specific Countries

In CDN Endpoint Dashboard click Geo-Filtering in left pane> In right pane select an action (Allow or Block) from Dropdown box and select the countries on which action will applicable>Click save.

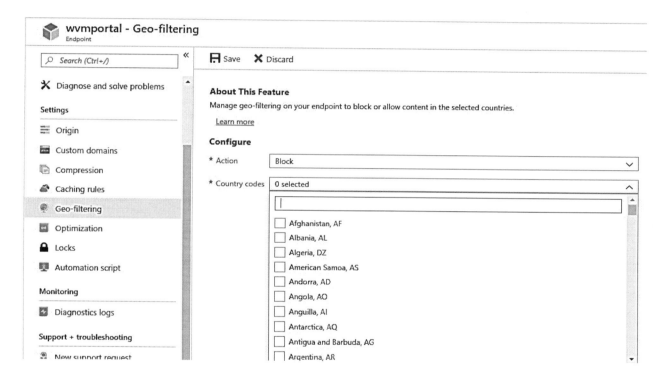

Chapter 9 Implement Storage with CLI and PowerShell

This Chapter covers following Lab Exercises

- Create Blob Storage Container using Azure CLI
- Create Blob Storage Container using PowerShell

Exercise 74: Create Blob Storage Container using Azure CLI

In this exercise we will create Blob Storage Container hk410cli in Storage Account stdcli410. Storage Account stdcli was created in Chapter 7, Exercise 60.

Connect to Azure using Azure CLI
Open command prompt (cmd) on your desktop and enter **az login** command for connecting and authenticating to Subscription.

Create Storage Container
az storage container create --name hk410cli --account-name stdcli410

```
Administrator: Command Prompt

C:\WINDOWS\system32>az storage container create --name hk410cli --account-name stdcli410
{
  "created": true
```

This command creates container with permission private no anonymous access.

Check the Storage Container created
az storage container list --account-name stdcli410

```
Administrator: Command Prompt

C:\WINDOWS\system32>az storage container list --account-name stdcli410
[
  {
    "metadata": null,
    "name": "hk410cli",
    "properties": {
      "etag": "\"0x8D642D93574F37D\"",
      "hasImmutabilityPolicy": "false",
      "hasLegalHold": "false",
      "lastModified": "2018-11-05T04:43:19+00:00",
      "lease": {
        "duration": null,
        "state": null,
        "status": null
```

Exercise 75: Create Blob Storage Container using PowerShell

In this exercise we will create Blob Storage Container hk410ps in Storage Account stdps410 and in Resource Group HKPS. Storage Account stdps410 was created in Chapter 7, Exercise 61. Resource Group HKPS was created in Chapter 2, Ex 20.

Connect to Azure using PowerShell
Open PowerShell command prompt on your desktop and login using Connect-AzureRmAccount.

Create Storage Container
New-AzureRmStorageContainer -Name hk410ps –StorageAccountName stdps410 –ResourceGroupName HKPS

```
PS C:\Users\Harinder Kohli> New-AzureRmStorageContainer -Name hk410ps -StorageAccountName stdps410 -ResourceGroupName HKPS

ResourceGroupName     : HKPS
StorageAccountName    : stdps410
Id                    : /subscriptions/7593a7e7-0d4e-493a-922e-c433ef24df3b/resourceGroups/HKPS/providers/Microsoft.Sto
                        rage/storageAccounts/stdps410/blobServices/default/containers/hk410ps
Name                  : hk410ps
Type                  : Microsoft.Storage/storageAccounts/blobServices/containers
Etag                  :
Metadata              :
PublicAccess          :
ImmutabilityPolicy    :
LegalHold             :
LastModifiedTime      :
LeaseStatus           :
LeaseState            :
LeaseDuration         :
HasLegalHold          :
HasImmutabilityPolicy :
```

This command creates container with permission private no anonymous access.

Check the Storage Container created
Get-AzureRmStorageContainer –Name hk410ps –StorageAccountName stdps410 –ResourceGroupName HKPS or
Get-AzureRmStorageContainer –StorageAccountName stdps410 –ResourceGroupName HKPS

```
PS C:\Users\Harinder Kohli> Get-AzureRmStorageContainer -Name hk410ps -StorageAccountName stdps410 -ResourceGroupName HKPS

ResourceGroupName     : HKPS
StorageAccountName    : stdps410
Id                    : /subscriptions/7593a7e7-0d4e-493a-922e-c433ef24df3b/resourceGroups/HKPS/providers/Microsoft.Storage
                        /storageAccounts/stdps410/blobServices/default/containers/hk410ps
Name                  : hk410ps
Type                  : Microsoft.Storage/storageAccounts/blobServices/containers
Etag                  : "0x8D642FDC9386C07"
Metadata              :
PublicAccess          : None
ImmutabilityPolicy    :
LegalHold             : Microsoft.Azure.Commands.Management.Storage.Models.PSLegalHoldProperties
LastModifiedTime      : 05-11-2018 09:05:08
LeaseStatus           : Unlocked
LeaseState            : Available
```

Chapter 10 Implement Azure Backup

This Chapter covers following

- Azure Backup
- Recovery services Vault
- Backup scenarios with Azure Backup
- Architecture of Azure Backup using Azure Backup Agent
- Architecture of Azure Backup using System Center Data Protection Manager
- Architecture of Azure Backup using Azure Backup Server
- Azure IaaS VM Backup
- Backup Reports

This Chapter Covers following Lab Exercises to build below topology

- Create Recovery Services Vault
- Backup Files & Folder using Azure Backup Agent
- Azure VM-level backup
- Restoring Azure VM-level backup
- Create Custom Backup Policy
- Associating Custom Policy with VM wvmportal Backup Job

Chapter Topology

In this chapter we will add Recovery Services Vault & Azure Backup to the Topology. We will also install Azure Backup Agent in VM wvmportal.

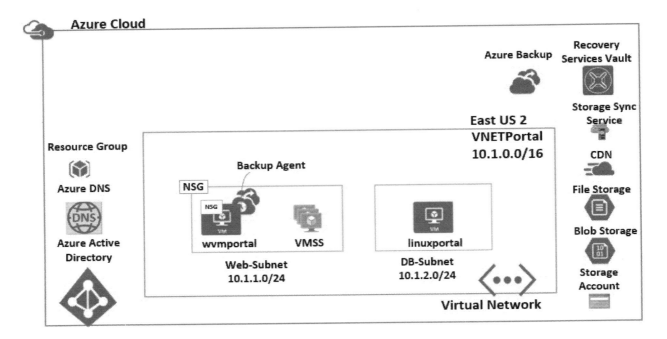

Azure Backup

Azure Backup is Backup as a service (BaaS) which you can use to backup and restore your data in Azure cloud.
You can backup both on Premises workloads and Azure workloads.
Azure Backups are stored in Recovery Services Vault.
Advantage of Azure backup is that we don't have to set up Backup infrastructure.

Feature of Azure Backup

1. No backup infrastructure to setup. It uses pay-as-you-use model.
2. Azure Backup manages backup storage scalability and high availability. Azure Recovery Services Vault offers unlimited Storage. For high availability, Azure Backup offers two types of replication: locally redundant storage and geo-redundant storage.
3. Azure Backup supports incremental backup. Incremental backup transfers changes made since the last full backup.
4. Data is encrypted for secure transmission between on-premises and Azure Cloud. The backup data is stored in the Recovery Services vault in encrypted form.
5. Backups are compressed to reduce the required storage space in Vault.
6. Azure Backup provides application-consistent backups, which ensured additional fixes are not needed to restore the data. Restoring application consistent data reduces the restoration time, allowing you to quickly return to a running state. This option is only available when we use either System Center DPM or Azure Backup server.

Recovery services Vault

A Recovery Services Vault is a storage entity in Azure that houses backup data.

You can use Recovery Services vaults to hold backup data for on-premises workload and for various Azure services such as IaaS VMs (Linux or Windows) and Azure SQL databases. **Azure Backup offers two types of replication:** locally redundant storage (LRS) and geo-redundant storage (GRS).

Backup scenarios with Azure Backup

Azure Backup provides 4 options to Backup on-premises and Cloud workloads – Azure Backup Agent, System Center DPM Server, Azure Backup Server and Azure IaaS VM Backup.

Table below shows comparison of Azure Backup options.

Backup Option	Features	Deployment	Target Storage
Azure Backup Agent	Backs up Files and Folders on Windows Server and VMs. No Linux support. No backup server required.	On-premises and Cloud	RSV
System Center DPM	Backs up Files, folders, Volumes, VMs & Application aware backup (SQL, Exchange). Other features include Restore granuality and Linux support. Cannot back up Oracle workload.	On-premises and Cloud	RSV, Local Disk on DPM server and Tape (on-site only)
Azure Backup Server	Backs up Files, folders, Volumes, VMs & Application aware backup (SQL, Exchange). Restore granuality and Linux support. Cannot back up Oracle workload. Requires live Azure subscription. No support for tape backup. Does not require a System Center license	On-premises and Cloud	RSV, Local Disk on Azure Backup Server
Azure IaaS VM Backup	Backup Integrated in VM dashboard. Backs up VMs and Disks. No specific agent installation required. Fabric-level backup with no backup infrastructure needed	Cloud only	RSV

RSV: Recovery Services Vault

Architecture of Azure Backup using Azure Backup Agent

Azure Backup agent backs up Windows server or Windows VM to Recovery Services Vault in Azure. Azure Backup Agent option can be used to backup both on-premises and cloud workloads.

Backup to Azure requires following components.
Recovery services Vault.
Azure Backup Agent.

Azure Backup Agent can backup following workloads

Files & Folders: Azure Backup agent backs up files and folders on Window server or Windows VM to Recovery Services Vault.

Windows System State

Backup Location

Backs up data to Recovery Services Vault in Azure. There is no option to backup Data locally.

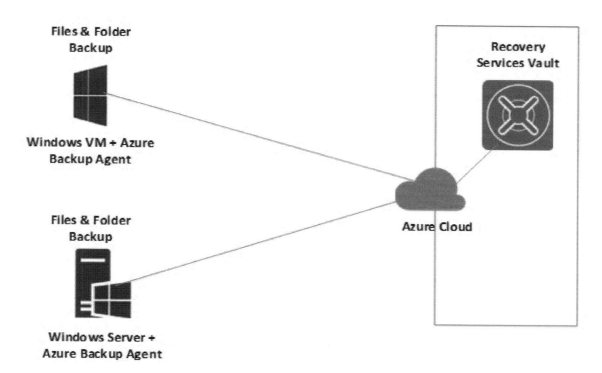

Installing & Working of Azure Backup Agent

1. Create Recovery Services vault.
2. Download Backup Agent and Vault Credentials to the on Premises server by configuring the Backup goal in Recovery services vault dashboard.
3. Install Azure Backup Agent on the on Premises Server and register the server with Recovery Services vault using Vault credentials.
4. Schedule the backup by opening Azure backup agent in the on premises server and configuring the backup policy.

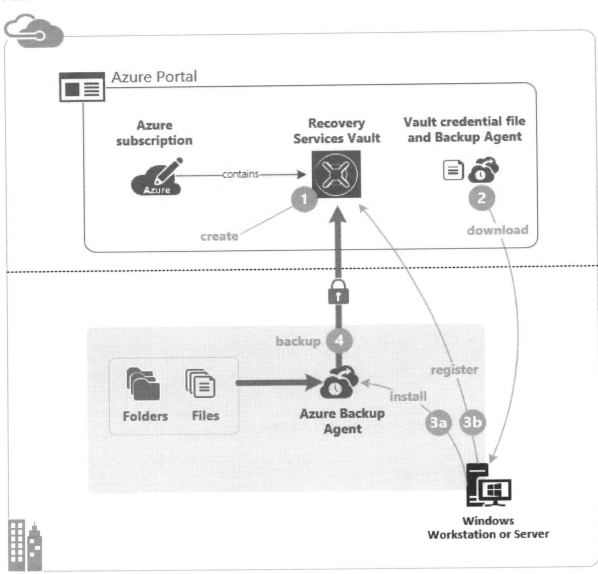

Architecture of Azure Backup using System Center DPM

Azure Backup using System Center Data Protection Manager (DPM) option not only backs up workload to Azure Recovery Service Vault but backup is also available locally on disk as well as on tape. This option can be used to backup both on-premises and cloud workloads.

Backup to Azure requires following components

Recovery services Vault.
Azure backup agent.
System Center Data Protection Manager (DPM).

In this case backup agent will be installed on DPM server.

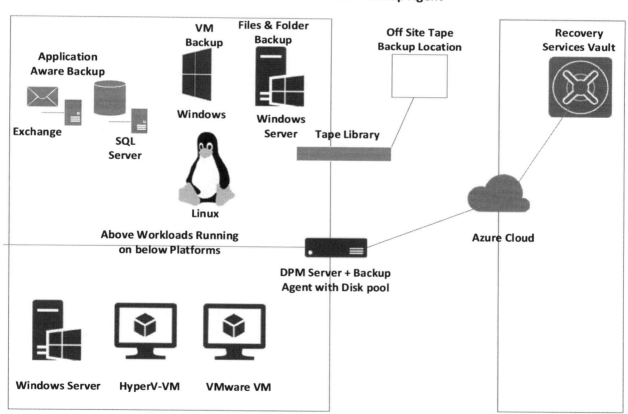

DPM can backup following workloads

Application-aware backup: Application-aware back up of Microsoft workloads, including SQL Server, Exchange, and SharePoint.

File backup: Back up files, folders and volumes for computers running Windows server and Windows client operating systems.

System backup: Back up system state or run full, bare-metal backups of physical computers running Windows server or Windows client operating systems.

Hyper-V backup: Back up Hyper-V virtual machines (VM) running Windows or Linux. You can back up an entire VM, or run application-aware backups of Microsoft workloads on Hyper-V VMs running Windows.

VMware VMs backup

DPM Backup Workload Locations

Disk: For short-term storage DPM backs up data to disk pools.

Azure Recovery Services Vault: For both short-term and long-term storage off-premises, DPM data stored in disk pools can be backed up to the Azure Recovery Services Vault using the Azure Backup service.

Tape: For long-term storage you can back up data to tape, which can then be stored offsite. This option is only available for on-premises workload.

Advantages of DPM backup

Backup is also available locally.
Linux VM backup.
Application Aware Backup.
Tape Backup option.

Architecture of Azure Backup using Azure Backup Server

This option is same as DPM option except for following 2 differences.

1. Tape option is not there with Azure backup server.
2. You don't have to pay license for Azure Backup server.

Backup to Azure requires following components

1. Recovery services Vault
2. Azure backup agent
3. Azure Backup Server

In this case backup agent will be installed on Azure Backup Server.

Rest everything is same as discussed in Data protection Server in previous section.

Azure Backup Server + Azure Backup Agent

Azure IaaS VM Backup

Azure IaaS VM Backup provides Native backups for Windows/Linux. This option can be used to backup Azure VMs only. The benefit of this option is that Backup option is built in VM dashboard.

Backup to Azure requires following components

1. Recovery services Vault.
2. Azure backup agent extension is automatically enabled when backup is enabled in the VM.

Azure IaaS VM Backup can backup following workloads

Full Azure Windows/Linux VM backup.
VM Disk Backups (Using Powershell).

Backup Location

Backs up data to Recovery Services Vault in Azure.

Azure IaaS VM Backup Working

The Backup service uses the *VMSnapshot*extension to backup workloads. The Backup service coordinates with the Volume Shadow Copy Service (VSS) to get a consistent snapshot of the virtual machine's disks. Once the Azure Backup service takes the snapshot, the data is transferred to the vault.

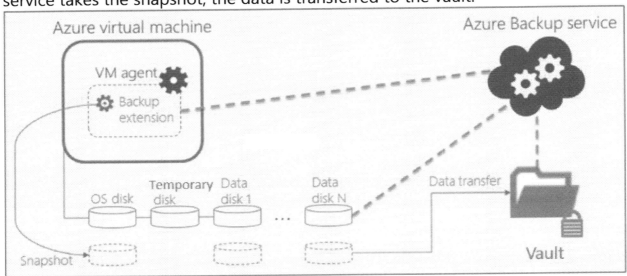

Exercise 76: Create Recovery Services Vault

1. In Azure Portal click create a resource> Storage> Backup and Site Recovery (OMS)> Create Recovery Services Vault Blade opens> Enter a name, select HKPortal Resource Group and select region and click create.

2. Figure below shows Dashboard of Recovery Services Vault.

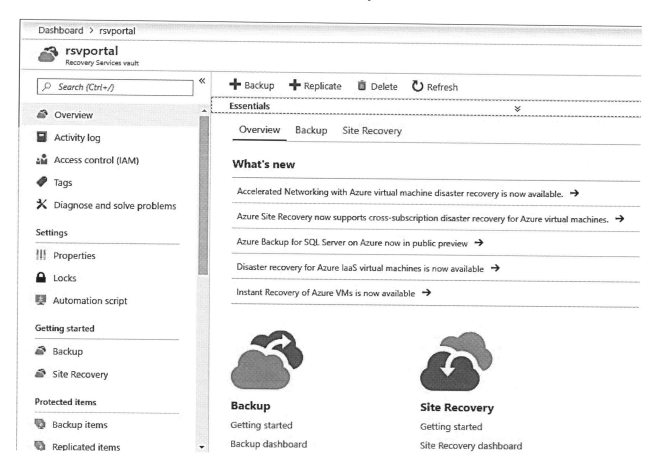

Exercise 77: Backup Files & Folder using Azure Backup Agent

In this exercise we will backup Files & Folders & System State of Azure VM wvmportal using Azure Backup Agent option. The same procedure is applicable for on-premises Windows Server or VM.

1. RDP into wvmportal.
2. Create an empty folder name test on the wvmportal desktop. Create a empty file HelloWorld.txt in the test folder.
3. In wvmportal Open internet explorer and log on to Azure portal> Go to Recovery Services Vault Dashboard>Click Backup in left pane>Select **on-premises** and select Files and Folder & System State>Click Prepare Infrastructure>Prepare Infrastructure Blade opens.

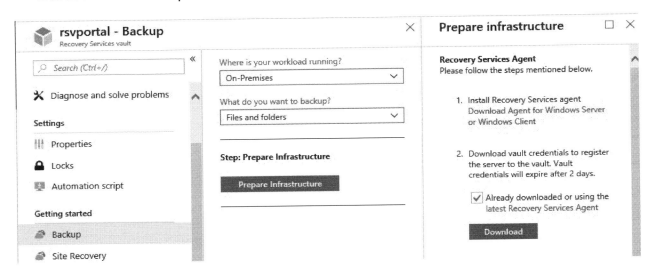

4. Click Download Agent for Windows Server.

5. Check mark the Vault credential and click download.

6. On the wvmportal VM double click MARSAgentInstaller.exe and start installation of the agent. At the end of installation click Proceed to Registration to register your on wvmportal VM to Recovery Services Vault>Click Browse and upload Vault credential file downloaded in step 5.

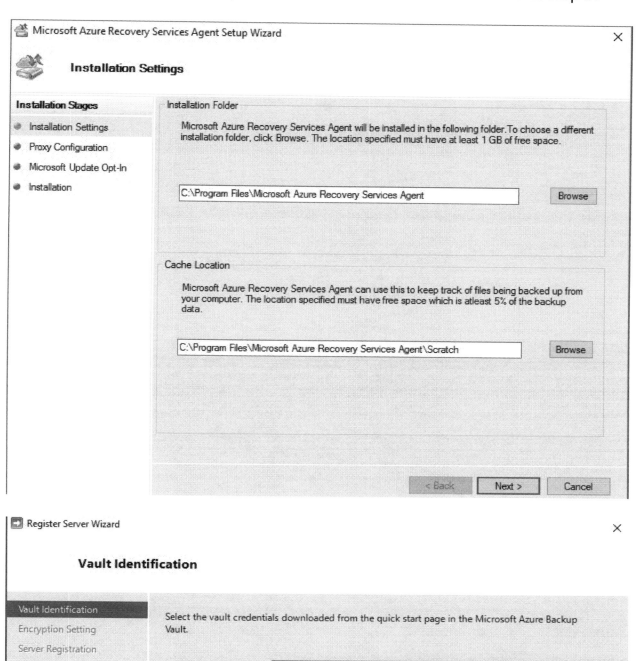

7. In Encryption setting enter a passphrase or generate passphrase and specify the location to save passphrase>Click finish.

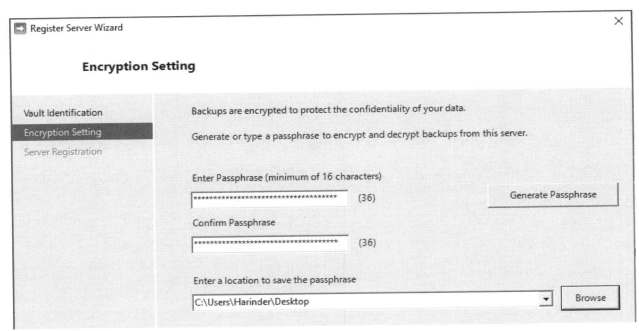

8. Microsoft Azure Backup Agent is installed and an icon shows on the desktop.

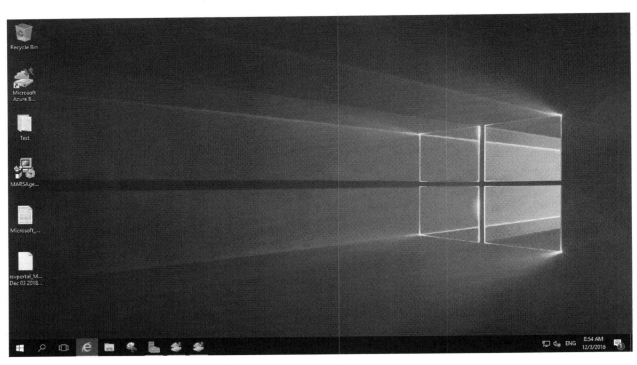

9. **Create a Backup Schedule & Select Backup items.** Open the Microsoft Azure Backup agent in wvmportal>Click Action> Click schedule backup> Schedule Backup Wizard opens> In Select Items to backup click Add items and select test folder created in step 2 and for rest select all default values> Click Finish>Click close.

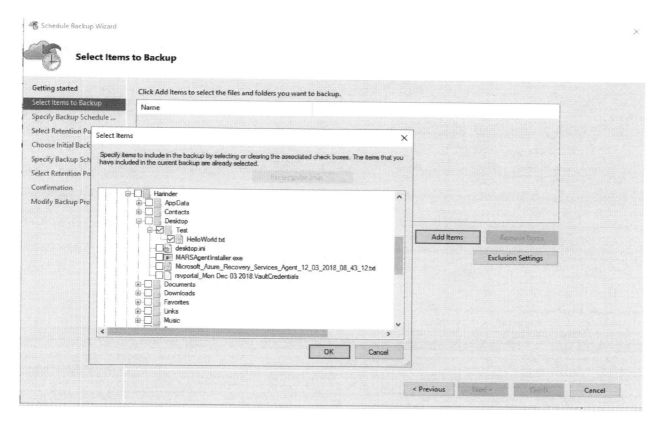

10. **To back up files and folders for the first time immediately** >open Microsoft Azure Backup Agent>Action>Backup now>Select Files & Folder and click next>On confirmation page click back up> Monitor the progress in agent console> Click close when backup is completed.

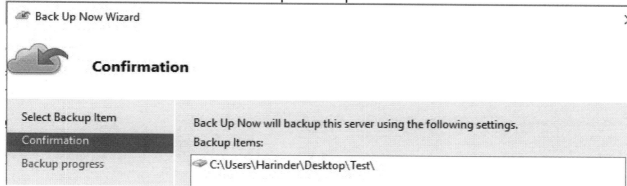

11. Once the backup is completed go the Recovery Services Vault Dashboard> Click Backup Items in left pane> Here you can see Backup Item Count against Azure Backup Agent.

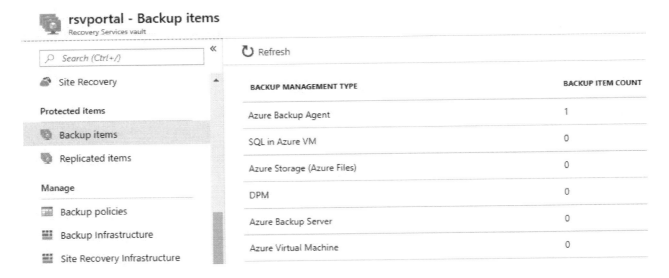

12. Click Azure Backup Agent and and Backup Items pane opens and you can see the backup is complete.

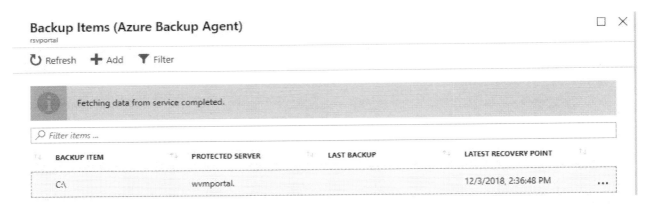

Exercise 78: Azure VM-level backup

1. In Azure Portal go to VM wvmportal dashboard.

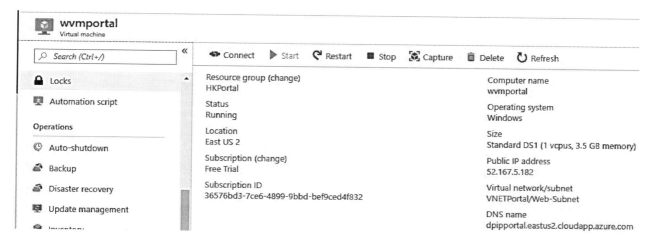

2. In left pane scroll down and Click Backup in left pane>Enable Backup blade opens> Select RSV created in Ex 76 and click enable backup (Not shown).

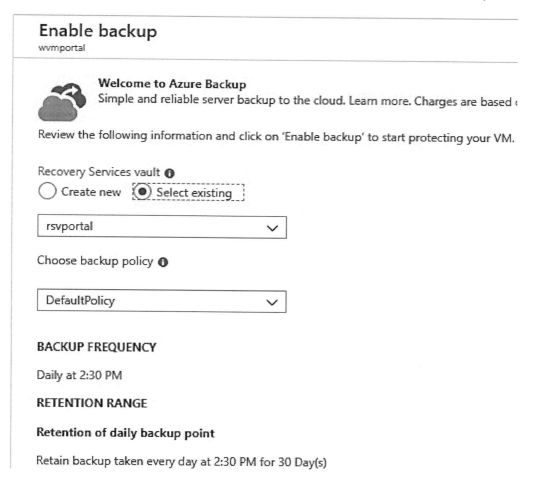

3. The default policy is to take Backup at 2.30 PM. Figure below shows the Backup status. It shows initial backup pending. This first backup job creates a full recovery point. Each backup job after this initial backup creates incremental recovery points. Incremental recovery points are storage and time-efficient, as they only transfer changes made since the last backup.

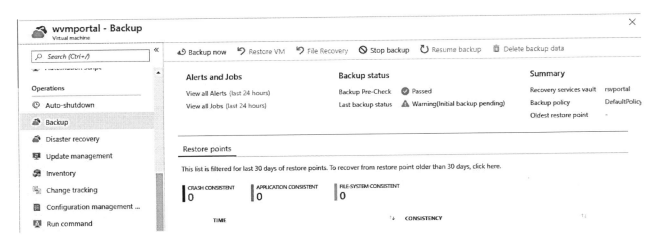

4. To start Backup instead of waiting for default policy to kick in Click Backup now in top right pane>Backup Now Blade opens.

5. Click OK to start Backup now. You can monitor the Progress by Clicking **View all Jobs** in Right pane as shown in top figure.

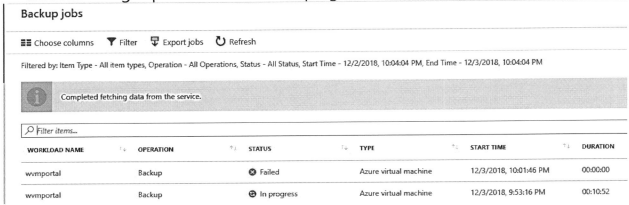

6. Just keep refreshing the backup job pane. You can see backup job completed. It took 1.45 hours to complete.

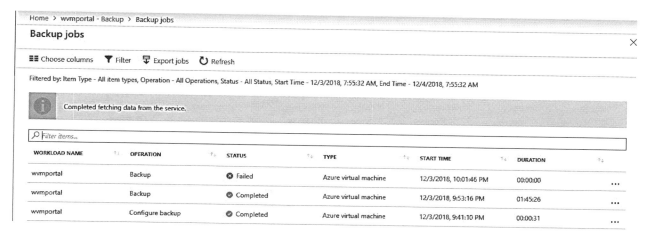

7. You can also track progress of backup in Recovery Services Vault. Click Backup items in Recovery Services vault. It will show Backup for Various Types.

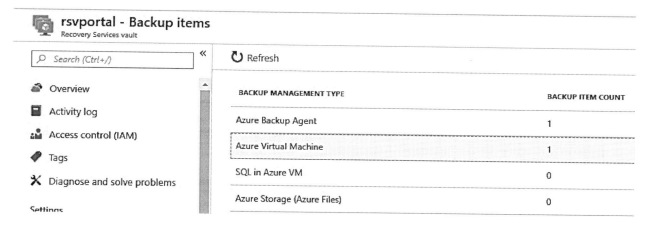

Click on Azure Virtual Machine and you can see backup Items for Azure VM.

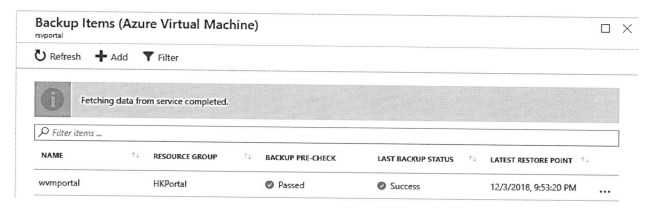

Exercise 79: Restoring Azure VM-level backup

In this exercise we will demonstrate Restoration operation. We will show options for creating new VM from backup and replacing Disks of existing VM with Restore point disks.

1. Click Backup in wvmportal Dashboard> Backup Pane opens. In right pane you can see option for Restore VM and File Recovery.

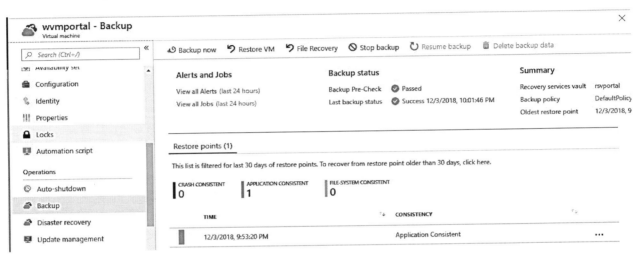

2. Click Restore VM in Right pane>Select your restore point>Click OK.

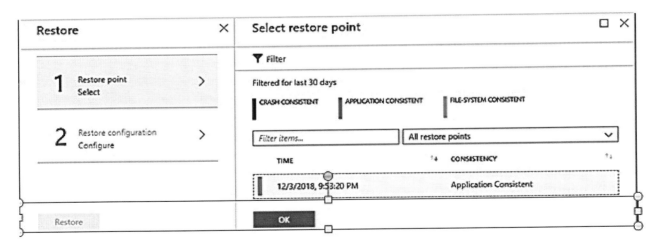

3. Restore Configuration pane. Here you have 2 options to Restore. Option 1 shown below is to create a new VM with the backup.

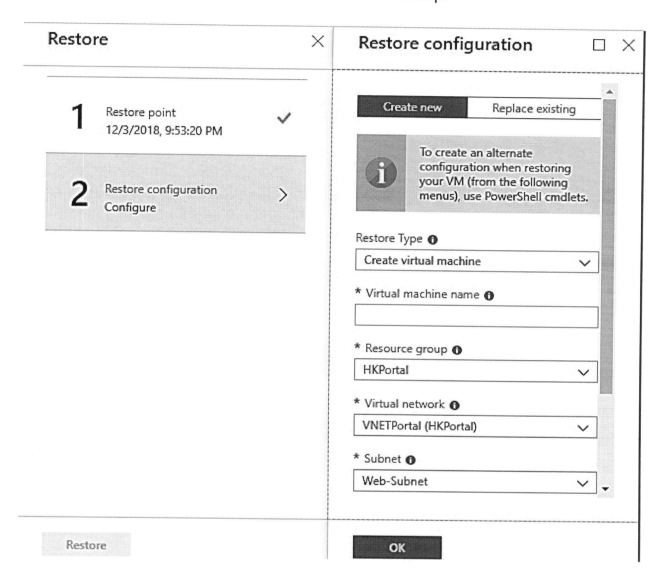

4. Second option in Restore Configuration pane is to replace disks in existing VM with disks from Restore points.

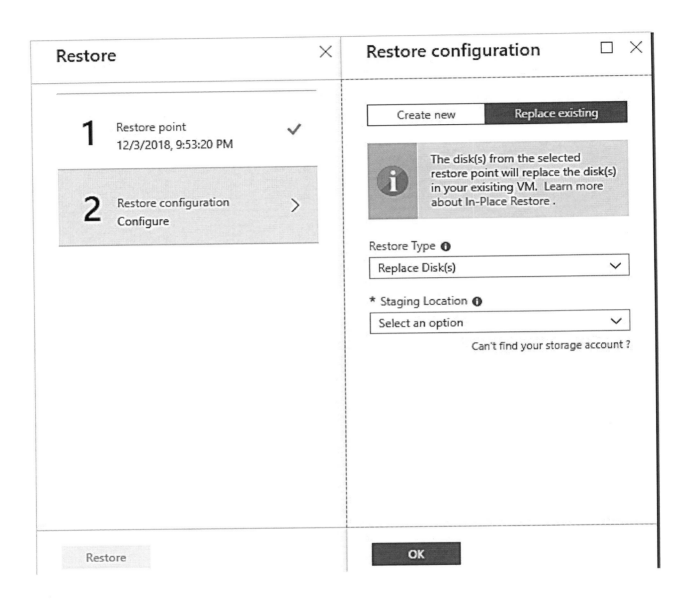

As an exercise for the readers use option 1 to create a new VM.

Virtual Machine Backup Policy

A backup policy defines a matrix of when the data snapshots are taken, and how long those snapshots are retained. When defining a policy for backing up a VM, you can trigger a backup job once a day or weekly.

A **default back policy** is applied when you create Backup job. With Default Policy backup is taken at 2.30 PM and Backup is retained for 30 days.

You can create a **Custom Policy** according to your requirements. Custom policy can be created during backup job creation time or afterwards.

Exercise 80: Create Custom Backup Policy

1. Go Recovery Service Vault rsvportal dashboard>Click Backup Polices in left pane>Backup policy blade opens.

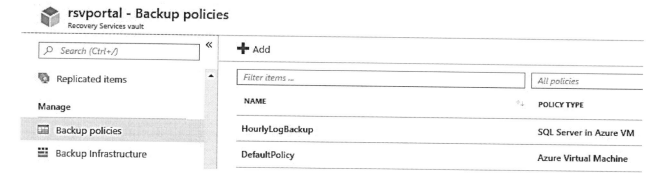

2. Click +Add> Click Azure Virtual Machine>Create Policy blade opens> give a name and select Backup Frequency (Daily or weekly) and select retention of snapshots (daily, weekly, Monthly and Yearly). Selecting Weekly, Monthly and Yearly is optional>Click create (Not shown).

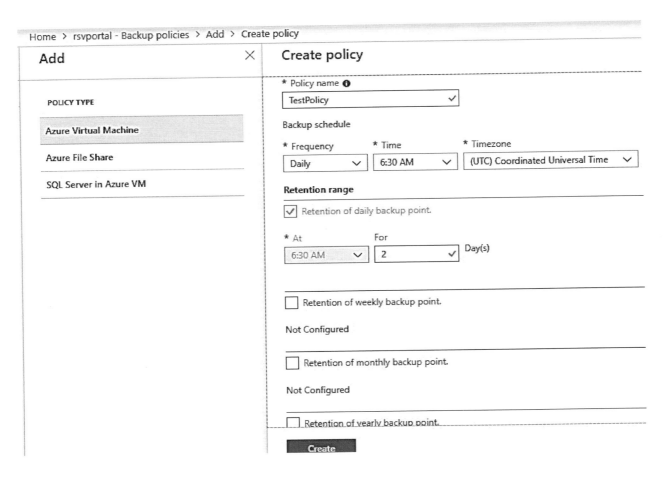

3. Figure below shows TestPolicy created Successfully.

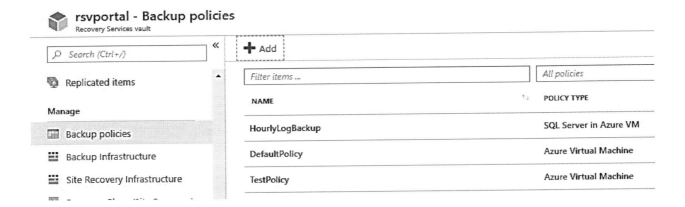

Exercise 81: Associating Custom Policy with VM wvmportal Backup Job

In this exercise we will associate Custom Policy created in previous exercise with VM wvmportal Backup job.

1. In Azure Portal go to wvmportal dashboard> Click Backup in left pane. You can see a default backup policy is associated with Backup.

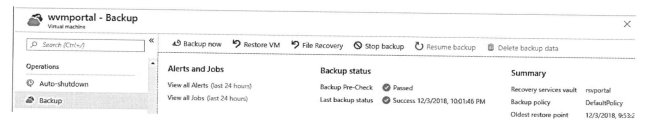

2. Click DefaultPolicy in right pane>Backup Policy blade opens>Choose TestPolicy from the dropdown box>Click save.

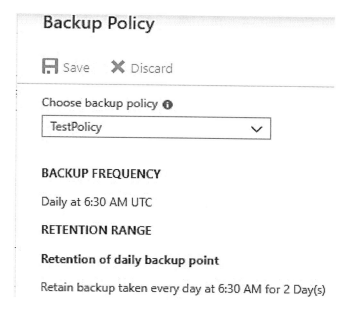

3. You can see in right pane that TestPolicy is applied to backup job.

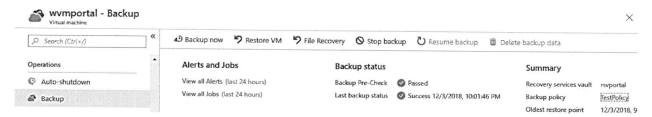

Backup Reports

Azure Backup reports are supported for Azure virtual machine backup and Azure Recovery Services Backup Agent option.

Requirement for Creating Backup Reports

Azure Storage Account: Storage account is used to store reports-related data.
Power BI account: Power BI account is used to view, customize and create reports by using the Power BI portal.

Create Backup Reports

In Recovery Services Vault Dashboard click Backup Reports in left pane> Backup Report pane opens. Enable diagnostic settings and select logs according to your requirement. You have the option to view reports Graphically in Power BI.

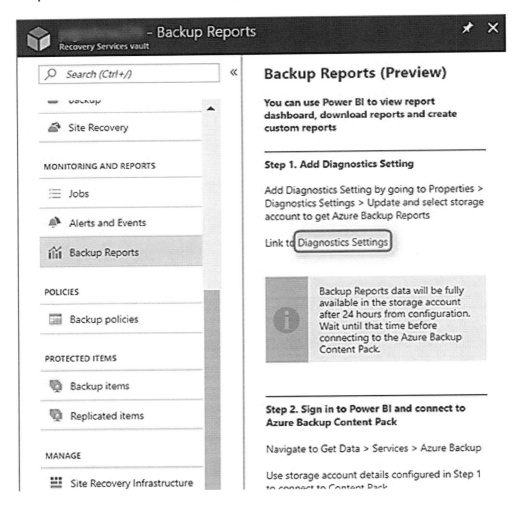

Chapter 11 Implementing and Managing Azure AD

This Chapter covers following Topic Lessons

Azure AD Introduction
Azure AD Basic & Premium License upgrade options
Azure AD Users
Azure AD Groups
Custom Domains
Self Service Password Reset (SSPR)
Azure AD Join
Azure AD Conditional Access
Azure AD Identity Protection
Managing Multiple Azure AD Directories

This Chapter covers following Lab Exercises

Exploring Dashboard of Default Azure AD
Activating Premium P2 Free Trial Licenses
Create User (User1 with Global Administrator Role)
Create User (User2 with Limited Administrator Role)
Create User (User3 with Directory Role User)
Exploring Dashboard of User
Checking User3 Access level
Create Group and add users manually
Assigning Azure AD Premium P2 License to Users
Create Test Group and add users
Add Custom Domain
Create TXT record in Domain Name Registrar
Verify the Custom Domain in Azure AD
Change Azure AD Login names to custom domain for User2
Enabling SSPR for Cloud Users (User2 & User3)
Setup SSPR Authentications for User3
Test SSPR for User3
Checking Device Settings for Azure AD Users
Joining Windows 10 PC to Azure AD using Azure AD Join
Log on to Windows 10 PC with User2

Enabling Enterprise State Roaming for Users
Create Conditional Access Policy
Testing CA Policy from Location outside India
Testing the CA Policy from Location in India
Simulate suspicious locations using TOR Browser
Enabling Azure Active Directory Identity Protection
Accessing Azure AD Identity Protection Dashboard
Demonstrating Resetting Compromised User Password
Investigating Risk Events
Investigating Vulnerabilities
Implementing Sign-in Risk Conditional Access Policy
Creating New Azure AD Tenant
Associating Azure AD Tenant with the Subscription

Chapter Topology

In this chapter we will configure Default Azure AD Tenant. We will also create a New Azure AD Tenant.

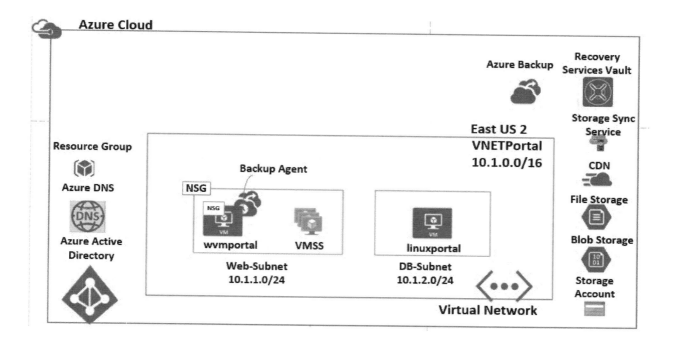

Azure AD Introduction

Microsoft Azure Active Directory (Azure AD) is a Multi-tenant cloud-based directory & identity management solution that combines core directory services, application access management, and identity protection into a single solution.

Azure AD also provides enterprise service's such as multifactor authentication service, a centralized application access panel for SaaS applications, an application proxy by which you can setup remote access for your on premises applications as well as Graph API that you can use to directly interact with Azure AD objects.

One of the Advantage of Azure AD is that application developers can easily integrate identity management in their application without writing complex code.

Azure AD can also act as SAML Identity provider. It Provides identity and authentication services to application using SAML, WS-Federation and OpenID connect protocols.

Azure Active Directory editions

Azure AD is offered in 4 Tiers: Free, Basic, Premium P1 and Premium P2.

Azure Active Directory Free edition can manage users and groups, synchronize with on-premises directories, get single sign-on across Azure, Office 365, and thousands of popular SaaS applications.

Azure AD Basic edition adds features such as group-based access management, self-service password reset for cloud applications, and Azure Active Directory Application Proxy.

Azure Active Directory Premium P1 edition add enterprise class features such as enhanced monitoring & security reporting, Multi-Factor Authentication (MFA), and secure access for your mobile workforce.

Azure Active Directory Premium P2 edition adds Identity Protection and Privileged Identity Management features.

Comparing Azure AD Editions

Features	Free	Basic	Premium (P1 & P2)
Directory Objects	50000	No Limit	No Limit
User/Group Management	√	√	√
Single sign-on (SSO)	10 apps/user	10 apps/user	No limit
Self-Service Password Change for cloud users	√	√	√
AD Connect	√	√	√
Security/Usage Reports	3 Basic Reports	3 Basic Reports	Advanced Reports
Group based access Management		√	√
Self Service password reset for cloud users		√	√
Logon page customization		√	√
SLA 99.9%		√	√
Self Service Group and app management			√
Self Service Password reset with on premises write back			√
Multi Factor Authentication	√ (See note 1)	√ (See note 1)	√
Microsoft Identity Manager user CAL + MIM Server			√
Azure AD Connect Health			√
Conditional access based on group and location			√
Conditional access based on device state (allow access from managed/domain joined devices)			√
Identity Protection			Premium P2
Privileged Identity Management			Premium P2

Note 1: Multi-Factor Authentication is available for Azure AD Free and Azure AD Basic, when you create a Multi-Factor Authentication Provider by the 'per user' or 'per authentication' billing/usage model.

Note 2: A default Azure AD (Free Edition) tenant is automatically created when you sign for Azure Subscription.

Azure AD Identity Management Features

- **Connect on-premises Active Directory with Azure AD**: In today's scenario, Organizations have large number of on-premises Active Directory users. Using Azure AD connect synchronize on-premises directory objects (users and groups) with Azure AD. This makes users more productive by providing a **common identity** for accessing resources regardless of location. Users and organizations can then use **single sign on (SSO)** to access both on-premises resources and Azure cloud services.

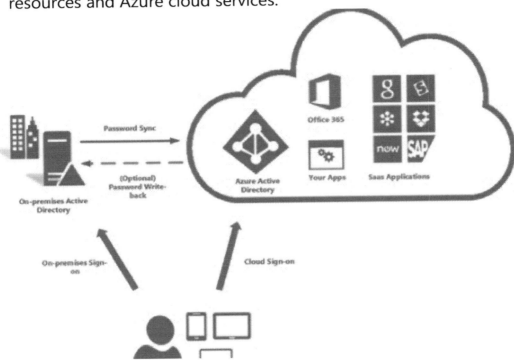

- **Manage and control access to corporate resources**: Enable application access security by using **Multi-Factor Authentication** for both on-premises and cloud applications.
- **Improve user productivity** with self-service password reset (**SSPR**).
- **Protecting Administrative Accounts**: Using Azure AD **Privileged Identity** Management you can restrict and monitor administrators and their access to resources and provide just-in-time access when needed.
- Provide **secure remote access** to on-premises application using Application Proxy without configuring VPN.

Default Azure AD Domain

A Default Azure AD Free Edition is automatically created with the subscription. You can upgrade Default Free edition to Basic or Premium Edition.

Domain name of the default Azure AD is in the following format:
<System generated Name>.onmicrosoft.com

System generated Name is based on the name and mail id used to create the subscription. You can check default Azure AD by going to Azure AD Dashboard and click Azure Active Directory in left pane.

Figure below shows dashboard of default Azure AD Tenant
harinderkohli543hotmail.onmicrosoft.com which I am using for this book.

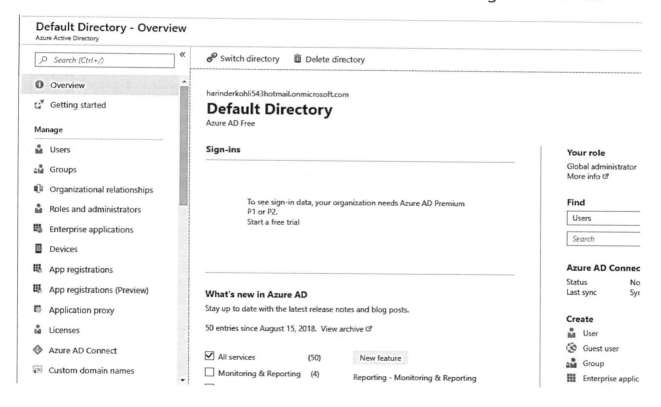

Note 1: user login name will be in following format for the above domain.
xyzxyz@harinderkohli543outlook.onmicrosoft.com

Note 2: You can assign custom Domain to your Default Azure AD. For example you can assign test.com. User login names will then be xyzxyz@test.com

Exercise 82: Exploring Dashboard of Default Azure AD

Login to Azure Portal @ https://portal.azure.com> Click Azure Active Directory in left Pane> Default Azure AD Tenant Dashboard Opens.

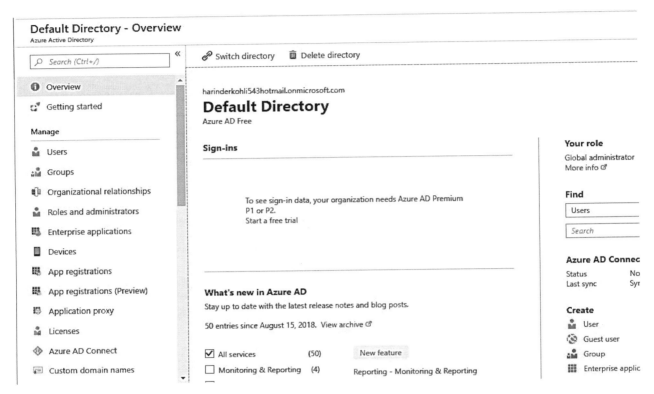

With **Users and Groups** option you can create user and Groups and Add users to groups.

With **Enterprise application** optio you can provide single sign-on to SaaS and custom application.

With **Licenses** option you can assign Basic or Premium licenses to Users.

With **Custom domain Name** option you can assign custom Domain Names to Default Azure AD.

With **Application Proxy** option you can provide secure remote access to on-premises application.

With **AD Connect** option you can synchronize on-premises users to Azure AD.

Azure AD Basic & Premium License upgrade options

The Basic and Premium editions Licenses are available for purchase through following options:

1. Microsoft Enterprise Agreement.
2. Open Volume License Program.
3. Cloud Solution Providers.
4. Online using credit card (Azure Subscribers only).
5. Premium P2 Free Trial licenses.

After you have purchased license through one of the above method the licenses will then be available in Azure Portal after activation. You can then assign these licenses to Azure users or groups.

Exercise 83: Activating Premium P2 Free Trial Licenses

In Azure Portal you get 2 options to activate Premium P2 Free Trial Licenses.

One option is Enterprise Mobility + Security E5 option which includes Azure Active Directory Premium P2, Microsoft Intune and Azure Rights Management Trial Licenses for 250 users for 90 days.

Second is Azure AD Premium P2 trial licenses for 100 users for 30 days.

1. Go to Default Azure AD dashboard> In the middle pane click start a free trial> Activate Blade opens> For this book I selected Azure AD Premium P2 license>Click Free trial>Activate Premium P2 trial blade opens> Click Activate> Close the activate pane.

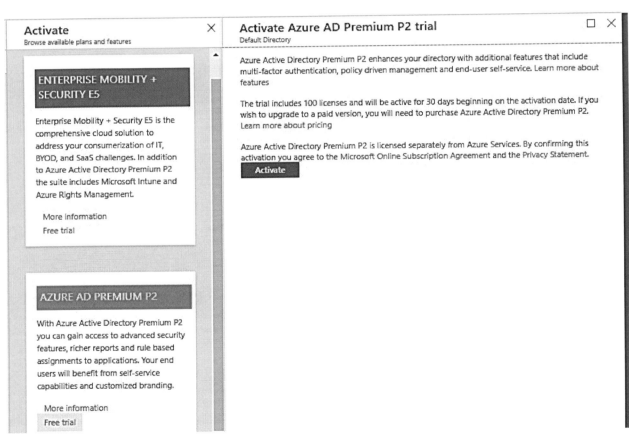

2. Refresh your Azure AD Dashboard using F5 keyboard button> You can now see the Premium P2 license available.

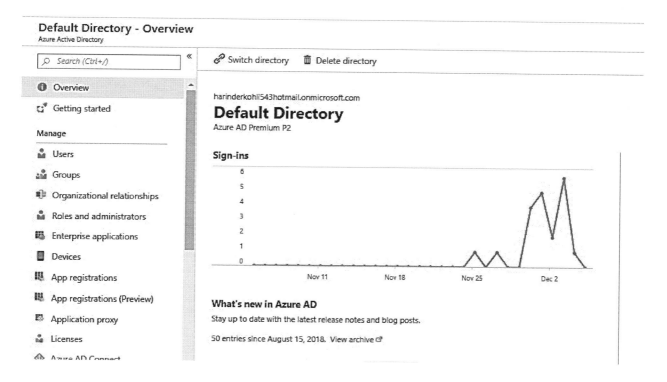

3. Click licenses in left pane> You can see 100 licenses. None of the license is assigned.

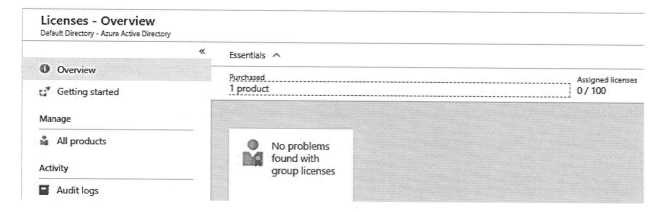

Azure AD Users

User name in Azure AD should be in email format with a verified domain. Verified domain can be default domain or custom Domain.

Directory Role for User

User is assigned Directory role during user creation time. A user can be assigned one of the following 3 directory roles:

User: User can login to Azure portal but cannot create, manage or view a resource. For a user to create, view or manage a resource in Azure Portal it needs to be assigned permissions Using Role based Access Control (RBAC).

Global Administrator: The Global administrators have full control over all **directory** (Azure AD) resources.

Limited Administrator: Limited administrator role has full access to particular Azure AD feature. Following Limited Administrative roles are available in Azure.

Billing Administrator	Exchange Service Administrator	Password Administrator / Helpdesk Administrator
Compliance Administrator	Global Administrator / Company Administrator	Power BI Service Administrator
Conditional Access Administrator	Guest Inviter	Privileged Role Administrator
Dynamics 365 service administrator	Information Protection Administrator	Security Administrator
Device Administrators	Intune Service Administrator	Service Support Administrator
Directory Readers	Mailbox Administrator	SharePoint Service Administrator
Directory Synchronization Accounts	Skype for Business / Lync Service Administrator	
Directory Writers	User Account Administrator	

Note: You can change user Directory role from Azure AD Dashboard.

Azure AD Password Policies for Cloud Users

The following table describes the available password policy settings that can be applied to user accounts that are created and managed in Azure AD:

Characters Allowed	A – Z, a – z, 0 – 9, @ # $ % ^ & * - _ ! + = [ ] { } | \ : ' , . ? / ` ~ " ( ) ;
Password restrictions	A minimum of 8 characters and a maximum of 16 characters. Strong passwords only: Requires three out of four of the following: • Lowercase characters. • Uppercase characters. • Numbers (0-9). • Symbols
Password expiry duration	• Default value: **90** days. • The value is configurable by using the `Set-MsolPasswordPolicy` cmdlet from the Azure Active Directory Module for Windows PowerShell.
Password expiry notification	• Default value: **14** days (before password expires). • The value is configurable by using the `Set-MsolPasswordPolicy` cmdlet.
Password expiry	• Default value: **false** days (indicates that password expiry is enabled). • The value can be configured for individual user accounts by using the `Set-MsolUser` cmdlet.
Password change history	The last password *can't* be used again when the user changes a password.
Password reset history	The last password *can* be used again when the user resets a forgotten password.
Account lockout	After 10 unsuccessful sign-in attempts with the wrong password, the user is locked out for one minute. Further incorrect sign-in attempts lock out the user for increasing durations of time.

Exercise 84: Create User (User1 with Global Administrator Role)

1. In Azure AD Dashboard>Click Users in left pane> All Users blade open>+New User> Add user blade opens> Enter name User1 and User name as user1@harinderkohli543hotmail.onmicrosoft.com>Assign Directory role of Global Administrator to user1> Click Ok>Click Show Password>Click create.

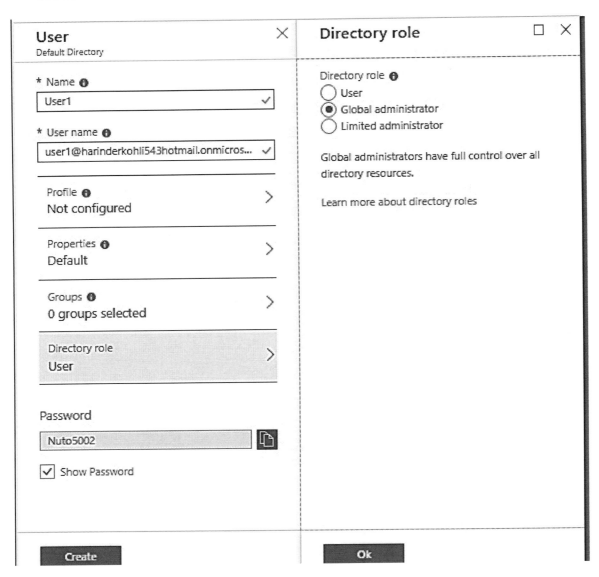

2. Note down the system generated Password and Log on with User1 Credentials and change the password. Please do this step.

User Name: User name should be in email format with a verified domain. Verified domain can be default domain or custom Domain. In this case we are using default domain harinderkohli543hotmail.onmicrosoft.com

Exercise 85: Create User (User2 with Limited Administrator Role)

1. In Azure AD Dashboard>Click Users in left pane> All Users blade open>+New User> Add user blade opens> Enter name User2 and User name as user2@harinderkohli543hotmail.onmicrosoft.com>Assign Directory role of Limited Administrator to user2 and Choose Billing Administrator Role>Click OK>Click Create.

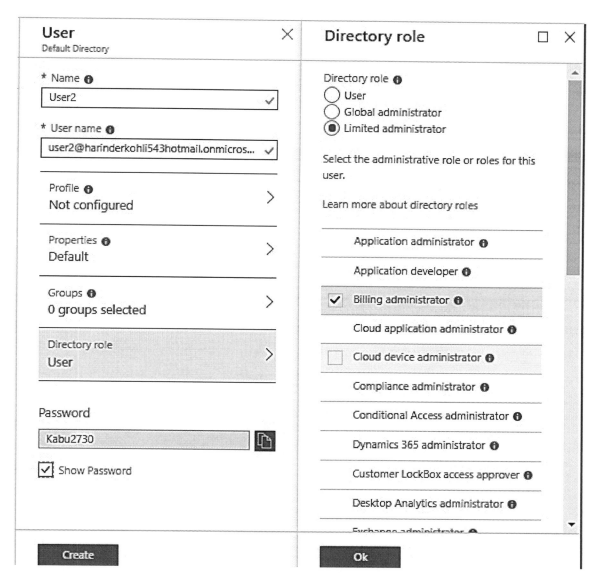

2. Note down the system generated Password and Log on with User2 Credentials and change the password. Please do this step.

Exercise 86: Create User (User3 with Directory Role User)

1. In Azure AD Dashboard>Click Users in left pane> All Users blade open>+New User> Add user blade opens> Enter name User3 and User name as user3@harinderkohli543hotmail.onmicrosoft.com>Assign Directory role of User to user3> Click Show password>Click Create.

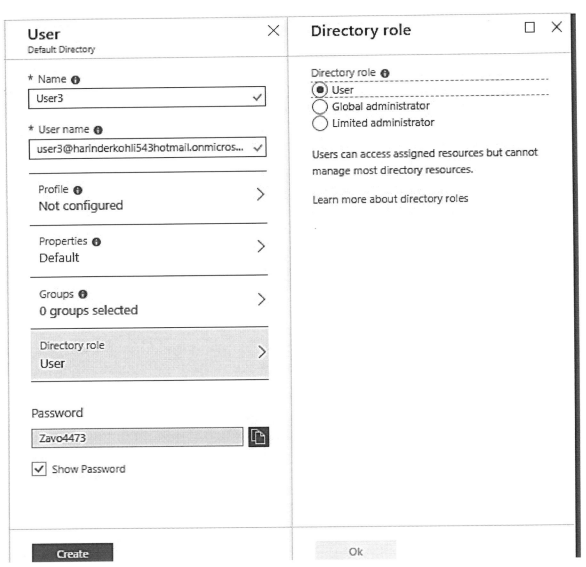

2. Note down the system generated Password and using Browser Log on with User3 Credentials and change the password. Please do this step.

Exercise 87: Exploring Dashboard of User

1. In Azure AD Dashboard>Click Users in left pane>All Users blade open> Dashboard shows administrator and 3 users (User1, User2 & User3) we created in previous exercises.

2. Select User3>user3 blade opens>From here you can assign Azure AD license, Change Directory role, Reset Password or delete the User etc.

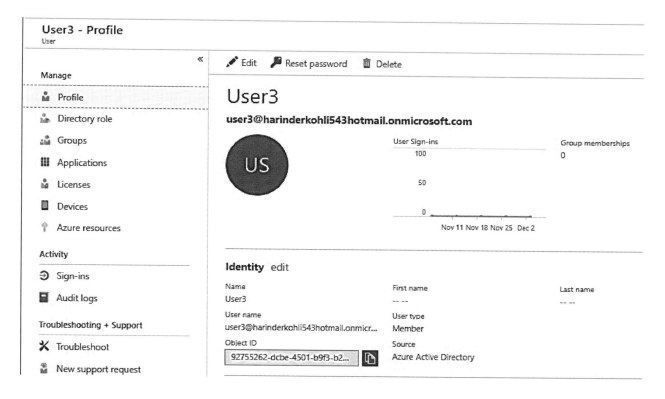

Exercise 88: Checking User3 Access level

In this exercise we will check User3 Access level in Azure Portal.

Log on to Azure portal @ https://portal.azure.com with User3 email-id and password. You can see there are no resources to display for User3 and user has no access to resources and User cannot create any resources.

In Subscription chapter we will discuss how we can assign Administrative permissions and Roles to Users.

Azure AD Groups

Group is a collection of users. The advantage of group is that it lowers administrative overhead of managing users. For Example instead of assigning Azure AD Basic or premium licenses to individual users, assign to group.

Adding users to group: Users can be added to group by manual selection or by using dynamic membership rules. Adding users by Dynamic rules requires an Azure AD Premium P1 or P2 license for each user member added.

Creating Group and Adding members manually: In Azure AD Dashboard>Click Users and Groups >All Groups>+ New Group> Add Group Blade opens>Select **Membership type assigned.**

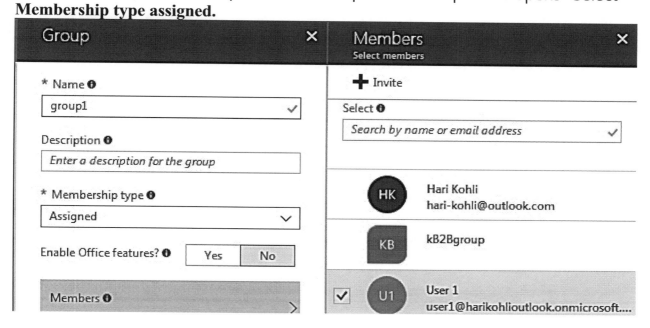

Adding members by Dynamic rules: Select **membership type Dynamic user**.

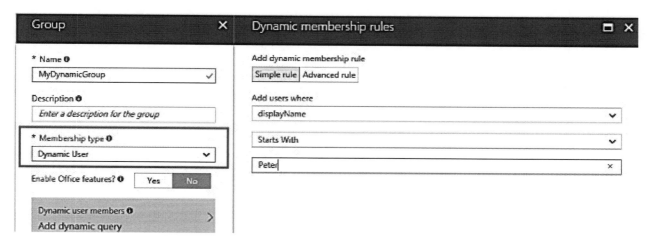

Exercise 89: Create Group and add users manually

In this exercise we will add 4 users to the group.

1. In Azure AD Dashboard>Click Groups >All Groups Blade open>+ New Group> Add Group Blade opens>Select Group type as Security>For name I entered AZ>Select Membership type assigned and Select Harinder Kohli, User1, User2 and User3 and click select and then create.

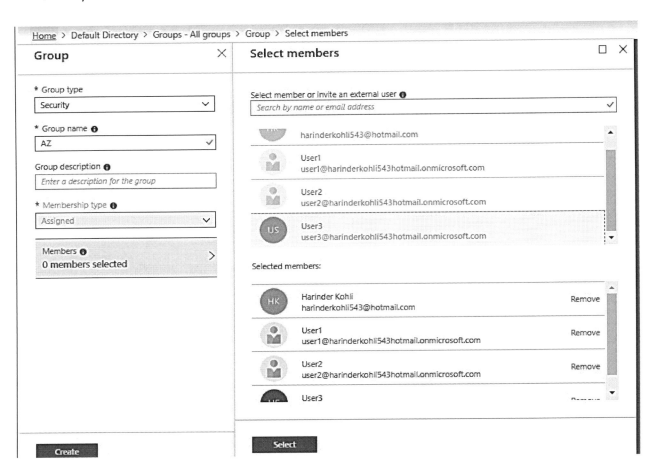

2. Figure below shows AZ Group.

3. Click on AZ Group and AZ group dashboard opens.

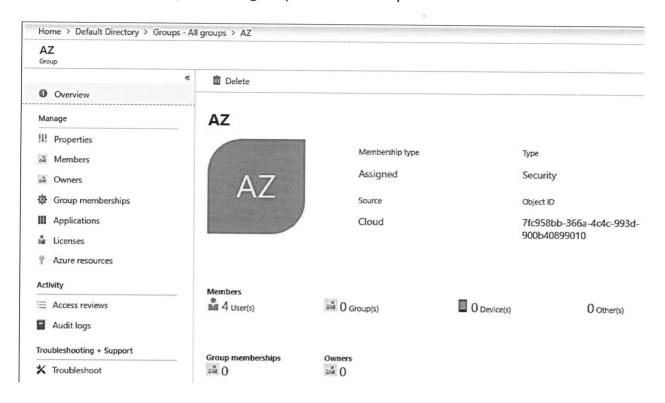

Exercise 90: Assigning Azure AD Premium P2 License to Users

In this exercise we will assign Premium P2 license to users. Instead of assigning to users individually we will assign to AZ group created in previous exercise.

1. In Azure AD Dashboard>Click Groups in left pane>All Groups Blade open>Click AZ Group Created in previous exercise>AZ Group dashboard opens>Click licenses in left pane> License blade opens.

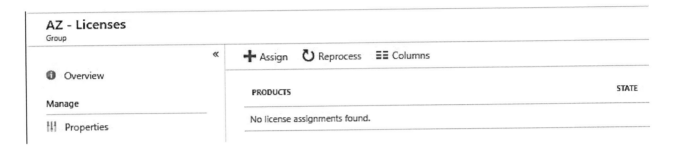

2. Click + Assign>Assign License blade opens>Click Products>In Right pane select Premium P2 >Click select (Not shown)> Click Assign (Not shown).

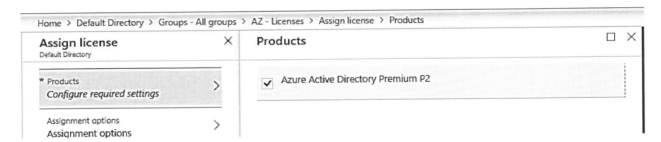

3. In AZ group license blade refresh the screen and you can see the licenses.

Note 1: When I tried to assign licenses to individual users it gave error.
Note 2: It will take 3-4 minutes for licenses to get updated in Azure AD license Dashboard.

Exercise 91: Create Test Group and add users

In this Exercise we will create Test Group which will include User2 and User3. We will use Test Group in SSPR lab.

1. In Azure AD Dashboard>Click Groups >All Groups Blade open>+ New Group> Add Group Blade opens>Select Group type as Security>For name I entered Test>Select Membership type assigned and Select User2 and User3 and click select and then create.

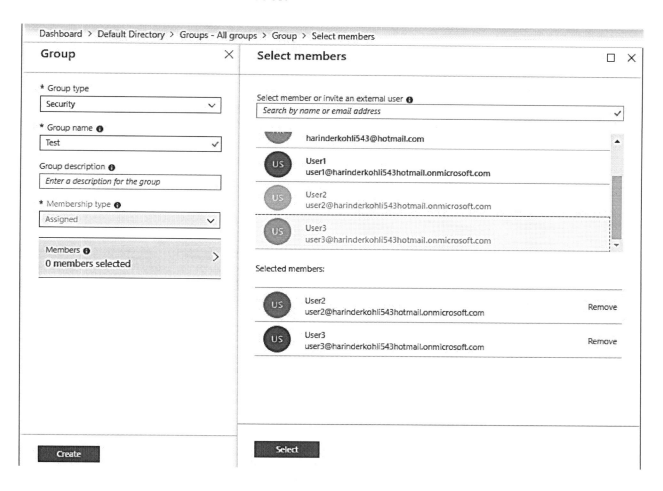

Create Bulk Users using CSV files and PowerShell

You can create Bulk users by importing a list of users from CSV files which then will create corresponding users in Azure Active Directory.

Step by Step Creating Bulk Users

1. Make sure Azure AD PowerShell Module is installed on your desktop.
2. Create CSV file with required user updates.
3. Create PowerShell script (*.ps1) for User Creation. This script will refer to CSV file on your system.
   Alternatively you can download and edit sample PS script from link shown below.
   https://gallery.technet.microsoft.com/scriptcenter/Update-Active-Directory-cd5c5513/file/168800/1/UpdateUsersCsv.ps1
4. Run the PowerShell script (*.ps1) which was created in step 3 with required new user information.

Add Custom Domains

Every Azure AD directory comes with an initial domain name in the form of <System generated Name>.onmicrosoft.com. System generated Name is based on the name and mail id used to create the subscription.

It would be difficult for users to remember the format of Default Azure AD domain name. Adding custom domain names to Azure AD allows you to assign user names in the format such as hari@fabrikam.com instead of hari@<System generated Name>.onmicrosoft.com.

Pre-Requisite for Adding Custom domain

You own a domain name and have sign-in rights to update DNS records with the Domain Name Registrar.

Note about Adding Custom Domain lab Exercise

In next page we will add Custom Domain mykloud.in to Azure AD Tenant.

I did this exercise at the end of the Book. I suggest that readers should also do this exercise at end of the book as it might create problems in succeeding exercises.

Readers are requested to Exercise 92- 95 at the end of the book.

Exercise 92: Add Custom Domain

In this exercise we will add Domain **mykloud.in**. Recall that in Chapter 1, Ex 14 we delegated administration of mykloud.in domain to Azure DNS from Registrar Go Daddy.

Step 1: Add domain mykloud.in to Azure AD

In Azure AD dashboard click Custom domain names in left pane>In right pane click + Add Custom Domain> Add Custom Domain pane opens>Enter domain name mykloud.in and click Add Domain (Not shown).

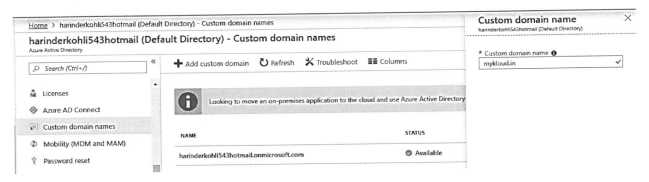

Step 2: Copy TXT Record Information from Custom Domain name pane.

Click Custom Domain created >Copy TXT Record information.

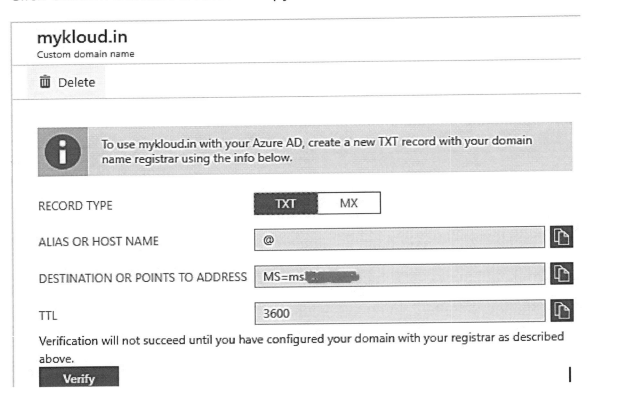

Exercise 93: Create TXT record in Domain Name Registrar

Recall that in Chapter 1, Ex 14 we delegated administration of mykloud.in domain to Azure DNS from Registrar Go Daddy. In Azure DNS we will create TXT record with TXT record information copied from previous Exercise.

1. In Azure Portal Click All Services in left pane> In Right pane under Networking click DNS Zones>DNS Zones pane opens>Click DNS Zone mykloud.in> DNS Zone dashboard opens as shown below.

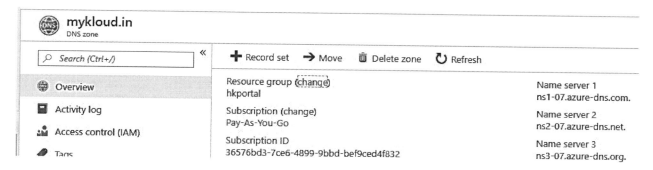

2. Click + Record Set in right pane> Add Record set blade opens>In name enter @>Select TXT from Dropdown box>In Value enter destination or point copied from step 2> Click OK (Not shown).

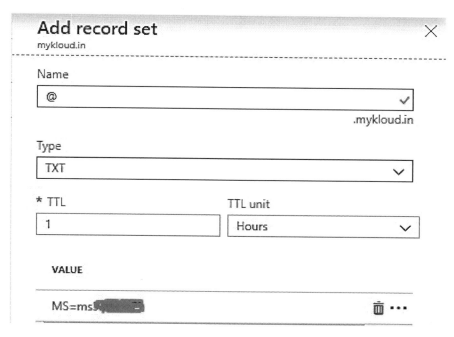

3. Txt Record is created and you can see in DNS Zone Dashboard.

Exercise 94: Verify the Custom Domain in Azure AD

In Azure AD dashboard click Custom domain names in left pane>In Right pane click the custom domain mykloud.in>Custom Domain pane opens>Click verify.

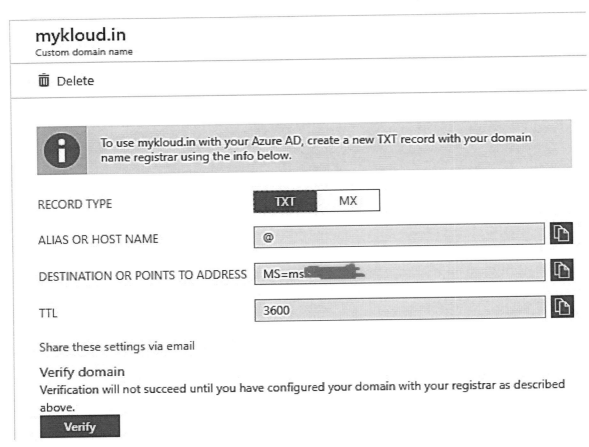

New pane opens and it shows verification is successful.

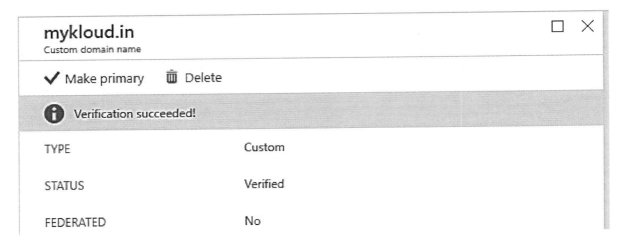

Exercise 95: Change Azure AD Login names to custom domain for User2

1. In Azure AD dashboard click Users in left pane>All Users pane opens>Click
   User2>User2 Profile opens>Click Edit> In user name box change
   user2@harinderkohli543hotmail.onmicrosoft.com to user2@mykloud.in> Click
   save.

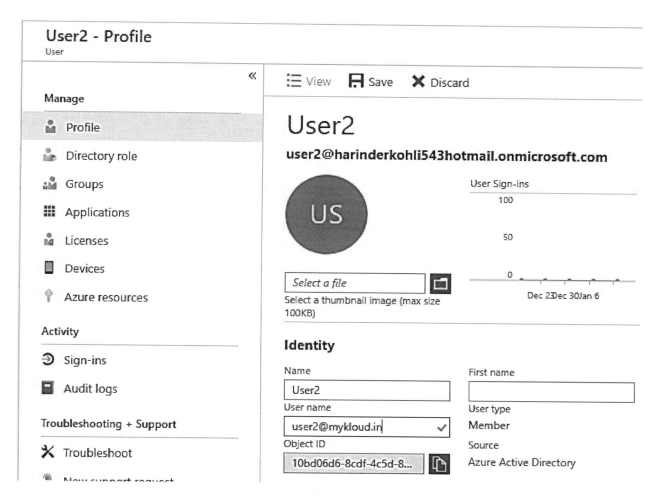

2. Open Firefox Browser and log on to Azure portal with user2@mykloud.in>
   Login was successful. In top right you can see user2@mykloud.in.

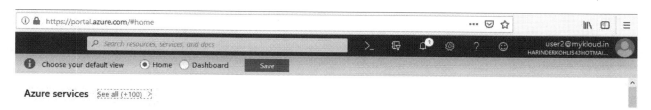

Self Service Password Reset (SSPR)

SSPR options allows users to change, reset and unlock there Azure AD login passwords.

SSPR option free's the helpdesk of password service queries and allow them to concentrate on more pressing issues. Helpdesk is an expensive resource. With SSPR option you can reduce the helpdesk cost.

Azure AD license Requirement for SSPC and SSPR

Self-Service Password Reset for cloud users: Requires AD Basic or Premium P1 or Premium P2 editions.
Self-Service Password Reset/Change/Unlock with on-premises writeback for hybrid users: Requires AD Premium P1 or Premium P2 editions.

Number of authentication methods required

This option determines the minimum number of the available authentication methods a user must go through to reset or unlock their password. **It can be set to either one or two.**

Authentication methods available for Self-Service Password Reset

If SSPR is enabled, you must select at least one or two of the following options for the authentication methods.

Mobile app notification (preview)
Mobile app code (preview)
Email
Mobile phone
Office phone
Security questions

Figure below shows Authentication methods available for password reset.

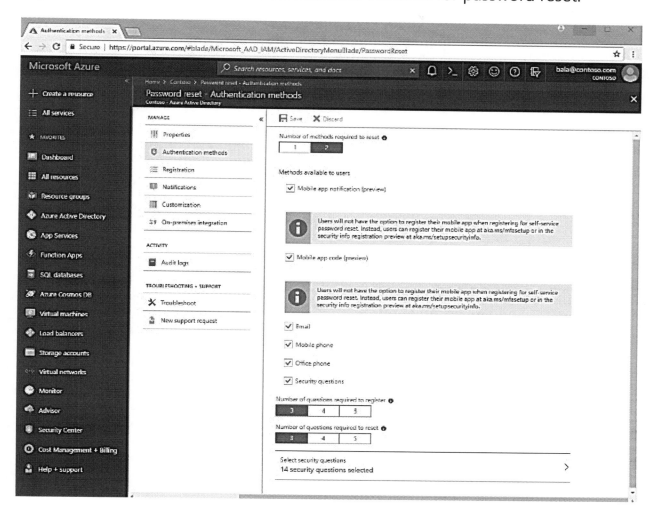

Exercise 96: Enabling SSPR for Cloud Users (User2 & User3)

1. In Azure AD Dashboard Click Password reset in left pane>Password Reset Blade opens> select either **Selected** or **All.** For this exercise Click **Selected**> Select Test Group created in Exercise 91 and click Select (Not Shown)> Click save.

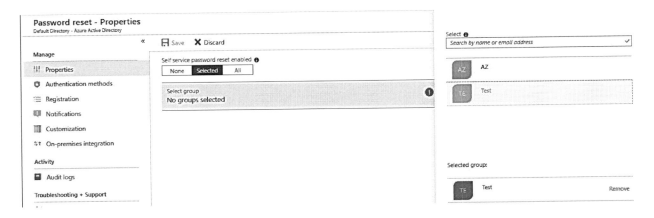

2. In Password reset blade click Authentication Methods>Select **1** and select **Email & Mobile Phone**. Note that save option is not highlighted as these are default options.

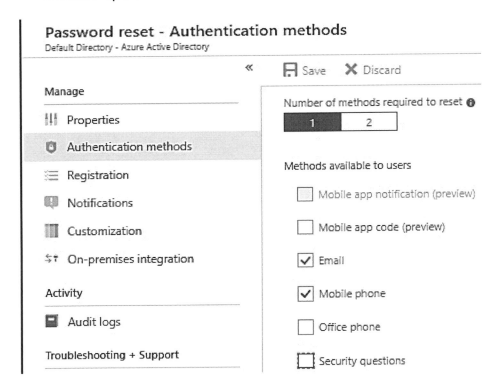

3. In Password reset blade click Registration> Select Yes. Note that save option is not highlighted as Yes is default option.

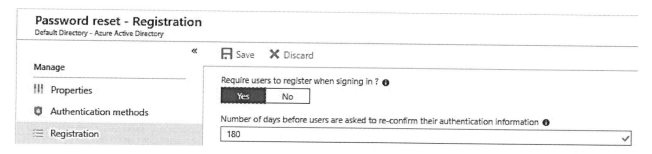

Note 1: After these steps are enabled whenever users of Test Group log in, they will be asked to update their Email and Mobile Number.

Note 2: If we selected No option, than it this case Administrator has to update Email and Mobile Number in User Profile dashboard.

Exercise 97: Setup SSPR Authentications for User3

Open a different Browser than what is used for Administrator. I am using Chrome for Administrator. I will use Firefox for users.

1. Open Firefox and log on with **user3@harinderkohli543hotmail.onmicrosoft.com** > System will ask to update your Authentication Phone and Email.

Note: Admin can also update User email and phone from User Profile dashboard.

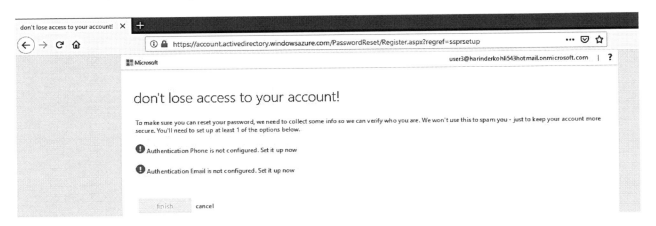

2. Using the link **set it up now** in browser update User3 Phone and email.
3. After you have updated click Finish to close the page.

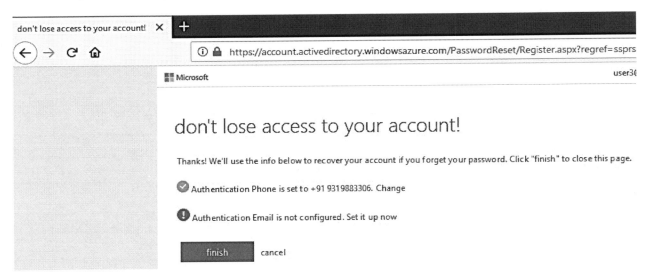

4. Log out of User3 account.
5. **Similarly repeat the above process for User2 also.**

Exercise 98: Test SSPR for User3

1. In Firefox open https://portal.azure.com and enter username but don't enter password. **user3@harinderkohli543hotmail.onmicrosoft.com**
2. In browser windows click Forgot my password>Get back into your account pane opens> enter User3 user-id and capcha and click next.

Microsoft

Get back into your account

Who are you?

To recover your account, begin by entering your user ID and the characters in the picture or audio below.

User ID:

| user3@harinderkohli543hotmail.onmicrosoft.com |

Example: user@contoso.onmicrosoft.com or user@contoso.com

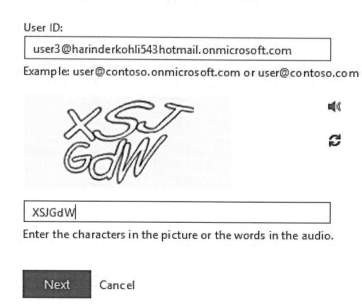

| XSJGdW |

Enter the characters in the picture or the words in the audio.

Next   Cancel

3. Enter Your Mobile Number and click text.

Microsoft

Get back into your account

verification step 1 > choose a new password

Please choose the contact method we should use for verification:

⦿ Text my mobile phone

◯ Call my mobile phone

In order to protect your account, we need you to enter your complete mobile phone number (************06) below. You will then receive a text message with a verification code which can be used to reset your password.

> Enter your phone number

> Text

4. Enter Verification code sent to your number and click next.

Get back into your account

verification step 1 > choose a new password

Please choose the contact method we should use for verification:

⦿ Text my mobile phone

◯ Call my mobile phone

We've sent you a text message containing a verification code to your phone.

> 349787

> Next   Try again   Contact your administrator

5. Password change pane opens> Enter your new password and click finish.

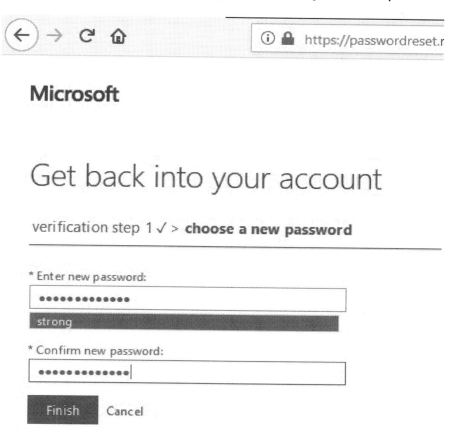

6. You can now log on with your new password.

You can see from above that User3 Reset its password without involving helpdesk.

Device Management in Azure AD

In Today's scenario users are accessing corporate applications not only from on-premises but also from home using corporate owned or personal devices.

In Security paranoid world IT administrators want to make sure that devices accessing corporate resources meet their standards for security and compliance.

Device management using Azure AD is foundation for device-based conditional access. With device-based conditional access, you can ensure that access to resources in your environment is only possible with trusted devices.

To manage devices using Azure AD you have 2 options:
1. Registering
2. Joining (AD Join or Hybrid AD Join).

In this Chapter we will focus on Azure AD Join only.

Azure AD Join

With Azure AD Join you join Windows 10 (Professional or Enterprise) computer to Azure AD using user's Azure AD identity. Joining the Device to Azure AD enables you to manage device identity. With Azure AD Join you sign-in to a device using an organizational work or school account instead of a personal account.

Azure AD Join is intended for organizations that are cloud-first / cloud-only. These are typically small- and medium-sized businesses that do not have an on-premises Windows Server Active Directory infrastructure.

Benefits of Azure AD Join

1. With Azure AD Join you can separate the personal and official work on Windows 10 Computer as you get separate screen for official work when you logon with your Azure AD Identity.
2. With Azure AD Join you can provide Single-Sign-On (SSO) to Azure managed SaaS apps and services.
3. With Azure AD Join you can restrict access to apps from devices that meet compliance policy.

4. Enterprise compliant roaming of user settings across joined devices. Users don't need to connect a Microsoft account (for example, Hotmail) to see settings across devices.

5. Access to Windows Store for Business using an Azure AD account. Your users can choose from an inventory of applications pre-selected by the organization.

6. Windows Hello support for secure and convenient access to work resources.

7. Seamless access to on-premises resources when the device has line of sight to the on-premises domain controller.

Exercise 99: Checking Device Settings for Azure AD Users

By default all users can AD Join Devices to Azure AD.

In Azure AD Dashboard Click **Devices** in left pane>Devices pane opens>Click Device Settings in left pane> In right pane you can see All Users can join devices to Azure AD (First Row).

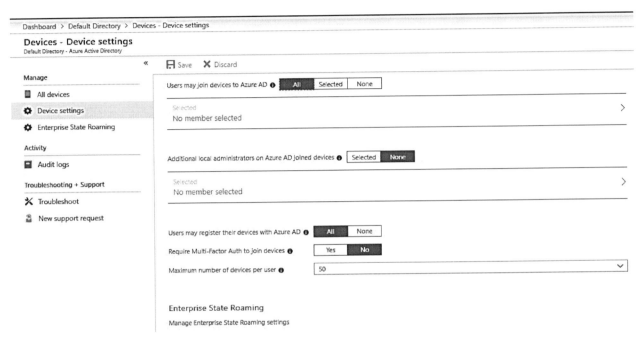

Word of Caution for Next Exercise: I joined my Windows 10 device to Azure AD using AD Join and User2 Credentials. It worked perfectly well. But after a recent Windows update a serious problem arose. I logged in using User2 credentials. When I logged out of system I could not get any option to log on my local desktop with my Local user account. It took me 4-5 hours of R&D to get back to my local desktop.

I would suggest avoid this Exercise.

Exercise 100: Joining Windows 10 PC to Azure AD using Azure AD Join

1. On your Windows 10 Pro Laptop>Click start>Settings Icon>Accounts>Access Work or School>+Connect> In bottom click join this device to Azure Active Directory> In Sign-in page enter User-id of User2 and click next.

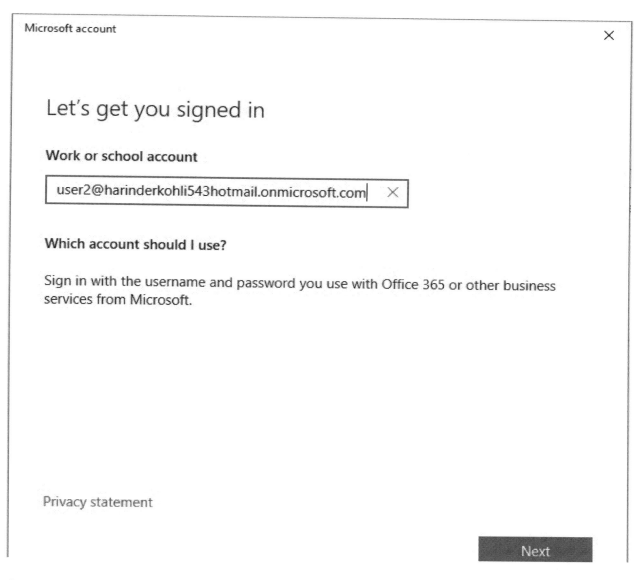

2. Enter your password and click sign-in

3. After Sign-in you get following message>Click Done (not Shown).

You're all set!

This device is connected to Default Directory.

When you're ready to use this new account, select the Start button, select your current account picture, and then select 'Switch account'. Sign in using your user2@harinderkohli543hotmail.onmicrosoft.com email and password.

4. Setting Pane now shows User2 Connected to Default AD>Close the Pane.

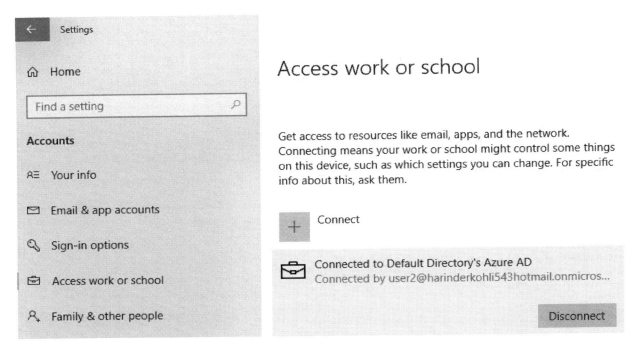

5. Devices Blade now shows Windows 10 AD Joined.

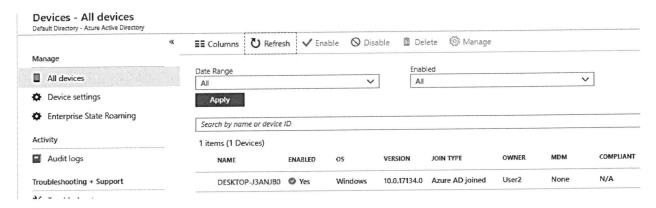

Exercise 101: Log on to Windows 10 PC with User2

1. On your Windows 10 laptop Logout of your personal account.
2. Log on with User2-id - user2@harinderkohli543hotmail.onmicrosoft.com.
3. System will ask you verify your account. Use Text message for verifying the account.
4. System will ask you to generate a Pin.
5. You are now logged on to the system.

The laptop screen will now show your work account with no files or folders from your personal Account.

If you are logging from multiple devices then you can sync settings and app data from work account using Enterprise State Roaming

Enterprise State Roaming

With Enterprise State Roaming Users can sync settings and app data across devices.
By default users are not enabled for Enterprise State Roaming. You can enable Enterprise State Roaming for all the users or for Selected Users.

Exercise 102: Enabling Enterprise State Roaming for Users

1. In Azure AD Dashboard Click **Devices** in left pane>Devices pane opens>Click Enterprise State Roaming in left pane> ESR pane opens.

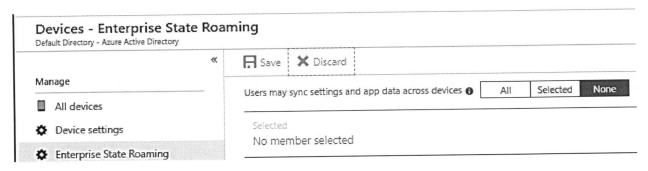

2. Click Selected>Click arrow icon below>+ Add Members>Click Test Group> Click Select>Click Ok.

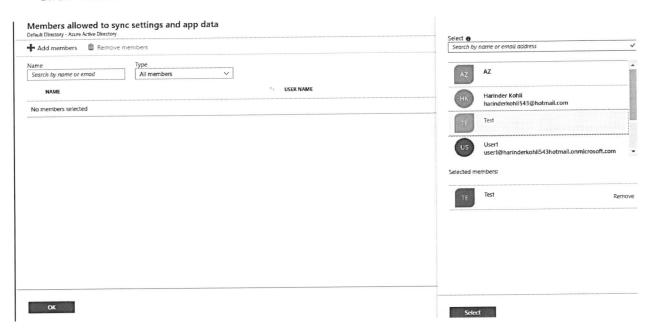

Enterprise State Roaming data

Enterprise State Roaming data is hosted in one or more Azure regions that best align with the country/region value set in the Azure Active Directory instance.

Data synced to the Microsoft cloud using Enterprise State Roaming is retained until it is manually deleted or until the data in question is determined to be stale.

Conditional Access in Azure AD

Azure Conditional Access is a feature of the Azure AD Premium P2 edition.

Before going into Conditional Access in Azure AD let's discuss why we need it in first place. In today's Cloud and Mobile era users are accessing corporate applications & services not only from on-premises but also from home or anywhere in world using corporate owned or personal devices.

Corporate IT Administrators are faced with two opposing goals:

1. Empower the end users to be productive wherever and whenever.
2. Protect the corporate assets.

With Conditional Access you can balance both the above goals.

Conditional access is a capability of Azure Active Directory that enables you to enforce controls on the access to apps in your environment based on specific conditions.
With controls, you can either **block access** or **allow access** or **allow access with additional requirements**. The implementation of conditional access is based on policies.

Figure below shows that up to 6 conditions can be applied before access to cloud apps is allowed or blocked.

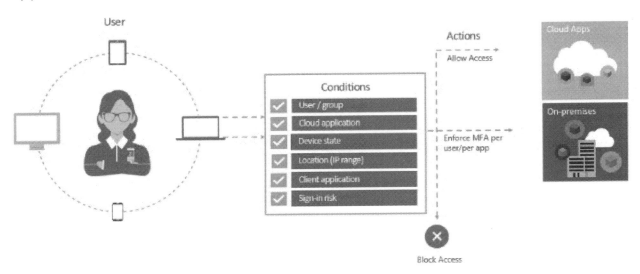

Conditional Access Policy

The combination of a condition statement with controls represents a conditional access policy. Figure below shows components of conditional access policy.

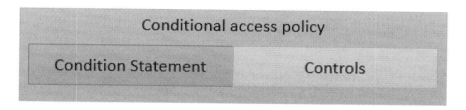

Based on the result of condition statement, controls are applied.

Condition Statements

In a conditional access policy, condition statements are criteria that need to be met for your controls to be applied.

You can include the **following 7criteria's** into your condition statement:

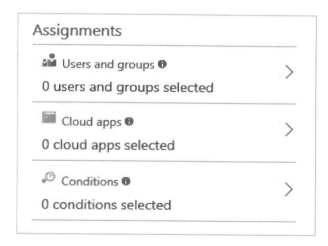

1. **Users & Groups**: In conditional access policy, you need to select the users or groups your policy applies to.

2. **Cloud Application**: In conditional access policy, you need to select the cloud application your policy applies to.

Conditions: In conditional access policy, you can define 5 conditions:

Sign-in risk | Device platforms | Locations | Client application | Device State

3. **Sign-in risk**: Sign-in risk level is used as a condition in a conditional access policy.

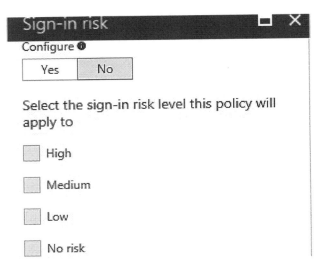

4. **Device Platform**: In a conditional access policy, you can configure the device platform condition to tie the policy to the operating system on a client. Azure AD conditional access supports the following device platforms:

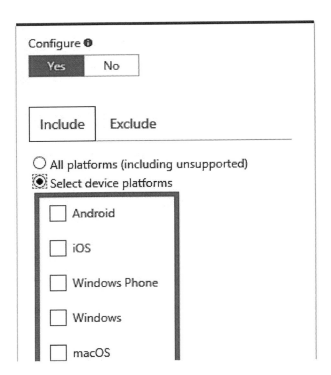

5. **Location**: In a conditional access policy, you can define conditions that are based on where a connection attempt was initiated from. The entries in the locations list are either **named locations** or **MFA trusted IPs**.

Named locations is a feature of Azure Active Directory that allows you to define labels for the locations connection attempts were made from. To define a location, you can either configure an IP address ranges or you select a country / region.

MFA trusted IPs is a feature of multi-factor authentication that enables you to define trusted IP address ranges representing your organization's local intranet. When you configure a location condition, Trusted IPs enables you to distinguish between connections made from your organization's network and all other locations.

6. **Client Apps**: The client apps condition allows you to apply a policy based on Client application type – Browser, Mobile apps or Desktop client.

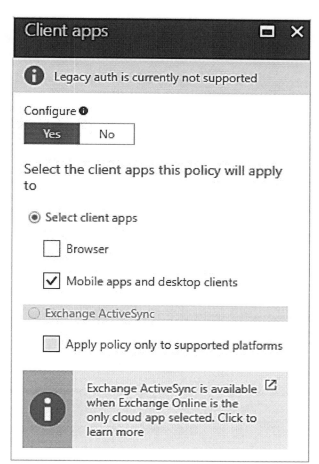

Controls

In a conditional access policy, controls define what it is that should happen when a condition statement has been satisfied.
With controls, you can either **block access** or **allow access with additional requirements**. When you configure a policy that allows access, you need to select at least one requirement.

There are two types of controls: Grant Control and Session Control.

Grant Control: Grant controls govern whether or not a user can complete authentication and reach the resource that they're attempting to sign-in to. Azure AD enables you to configure the following grant control requirements:

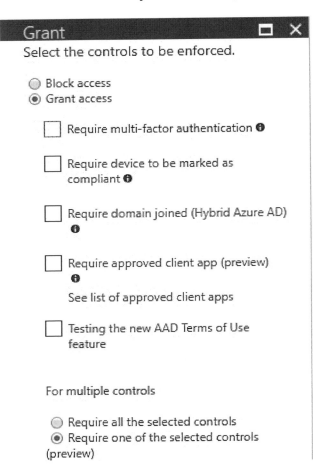

Session Control: Session controls enable limiting experience within a cloud app. The session controls are enforced by cloud apps and rely on additional information provided by Azure AD to the app about the session.

Exercise 103: Create Conditional Access (CA) Policy

In this exercise we will create Conditional Access Policy which will allow User3 to access Cloud app **Microsoft Azure Management or Azure Portal** only if User3 is accessing the Cloud app from India.

1. In Azure AD Dashboard Click **Conditional Access** in left pane> Conditional Access Blade opens>Click Named Location in left pane.

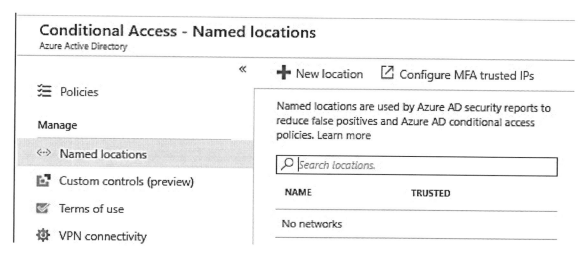

2. Click + New Location>New Location Blade opens>Enter a name, Select Countries/Region> From drop down box check select all> Deselect India> click Create (Not shown).

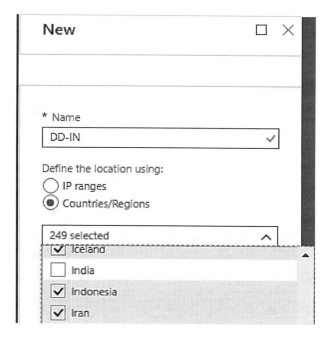

3. In Conditional Access Blade click Policies in left pane.

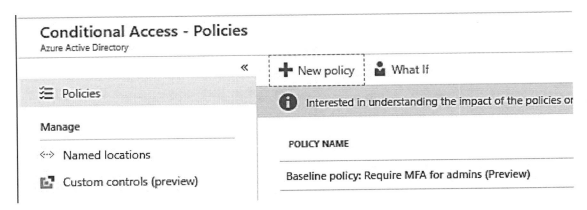

4. Click + New Policy> Create New Policy Blade opens>Enter a name>In users and groups Select **User3**>In Cloud App Select **Microsoft Azure Management**> In Conditions select Location, click Yes, Click selected Location radio Button, Click Select and then select **DD-IN** Location created in step 1& 2> Click Select>Click Done>Click Done> In Access Control select **Block** Access>Click **On** for Enable Policy> Click Create.

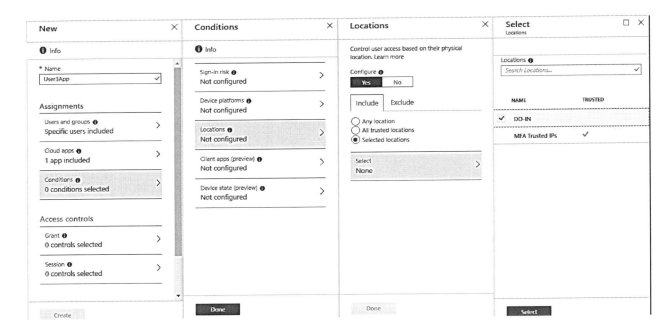

Note: Readers are advised to deselect the country from which they will be doing this Exercise.

Exercise 104:Testing CA Policy from Location outside India

For this Exercise we will use TOR Browser. You can check IP address and Location by using link https://www.iplocation.net/find-ip-address. In my case it was a European location with IP Address X.10.X.200.

1. Open Tor Browser on your laptop and go to portal.azure.com and log on with User3 Credentials> You cannot access the Azure Portal.

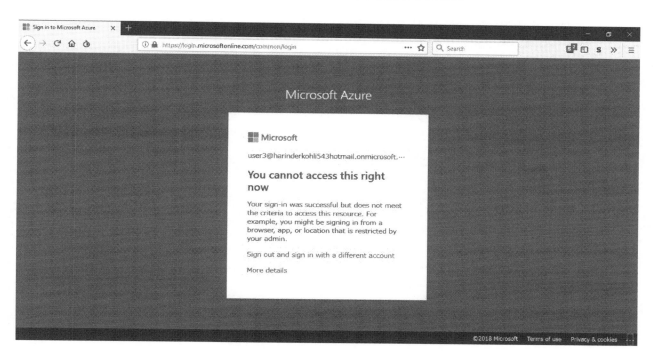

Exercise 105: Testing the CA Policy from Location in India

1. Open Firefox Browser on your laptop and go to portal.azure.com and log on with User3 Credentials> You can access the Azure Portal.

Exercise 106: Testing the Conditional Access Policy using What If option

1. In Azure AD Dashboard Click **Conditional Access** in left pane> Conditional Access Blade opens> In Conditional Access Blade click Policies in left pane>In Right pane click **What If** in Right pane>What If Pane opens>Select User3, Select Microsoft Azure Management, Select Country as Switzerland and IP Address as 176.10.99.200> click What If>Evaluation Result shows Block access.

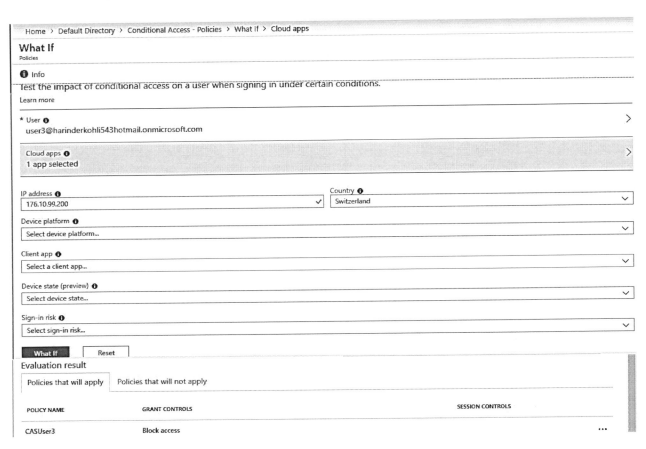

2. If I use India as Location and IP address as 139.167.240.27 then no Conditional Access Policy is applied. The reason is that in named location we did not selected India.

Evaluation result

Policies that will apply	Policies that will not apply	
POLICY NAME	GRANT CONTROLS	SESSION CONTROLS
No policies		

Azure Active Directory Identity Protection

Before going into Azure AD Identity Protection let's discuss why we need it in first place. The vast majority of security breaches take place when attackers gain access to an environment by stealing a user's identity.

<u>Azure AD Identity Protection helps in detecting and remediating compromised user identities by configuring risk-based policies that automatically respond to detected issues when a specified risk level has been reached.</u>

Azure Active Directory Identity Protection provides risk-based conditional access to your applications and critical company data. Identity Protection uses adaptive machine learning algorithms and heuristics to detect anomalies and risk events that may indicate that an identity has been compromised. Using this data, Identity Protection generates reports and alerts that enable you to investigate these risk events and take appropriate remediation or mitigation action.

Azure Active Directory Identity Protection is a feature of the Azure AD Premium P2 edition.

Azure AD Identity Protection Function

1. Get a consolidated view of flagged users and risk events detected using machine learning algorithms.
2. Improve security posture by acting on vulnerabilities.
3. Set risk-based Conditional Access policies to automatically protect your users from impending security breaches. Identity protection offers following 3 Risk based policies to configure.
   Azure Multi-factor Authentication registration policy.
   User risk policy .
   Sign-in risk policy.

Exercise 107: Simulate suspicious locations using TOR Browser

1. Using User2 and User3 credential log on to Azure Portal using TOR Browser. Do it couple of times using different TOR locations.

Exercise 108: Enabling Azure Active Directory Identity Protection

1. In Azure Portal Click +Create a resource> Identity>Azure AD Identity Protection> Azure AD Identity Protection Blade opens>Click Create.

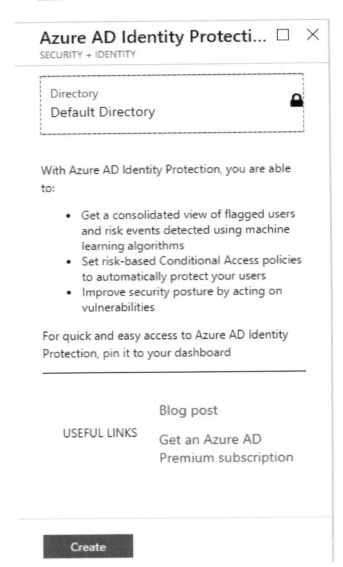

Exercise 109: Accessing Azure AD Identity Protection Dashboard

1. Open Browser and go to the AD Identity Protection Dashboard URL at https://portal.azure.com/#blade/Microsoft_AAD_ProtectionCenter/IdentitySecurityDashboardMenuBlade/Overview

2. Figure below show Identity Protection dashboard. It has 3 Mini Dashboards – **Users flagged for Risk, Risk Events and Vulnerabilities**.

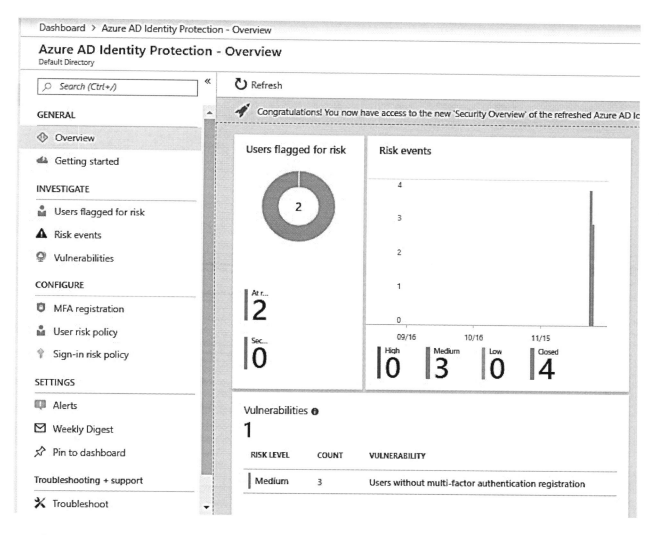

Under Configure you can see 3 risk based policies - Azure Multi-factor Authentication registration policy, User risk policy & sign-in risk policy.

3. Click **User flagged for Risk** in left pane>In right pane you can see security risk & status information about the user.

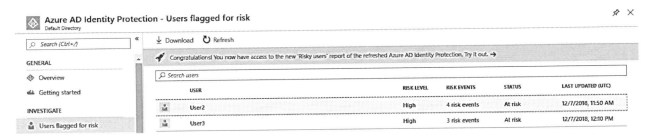

4. Click **Risk events** in left pane> You can see risk event type.

5. Click **Vulnerabilities** in left pane> You can see the risk level and type of Vulnerability which in this case is that there is no MFA for users.

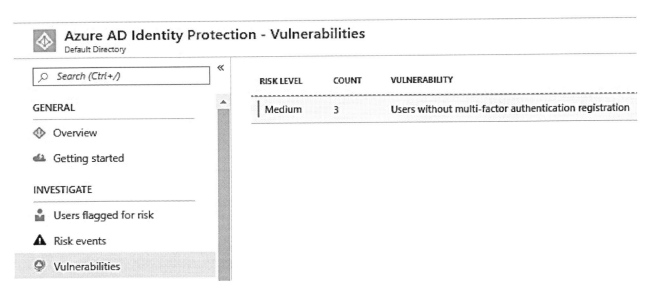

Users Flagged for Risk

These are users in your directory whose credentials might be compromised based on observed patterns of behaviour. Identity Protection Dashboard chart shows you the number of users who are currently at risk as well as users who had risk events that were already remediated.

Remediating Risk: After you have investigated, you can remediate risk events by resetting the user's password—this takes control away from any attacker who had the previous password.

Exercise 110: Demonstrating Resetting Compromised User Password

In Identity Protection Dashboard click **User flagged for Risk** in left pane.

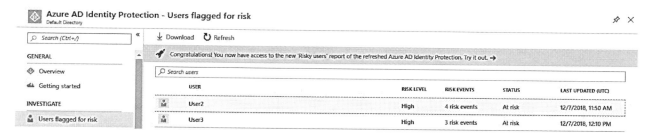

In right pane click one of the user listed. In this case I selected User3>In User3 pane click Reset password>Reset Password pane opens. From here you can reset User password.

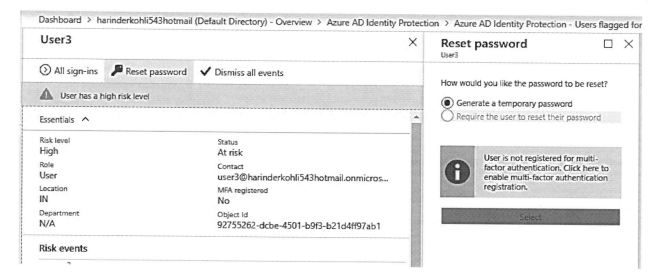

Risk events

These are events that Identity Protection has flagged as high risk and indicate that an identity may have been compromised. Some of the Risk events include:
1. Users with leaked credentials.
2. Irregular sign-in activity.
3. Sign-ins from possibly infected devices.
4. Sign-ins from unfamiliar locations.
5. Sign-ins from IP addresses with suspicious activity.
6. Sign-ins from impossible travel.

Remediating Risk Events: After you have investigated, you can remediate risk events by applying Sign-in risk policies.

Exercise 111: Investigating Risk Events

In Identity Protection Dashboard click **Risk Events** in left pane> In right pane click one of Risk Event> You can see the Risk Event- **Sign-ins from anonymous IP Addresses**. I had tried to log on with User2 & User3 using TOR Browser from one of the European locations before starting this exercise.

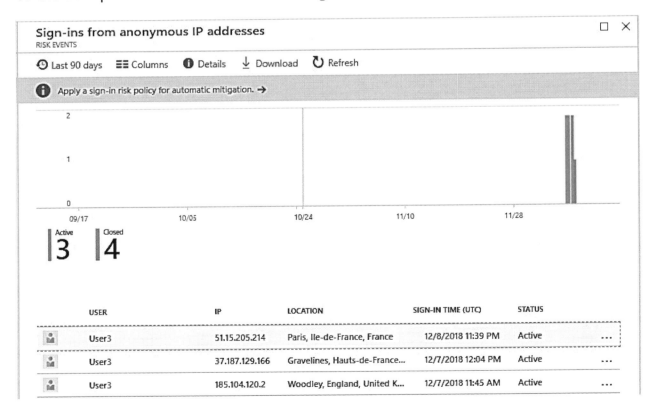

Vulnerabilities

These are weaknesses in your environment that can be exploited by an attacker. It is recommended that you address these vulnerabilities to improve the security posture of your organization and prevent attackers from exploiting these vulnerabilities. Following are some of the vulnerabilities that Identity Protection detects.

1. Users not registered for multi-factor authentication.
2. Unmanaged apps discovered in last 7 days.
3. Security Alerts from Privileged Identity Management.

Remediating Vulnerabilities: After you have investigated, you can remediate Vulnerabilities by applying MFA Registration Policy.

Exercise 112: Investigating Vulnerabilities

1. Click **Vulnerabilities** in left pane> In right pane you can see the risk level and type of Vulnerability which in this case is that there is no MFA for users.

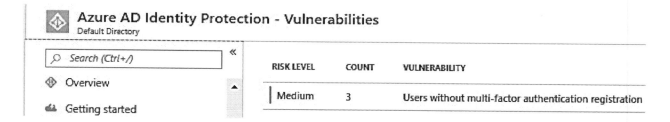

2. In right pane click on the Vulnerability discovered> MFA Policy pane opens. Here you can MFA policy for all or selected users.

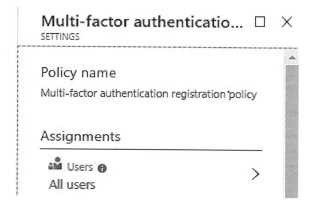

Security Policies

Identity Protection offers 3 types of security policies to help protect your organization- Multi-factor Authentication registration policy, User risk policy & sign-in risk policy.

Azure Multi-factor Authentication registration policy: Azure Multi-factor Authentication registration policy helps you manage and monitor the roll-out of multi-factor authentication registration by enabling you to define which employees are included in the policy and view the current registration state of impacted users.

In Identity Protection dashboard> Click MFA Registration in left pane>MFA Registration Policy opens.

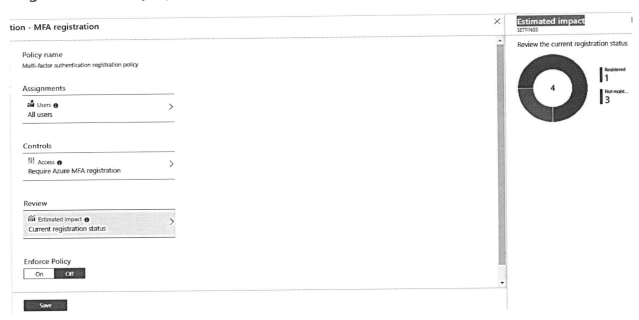

Note 1: We will not enable this policy as MFA is not in the scope of AZ100. MFA is part of AZ101.

Note 2: Readers are advised to check all the options in the policy.

User risk policy: This is a Conditional Access policy which helps block risky users from signing in, or forces them to securely change their password. You can control which action (block or secure password change) is triggered at different risk levels depending your organization's risk tolerance.

In Identity Protection dashboard> Click User Risk Policy in left pane>User risk remediation Policy opens.

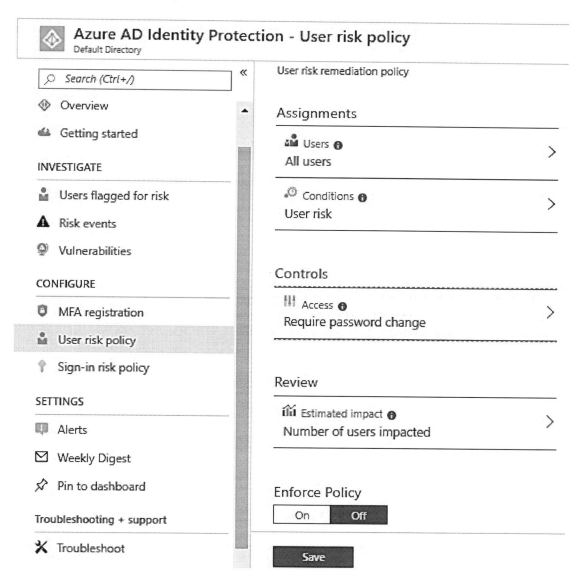

Note: Readers are advised to check all the options in the policy by clicking arrow button.

Figure below shows Condition options in User Risk Policy.

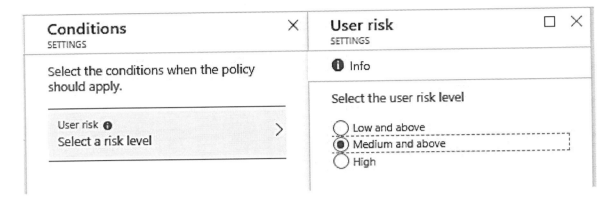

Figure below shows Control options in User Risk Policy.

Both the above are same in User Sign-in Risk policy also.

Sign-in risk policy: You can configure a sign-in risk policy to block user sign-in or require multi-factor authentication at different risk thresholds. Click sign-in risk policy in Identity Protection dashboard to open the policy.

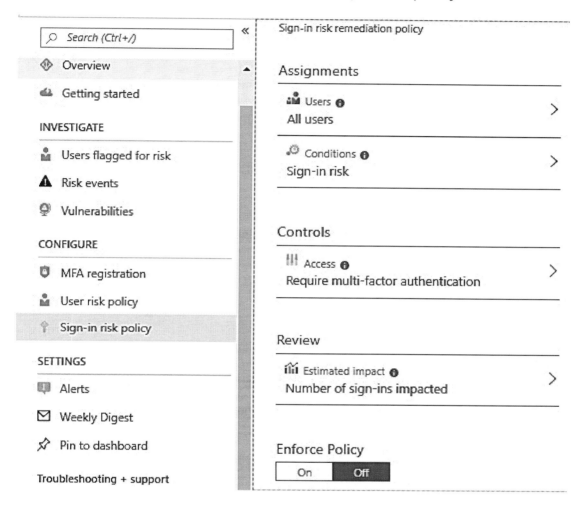

Figure below shows Condition options.

Note: Readers are advised to check Control option also.

Exercise 113: Implementing Sign-in Risk Conditional Access Policy

In this exercise we will create Sign-in Risk Conditional Access Policy which will block access if Identity Protection detects that a sign-in attempt was not performed by the legitimate owner of a user account. We will use TOR Browser for this exercise.

1. Go to Identity Protection Dashboard>Click Sign-in risk policy in left pane>Sign-in risk policy blade opens>Select **User3**>In Condition Select Medium and above> In Control Select Block Access>Click On for Enforce Policy>Click Save

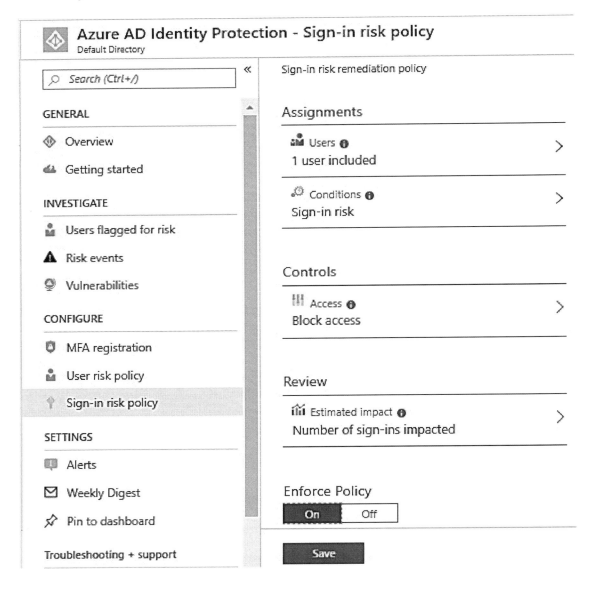

2. Open **Tor Browser** and log on to portal.azure.com with User3 credentials. Your sign-in attempt is blocked by Sign-in risk conditional access policy.

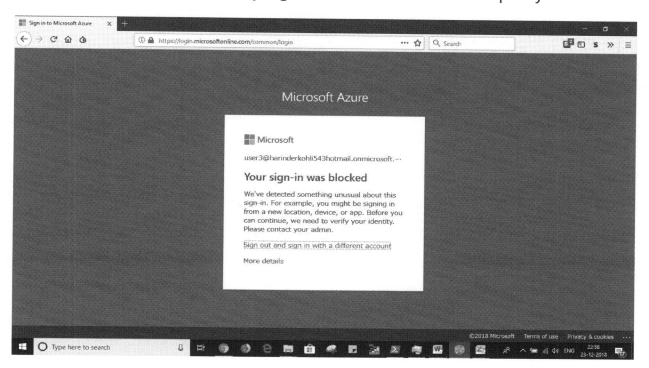

Managing Multiple Directories

A Subscription can be associated with a Single Azure AD Tenant only. But Azure AD tenant can be associated with Multiple Subscriptions.

Instead of Default Azure AD Tenant you can associate a New Azure AD Tenant with the Subscription.

Exercise 114: Creating New Azure AD Tenant

2. In Azure Portal Click +Create a Resource in left pane> Identity> Azure Active Directory> Create Azure Active Directory blade opens> Enter a name, **aadPortal** for initial Domain name and select Country and click create.

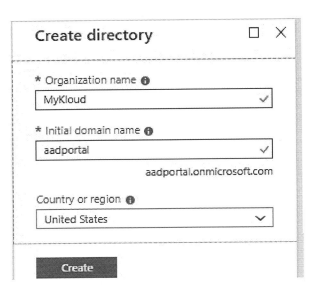

3. After you get the notification that successfully created Directory MyKloud >Click Azure Active Directory in Left pane you can see MyKloud Azure AD.

4. To go to Defualt Azure AD Tenant>Click Switch Directory>In Right Pane Select your Default Azure AD Tenant.

Exercise 115: Associating Azure AD Tenant with the Subscription

In this exercise we will just demonstrate how to associate our subscription with AD tenant created in previous Exercise. Actual association will not happen as we have to do more exercises with default AD tenant.

1. In Azure Portal Click **Cost Management + Billing** in left pane> Cost Management + Billing Dashboard opens>Click Subscriptions in left pane> In right pane click your subscription>Subscription Dashboard opens> You can see Subscription is associated with Default Azure AD Tenant.

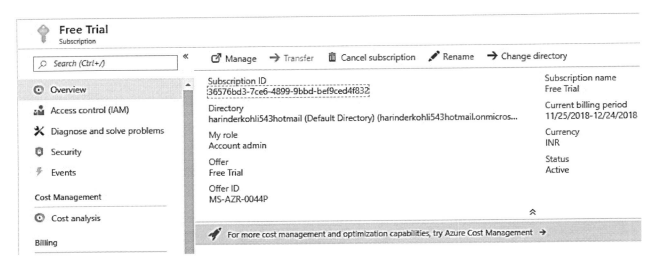

2. Click Change Directory in Right pane>Change Directory Blade opens>From Drop Down Box Select Your New Azure AD Tenant created in Previous Exercise. Don't proceed further as we need to more exercises with Default Tenant. Close the Change Directory Blade.

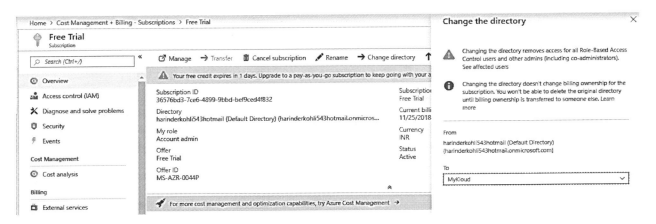

Chapter 12 Implementing Azure AD Hybrid Identities

This Chapter covers following Topic Lessons

- Azure AD Hybrid Identity options with AD Connect
- Components of AD Connect
- Requirements for deploying AD Connect Server
- AD Connect with Federation with ADFS option
- Seamless Single Sign-on
- Password Writeback

This Chapter covers following Lab Exercises

- Install AD Connect with Password Hash Synchronisation
- Check Users Test1 & Test2 synchronization to Azure AD
- Check AD Connect options
- AD Connect Health

Chapter Topology

In this chapter we will add **AD Connect** and **AD Connect health Agent** to the topology. They will be installed on VM OnPremAD. AD Connect will synchronize on-premises users in Active Directory Domain Services (AD DS) to Default Azure AD Tenant. **AD Connect health Agent** will monitor health of On-premises Active Directory (AD DS). AD DS role was installed on VM OnPremAD in Compute Chapter.

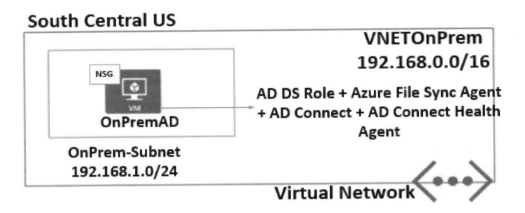

Users in on-premises AD DS will be synchronized to Default Azure AD Tenant.

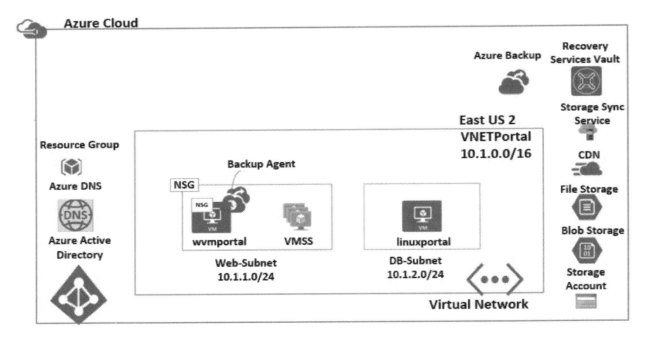

Azure AD Hybrid Identity options with AD Connect

Azure AD Connect integrates on-premises directories with Azure Active Directory. AD Connect synchronizes on-premises users in Active Directory Domain Services (AD DS) or any other compatible Directory Services to Azure Active Directory.

The **advantage** of AD Connect is that Users can access cloud and on-premises resources with the single identity. Another advantage is that we don't have to manually create user in Azure Active Directory as they synced from on-premises AD. Third advantage is that by enabling single sign-on, users who are logged on to on-premises can access cloud resources without logging to Azure.

You need to just manage your on-premises AD and all changes are synchronized with Azure AD.

AD Connect is usually installed on-premises with a service component in Azure. Figure below shows Architecture of AD Connect.

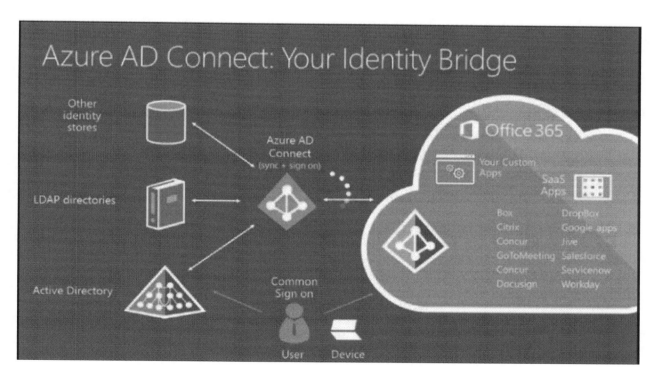

Following 5 identity options are available with Azure AD when used in conjunction with AD Connect. Figure below shows various Identity options available.

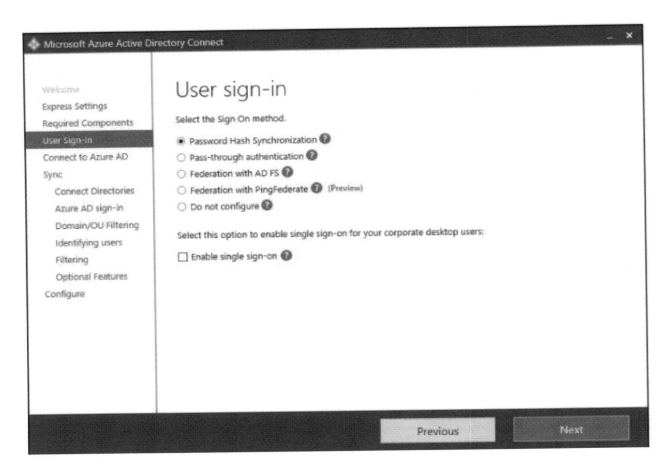

Synced Identity or Password Hash Synchronization: Identity is maintained both in cloud and on-premises. Authentication happens in cloud.

AD Connect installed on-premises with password synchronization option, synchronizes users and password hash of on-premises Active Directory users to Azure AD.

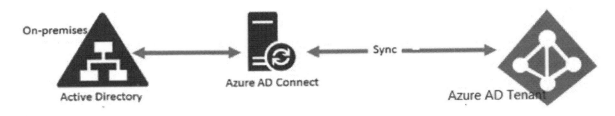

One advantage of this option is that you can enable single sign-on during AD Connect Installation without requiring any complex hardware setup.

Requires Azure AD Subscription, AD Connect Installed on-premises and on-premises AD DS.

Pass-through Authentication Option: Identity is maintained in both cloud and on-premises. Authentication happen on-premises with Active Directory.

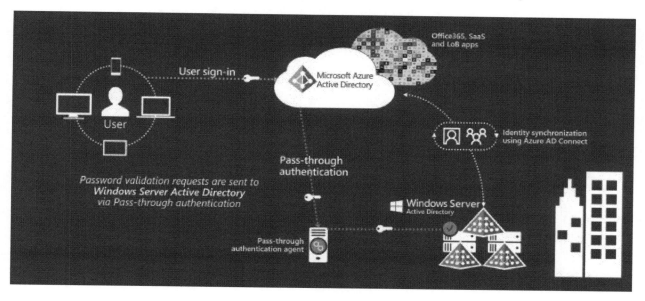

AD Connect installed on-premises with Pass-through Authentication Option, Synchronizes on premises Active Directory users to Azure AD. In this case Password Hash of users are not Synchronized.

A Pass through agent is installed on-premises on a windows server. The agent listens for and responds to password validation requests only. It receives encrypted password from Azure AD. It Decrypts it and validates it against Local Active Directory. The communication between Azure AD and Pass through agent is over Azure Service Bus. Azure SQL Database in cloud is used to holds information about metadata and encryption keys of Authentication Agents.

The advantage of this option is that there is no need for complex on-premises deployments or network configuration as in the case of ADFS. Second advantage is that you can enable seamless single sign-on during AD Connect Installation.

Requires Azure AD Subscription, AD Connect installed on-premises, Pass through agent installed on-premises, Azure SQL Database, Azure Service Bus and on-premises Active Directory.

Federated Identity with ADFS: Identity is maintained in both cloud and on-premises. User Authentication happen on-premises by Active Directory Federation Services (ADFS) server against local Active Directory.

AD Connect installed on-premises with Federation with ADFS option, Synchronizes on premises Active Directory users to Azure AD. In this case Password Hash of users are not Synchronized.

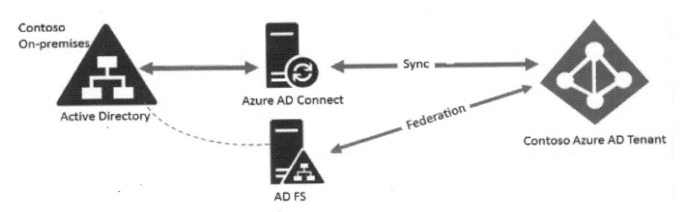

Active Directory Federation Services (ADFS) server installed on-premises and ADFS component in AD Connect, federate the 2 directories which results in one-way trust with Azure AD **Trusting** on-premises ADFS. User Login happens in cloud but user authentication is redirected to on-premises ADFS.

Requires Azure AD Subscription, AD Connect Installed on-premises, on-premises Active Directory Domain Services (AD DS) and on-premises Active Directory Federation services (AD FS).

ADFS option is used by organizations to address complex deployments such as enforcement of on-premises AD sign-in policy, Single Sign-on (SSO) and smart card or 3rd party MFA.

Federated Identity with PingFederate: Identity is maintained in both cloud and on-premises. User Authentication happen on-premises by PingFederate Instance against local Active Directory or any other LDAP Server.

AD Connect installed on-premises with Federation with PingFederate option, Synchronizes on premises users to Azure AD. In this case Password Hash of users are not Synchronized.

Requires Azure AD Subscription, AD Connect Installed on-premises, on-premises Active Directory and on-premises PingFederate Instance.

Federated Identity with 3rd Party Identity Manager: Identity is maintained in both cloud and on-premises. User Authentication happen on-premises by 3rd party identity manager server against local Active Directory.

3rd Party Identity Manager can be from Okta, Big-IP Access Policy Manager & IBM Tivoli Federated Identity Manager etc.

Requires Azure AD Subscription, AD Connect installed on-premises, on-premises Active Directory and on-premises 3rd Party Identity Manager.

Important Note: In this case Federation between 3rd party identity manager and Azure AD requires integration to be provided by 3rd party identity manager.

Components of AD Connect

Azure Active Directory Connect is made up of **three components**: the **synchronization services**, the optional **Active Directory Federation Services (ADFS)** component and the monitoring component named **Azure AD Connect Health**.

Synchronization Service

It synchronizes identity data between your on-premises Active Directory and Azure AD. The synchronization feature of Azure AD Connect has two components.

1. The on-premises component Azure AD Connect sync, also called sync engine.
2. The service residing in Azure AD also known as Azure AD Connect sync service.

Synchronization service copies usernames and password hash from on-premises active directory to Azure AD tenant. This allows users to authenticate against Azure AD using there on-premises credentials.

Note: We will not discuss ADFS here as we have already covered it in previuos section and we also cover it in next sections.

AD Connect Health

Azure AD Connect Health helps you monitor and gain insight into your on-premises identity infrastructure and the synchronization services.

AD Connect Health Monitors - Active Directory Federation Servers (AD FS), Azure AD Connect servers (Sync Engine), Active Directory Domain Controllers (AD DS).

Azure Connect Health requires Azure AD Premium edition. You also require an agent on each of your on-premises identity servers.

Figure below shows Azure AD Connect Health portal which is used to view alerts, performance monitoring, usage analytics, and other information for your identity Infrastructure.

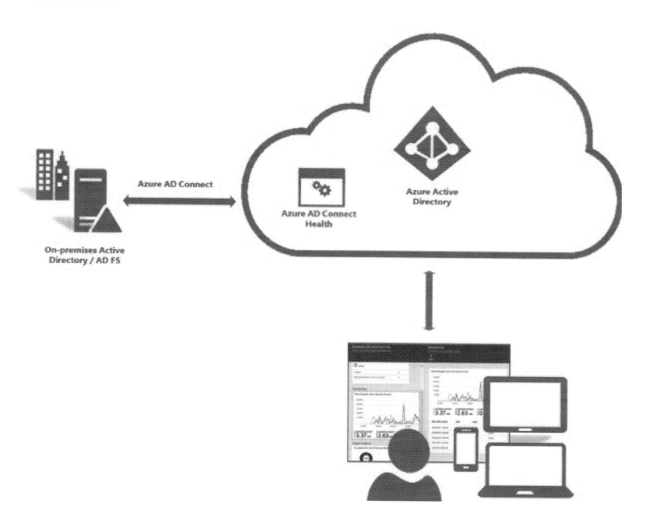

The AD Connect Health Portal URL is at https://aka.ms/aadconnecthealth. On the Portal you can see the identity services which are being monitored and the severity level of the services. You can drill down on the service further by clicking one of the tiles. Figure bellows AD Connect Health Portal dashboard showing monitoring of ADFS, AD Connect & AD DS.

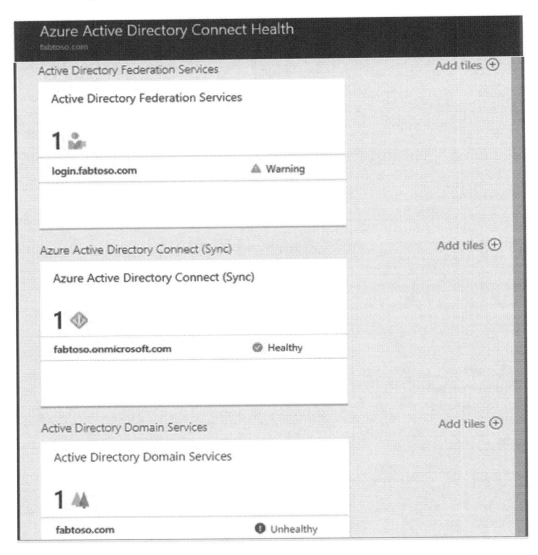

Requirements for deploying AD Connect Server

Hardware Requirement for AD Connect Server

CPU: Dual Core 1.6 GHz or Higher.
Memory: 4GB or Higher (Depends on number of objects in Active Directory).
HDD: 70 GB to 500 GB (Depends on number of objects in Active Directory).
Table below shows Database, Memory and HDD requirement for AD Connect based on number of objects in Active Directory. CPU Requirement remains same.

Number of objects in AD	Database	Memory	HDD
Upto 50000	SQL Server Express or SQL Server	4 GB	70 GB
50,000–100,000	SQL Server Express or SQL Server	16 GB	100 GB
100,000–300,000	SQL Server	32 GB	300 GB
300,000–600,000	SQL Server	32 GB	450 GB
More than 600,000	SQL Server	32 GB	500 GB

Software Requirements for AD Connect Server

Operating System: Recommended is to install on windows Server 2008 R2 SP1 Standard or higher version. The Azure AD Connect server must have .NET Framework 4.5.1 or later and Microsoft PowerShell 3.0 or later installed.
Database: SQL Server Express or SQL Server. By default a SQL Server 2012 Express is installed that enables you to manage approximately 100,000 objects. To manage more than 100000 objects you need SQL Server 2008 onwards.
Note 1: Certain feature like group managed service account require Windows server 2012.

DNS Requirement (Important Concept)

The Azure AD Connect server needs DNS resolution for both intranet and internet.

Exercise 116: Install AD Connect with Pass Hash Synchronisation

We will install AD connect with Password Hash Synchronisation option on VM OnPremAD. VM OnPremAD was configured with AD DS role in Chapter 3, Exercise 32.

We will use User1 to connect to Azure AD during AD Connect Installation. User1 was created in Exercise 84. AD connect will synchronise on-premises users to Azure AD Tenant. You cannot use Subscription user with MS Hotmail Account.

Create 2 Users (Test1 & Test 2) in AD DS to be synced with Azure AD Tenant

1. RDP to VM OnPremAD.
2. Open Active Directory Users and Computers>Click on domain AZX0X.local> Right Click Users>New>User>Create User pane opens. Create 2 Users Test1 & Test2.

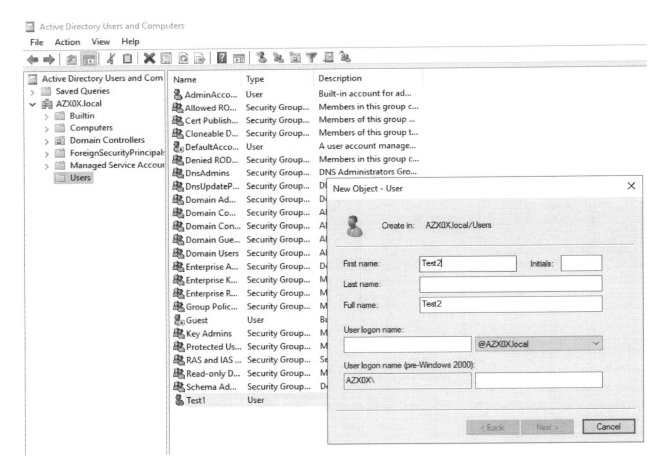

3. Close Active Directory Users and Computers.

Download and Install AD Connect

1. RDP to VM OnPremAD.
2. Open Internet Explorer and log on to https://portal.azure.com with **User1** Credentials user1@harinderkohli543hotmail.onmicrosoft.com.
3. Click Azure Active Directory in left pane>In Azure AD Dashboard click AD Connect in left pane>In right pane Click Download Azure AD Connect>New Browser windows opens> click download to download AD Connect.

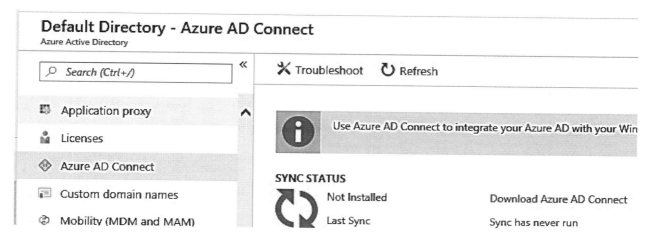

4. Click the AD Connect downloaded file to start the installation>AD Connect Installation wizard opens>Select License check box>Click Continue (Not shown).

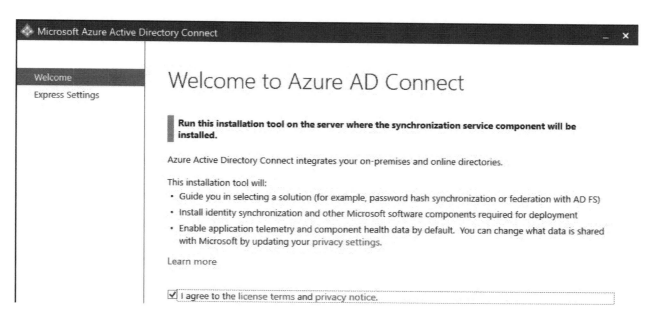

4. Click Continue>Express Setting Installation option opens> Click Customize in bottom.

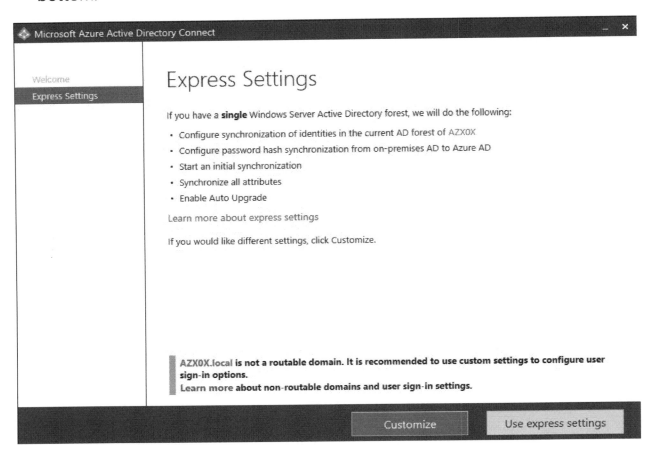

5. Install Required Components pane opens>Click Install in Bottom right (Not shown)> Installation starts. (Don't select any components here).

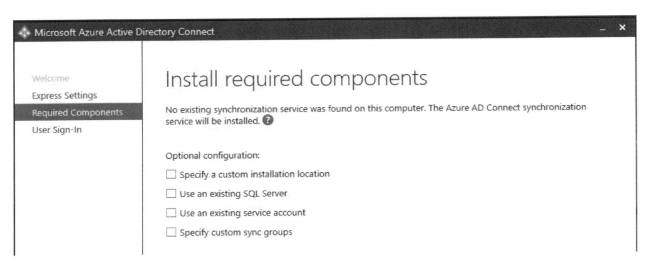

6. User Sign-in pane opens>Select Password Hash-Synchronization>Click next.

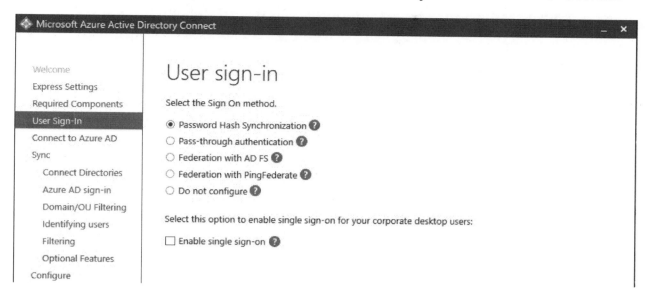

Note: There is Enable single sign-on check box. This enables seamless single sign-on for domain users. If you are logged on to on-premises Domain controller then you can log on to Azure AD without signing again.

7. In Connect to Azure AD pane Enter **User1** Credential and password>click next.

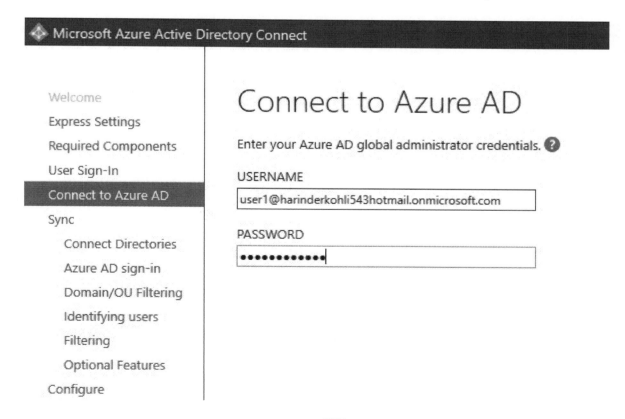

8. Connect Directories pane select Active directory and enter domain name AZX0X.local. This domain was configured in Chapter 3, Exercise 32.

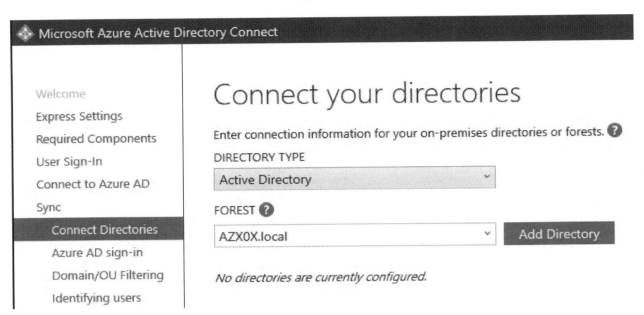

9. Click Add Directory>AD Forest Account pane pops up>Enter Administrator credentials in the format **AZX0X.local\AdminAccount**>Enter password>Click Ok>Click Next.

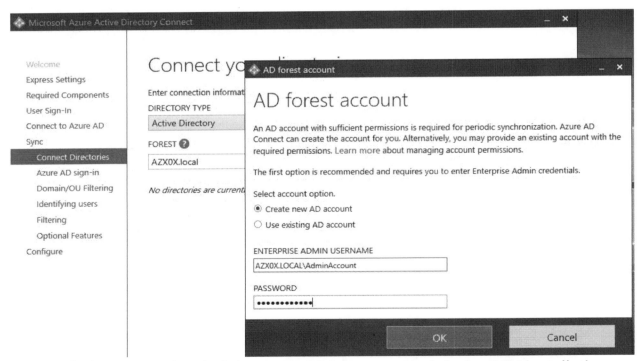

Note: AdminAccount is administrator which was created during VM installation.

10. In Azure AD sign-in pane>check mark Continue without matching all UPN suffixes to verified domains>Click Next.

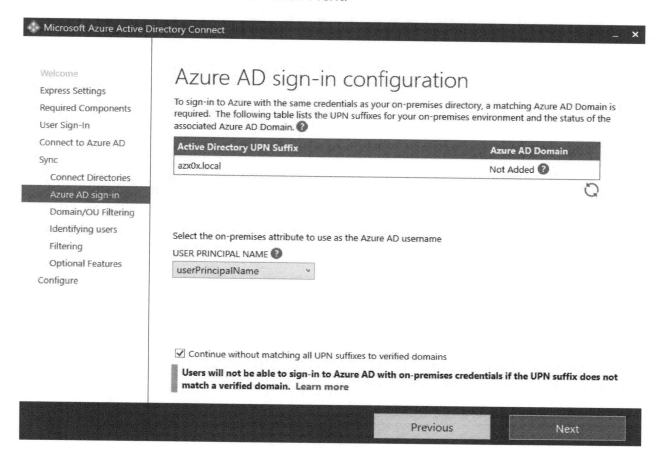

11. In Domain and OU Filtering pane>Select Sync all domains and OUs> Click Next. This allows you to select specific OUs or all OUs.

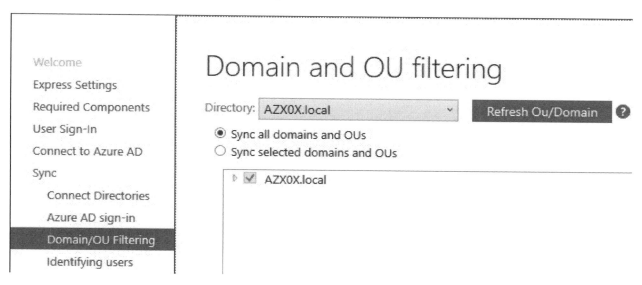

12.In identifying Users pane select the default values>Click next.

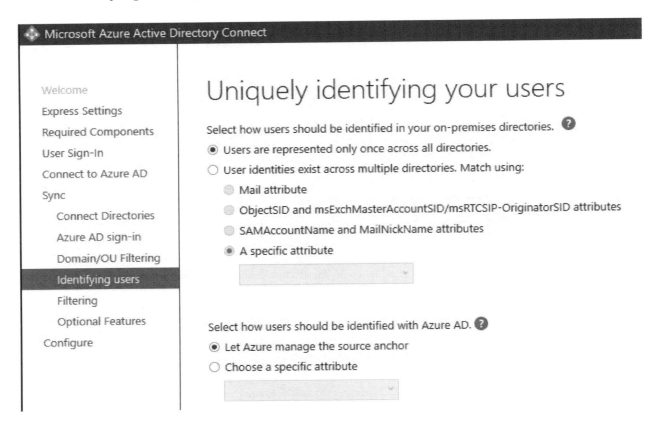

13.In Filtering pane select the default and click next.

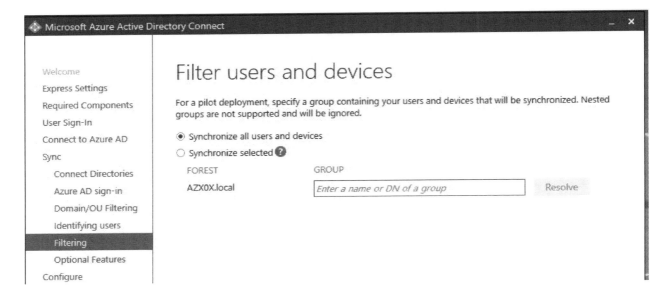

14.In optional make sure default option Password Hash Synchronization is selected and click next.

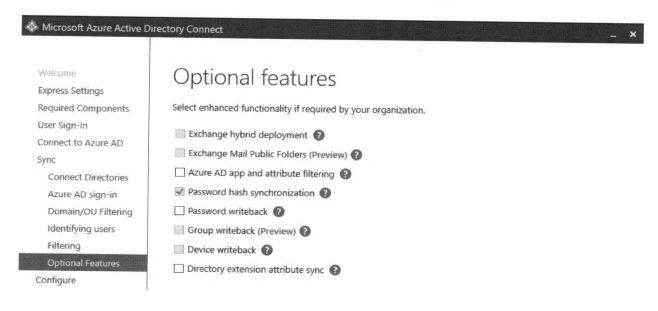

Note: Note the password Write Back Option. We will discuss it in next section.

15.In Configure select the default option and click install.

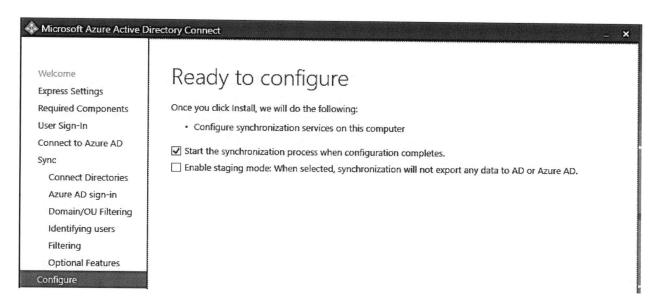

16.After Configuration Process gets complete click exit to close the Azure AD Connect Installation wizard.

17.In Windows VM OnPremAD logout User1 and close RDP session.

Exercise117: Check Users Test1 & Test2 synchronization to Azure AD

In Azure AD Portal Click Azure Active Directory in left pane>Azure AD Dashboard opens>Click Users in left pane>User Dashboard opens> You can see Test1 and Test2 users are synchronized to Azure AD and the source is Windows Server AD. User id have become Test1@harinderkohli543hotmail.onmicrosoft.com.

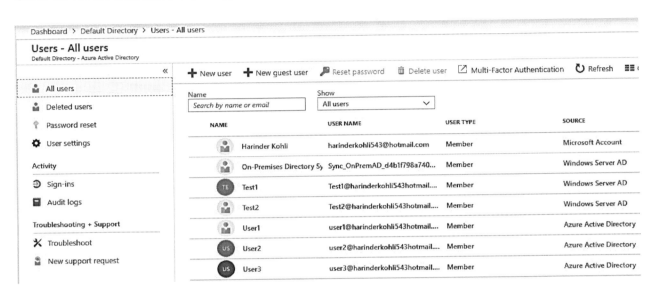

Exercise 118: Check AD Connect options

In this exercise we will check options available to Operate and configure AD connect after Installation of AD Connect.

1. RDP to windows VM OnPremAD> click Start icon>Under AD Connect you can see following 4 applications installed.
   AD Connect.
   Synchronization Rules Editor.
   Synchronization Service.
   Synchronization Service Webservice Connector Config.

2. Click on AD connect icon on desktop which was installed in Previous exercise>AD Connect welcome screen opens>Click Configure> You can see various task available for configuration.

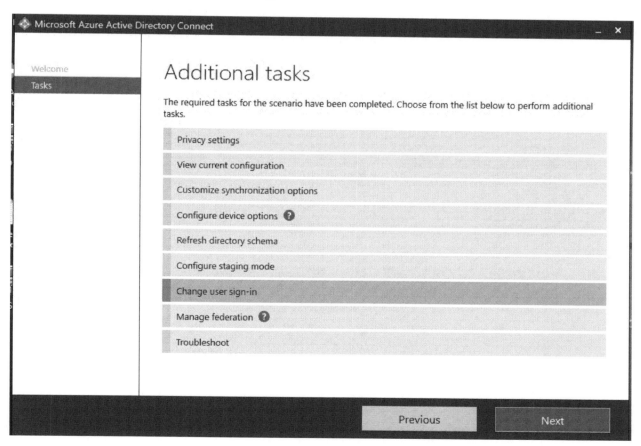

Note 1: Readers are advised to go through all tasks by selecting a task and clicking Next.

3. On VM OnPremAD click Start icon>Under AD Connect Click Synchronization Service> Synchronization Service Manager opens.

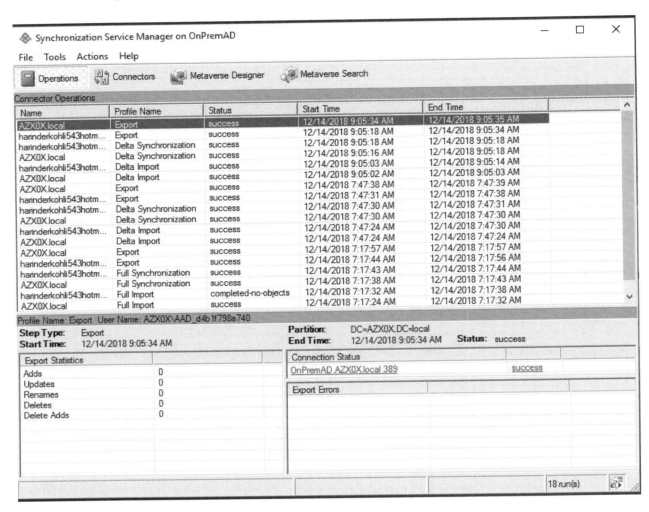

Readers are advised to click connectors tab and check the options available.

Exercise 119: AD Connect Health

In this exercise we will monitor Sync services and Active Directory Domain Services (AD DS) running on VM OnPremAD. To Monitor AD DS we will download and install AD Connect Health agent on VM OnPremAD.

Accessing AD Connect Health Dashboard

1. Open Browser and go to the AD Connect Health Portal URL at https://aka.ms/aadconnecthealth or Go to Azure Active Directory Dashboard >Click Azure AD Connect in left pane>Click Azure AD Connect Health in Right pane under Health and Analytics> Azure AD Connect Health pane opens.

Azure Active Directory Connect Health - Quick start
harinderkohli543hotmail (Default Directory)

«	**What's New**
📇 Quick start	Azure AD Connect Health for Sync - Diagnose and remediate duplicated attribute sync errors from the portal is now in preview!
Azure Active Directory Connect (Sync)	Learn more about release history
ⓘ Sync errors	
◈ Sync services	**Get tools**
Active Directory Federation Services	Download and install Azure AD Connect Health Agents to get health and usage information of your on premise services.
🔧 AD FS services	- Download Azure AD Connect Health Agent for AD FS
Active Directory Domain Services	- Download Azure AD Connect (configures Azure AD Connect Health agent for sync)
🔺 AD DS services	- Download Azure AD Connect Health Agent for AD DS
Configure	**Provide feedback**
⚙ Settings	Report an issue, ask a question or provide feedback on the Azure Active Directory Connect Health Service
👤 Role based access control (IAM)	
TROUBLESHOOTING + SUPPORT	**Learn more**
✗ Troubleshoot	Documentation and FAQs for using Azure AD Connect Health
📋 New support request	

Note 1: In left pane you can see 3 Services which can be monitored – Sync Service, Active Directory Federation Services and Active Directory Domain Services.
Note 2: From right pane you can download AD Connect Health Agents.

Download and Install Agent for AD DS on VM OnPremAD

1. RDP to VM OnPremAD> Open Browser and log on to AD Connect Health Portal URL at https://aka.ms/aadconnecthealth
2. In Right pane Click Download Azure AD Connect <u>Health Agents</u> AD DS>New Browser window opens>Click download and save exe file on desktop.

3. Click exe file downloaded>Run>Install>After Setup is complete>Click Configure now>Some PowerShell scripts are automatically run and Sign in to your account box opens>Enter **User1 Credentials** and click next>enter password and click sign in.

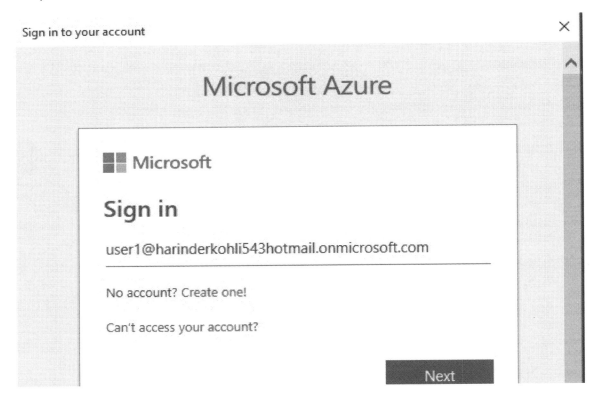

Agent registration completed successfully as shown.

```
2018-12-14 10:01:23.262 Started agent services successfully...
2018-12-14 10:01:28.747 Agent registration completed successfully.

Detailed log file created in temporary directory:
C:\Users\AdminAccount\AppData\Local\Temp\2\AdHealthAddsAgentConfiguration.2018-12-14_09-59-21.log
PS C:\Users\AdminAccount\Desktop>
```

Monitoring Active Directory Domain Services

1. Go to Azure AD Connect Health Dashboard> Click AD DS Services in left pane> In Right pane you can see that Domain Controller is Healthy.

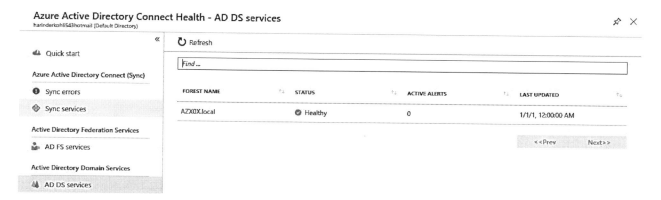

2. In Right pane click the domain name>Domain pane open>Scroll down to see more options.

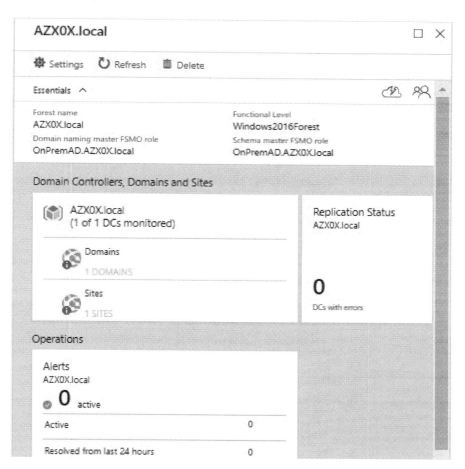

Monitoring Sync Services

1. Go to Azure AD Connect Health Dashboard> Click Sync Services in left pane> In Right pane you can see that sync status is Healthy.

2. In Right pane click the sync service>Sync service pane open>Scroll down to see more options.

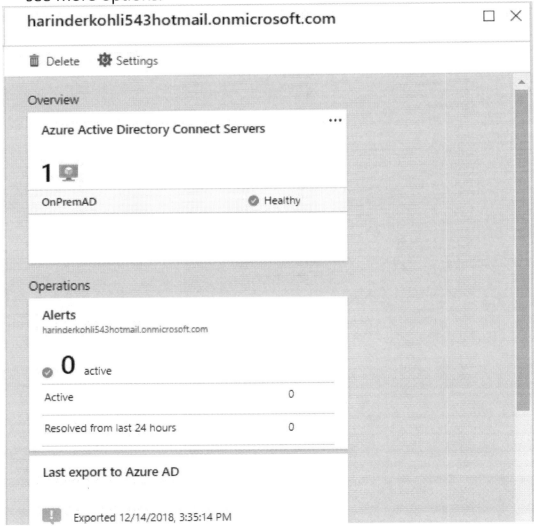

Seamless Single Sign-on

Note: Enable single sign-on option is only available for Password Hash Synchronization option and Pass-through Authentication option. It is not applicable for Federation with ADFS option.

With seamless single sign-on users who are already logged on to their corporate network on domain-joined machines can sign on to Azure AD without entering there on-premises password again.

The advantage of this feature is that it can be enabled without creating any complex on-premises deployments and network configuration as in the case of Federation with ADFS.

Enabling Seamless Single sign-on Step 1

Seamless Single sign-on is enabled during installation of AD Connect with either Password Hash Synchronization option or Pass-through Authentication option as shown in figure below. You to need to just check the Enable single sign-on box.

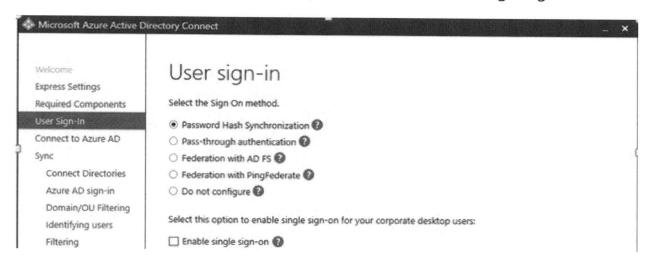

Enabling Seamless Single sign-on Step 2 - Configure the Intranet Zone for client machines

To ensure that the client sign-ins automatically in the intranet zone you need to ensure that two URLs are part of the intranet zone. This ensures that the domain joined computer automatically sends a Kerberos ticket to Azure AD when it is connected to the corporate network.

Create or Edit existing Group Policy which applies to all synchronized users.

1. Open the Group Policy Management tool on Domain Controller Machine.
2. Edit the Default Domain Group policy that will be applied to all users.
3. Navigate to **User Configuration\Administrative Templates\Windows Components\Internet Explorer\Internet Control Panel\Security Page** and select **Site to Zone Assignment List** as shown below.
4. Enable the policy, and enter the following item in the dialog box.

Value: `https://autologon.microsoftazuread-sso.com`
Data: 1

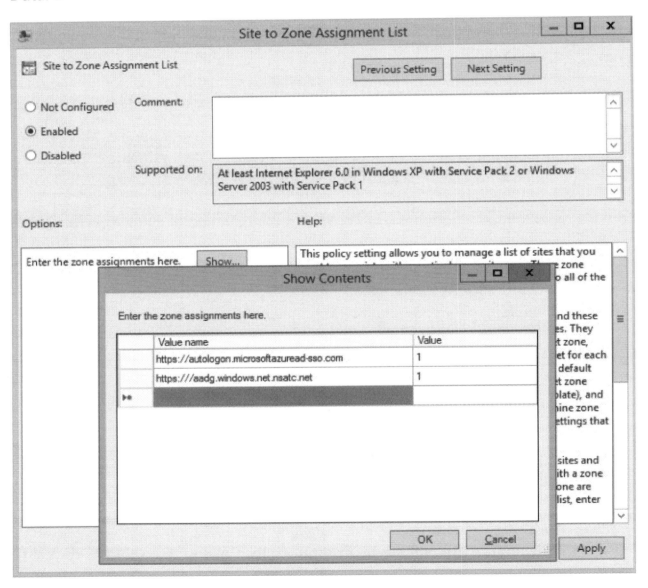

Key Features of Seamless Single sign-on

1. Users are automatically signed into both on-premises and cloud-based applications.
2. Works with Password Hash Synchronization or Pass-through Authentication option only.
3. Register Domain joined non-Windows 10 devices with Azure AD to **enable device based conditional access.** This capability needs you to install version 2.1 or later of the workplace-join client. Version 2.1 has added support for Azure Active Directory Seamless Single Sign On (https://aka.ms/hybrid/sso).

Note: For Windows 10, the recommendation is to use Azure AD Join for the optimal single sign-on experience with Azure AD.

Figure below shows using seamless single sign-on users logged on to domain joined machines can access Azure AD application without entering there passwords.

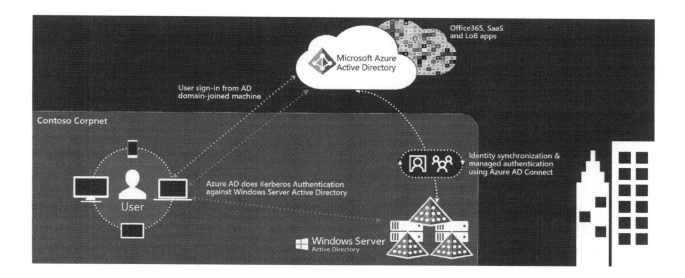

Password Writeback

Password Writeback is a feature enabled with Azure AD Connect that allows password changes in the cloud to be written back to an existing on-premises directory in real time.

This feature can be enabled during AD Connect Installation.

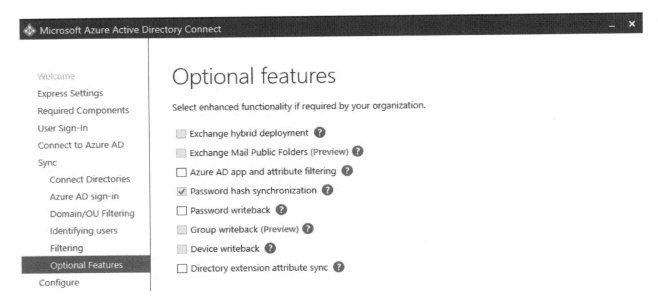

Password writeback is supported in following options only:

1. Active Directory Federation Services
2. Password hash synchronization
3. Pass-through authentication

License Requirement for Password Writeback option

Self-Service Password Reset/Change/Unlock with on-premises Writeback is a premium feature of Azure AD and requires Azure AD Premium P1 or Azure AD Premium P2 licenses.

AD Connect with Federation with ADFS option

Federation is a collection of domains that have established trust for shared access to a set of resources. Trust can be one way or 2 way. Trust with ADFS option includes authentication and authorization. This results that all user authentication occurs on-premises. This method allows administrators to implement more rigorous levels of access control including implementing on-premises password policies. This method also enables Single sign-on.

In ADFS, identity federation is established between two organizations by establishing trust between two security realms. A federation server on one side (Account side) authenticates the users against Active Directory Domain Services and then issues a token containing a series of claims about user. On the other side, resource side another federation server validates the token and issues another for the local servers to accept the claimed identity. This allows a system to provide controlled Access to its resources to a user that belongs to another security realm without requiring the user to authenticate directly to the system and without the two systems sharing a database of user identities or passwords.

Trust can be one-way or two-way trust. In one-way trust, trusted organization authenticates and issues claim based token to user of trusted organization who are connecting to trusting organization for resource access. In this way trusting organization need not maintain the identity infrastructure.

Note: Federation option is only available with ADFS and Ping Federate. ADFS or Ping Federate are option is chosen during AD Connect installation.

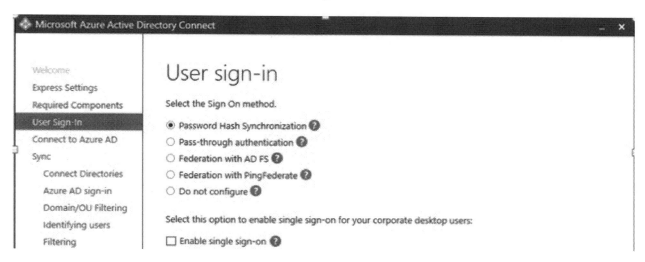

AD Connect installed on-premises with Federation with ADFS option, Synchronizes on premises Active Directory users to Azure AD. In this case Password Hash of users are not Synchronized.

Active Directory Federation Services (ADFS) server installed on-premises and ADFS component in AD Connect, federate the 2 directories which results in one-way trust with Azure AD **Trusting** on-premises ADFS. User Login happens in cloud but user authentication is redirected to on-premises ADFS.

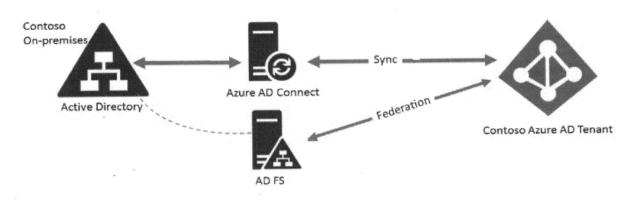

Federation can be used to configure a hybrid environment using an on-premises AD infrastructure. This can be used by organizations to address complex deployments, such as enforcement of on-premises AD sign-in policy, SSO and smart card or 3rd party MFA.

Single sign-on with ADFS

ADFS also enables single sign-on. Users who are already logged on to their corporate network can sign on to Azure AD without entering there on-premises password again.

Figure below show users accessing Corporate resources and Azure AD from within or outside the Corporate Headquaters using a single identity. Single sign-on is also enabled.

Note 1: Web Application proxy server is required when users are accessing from outside the Company premises.

Note 2: AD connect is not shown in the figure but is always required.

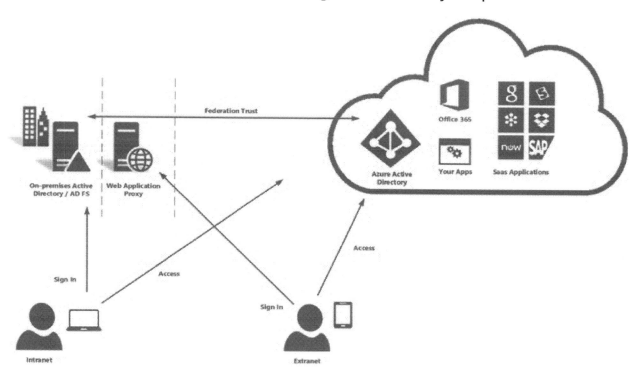

Installation of AD Connect with ADFS Option

Pre-Requisite

19 Azure AD Tenant.

20 On-premises Active Directory Domain Services (AD DS).

21 On-premises ADFS Server or ADFS Server farm. ADFS server requires SSL certificate. ADFS server also requires DNS records for the AD FS federation service name (for example adfs.test.com) for both the intranet (your internal DNS server) and the extranet (public DNS through your domain registrar). For the intranet DNS record, ensure that you use A records and not CNAME records.

22 On-Premises ADFS Web Application Proxy Server (Required only if users are accessing resources from outside the corporate HQ). ADFS Web Application Proxy Server requires SSL certificate.

AD Connect Installation

You need to install AD connect with Federation with AD FS option. The Azure AD Connect server needs DNS resolution for both intranet and internet.

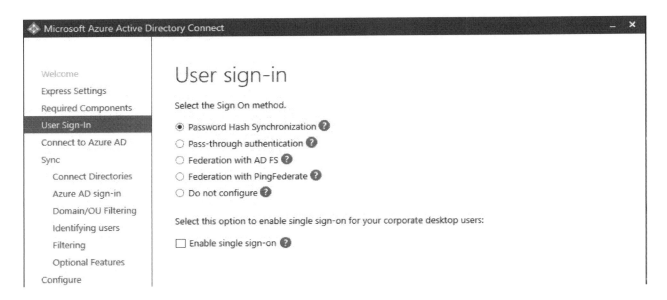

IDFIX tool

IdFix is used to perform **discovery** and **remediation** of identity objects and their attributes in an on-premises Active Directory Domain Services (AD DS) environment in preparation for migration to Azure Active Directory.

The purpose of IdFix is to reduce the time involved in remediating the Active Directory errors reported by Azure AD Connect.

Download IDFIX Tool
https://www.microsoft.com/en-us/download/details.aspx?id=36832

Installation Requirement

Windows 7, Windows 10 or Windows Server 2008R2 and above.
Net 4.0 must running on the workstation running the IDFIX application.

Chapter 13 Azure Subscription Management

This Chapter covers following Topic Lessons

- Azure Subscription
- Subscription Usage & Quota
- Cost or Spend Analysis
- Monitor Azure Spend and Create Billing Alarms using Budgets
- Identify unused or underutilized Resources and Optimize Azure Cost
- Implementing IT Governance using Azure Policy
- Assign Administrative Permissions using Azure AD Directory Role
- Assigning Administrative Permissions using Role Based Access Control

This Chapter covers following Lab Exercises

- Exploring Subscription Dashboard
- Checking Subscription Usage & Quota
- Cost Analysis in Subscription Dashboard
- Explore Cost Analysis in Cost Management Dashboard
- Create Budgets with Billing Notification alarms
- Advisor Recommendations
- Applying Azure Policy at Subscription Level
- Test the Allowed Virtual Machine SKU Policy
- Assign User3 Directory role of Limited Administrator
- Check User3 Access by creating a User
- Assigning User3 Role of Reader in Resource Group
- Check User3 Access level in Azure Portal
- Adding Co-Administrators to the subscription
- Check User3 Access level in Azure Portal

Chapter Topology

In this chapter we will explore Azure Subscription Dashboard and monitor Azure spend through options like Cost Analysis and Budget feature. We will configure Azure policy at subscription level. We will also configure RBAC.

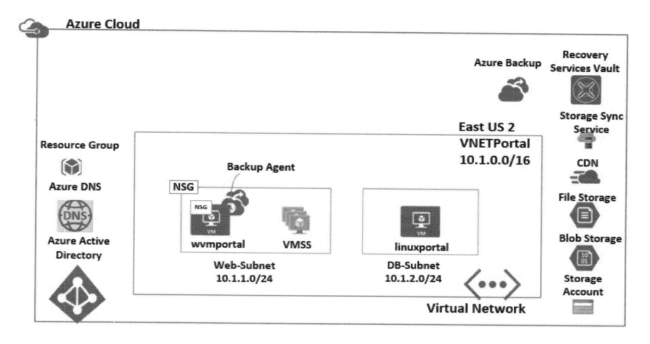

Azure Subscription

Management of Subscription happens through subscription dashboard.

Exercise120: Exploring Subscription Dashboard

3. In Azure Portal Click **Cost Management + Billing** in left pane> Cost Management + Billing Dashboard opens>Click Subscriptions in left pane.

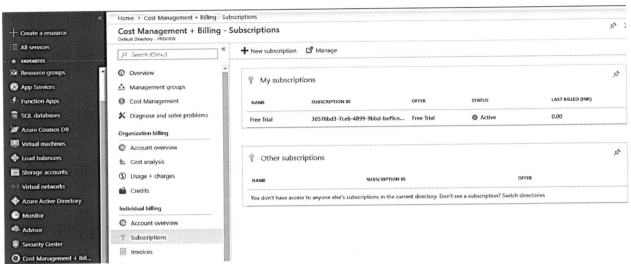

4. In right pane click your subscription>Subscription Dashboard opens.

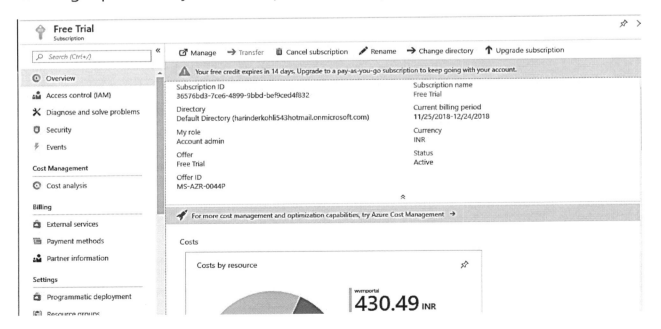

Note: Readers are advised to go through all options in Subscription dashboard and Cost Management + Billing Dashboard.

Subscription Usage & Quota

Each subscription has quota cap for resources. Resource usage is tracked per subscription. If you reach a quota cap, you can request an increase.

Usage +Quota tab in left pane will show you the usage as well as the quota associated with that resource.

Exercise 121: Checking Subscription Usage & Quota

In Subscription Dashboard Click Usage + quotas in left pane>In right pane you can see Usage + quotas for various resources> Select Microsoft.Compute from Dropdown box in Provider option.

Figure below shows usage and quota for Microsoft Compute only. You have the option to select other resources also. Readers are advised to click the drop down boxes and check other options available.

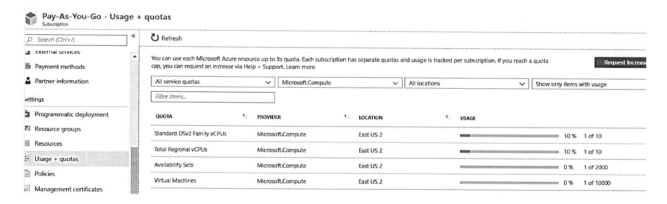

Cost or Spend Analysis

Cost Analysis helps understand where costs originated within the organization. You can view monthly, Quarterly or Custom dates cost in Cost Analysis. You can view Total cost in subscription or Cost by resource type or Resource Group or custom cost using tags.

Exercise in Resource group Chapter will show how to create Cost Analysis using Tags.

You can view Cost Analysis in Subscription or in Cost Management dashboard. Cost Analysis in Cost Management dashboard gives much more detailed analysis. Cost Analysis in Cost Management dashboard is only available for Enterprise Agreement (EA) customers.

Exercise 122: Cost Analysis in Subscription Dashboard

In Azure Portal Click Cost Management + Billing in left pane> Cost Management + Billing Pane opens> Click Subscription in left Pane>In Right pane select your subscription> Subscription Dashboard opens>Click Cost Analysis in left pane. Cost Analysis tab in left pane shows the total cost incurred during the billing period as well as cost by resources.

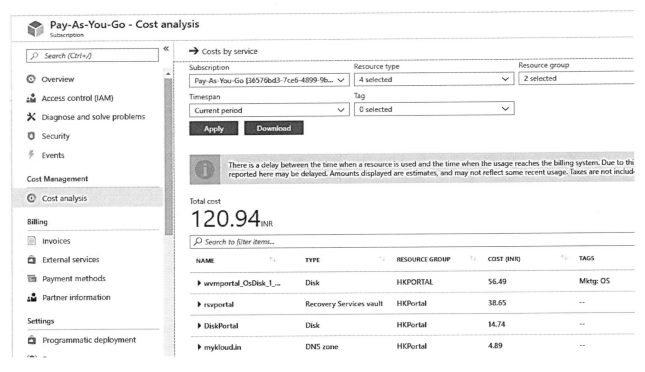

Cost Analysis by Resource Type: You can also see total cost by Resource type like VM etc by selecting Resource type from Drop Down Box or cost by Resource Group or cost by Tags from Drop down box.

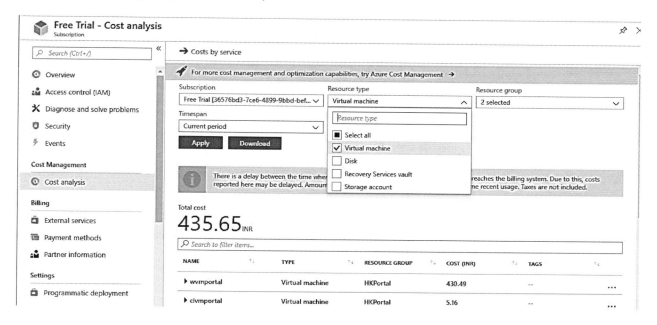

Exercise 123: Exploring Cost Analysis in Cost Management Dashboard

1. In Azure Portal Click Cost Management + Billing in left pane> Cost Management + Billing Pane opens> Click Cost Management in left pane>Cost Analysis and Budgets tabs are greyed out and are only available for EA customers.

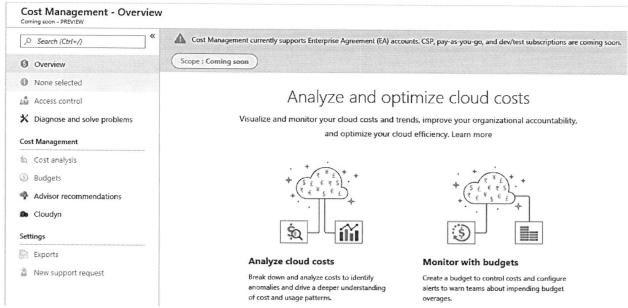

2. Click Cost Analysis in left pane>You can see Cost analysis Graphically.

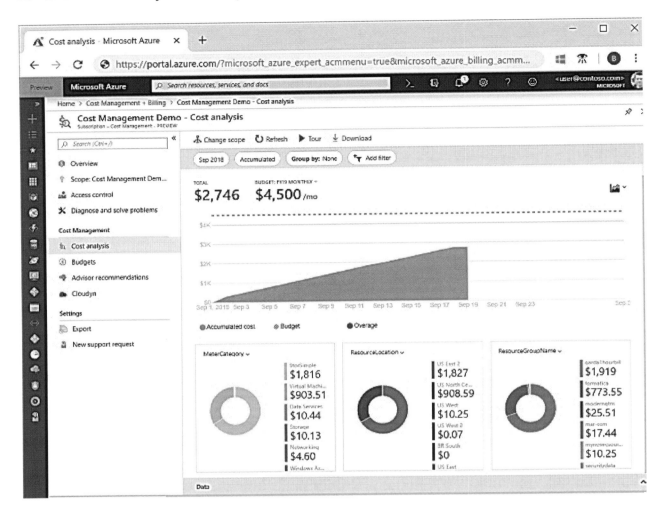

Monitor Azure Spend and Create Billing Alarms using Budgets

Budgets feature in Cost Management helps you proactively monitor Cloud cost spending over time. You can use budgets to compare and track spending as you analyze costs.

Budgets feature is available to Azure Enterprise Agreement (EA) customers only. This feature is not available in Pay as you go or Free trial Subscription.

When the budget thresholds are exceeded, notifications Billing alarms are triggered. Budget feature dosen't affects consumption and none of the resources are stopped.

You can create monthly, quarterly or Yearly Budgets.

Exercise 124: Create Budgets with Billing Notification alarms

1. In Azure Portal Click Cost Management + Billing in left pane> Cost Management + Billing Pane opens> Click Cost Management in left pane>Cost Management Pane opens. Note the Budgets tab in left pane.

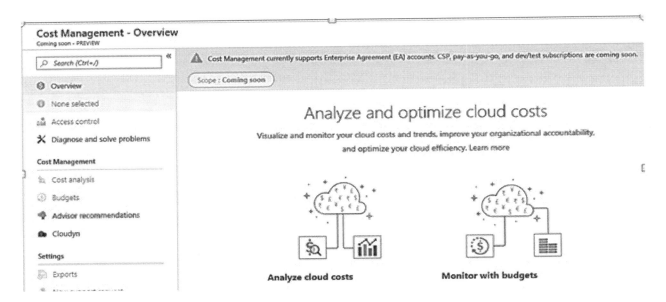

Note 1: Budget Tab in left pane is not available for Free Trial or Pay as you go subscription.

Note 2: For This Exercise I will be using Screenshots from Azure Docs.

2. Click Budgets in left pane>Budgets pane opens in right pane.

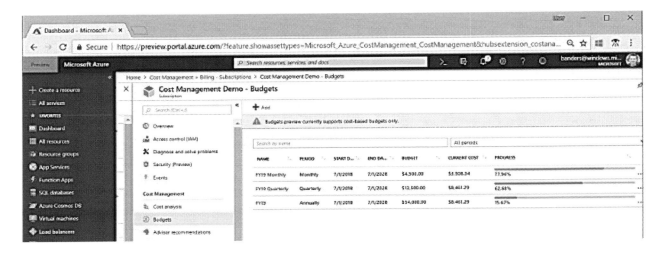

3. Click + Add in right pane> Create Budget blade opens> Enter a name> Enter
   Budget amount> Select Time Frame period (Monthly, Quarterly or Yearly)
   from dropdown box. I selected Monthly> Select Budget start and Expiration
   Date> Set **Billing alert condition** in terms of percentage of Budget. This will
   trigger an email notification alerts if the percentage threshold is reached>
   Add an alert email and click create.

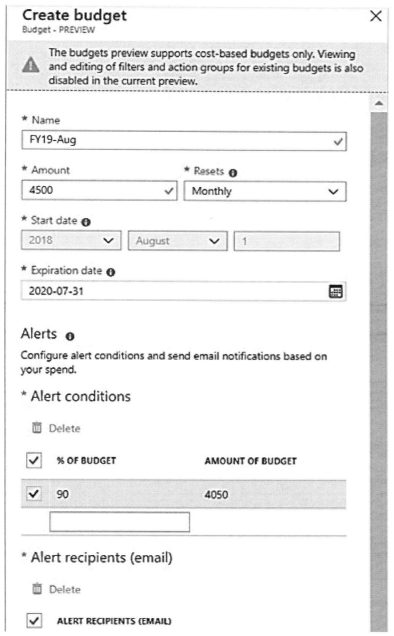

This will create a Monthly Budget of 4500 USD. If Cloud spending reaches 90% of
4500 USD a Billing alert email will be send.

4. Similarly create quarterly and Yearly Budgets.
5. In Budget pane you can see the current spending against the Budget. It shows current Monthly Cloud spend is USD 4151 against a budget of USD 4500. It is still within the budget but has crossed the 90% Billing Alert Threshold. Whereas Quarterly and Yearly Budget are within budget and also have not crossed the Billing Alert threshold.

NAME	RESET ...	START...	END D...	BUDGET	CURRENT C...	PROGRESS	
FY19 Monthly	Monthly	7/1/2018	7/1/2028	$4,500.00	$4,151.29	92.25%	...
FY19 Quarterly	Quarterly	7/1/2018	7/1/2028	$13,500.00	$9,104.24	67.44%	...
FY19	Annually	7/1/2018	7/1/2028	$54,000.00	$9,104.24	16.86%	...

Identify unused or underutilized Resources and Optimize Azure Cost

Azure Advisor Recommendations identifies idle and underutilized resources. It then gives recommendations to optimize the Azure Cost Spend.

Example: Optimizing Azure Cost Spend on Virtual Machines

Azure Advisor monitors your virtual machine usage for 14 days and then identifies underutilized virtual machines. Virtual Machines whose CPU utilization is five percent or less and network usage is seven MB or less for four or more days are considered low-utilization virtual machines.
The 5% or less CPU utilization setting is the default, but you can adjust the settings.

It will then give you recommendations to change the size of the Virtual Machine to save on Potential Cost or shutdown underutilized virtual machines to save cost.

Exercise 125: Advisor Recommendations

1. In Azure Portal scroll down and click Cost Management + Billing in left pane >Cost Management>Advisor recommendations.

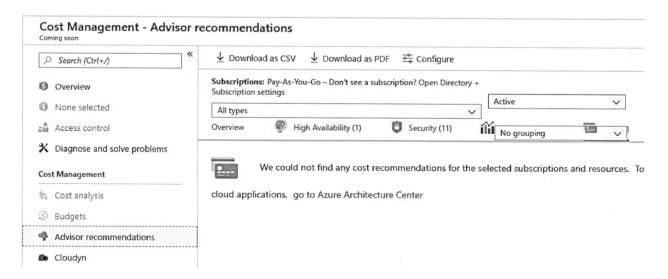

Note: My Subscription did not had any cost recommendation for Virtual Machines. In next step I will use screen shot from Azure Docs.

2. In Recommendation details in Advisor Recommendation dashboard click Resize the Virtual Machine. In the following example, the option chosen resizes current size to a DS13_V2. **The recommendation saves $551.30/month or $6,615.60/year.** This below screen shot is taken from Azure Docs.

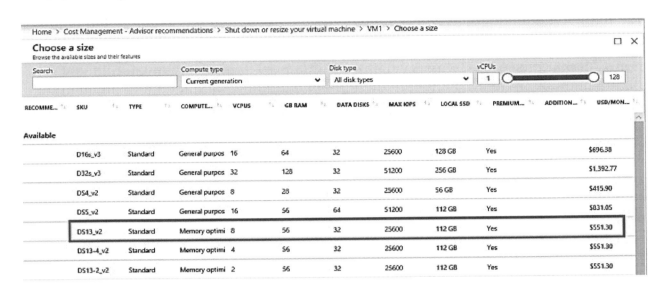

	SKU	TYPE	COMPUTE...	VCPUS	GB RAM	DATA DISKS	MAX IOPS	LOCAL SSD	PREMIUM...	ADDITION...	USD/MON...
Available											
	D16s_v3	Standard	General purpos	16	64	32	25600	128 GB	Yes		$696.38
	D32s_v3	Standard	General purpos	32	128	32	51200	256 GB	Yes		$1,392.77
	DS4_v2	Standard	General purpos	8	28	32	25600	56 GB	Yes		$415.90
	DS5_v2	Standard	General purpos	16	56	64	51200	112 GB	Yes		$831.05
	DS13_v2	Standard	Memory optimi	8	56	32	25600	112 GB	Yes		$551.30
	DS13-4_v2	Standard	Memory optimi	4	56	32	25600	112 GB	Yes		$551.30
	DS13-2_v2	Standard	Memory optimi	2	56	32	25600	112 GB	Yes		$551.30

Implementing IT Governance using Azure Policy

Azure Policy helps in implementing IT Governance in an organisation. IT Governance ensures that your organization is able to achieve its goals through an effective and efficient use of IT. IT Governance involves planning and initiative at strategic level to prevent IT issues from derailing IT projects.

Azure Policy is a managed service in Azure that is used to assign and manage policies. These policies enforce rules so that resources stay compliant with your corporate standards and service level agreements.

Azure Policy Example

You have assigned a policy to allow only a DSv2 SKU size of virtual machines in your environment. Once this policy has been implemented it will only allow DSv2 Size Virtual Machines to be created in your environment. Secondly any non DSv2 Virtual Machine which was their before this Policy was assigned will be marked as non-compliant. Azure Policy runs evaluations of your resources and scans for those not compliant with the policies you have created.

Policy Assignment Scope

Azure Policy can be applied at Subscription, Resource Group or at Management Group level. Policy assignments are inherited by all child resources. However, you can exclude a subscope from the policy assignment.

Built in Policies

There are Hundred built in Policies. Some of the built in policies include:

Allowed Storage Account SKUs: This policy definition has a set of conditions/rules that determine if a storage account that is being deployed is within a set of SKU sizes. Its effect is to deny all storage accounts that do not adhere to the set of defined SKU sizes.

Allowed Resource Type: This policy definition has a set of conditions/rules to specify the resource types that your organization can deploy. Its effect is to deny all resources that are not part of this defined list.

Allowed Locations: This policy enables you to restrict the locations that your organization can specify when deploying resources. Its effect is used to enforce your geo-compliance requirements.

Allowed Virtual Machine SKUs: This policy enables you to specify a set of virtual machine SKUs that your organization can deploy.

Apply tag and its default value: Applies a required tag and its default value if it's not specified by the deploy request.

Not allowed resource types: Prevents a list of resource types from being deployed.

Exercise 126: Applying Azure Policy at Subscription Level

1. Go to Subscription Dashboard>Click Policies in left pane>Policies Blade open>Click Compliance in left pane.

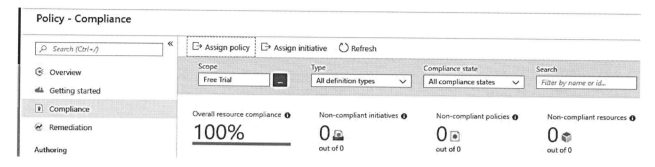

2. Click Assign Policy>Assign Policy Blade opens as shown below.

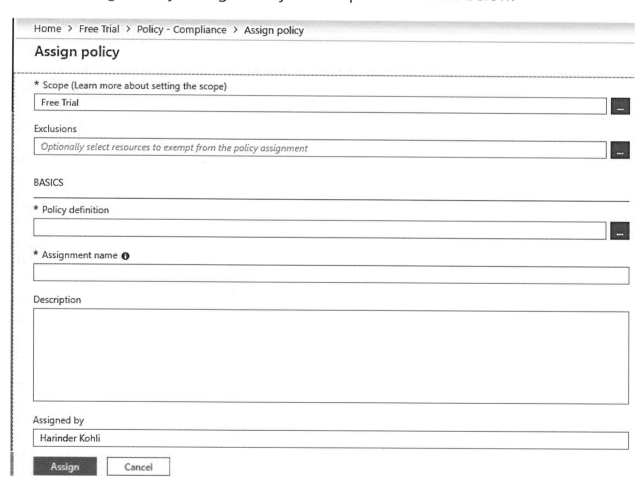

3. Under Policy Defination click ellipsis (...) Box>Available Defination Blade opens>Scroll down and select **Allowed Virtual Machine SKU**s.

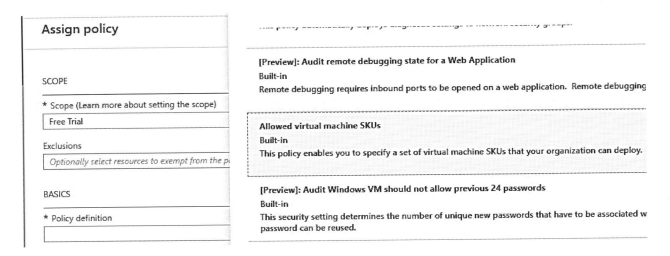

4. Select Allowed Virtual Machine SKU>Click Select> A drop down Box is created in Azure Policy Blade to select the required SKU> Here I selected Standard_D1 SKU>Click Assign in Bottom of the pane (Not shown).

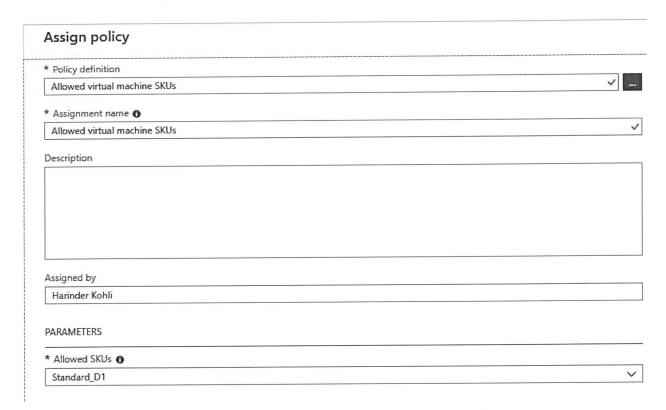

Note: An Assignment name is automatically generated. You can change it.

5. Policies dashboard shows the Policy created. It takes 15-20 minutes for Policy to take effect. You need to refresh it continuously.
   It shows 1 Resource as non-compliant.

6. Click the Policy in the right pane to get the detail of Non-Compliant Resource. wvmportal VM is non-compliant. wvmportal is DS1 size SKU whereas our policy allows Standard D1 type VM.

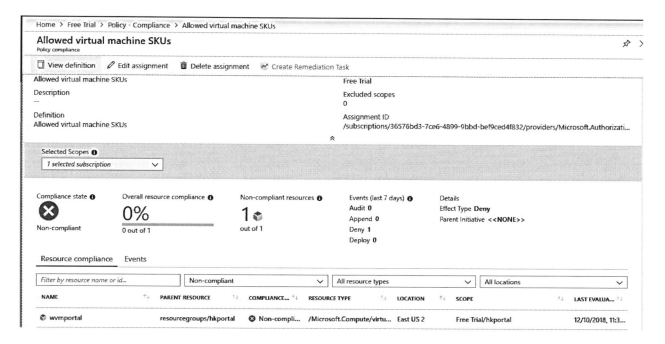

Exercise 127: Test the Allowed Virtual Machine SKU Policy

In this Exercise we will try to create A Series Virtual Machine and see whether system allows or not. Our Policy created in previous exercise at Subscription level allows Standard_D1 Machines only.

1. Click Create a Resource>Compute>Windows Server 2016 Datacenter >Create VM dashboard opens>Select Resource Group HKPortal>enter a name>In size click change size and Select VM size as A1 and enter username and password and click Review + Create> Validation fails and click on it to get the reason> Resource was disallowed by policy and Policy name was Allowed Virtual Machine SKUs. This Policy only allowed Standard_D1 Machines only.

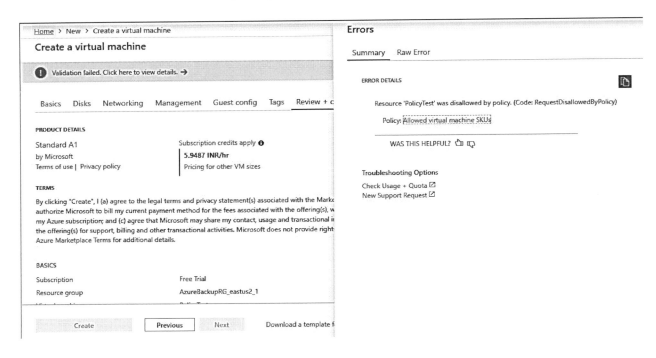

Assign Azure AD Directory Role to Users

User is assigned Directory role during user creation time. You also have the option to change user Directory role from Azure AD User Profile Dashboard.

A user can be assigned one of the following 3 directory roles:

User: User can login to Azure portal but cannot create, manage or view a resource. For a user to create, view or manage a resource in Azure Portal it needs to be assigned permissions Using Role based Access Control (RBAC).

Global Administrator: The Global administrators have full control over all **directory** (Azure AD) resources.

Limited Administrator: Limited administrator role has full access to particular Directory (Azure AD) feature. Following Limited Administrative roles are available in Azure.

Billing Administrator	Exchange Service Administrator	Password Administrator / Helpdesk Administrator
Compliance Administrator	Global Administrator / Company Administrator	Power BI Service Administrator
Conditional Access Administrator	Guest Inviter	Privileged Role Administrator
Dynamics 365 service administrator	Information Protection Administrator	Security Administrator
Device Administrators	Intune Service Administrator	Service Support Administrator
Directory Readers	Mailbox Administrator	SharePoint Service Administrator
Directory Synchronization Accounts	Skype for Business / Lync Service Administrator	
Directory Writers	User Account Administrator	

Note: You can change user Directory role from Azure AD Dashboard.

Exercise 128: Assign User3 Directory role of Limited Administrator

In this Exercise we will assign User3 Directory role of Limited Administrator with role of User Account Administrator. Users with this role can create and manage all aspects of users and Groups. User3 was created in Implementing and Managing Azure AD Chapter 11, Exercise 86 with Directory role of User.

1. In Azure AD Dashboard>Click Users in left pane> All Users blade open>Click User3 in right pane>User3 Profile blade opens>Click Directory Role in left pane>Click +Add Role>Directory Roles Blade opens>Scroll down and select User administrator and click select.

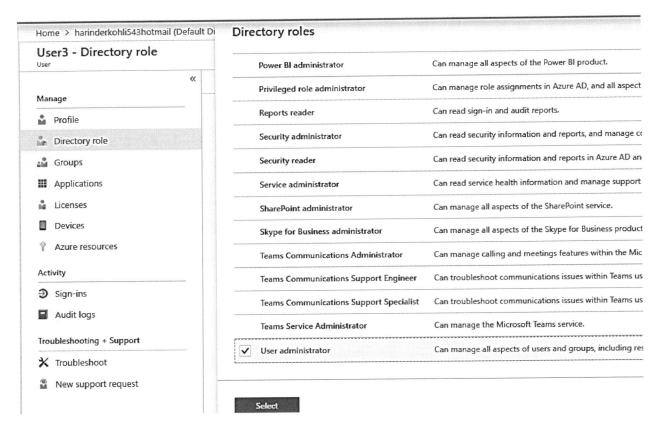

2. User3 is now assigned Directory role of User administrator.

Exercise 129: Check User3 Access by creating a User

In this exercise we will log on to Azure Portal with User3 credentials and will try to create a User.

1. Log on to Azure Portal @ https://portal.azure.com with User3 credentials-user3@harinderkohli543hotmail.onmicrosoft.com
2. In Azure Portal click Azure Active Directory in left pane>In Azure AD Dashboard click Users in left pane>All Users blade opens>Click + New User>Create User blade opens> Enter User4 in name and user4@harinderkohli543hotmail.onmicrosoft.com in user name and click create.

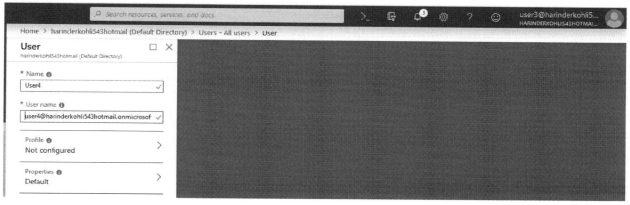

3. User4 was successfully created. Last row in below figure.

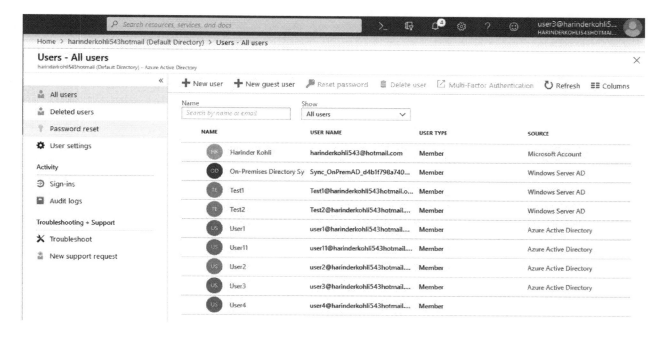

Assigning Administrative Permissions using Role Based Access Control

Before going into RBAC let's discuss why we need it in first place. Unlimited access to users in Azure can be security threat. Too few permissions means that users can't get their work done efficiently.

Azure Role-Based Access Control (RBAC) helps address above problem by offering fine-grained access management for Azure resources. With RBAC users are given amount of access based on their Job Roles. For example, use RBAC to let one employee manage virtual machines in a subscription, while another can manage SQL databases.

Role Based Access Management in Azure

You can assign roles to users, groups, and applications at a certain level. The level of a role assignment can be a subscription, a resource group, or a single resource.

Figure below shows RBAC can be assigned to User, Group & Application and can be applied at Subscription or Resource Group or single resource level.

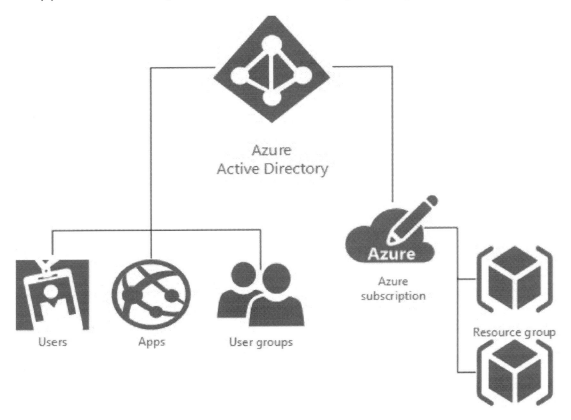

Azure RBAC Built-in roles

Owner has full access to all resources including the right to delegate access to others.

Contributor can create and manage all types of Azure resources but can't grant access to others.

Reader can view existing Azure resources.

Azure RBAC Scope and Assignment

Scope: RBAC role assignments are scoped to a specific subscription, resource group, or resource.

A user given access to a single resource cannot access any other resources in the same subscription.

A role assigned at a parent scope also grants access to the children contained within it. For example, a user with access to a resource group can manage all the resources it contains, like websites, virtual machines, and Virtual Networks etc.

Role: Within the scope of the assignment, access is narrowed even further by assigning a role. Roles can be high-level, like owner, or specific, like virtual machine reader.

Following is a **partial list** of built-in roles available.

RBAC Built in Roles	Description
Backup Contributor	Can manage backup in Recovery Services vault.
Backup Operator	Can manage backup except removing backup, in Recovery Services vault.
Backup Reader	Can view all backup management services.
BizTalk Contributor	Can manage BizTalk services.
Azure Cosmos DB Account Contributor	Can manage Azure Cosmos DB accounts.
Network Contributor	Can manage all network resources.
SQL DB Contributor	Can manage SQL databases, but not their security-related policies.
User Access Administrator	Can manage user access to Azure resources.
Virtual Machine Contributor	Can create and manage virtual machines, but not the virtual network or storage.

How Administrative Permissions are assigned

Administrative permissions are assigned to Users using **Access Control (IAM) Tab** in Resource or Resource Group or Subscription Dashboard.

Exercise 130: Assigning User3 Role of Reader in Resource Group

In this Exercise we will assign User3, Role of Reader in Resource Group HKPortal. User3 was created in Chapter 11, Exercise 86.

1. Go to Resource Group HKPortal Dashboard>Click Access control (IAM) in left pane>In Right pane Click +Add role assignment>In Add role assignment blade select reader from down box and select User3> Click save.

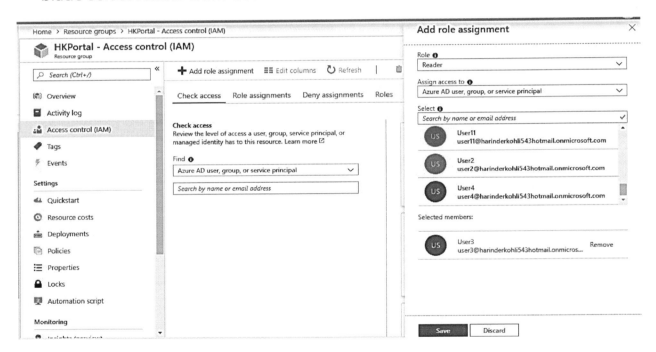

2. Click Role assignments and you can see User3 is assigned the role of Reader.

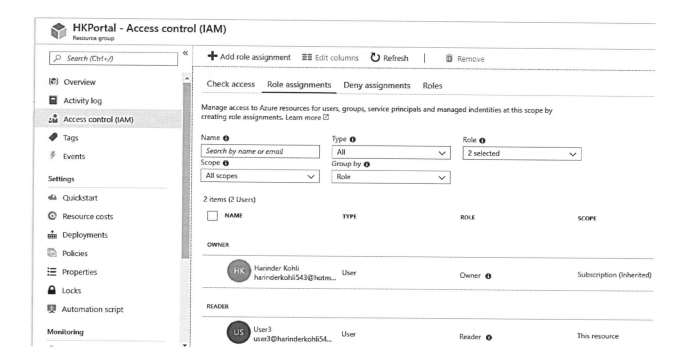

Exercise 131: Check User3 Access level in Azure Portal

1. Log on to Azure Portal @ https://portal.azure.com with User3 credentials-
   user3@harinderkohli543hotmail.onmicrosoft.com
2. Click Resource Groups in left pane> In right pane you can see User3 has
   access to only one Resource Group.

3. As an Exercise to users try to create a Resource in Resource Group HKPortal. It
   will fail as User3 has only Reader role assigned.

Exercise 132: Adding Co-Administrators to the subscription

In this exercise we will assign User3 role of Contributor at Subscription level. With Contributor role User3 can manage and create all resources in subscription but cannot delegate access to other users.

1. In subscription Dashboard click Access Control (IAM) in left pane> In Right pane Click +Add role assignment>In Add role assignment blade select contributor from down box and select User3> Click save.

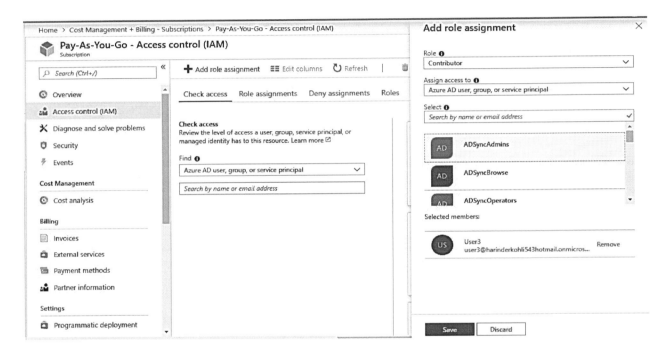

Exercise 133: Check User3 Access level in Azure Portal

1. Log on to Azure Portal @ https://portal.azure.com with User3 credentials-
   user3@harinderkohli543hotmail.onmicrosoft.com
2. Click All Resource in left pane> In right pane you can see User3 has access to
   All the Resources which we have created in the Subscription.

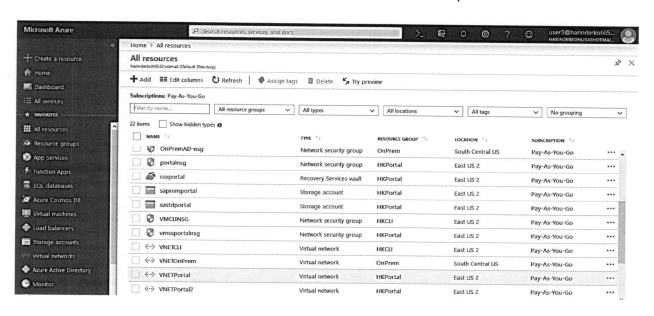

Chapter 14 Azure Resource Groups, Tags and Locks

This Chapter covers following Topic Lessons

- Resource Groups (RG)
- IT Governance at Resource Group Level using Azure Policy
- Moving Virtual Machines
- Tags
- Locks

This Chapter covers following Lab Exercises

- Create Resource Group HKTest
- Applying Azure Policy at Resource Group Level
- Test the Allowed storage accounts SKU Policy
- Move resources to new resource group
- Create Tag with name Mktg for VM wvmportal
- Create Tag with name Mktg for VM wvmportal OS Disk
- Find Cost of Resources Associated with Mktg
- Create CanNotDelete Lock on VM wvmportal
- Test the Lock

Chapter Topology

In this chapter we will add Resource Group, Tags and Locks to the Topology. We will configure Azure policy at Resource Group level.

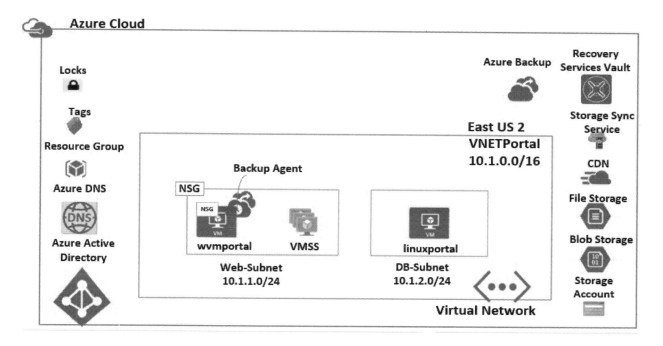

Resource Groups (RG)

Resource Groups are logical containers in which resources are grouped. All Resources in Azure are created in Resource Group. Resource Group can be created independently or can be created along with resource creation.

Resource groups allow you to manage related resources as a single unit. Using Resources Groups you can monitor, control access and manage billing for resources that are required to run an application.

Design Considerations for Resource Groups

1. A resource group can contain resources that reside in different regions.
2. All the resources in a resource group must be associated with a single subscription.
3. Each resource can only exist in one resource group.
4. You can move a resource from one resource group to another group.
5. Ideally all the resources in a resource group should share the same lifecycle. You deploy, update, and delete them together. If one resource, such as a database server, needs to exist on a different deployment cycle it should be in another resource group.
6. A RG can be used to scope access control for administrative actions.

Exercise 134: Create Resource Group HKTest

1. In Azure Portal click Resource groups in left pane>Click +Add>Add Resource Group blade opens>Enter as per your requirement and click create.

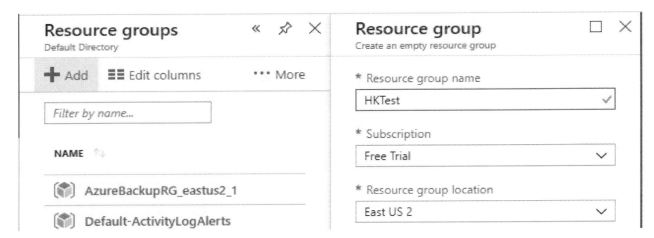

2. Figure below shows Resource Group HKTest Dashboard. Currently there are no resources to display as it is a new created group.

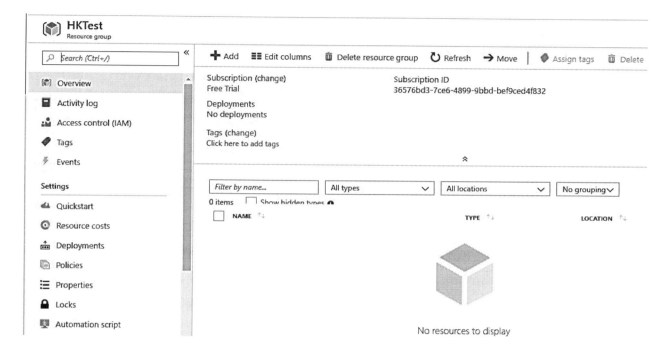

IT Governance at Resource Group level using Azure Policy

Note: Azure Policies is already discussed in Subscription Chapter. Policies can be applied at Subscription or Resource Group Level.

Azure Policy helps in implementing IT Governance in an organisation. IT Governance ensures that your organization is able to achieve its goals through an effective and efficient use of IT. IT Governance involves planning and initiative at strategic level to prevent IT issues from derailing IT projects.

Azure Policy is a managed service in Azure that is used to assign and manage policies. These policies enforce rules so that resources stay compliant with your corporate standards and service level agreements.

Policy Assignment Scope

Azure Policy can be applied at Subscription, Resource Group or at Management Group level. Policy assignments are inherited by all child resources. However, you can exclude a subscope from the policy assignment.

Built in Policies

There are Hundred built in Policies. Some of the built in policies include:

Allowed Storage Account SKUs: This policy definition has a set of conditions/rules that determine if a storage account that is being deployed is within a set of SKU sizes. Its effect is to deny all storage accounts that do not adhere to the set of defined SKU sizes.

Allowed Resource Type: This policy definition has a set of conditions/rules to specify the resource types that your organization can deploy. Its effect is to deny all resources that are not part of this defined list.

Allowed Locations: This policy enables you to restrict the locations that your organization can specify when deploying resources. Its effect is used to enforce your geo-compliance requirements.

Exercise 135: Applying Azure Policy at Resource Group Level

In this Exercise we will assign Policy to Resource Group HKTest. This Policy allows creation of Storage Account with RA GRS replication option only.

7. Go to Resource Group HKTest Dashboard>Click Policies in left pane>Policies Blade open>Click Compliance in left pane.

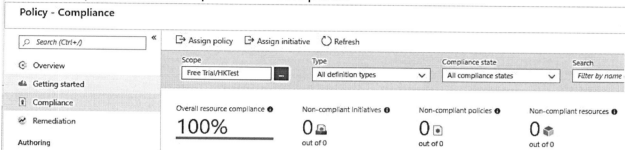

8. Click Assign Policy>Assign Policy Blade opens as shown below.

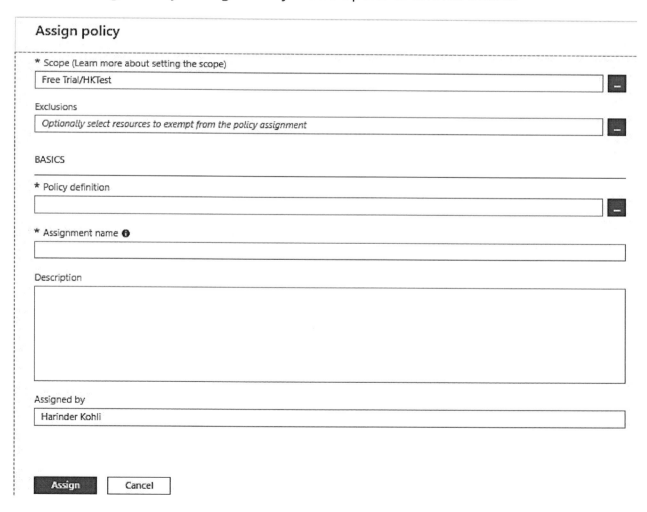

9. Under Policy Defination click ellipsis ... Box >Available Defination Blade opens>Scroll down to **Allowed storage accounts SKU**s.

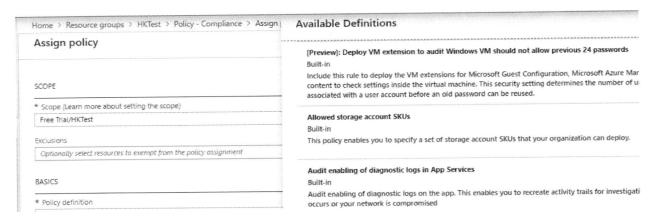

10. Select **Allowed storage accounts SKUs** >Click Select (Not shown)> A drop down Box is created in Azure Policy Blade to select the required SKU> Here I selected Standard_RAGRS>Click Assign in Bottom of the pane (Not shown).

11. Policies dashboard shows the Policy created. It takes 15-20 minutes for Policy to take effect. You need to refresh it continuously.

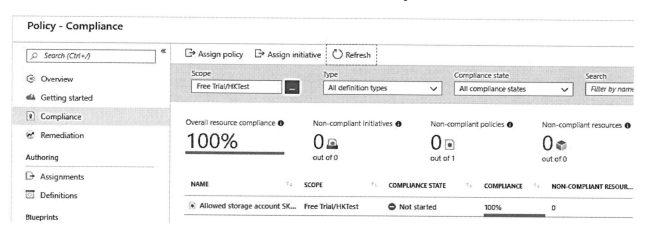

Exercise 136: Test the Allowed storage accounts SKU Policy

1. In Azure Portal click create a Resource>Storage> Storage Account>Create Storage Account Blade opens>Select Resource Group **HKTest**> Enter a name>Make sure Replication is **LRS**.

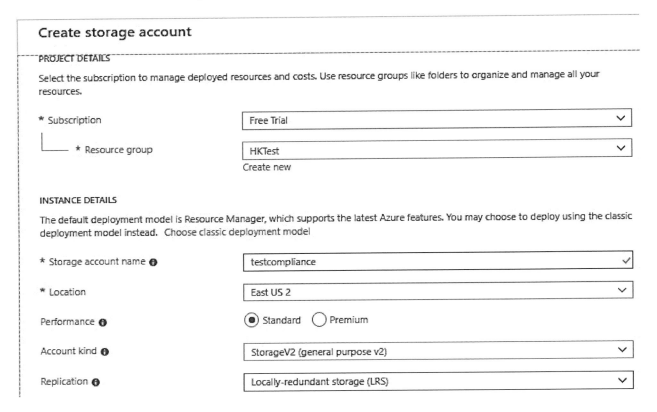

2. Click Review +Create (Not shown) in above screen>Validation fails because of Policy. Our Policy only allowed RA-GRS where as we were creating Storage Account with LRS Replication.

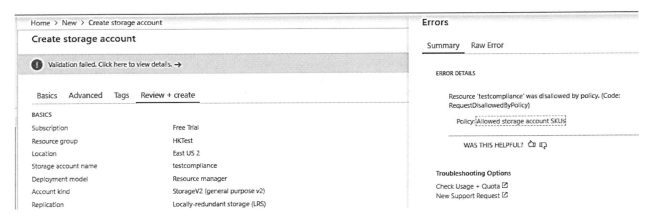

Moving Virtual Machines

You can move Azure VM to either a new subscription or a new resource group in the same subscription.

When moving resources, both the source group and the target group are locked during the operation. Write and delete operations are blocked on the resource groups until the move completes.

You can't change the location of the resource. Moving a resource only moves it to a new resource group. The new resource group may have a different location, but that doesn't change the location of the resource.

Requirement for moving resources

1. The source and destination subscriptions must exist within the same Azure Active Directory tenant.
2. The destination subscription must be registered for the resource provider of the resource being moved. If not, you receive an error stating that the **subscription is not registered for a resource type**. You might encounter this problem when moving a resource to a new subscription, but that subscription has never been used with that resource type.

Limitations

Managed disks don't support move. This restriction means that several related resources can't be moved too. You can't move:

Managed disks
Virtual machines with the managed disks
Images created from managed disks
Snapshots created from managed disks
Availability sets with virtual machines with managed disks

Exercise 137: Move resources to new resource group

In this exercise we will move VM OnPremAD in Resource Group OnPrem to Resource Group HKTest.

To move resources go to the resource group with those resources, and then select the **Move** button.

1. Go to Resource Group OnPrem Dashboard>Click Move> When You Click Move Button you get 2 options- Move to another Resource Group or Move to another Subscription.

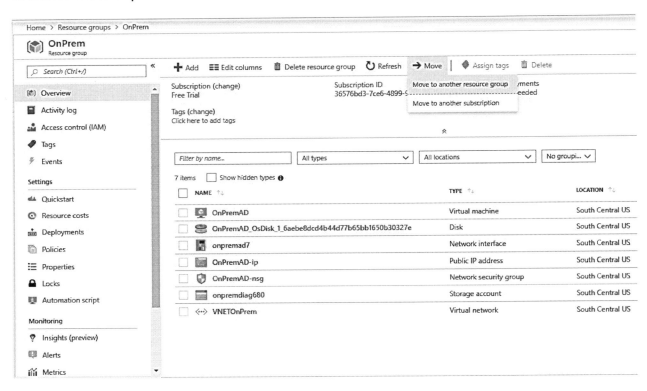

2. When You Click Move Button you get 2 options- Resource Groups or Subscription>Click Move to another Resource Group>Select VM OnPremAD >Select Resource Group HKTest>Check Mark Terms & Conditions>Click OK.

3. Go to Resource Group HKTest Dashboard>You can see VM OnPremAD has moved from Resource Group OnPrem to Resource Group HKTest.

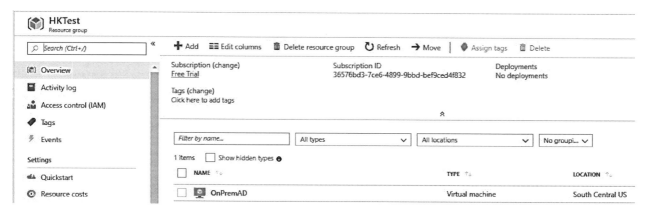

Tags

You can tag resource or resource group with name/value pairs to categorize and view resources across resource groups and across subscriptions. Using tags you can logically organize Azure resources by categories.

Each tag consists of a name and a value.

Tags enable you to retrieve related resources from different resource groups. This approach is helpful when you need to organize resources for billing or management.

Each resource or resource group can have a maximum of 15 tag name/value pairs. If you want to associate more than 15 values with a resource, use a JSON string for the tag value.

Exercise 138: Create Tag with name Mktg for VM wvmportal

In Azure Portal go to VM Resource wvmportal and click Tag in left pane>Add Tag opens in Right Pane> I entered **Mktg** in Name and **VM** in Value>Click Save.

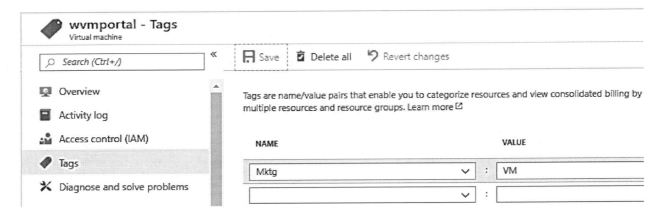

Exercise 139: Create Tag with name Mktg for VM wvmportal OS Disk

Go to VM wvmportal Dashboard> In left pane Click Disks> Click wvmportal_OS Disk> OS Disk Pane opens>Click Tag in left pane>In Right pane in Name enter **Mktg** and Value Enter **OS**>Click Save.

Exercise 140: Find Cost of Resources Associated with Mktg Tag

1. In Azure Portal click Cost Managemnt + Billing in left pane>Click Subscription in left pane> Click your subscription>In Subscription dashboard Click cost Analysis in left pane> In Tag Box select the Tags Mktg:VM & Mktg:OS and click Apply. You can see the Total & Break up cost associated with Mktg.

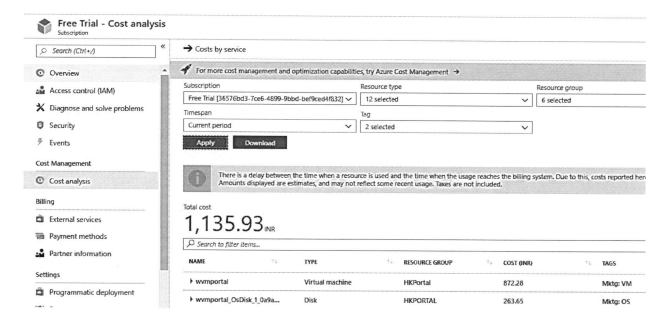

Locks

Locks are applied at subscription, resource group, or resource level to prevent users from accidentally deleting or modifying critical resources.

You can set the lock level to **CanNotDelete** or **ReadOnly**.

CanNotDelete means authorized users can still read and modify a resource, but they can't delete the resource.
ReadOnly means authorized users can read a resource, but they can't delete or update the resource.

When you apply a lock at a parent scope, all resources within that scope inherit the same lock.

Resource Manager Locks apply only to operations that happen in the management plane, which consists of operations sent to https://management.azure.com. The locks do not restrict how resources perform their own functions. Resource changes are restricted, but resource operations are not restricted.
For example a ReadOnly lock on a SQL Database prevents you from deleting or modifying the database but it does not prevent you from creating, updating or deleting data in the database. Data transactions are permitted because those operations are not sent to https://management.azure.com.

Exercise 141: Create CanNotDelete Lock on VM wvmportal

Go to wvmportal dashboard>Click Lock in left pane>In right pane Click + Add>
Add Lock blade opens>Enter a name and from dropdown box select Delete and
optionally add description about lock>Click OK.

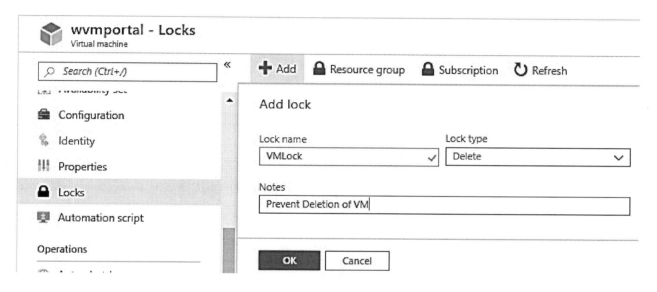

Exercise 142: Test the Lock

In wvmportal dashboard Click overview in left pane>In Right pane Click Delete>
Delete VM Box pops up>Click Yes> You get notification Failed to Delete the
Virtual Machine.

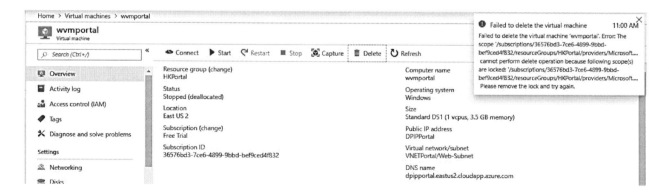

Chapter 15 Analyzing & Monitoring Azure Resources

This Chapter covers following Topic Lessons

- Azure Monitoring Solutions
- Azure Monitor
- Metrics & Logs
- Activity Log
- Diagnostic Logs (Non-Compute Resources)
- Diagnostic Logs (Compute Resource)
- Metrics
- Action Group
- Alerts
- Log Analytics
- Management Solutions
- Advisor
- Azure Service Health

This Chapter covers following Lab Exercises

- Accessing & Exploring Monitor Dashboard
- Accessing Activity Log from a Monitor Dashboard
- Accessing Activity Log from a Resource Dashboard
- Creating Alert on Activity Log
- Accessing Diagnostic Log from the Monitor Dashboard
- Enabling Diagnostic Logs for Recovery Services Vault
- Enabling Guest OS Diagnostic Logs in VM wvmportal
- Virtual Machine Percentage CPU Metrics
- Storage Account Used Capacity Metrics
- Accessing Metric from Resource (VM) Dashboard
- Create Action Group
- Create an alert on Metric (Percentage CPU)
- Accessing Alert from Resource (VM) Dashboard
- Monitoring IIS Web Server with Log Analytics
- Connect VM OnPremAD to Log Analytics
- Installing Management Agent (AD Heath Check)
- Installing Microsoft Monitoring Agent in On-Premises VM
- Checking Advisor Recommendations

- Checking Service Health Events
- Configuring Alerts for Service Health Events

Chapter Topology

In this chapter we will add Monitor, Log Analytics, Advisor & Service Health to the topology. We will Install Diagnostic Agent (DA) on VM wvmportal. We will connect VM wvmportal to Log Analytics by installing Microsoft Monitoring Agent (MMA) on VM wvmportal.

For Monitoring of resources we will enable or create Activity Logs, Diagnostic Logs, Alerts and Action Groups.

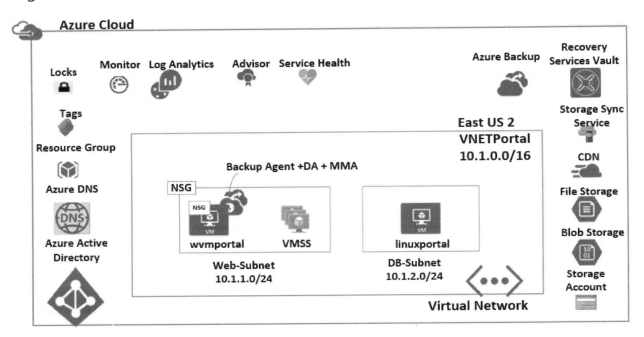

We will Install Microsoft Monitoring Agent (MMA) on VM OnPremAD which will connect it to Log Analytics. We will add Management Agent (AD Heath Check) in Log Analytics to Asses Health and Risk of Active Directory Domain services (AD DS). AD DS role is installed on VM OnPremAD.

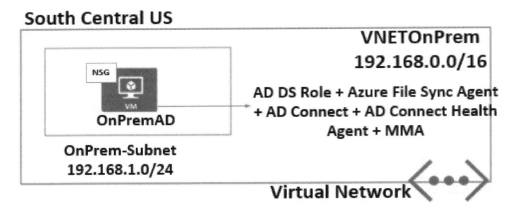

Azure Monitoring Solutions

Azure includes multiple services that individually perform a specific role or task in the monitoring space. Together, these services deliver a comprehensive solution for collecting, analyzing, and acting on telemetry from your application and the Azure resources that support them.

The figure below shows a conceptual view of the components that work together to provide monitoring of Azure resources.

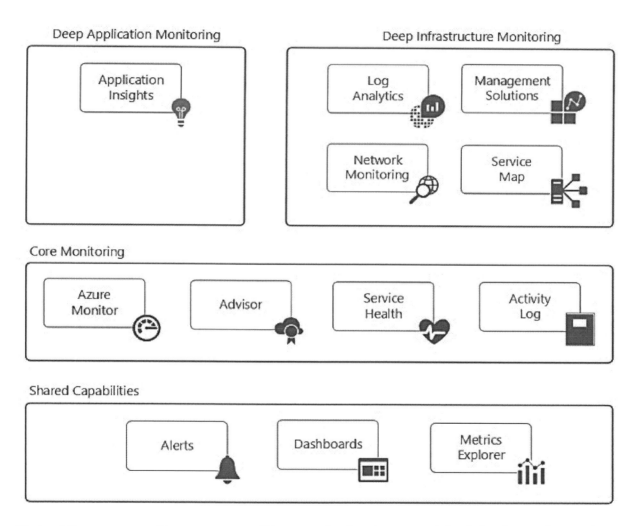

Note: We can monitor resource Diagnostic Settings and Activity logs through resource Dashboard or through Monitor Dashboard.

Azure Monitor

Azure Monitor provides centralized dashboard for viewing Logs, metrics & alerts for Azure resources.

Azure Monitor provides mini-dashboards for Metrics, Activity Log, Diagnostic logs, alerts, Service Health, Network Watcher & Application Insights etc. Data can be exported to Log Analytics and Power BI for further Analysis.

Metrics & Logs

All data collected by Azure Monitor fits into one of two fundamental types - Metrics and Logs.

Metrics are numerical values that describe some aspect of a system at a particular point in time. They are lightweight and capable of supporting near real-time scenarios.

Logs contain different kinds of data organized into records with different sets of properties for each type. Telemetry such as events and traces are stored as logs in addition to performance data so that it can all be combined for analysis.

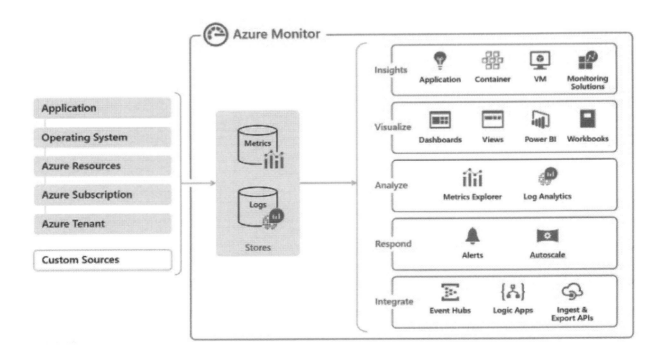

Exercise 143: Accessing & Exploring Monitor Dashboard

In Azure Portal click Monitor in Left pane> Monitor Dashboard opens> In the left pane you can see tabs for Alerts, Metrics, Activity Log, and Diagnostic settings etc.

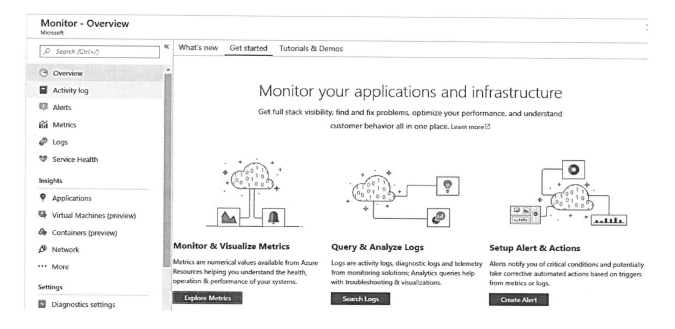

Activity Log

Activity Logs provide data about the operations on a resource from the outside. The Activity Log reports control-plane events for your subscriptions. For Example Azure Activity log will log an event when a virtual machine is created or a logic app is deleted. But any Activity performed by virtual Machine will not be reported by Activity Log.

You can monitor Activity log for Compute as well as non-compute Resources.

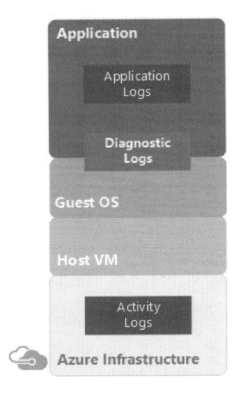

Compute resources only

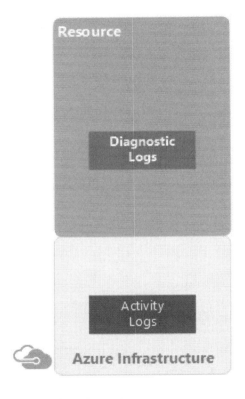

Non-Compute resources only

Activity Log is a Platform level Service. You don't require any agents to be installed. Events can be seen in Azure Portal. Events Logs can be exported to Azure Storage, Event Hubs, Power BI and OMS Log Analytics. You can create alerts on Events generated in Activity Log.

Exercise 144: Accessing Activity Log from a Monitor Dashboard

In Azure Portal click Monitor in Left pane> Monitor Dashboard opens> Click Activity Log. This will report control plane events for **all the resources**.
Note: By default Activity dashboard will show logs for last 6 Hours. To see Logs for different duration you need to select duration from Timespan dropdown box.

To see activity log for particular resource such as Virtual Network "VNETPortal"
Click Add Filter>Select Resource Group HKPortal>Select Resource VNETPortal.

Exercise 145: Accessing Activity Log from a Resource Dashboard
Go to Virtual Network "VNETPortal" Dashboard> Click Activity Log in left Pane.

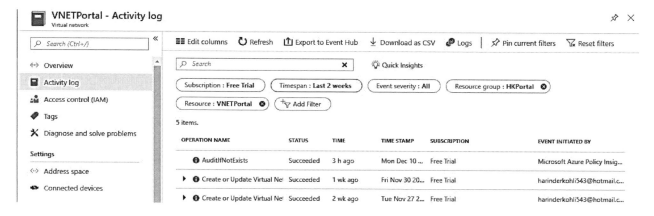

Exercise 146: Creating Alert on Activity Log

In this we will just demonstrate how to create alert on Activity Logs. Alerts will be discussed comprehensively in coming sections.
Go to Virtual Network VNETPortal Dashboard>Click Activity Log in left pane> Click the Log in right pane> In the Bottom you can see +Add activity log alert.

Click +Add activity log alert in right pane bottom>Create Alert rule Pane opens.

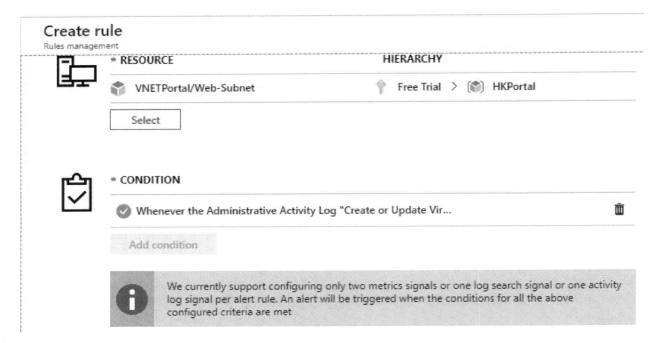

Diagnostic Logs (Non-Compute Resources)

Azure resource-level diagnostic logs are logs emitted by a resource about the operation of that resource. Diagnostic logs provide insight into operations that were performed within that resource itself, for example, getting a secret from a Key Vault.

Difference between Activity and Diagnostic Logs: Activity Logs provide data about the operations on a resource from the outside (the "control plane"). Diagnostics Logs are emitted by a resource and provide information about the operation of that resource (the "data plane").
You can monitor Diagnostic log for Compute as well as non-compute Resources.

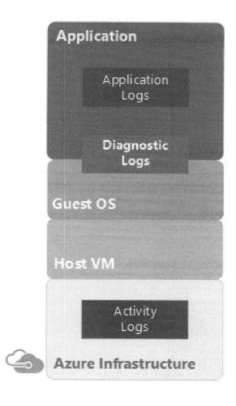

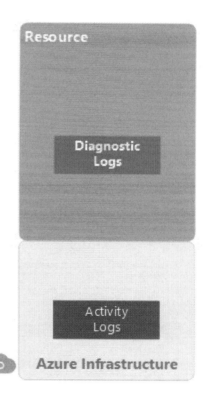

Compute resources only   Non-Compute resources only

Diagnostic log is a Platform level Service. **You don't require any agents to be installed** and nor you require any Azure Level service to be created. **You just need to enable diagnostic logs for the resource**.

Diagnostic Log Architecture

The Figure below shows the Architecture of Diagnostic Log.

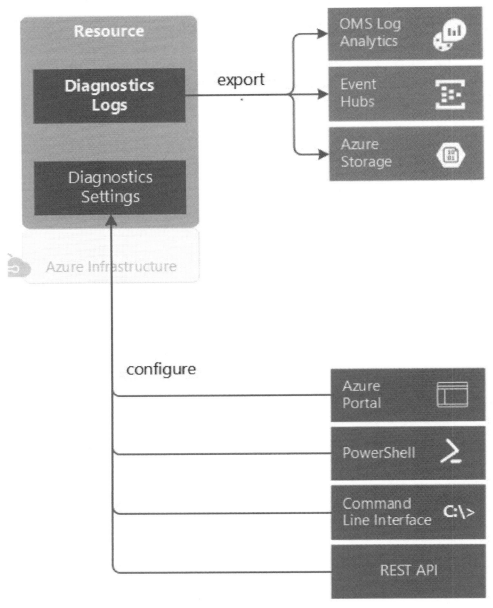

Diagnostic Log is a Platform level Resource which logs Events generated by the resource. Events Logs can be seen in Azure Portal.

Diagnostic Logs can be streamed to Event Hubs for ingestion by a third-party service or custom analytics solution such as PowerBI. You can Analyze logs with OMS Log Analytics.

Exercise 147: Accessing Diagnostic Log from the Monitor Dashboard

In Monitor Dashboard click Diagnostic settings in left pane> Right pane shows diagnostic logs status for all the Azure resources in the subscription.

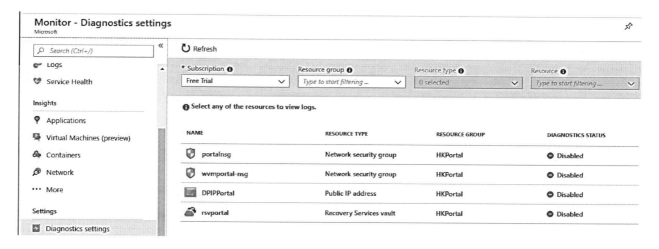

Exercise 148: Enabling Diagnostic Logs for Recovery Services Vault

1. In Monitor Dashboard click Diagnostic settings in left pane> In Right pane click rsvportal> From here you can enable Diagnostic setting for rsvportal.

2. Click Turn on diagnostics>Diagnostic Setting blade opens>Enter a name, Select Storage account and/or Event Hub and/or Log Analytics and select logs as per your requirement and click save.

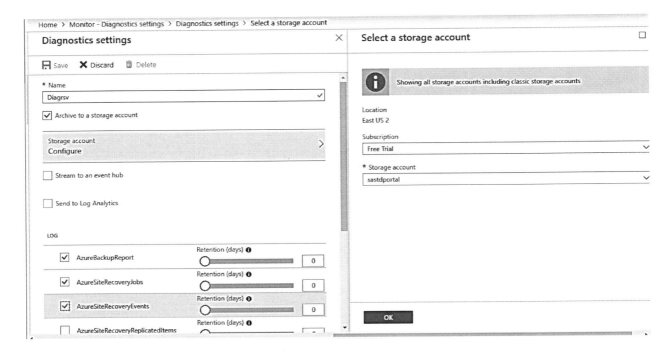

Diagnostic Logs (Compute Resource)

Guest OS-level diagnostic logs are collected by installing diagnostics agent on the Azure virtual machine.

Guest OS-level diagnostic logs capture data from the operating system and applications running on a virtual machine. Guest OS-level diagnostic logs collect following types of Metrics and Logs:

Performance counters
Application Logs
Windows Event Logs
.NET Event Source
IIS Logs
Manifest based ETW
Crash Dumps
Customer Error Logs

Exercise 149: Enabling Guest OS Diagnostic Logs in VM wvmportal

1. Go to VM wvmportal Dashboard>Click Diagnostic settings in left pane>In Right pane click Enable Guest Level Monitoring.

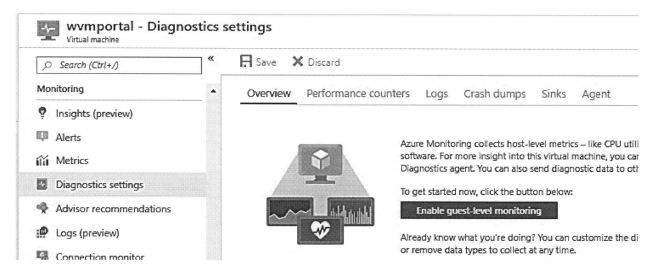

Compare this with Resource Level diagnostics logs which require no agent and capture resource-specific data from the Azure platform itself.

2. After enabling you can see following in overview screen

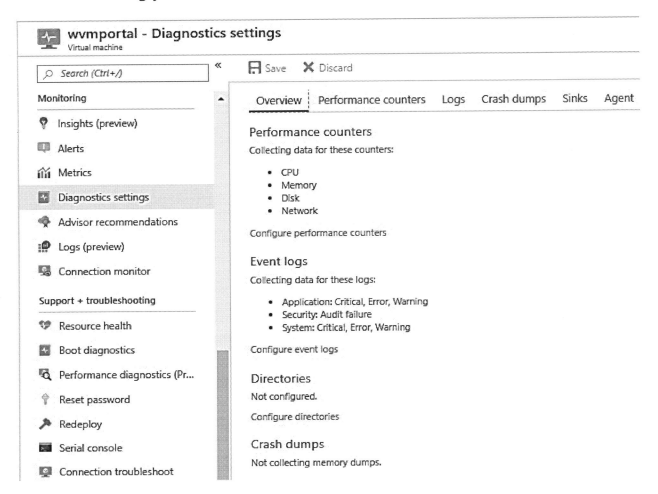

3. Click on Performance Counters>Custom><You can now see OS level/VM level counters.

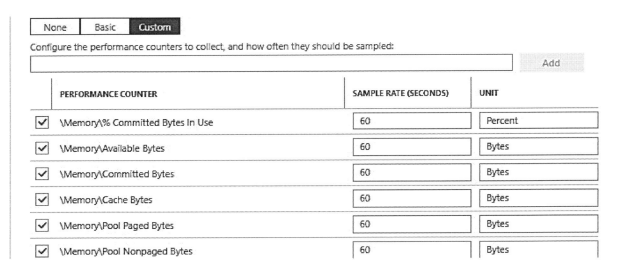

4. **Checking VM level Performance Counters**. In VM wvmportal dashboard click metrics in left pane> In Resource select wvmportal> In metric Namespace select **Microsoft.compute/virtualmachines/guest**> In Metric Dropdown box you can see VM level counters are available now.

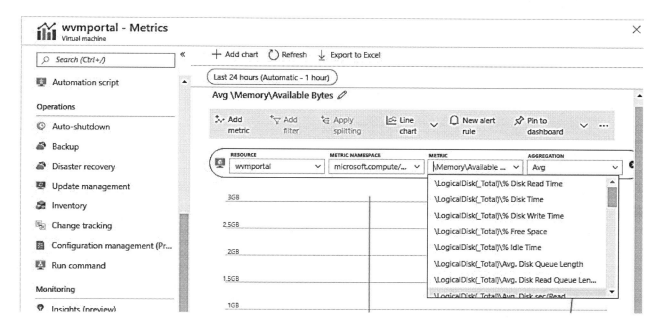

Note: Metric Namespace **Microsoft.compute/virtualmachines/guest is not available if you don't enable Guest Level Monitoring.**

Metrics

Metrics are numerical values that describe some aspect of a system (CPU or Memory utilization etc.) at a particular time. They are lightweight and capable of supporting near real-time scenarios. Metrics are collected at regular intervals whether or not the value changes.

They're useful for alerting because they can be sampled frequently, and an alert can be fired quickly with simple logic.

Metrics Example

Percentage CPU metric will collect processor utilization from a virtual machine every minute. You have the option to configure and fire an alert on the metric such as when one of those collected values exceeds a defined threshold.

Metric are Key value pairs. Metric for Percentage CPU and Network Throughput are shown below:

Percentage CPU

Timestamp	Metric Value
8/9/2017 8:14	70

Network Throughput

Timestamp	Metric Value
8/9/2017 8:15	1,141.4 Kbps

Metric Features

23 Collected at one-minute frequency unless specified otherwise in the metric's definition.
24 Uniquely identified by a metric name and a namespace that acts as a category.
25 Stored for 93 days. You can copy metrics to Log Analytics for long term trending.

Sources of metric data

There are three fundamental sources of metrics collected by Azure Monitor. All of these metrics are available in the metric store where they can be evaluated together regardless of their source.

Platform metrics are created by Azure resources and give you visibility into their health and performance. Each type of resource creates a distinct set of metrics without any configuration required.

Application metrics are created by Application Insights for your monitored applications and help you detect performance issues and track trends in how your application is being used. This includes such values as Server response time and Browser exceptions.

Custom metrics are metrics that you define in addition to the standard metric that are automatically available. Custom metrics must be created against a single resource in the same region as that resource.

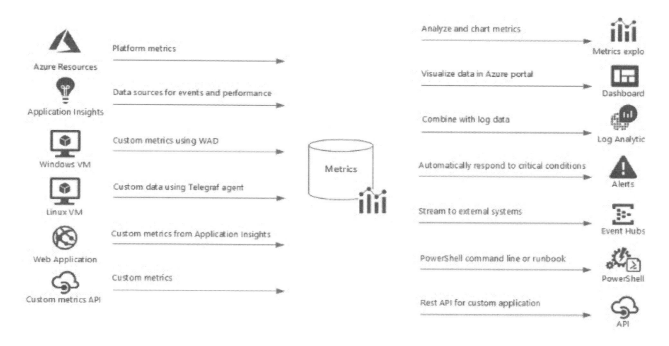

Exercise 150: Virtual Machine Percentage CPU Metrics

1. In Monitor Dashboard click Metrics in left pane> In Metric Pane Click Add Metric>Enlarge Resource Dailog Box>Under Resource Group Select HKPortal> Resource Type Select Virtual Machine>Select VM wvmportal

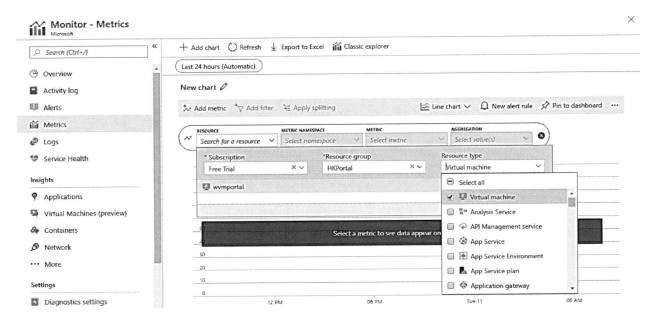

2. In Metric Drop Box select percentage CPU>You can now see real time chart for last 24 Hours.

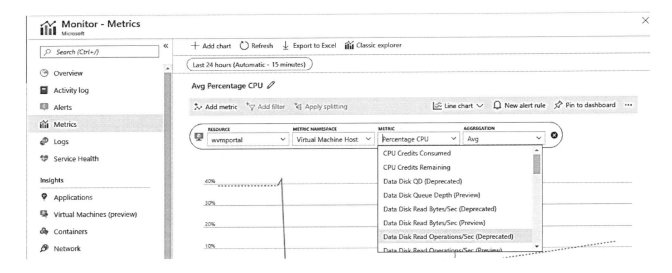

Note 1: Readers are advised to see metrics for other Resource Type also.
Note 2: You can also access Metric through VM dashboard.

Exercise 151: Storage Account Used Capacity Metrics

1. In Monitor Dashboard click Metrics in left pane> In Metric Pane Click Add Metric>Enlarge Resource Dailog Box>Under Resource Group Select HKPortal> Resource Type Select Storage Account>Select sasstdportal> In Metric Drop Box select Used Capacity>You can now see real time chart for last 24 Hours.

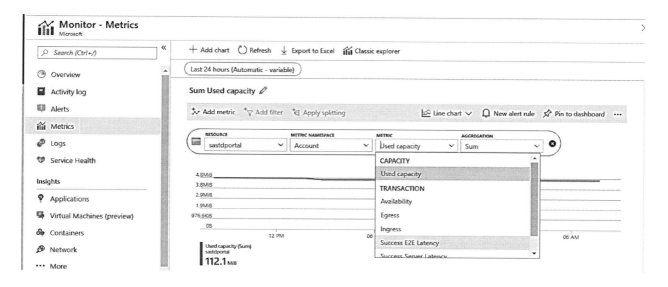

Exercise 152: Accessing Metric from Resource (VM) Dashboard

In Azure Portal go VM wvmportal dashboard> Under Monitoring Click Metrics in left pane>Metric Pane opens as shown below.

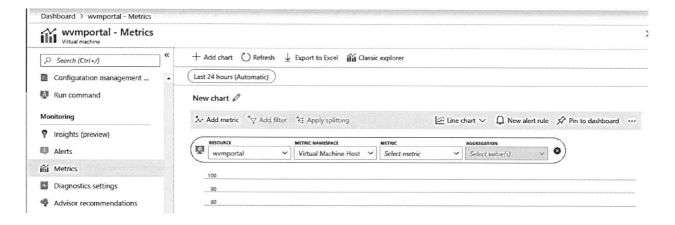

Action Group

An action group is a collection of **notification preferences** (Action Types) defined by the user. Various Alerts types use Action Groups when the alert is triggered.

Action Types

Email/SMS/Push/Voice
Azure Function
Logic App
Webhook
ITSM
Automation Runbook

Exercise 153: Create Action Group

In this exercise we will create Action group with Action type Email. We will use this Action Group with Alerts in Alert exercise.

1. In Azure Portal click Monitor in Left pane> Monitor Dashboard opens>Click Alert in left pane.

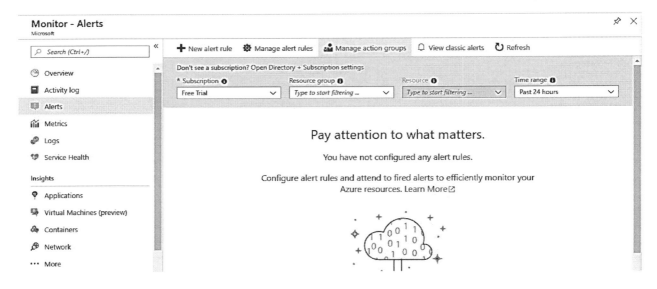

In Right pane you can see Manage Action groups.

2. Click Manage action groups in right pane>Action Group pane opens>Click +Add action Group>Add Action group blade opens>Give a name and short name> Select HKPortal Resource group from drop down box> Enter action name>Select Email/SMS/Push/Voice in Action type>Email/SMS/Push/Voice detail pane opens> Select Email check box and enter email id>Click OK>Click Ok.

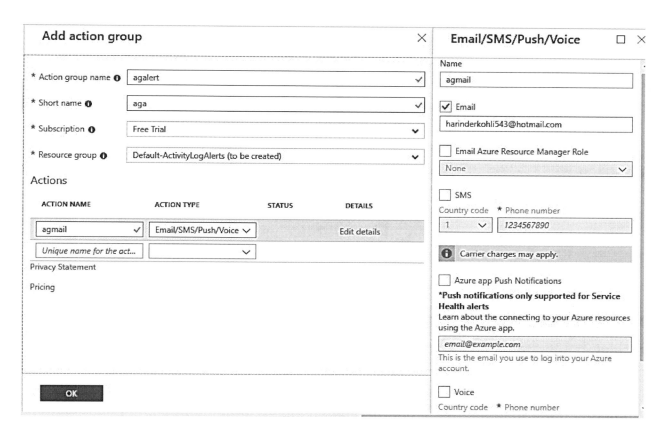

Note 1: You can add Multiple action types in a group.
Note 2: Readers are advised to check all action types and detail pane which opens for that Action type.

3. You can now see Action group created in Action Group pane.

Alerts

Alerts proactively notify you when important conditions are found in your monitoring data. They allow you to identify and address issues before the users of your system notice them.

For Example you can create an alert on Virtual Machine Metric that if CPU utilization goes above 70% then send an email or start an additional instance.

Architecture Overview of Alerts

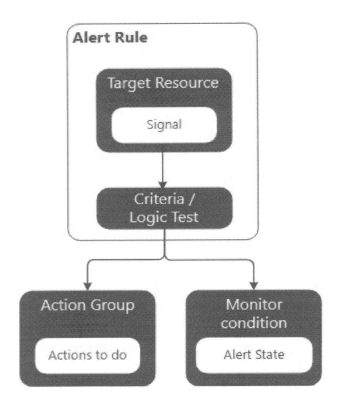

Alert Rule: The alert rule captures the target and criteria for alerting.
Target Resource: A target can be any Azure resource such as virtual machine, a storage account, a virtual machine scale set, a Log Analytics workspace, or an Application Insights resource.
Signal: Signals are emitted by the target resource and can be of several types - Metric, Activity log, Application Insights, and Log.
Criteria: Criteria is combination of Signal and Logic applied on a Target resource.
Action: A specific action taken when the alert is fired and is specified in Action Group.

Exercise 154: Create an alert on Metric (Percentage CPU) for VM

In this lab we will create Alert on Metric (Percentage CPU) with a criteria that if CPU utilization goes above 70% in VM wvmportal then notify through an e-mail. We will use Action group created in Exercise 153 for notification.

1. In Monitor Dashboard Click Alert in left pane>Alert Pane opens.

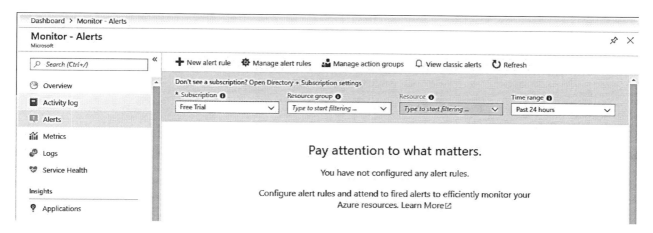

2. In Alert pane click + New Alert Rule> Create rule blade opens>Click select under Resource>Select a resource blade opens>In Resource type drop down box select Virtual Machines>Under resources select VM wvmportal>Done.

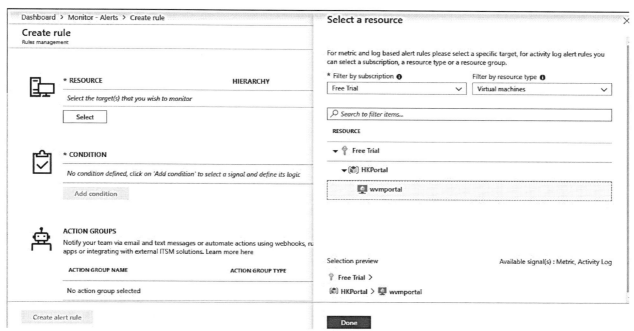

Note: You have option of accessing Alert from VM wvmportal dashboard also.

3. Click Add Condition> Configure Signal Logic Blade opens.

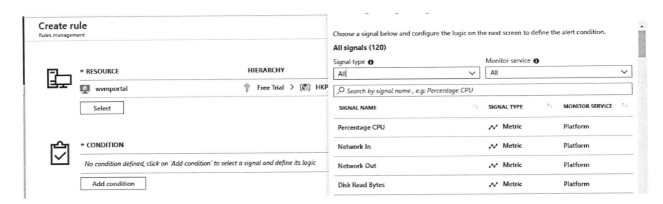

4. Select Percentage CPU>Percentage Platform blade opens>Scroll down> In Threshold Box enter 70>Click Done

5. In Action groups click select existing>Select an Action Group blade opens>Select action group Created in Exercise 153>Add>

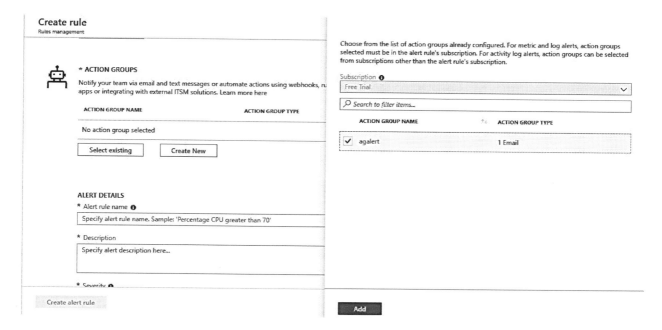

6. In Alert Details Enter a name for Alert Rule, Select Severity Level>Select Yes for Rule creation>Enter a description>Click Create Alert Rule.

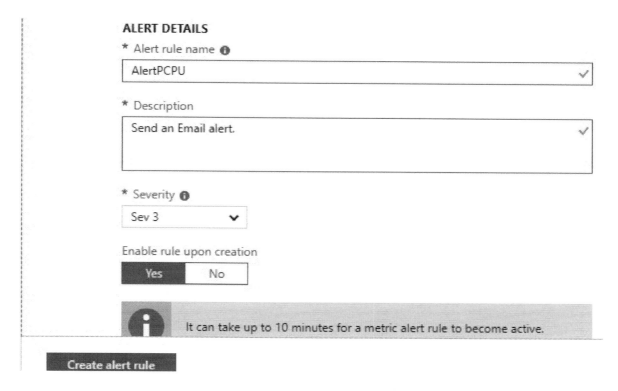

7. In Alert pane click Manage alert Rules>You can see the alert rule created> If required you can edit the rule also.

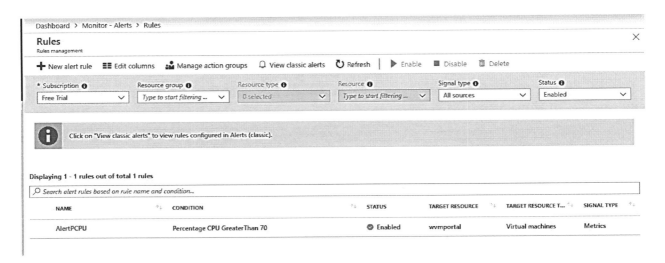

Exercise 155: Accessing Alert from Resource (VM) Dashboard

In Azure Portal go VM wvmportal dashboard> Under Monitoring Click Alerts in left pane>Alert Pane opens as shown below.

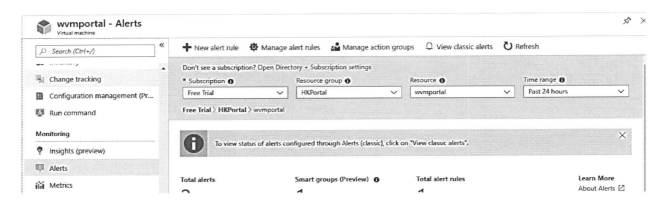

Log Analytics

Log Analytics is a service in Operations Management Suite (OMS) that helps you collect and analyze data generated by resources in your cloud and on-premises environments.

It gives you real-time insights using integrated search and custom dashboards to readily analyze millions of records across all of your workloads and servers regardless of their physical location.

Log Analytics Architecture

Log Analytics has 2 components – OMS Workspace & Monitoring Agent.

The combined solution of Log Analytics service and OMS repository is known as OMS Workspace. OMS repository is hosted in the Azure cloud.

Microsoft Monitoring Agent is installed on the connected source. Data is collected into the repository from connected sources.

Figure below shows Log Analytics collecting and analyzing data generated by resources in Azure, on-premises and other Clouds.

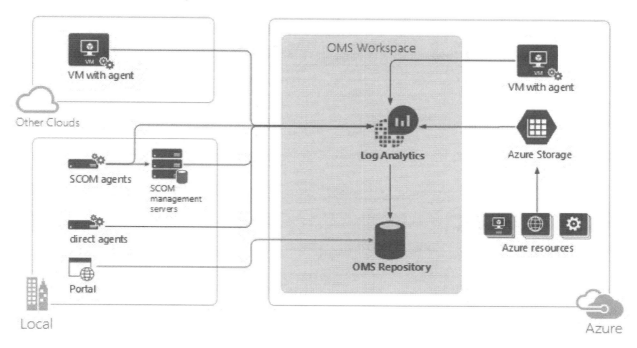

Data Collection from Connected Sources & Azure Managed Resources

Connected Sources can be on-premises or Cloud Resources. All Resources which you have created in your Subscription will appear in Log Analytics Dashboard under various Data Sources. You can add following Connected Sources in Log Analytics Services.

1. On-Premises Windows & Linux Servers with MS Monitoring Agent Installed.
2. Azure VMs with Microsoft Monitoring Agent virtual machine extension.
3. Azure Storage Accounts.
4. Azure Activity Logs
5. Azure Resources: You can add Azure Resources to Log Analytics which you have created in your subscription. For example following Azure Resources I have created in My Subscription and they appear under Azure Resources in Log Analytics Dashboard. You can enable all of them or enable as per your requirement to send Monitoring Data to Log Analytics Services.

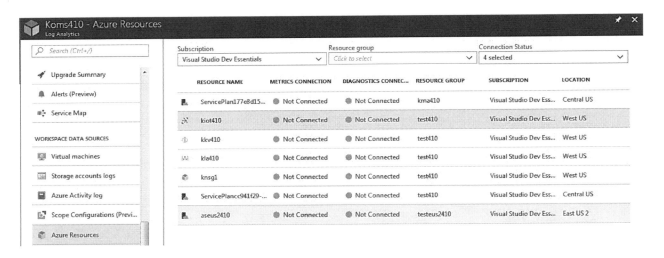

Data Sources

Data sources are configured on connected sources. Data sources can be IIS Logs, Performance Counters, Syslog, windows security events, windows firewall log, Network Security group.

Design Nuggets: You can create multiple workspaces in Azure Subscription. Workspaces are independent of each other and that data collected from each workspace cannot be viewed in another workspace.

Log Analytics Working, Reporting and Analyzing data

Log Analytics collects data from managed resources into a central repository. This data could include events, performance data, or custom data provided through the API. Once collected, the data is available for alerting, analysis, and export.

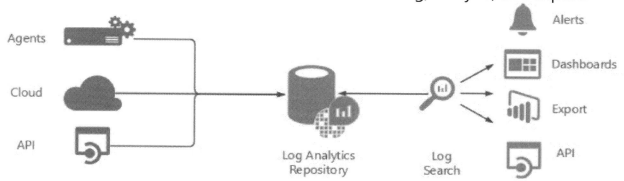

Log Analytics includes a powerful query language to extract data stored in the repository. The result of the query can be viewed in following ways:

Dashboard: You can view the result of the query in Log Analytics Dashboard.
Export: You can export the results of any query to analyze it outside of Log Analytics. You can schedule a regular export to Power BI which provides significant visualization and analysis capabilities.
Log Search API. Log Analytics has a REST API for collecting data from any client. This allows you to programmatically work with data collected in the repository or access it from another monitoring tool.

Alerting

You can create Alerts on the Log search data. In addition to creating an alert record in the Log Analytics repository, alerts can take the following actions.

Email. Send an email to proactively notify you of a detected issue.

Runbook. An alert in Log Analytics can start a runbook in Azure Automation. This is typically done to attempt to correct the detected issue. The runbook can be started in the cloud in the case of an issue in Azure or another cloud, or it could be started on a local agent for an issue on a physical or virtual machine.

Webhook. An alert can start a webhook and pass it data from the results of the log search. This allows integration with external services such as an alternate alerting system, or it may attempt to take corrective action for an external web site.

Exercise 156: Monitoring IIS Web Server with Log Analytics

In this exercise we will monitor IIS server running in Azure VM wvmportal. There are 4 steps involved in this: Creating Log Analytics workspace, Add Connected source, Add data source and Query IIS Log data using log search.

Step 1: Create Log Analytics workspace (Log Analytics service + OMS Repository)

1. Click + Create a resource > Management Tools > Log Analytics> create Log Analytics workspace blade opens>enter a name>I selected create new resource group with name mlogs> East US Location>Click ok.

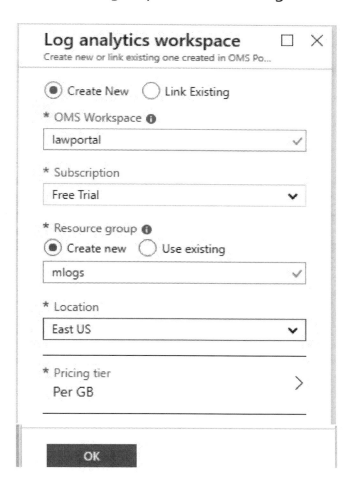

2. **Accessing Log Analytics workspace lawportal dashboard**> Click All resources in left pane>All Resources blade opens>Scroll down and you can see lawportal.

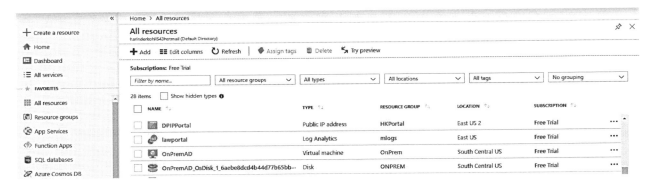

3. Click lawportal (second row in above figure)> lawportal dashboard opens as shown below> in left pane we scrolled down to see Workspace Data sources options.

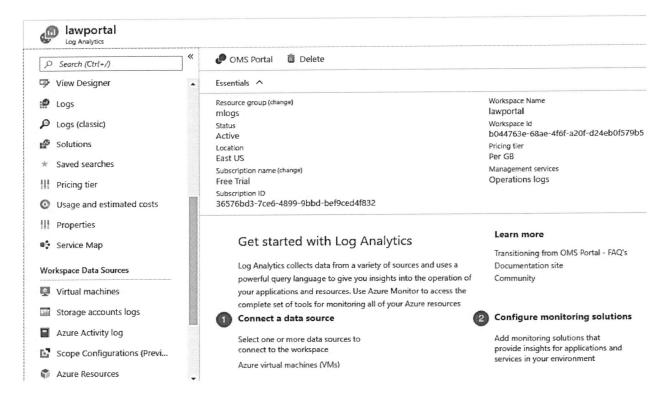

Step 2: Add Connected Source (Azure VM wvmportal running IIS Web Server) by installing Log Analytics VM Extension or Microsoft Monitoring Agent (MMA)

1. In Log Analytics workspace dashboard in left pane scroll down and under Workspace Data sources click Virtual Machines> Right pane shows the Virtual Machine wvmportal and the status of OMS Connection. Which in this case is not connected.

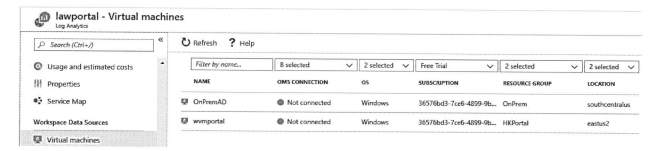

2. In right pane click VM wvmportal> Connect Blade opens> Click Connect. This will install Log Analytics Agent VM Extension> After a minute it gets connected. Status will show This workspace. Close the connect blade.

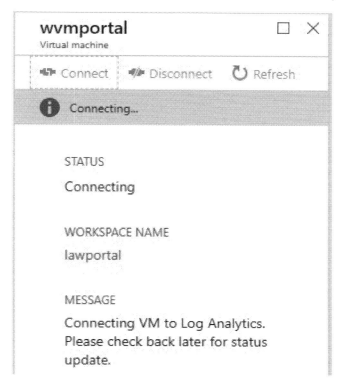

Note: Log Analytics VM Extension installs Microsoft Monitoring Agent on the machine.

Step 3: Add Data Source – IIS log

1. In Log Analytics workspace dashboard click **Advanced Settings** in left pane> In Advanced Setting pane click Data>Click IIS logs> Select Collect IIS Log files>Save> Close the Advance Settings pane.

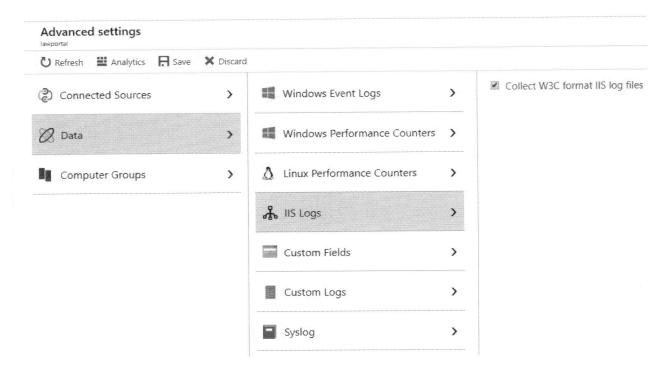

2. Click Windows Performance Counters>In right pane you can see various options for performance counters. We are not adding performance counters.

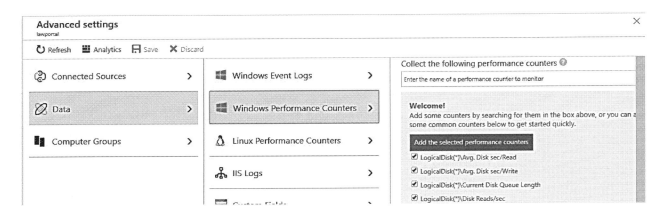

Readers are advised to scroll down and see all options for counters.

Step 4: Check IIS Log Data for Website on VM wvmportal

Wait for 30 minutes to 1 hour before proceeding with this exercise.

1. In Log Analytics workspace dashboard click **Logs (Classic)** in left pane> Logs Classic Pane opens as shown below.

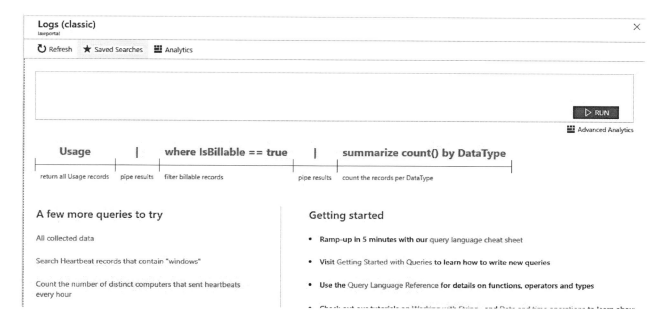

2. In Log (Classic) pane click All Collected Data> Select W3CIISLog check box>Click apply.

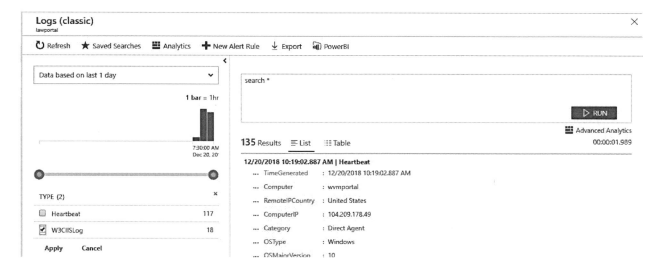

3. Now we can see all IIS Logs.

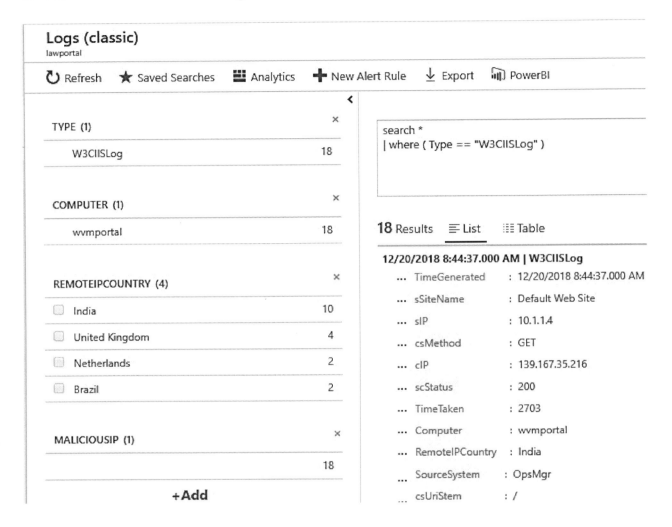

From the above figure following can be inferred.

1. The website on VM wvmportal has been accessed from 4 countries.
2. Just Scroll down the left pane and you can see IP addresses of hosts who have accessed this website.

Similar way you can monitor Performance counters, Event Logs of the connected source using Log analytics.

Note: To Add more options for IIS logs click +Add

4. To Add more options for IIS logs click +Add> Add Filter pane opens>Under W3CIISLog select the options.

Management Solutions

Management solution packs have Pre Built rules and Algorithms that perform analysis leveraging Log Analytics services. Management solutions are added to Log Analytics Workspace.

Management solutions are available both from Microsoft and partners.

Below are some of the Management solutions which can be added to Log Analytics service.

Active Directory Health Check: Active Directory Health Check solution assesses the risk and health of your server environments (Domain Controllers) on a regular interval. The solution provides a prioritized list of recommendations specific to your deployed server infrastructure.

AD Replication Status: The AD Replication Status solution pack regularly monitors your Active Directory environment for any replication failures.

Alert Management Solution: The Alert Management solution helps you analyze all of the alerts in your Log Analytics repository.

Network Performance Monitor (NPM): The Network Performance Monitor management solution is a network monitoring solution that monitors the health, availability and reachability of networks.

Network Security Group analytics solution: Network Security Group analytics management solutions collect diagnostics logs directly from Network Security Groups for analyzing them in Log analytics.

Container Monitoring Solution: Container Monitoring Solution shows which containers are running, what container image they're running, and where containers are running. You can view detailed audit information showing commands used with containers.

Key Vault Analytics solution: Azure Key Vault solution in Log Analytics reviews Azure Key Vault logs.

Office 365 management solution: Office 365 management solution allows you to monitor your Office 365 environment in Log Analytics.

Service Fabric Analytics: Identify and troubleshoot issues across Service fabric Clusters.

Service Maps: Automatically discovers and Maps servers and their dependencies in real-time. Service Map automatically discovers application components on Windows and Linux systems and maps the communication between services. It also consolidates data collected by other services and solutions to assist you in analyzing performance and identifying issues. Service Map shows connections between servers, processes, and ports across any TCP-connected architecture, with no configuration required other than the installation of an agent.

SQL Server Health Check: SQL Health Check solution assesses the risk and health of your SQL Server environments on a regular interval.

Update Management: Identifies and orchestrates the installation of missing system updates. This solution requires both Log Analytics and Automation account.

Change Tracking: Tracks configuration changes across your servers. This solution requires both Log Analytics and Automation account.

Antimalware Assessment: OMS Antimalware Assessment solution helps you identify servers that are infected or at increased risk of infection by malware.

Azure Site Recovery: Monitor's Virtual Machine replication status for your azure Site Recovery Vault.

IT Service Management (ITSM) connector: Connects Log Analytics with ITSM Products such as servicenow.

Exercise 157: Connect VM OnPremAD to Log Analytics

VM OnPremAD has Active Directory (AD DS) role installed. We will install Management Agent AD Heath Check to monitor AD DS. In this Exercise we will add VM OnPremAD to Log Analytics. In Next Exercise we will add the agent.

1. In Log Analytics workspace dashboard in left pane scroll down and under Workspace Data sources click Virtual Machines> Right pane shows the Virtual Machine status of OMS Connection. VM wvmportal is connected. This we did in previous exercise. VM OnPremAD is not connected to Log Analytics.

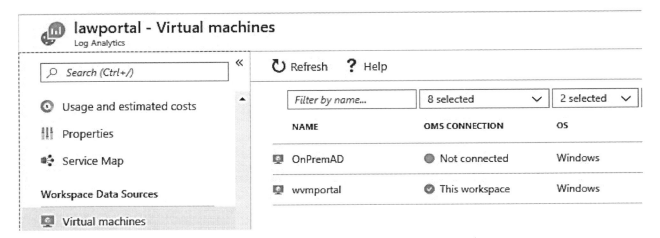

2. In right pane click VM OnPremAD> Connect Blade opens> Click Connect. This will install Log Analytics Agent VM Extension> After a minute it gets connected. Status will show This workspace. Close the connect blade.

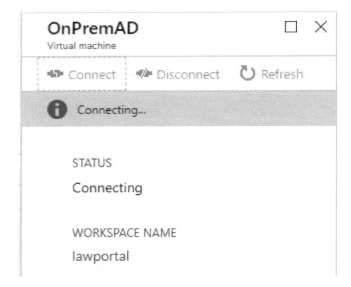

Exercise 158: Installing Management Agent (AD Heath Check)

1. Go to Log Analytics workspace dashboard> Make sure overview is selected in left pane> In Right pane under configure Monitoring Solutions click View Solutions.

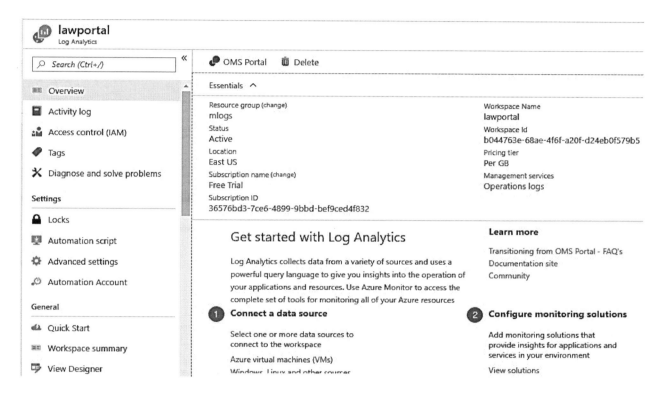

2. Add Solution Pane opens>Click +Add> Management Solution Blade opens>Scroll down and select Active Directory Health Check> Active Directory Health Check blade opens>Click Create (Not shown in Figure).

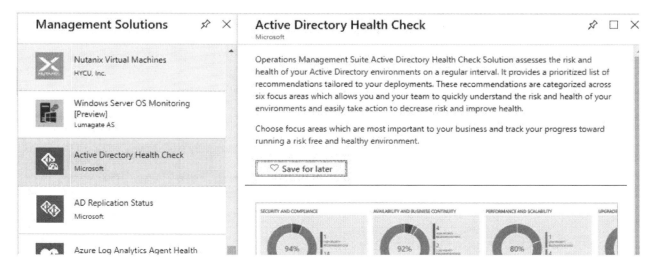

3. Create new Solution Blade opens> Click create.

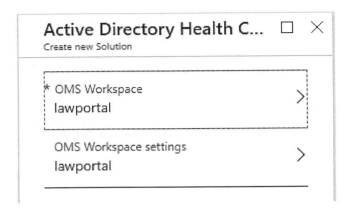

4. After Deployment is succeeded go to Log Analytics Dashboard and click Solutions in left pane> You can see ADAssessment Solution is added.

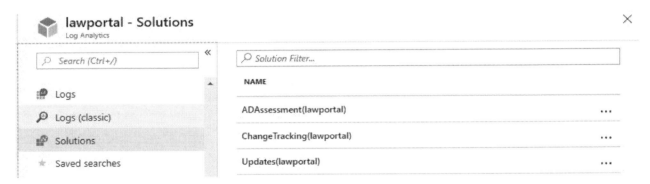

Note 1: This agent will monitor AD health Check in VM OnPremAD. Active Directory role was installed in VM OnPremAD in Chapter 3, Exercise 32.
Note 2: Readers are advised to scroll down and see all management solutions which are available.

5. Wait for 10-15 minutes and then Click on Solution ADAssessment as shown in previous figure> ADAssessment dashboard opens. You need to continuously refresh the screen with F5.

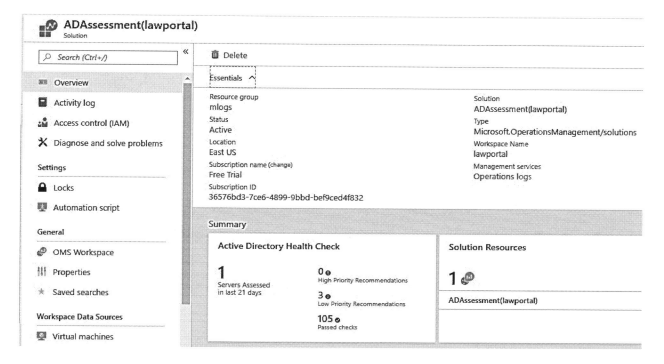

3. Click on Summary Pane> There are 3 low priority Recommendation Under Availability and Business Continuity.

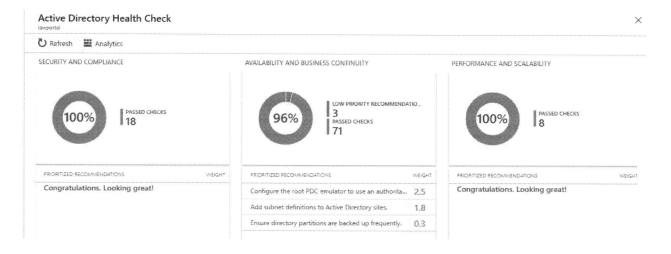

As an exercise to Readers go through all Management solutions and add Service Map Management Solution

Exercise 159: Installing Microsoft Monitoring Agent in On-Premises VM

In this exercise we will just demonstrate the steps on how to install MMA in On-Premises Server or VM.

1. From your on-premises VM open browser and log on to Azure Portal.
2. Go to Log Analytics Workspace dashboard> Click Advanced Settings in left pane>Connected Sources> Select Windows or Linux Servers as per your requirement>In right pane download the agent on your Windows or Linux Machine> Note down Workspace ID and Primary Key. This will be required to register the server with Log Analytics Workspace during installation.

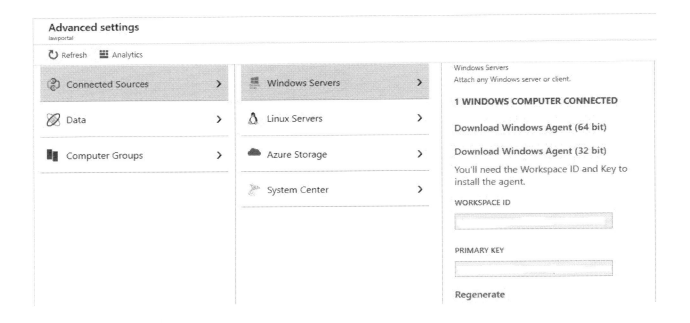

Advisor

Azure Advisor is a personalized recommendation engine that provides proactive best practices guidance for optimally configuring your Azure resources.

Azure Advisor gives recommendation to optimize across following **four** different areas.

High Availability
Performance
Security
Cost

All recommendations accessible in one place on the Azure portal. Azure Advisor is a free service.

Working

It analyzes your resource configuration and usage telemetry. It then recommends solutions to help improve the performance, security, and high availability of your resources while looking for opportunities to reduce your overall Azure spend.

Exercise 160: Checking Advisor Recommendations

1. In Azure Portal click Advisor in Left pane> Advisor Dashboard opens. It shows recommendation in 4 areas - High availability, Performance, Security and Cost.

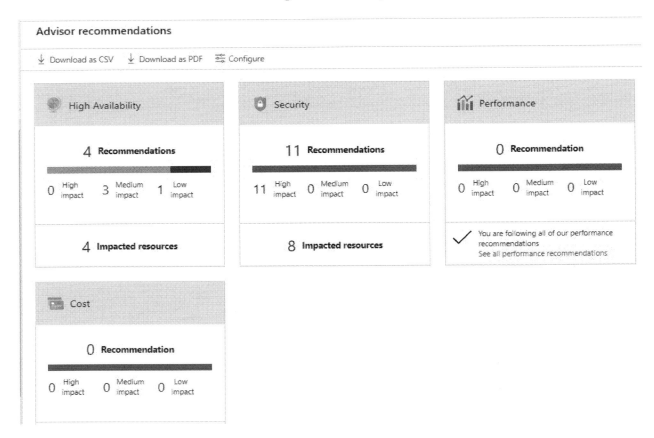

2. Click on High Availability Tab and you can see there are 4 Recommendations.

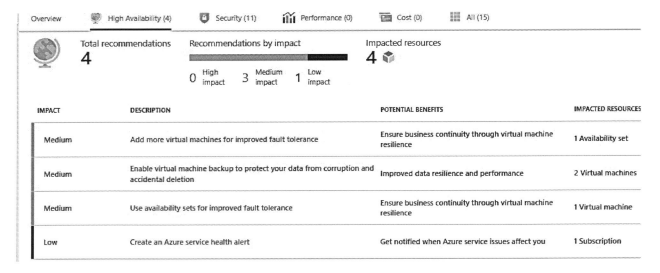

IMPACT	DESCRIPTION	POTENTIAL BENEFITS	IMPACTED RESOURCES
Medium	Add more virtual machines for improved fault tolerance	Ensure business continuity through virtual machine resilience	1 Availability set
Medium	Enable virtual machine backup to protect your data from corruption and accidental deletion	Improved data resilience and performance	2 Virtual machines
Medium	Use availability sets for improved fault tolerance	Ensure business continuity through virtual machine resilience	1 Virtual machine
Low	Create an Azure service health alert	Get notified when Azure service issues affect you	1 Subscription

3. Click on the 1ˢᵗ Recommendation. It is recommending that one more VM to be added to Availability Set asportal. Recall that we added only one VM wvmportal created in Exercise 24 to Availability Set created in Exercise 23.

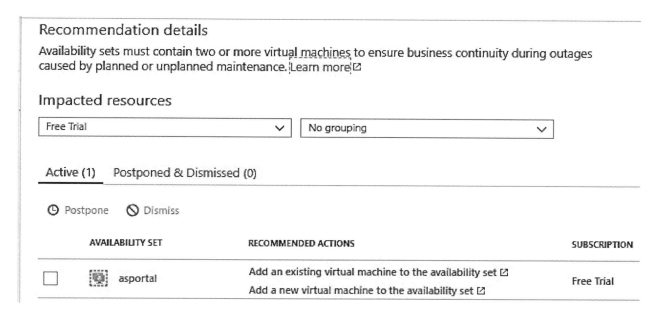

4. Click on Security Tab and you can see there are 11 Recommendations.

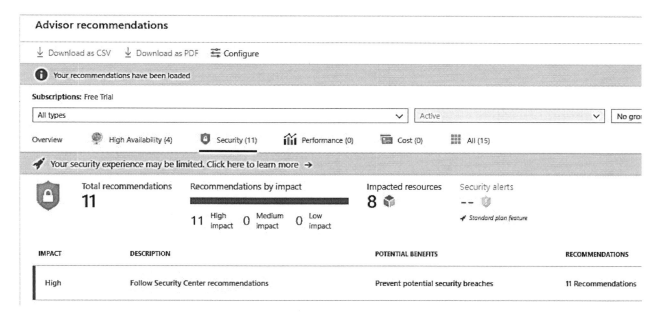

5. Click on the recommendation and its shows recommendation available from Security Center.

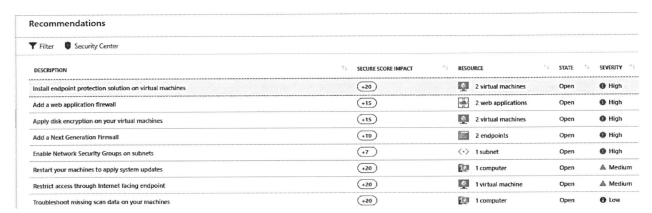

DESCRIPTION	SECURE SCORE IMPACT		RESOURCE	STATE	SEVERITY
Install endpoint protection solution on virtual machines	(+20)		2 virtual machines	Open	High
Add a web application firewall	(+15)		2 web applications	Open	High
Apply disk encryption on your virtual machines	(+15)		2 virtual machines	Open	High
Add a Next Generation Firewall	(+10)		2 endpoints	Open	High
Enable Network Security Groups on subnets	(+7)		1 subnet	Open	High
Restart your machines to apply system updates	(+20)		1 computer	Open	Medium
Restrict access through Internet facing endpoint	(+20)		1 virtual machine	Open	Medium
Troubleshoot missing scan data on your machines	(+20)		1 computer	Open	Low

Azure Service Health

Azure Service Health provides status of Azure services which can affect your business critical applications. It also helps you prepare for upcoming planned maintenance. Azure Service Health alerts you and your teams via targeted and flexible notifications.

Service Health Events

Service Health tracks following three types of health events that may impact your resources:

1. **Service issues** - Problems in the Azure services that affect you right now.
2. **Planned maintenance** - Upcoming maintenance that can affect the availability of your services in the future.
3. **Health advisories** - Changes in Azure services that require your attention. Examples include when Azure features are deprecated or if you exceed a usage quota.

Exercise 161: Checking Service Health Events

1. Go to Monitor Dashboard>Click Service Health Tile in left pane> Service Health Dashboard Opens> currently there are no Service issues.

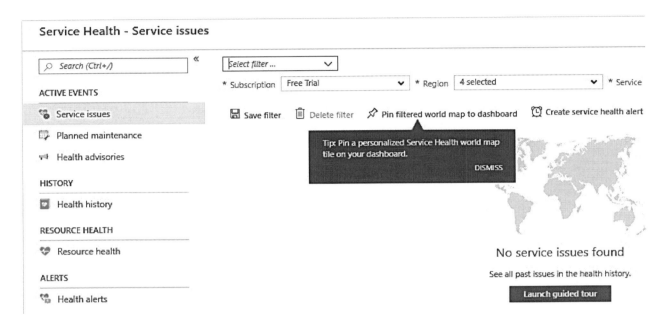

2. Click on Planned maintenance in left pane> No events are scheduled.

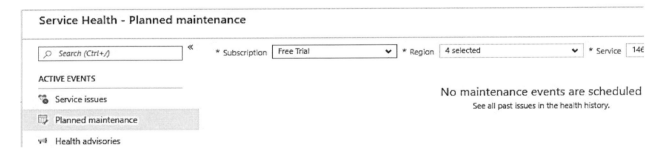

3. Click on Health advisories in left pane> No advisories are found.

Exercise 162: Configuring Alerts for Service Health Events

In this Exercise we will create email Alert on Service Health events – Service Issues, Planned maintenance and Health Advisories.

1. In Service Health Dashboard click Health alerts in left pane.

2. Click +Create Service Health Alert in Right pane>Add Rule Blade opens>Selects Events as per your req>Select Action Group created in Exercise 153>Give a name and description for alert rule> click Yes to enable rule and Click Create Alert Rule.

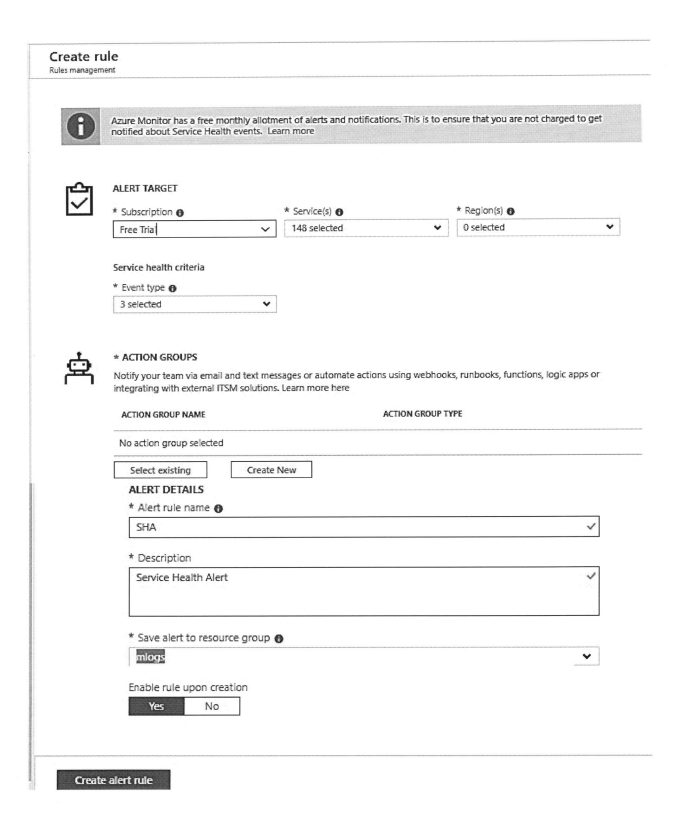

Chapter 16 Azure Automation

This Chapter covers following Topic Lessons

- Azure Automation
- Process Automation Working and Architecture
- Automate configuration management using Desired State Configuration
- Update Management
- Inventory Management
- Change Tracking

This Chapter covers following Lab Exercises

- Create Automation Account
- Desired State Configuration (DSC) using Azure Automation
- PowerShell DSC Extension
- Enabling Update Management and Add Azure VM
- Scheduling Update Deployment
- Enabling Inventory Management and Add VM wvmportal
- Checking Change Tracking for VM wvmportal

Chapter Topology

In this chapter we will add Azure Automation to the Topology.

From Automation Dashboard we will configure Desired State Configuration. From Automation Dashboard we will also enable Update, Inventory and Change Tracking Management for Azure Virtual Machines.

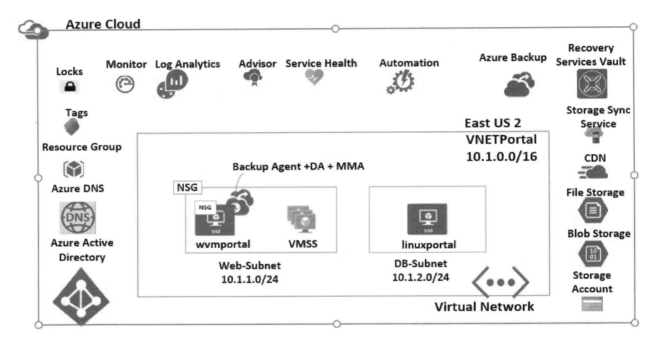

Azure Automation

Azure Automation is a managed service that provides **process automation, configuration management, update management, Inventory Management and Change Tracking.** It automates manual processes (Process Automation) and enforces configurations for physical and virtual computers (Desired State Configuration) and Update/Inventory/change tracking for Azure VMs or On-premises VMs or Physical Servers

Figure below shows the architecture of Azure Automation. Azure Automation provides it functionality to both Azure and on-premises resources.

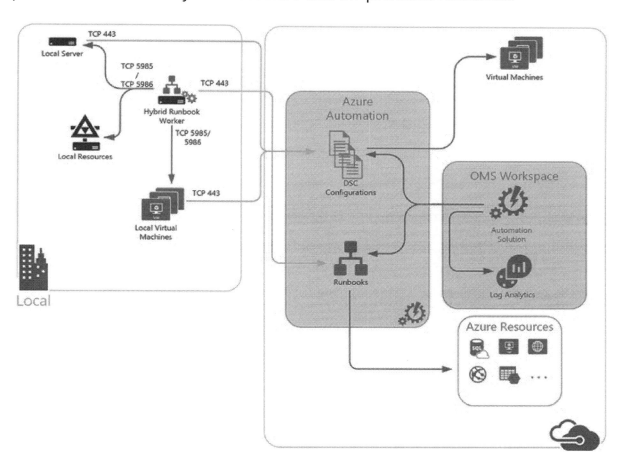

Log analytics workspace is required if you want to offer Update Management, change & Inventory tracking functionality and Hybrid worker solution. It also collects Runbook job status and receives configuration information from your Automation account.

Exercise 163: Create Automation Account

1. In Azure Portal click create a resource> Management Tools>Automation>
   Add Automation Account Blade opens>Enter a name, Select HKPortal in
   Resource Group and click create

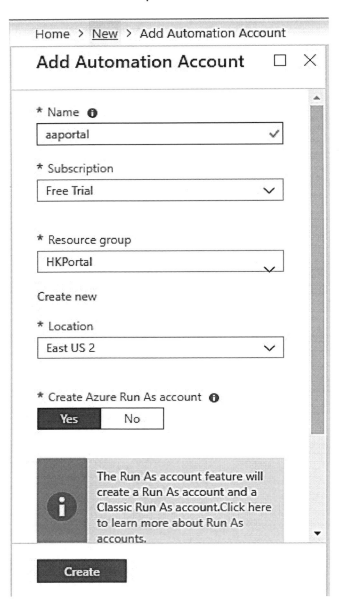

2. Figure below shows Automation Account Dashboard.

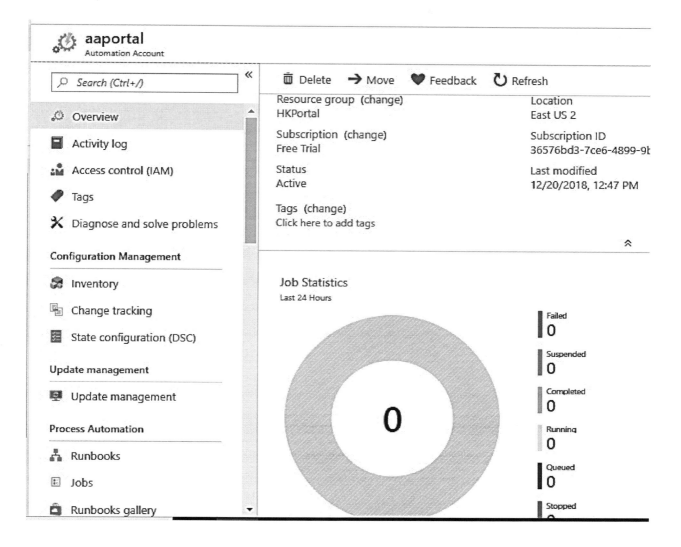

From Automation Dashboard you can configure Desired State Configuration and Process Automation. From Automation Dashboard you can also enable Update, Inventory and Change Tracking Management for Azure Virtual Machines or on-premises servers.

Process Automation Working and Architecture

Azure Process Automation automates manual processes using Runbooks against Azure Resources. Runbooks are containers for custom scripts and workflows. You can invoke and run runbooks on demand or according to schedule by using Automation Schedule assets or based on alerts in OMS Log Analytics.

Figure below shows Architecture of Process Automation.

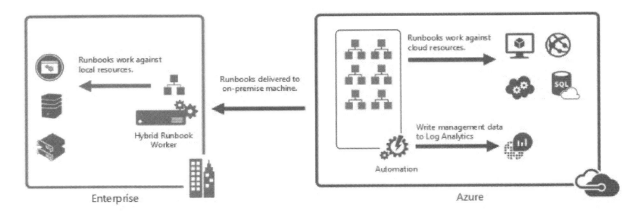

Runbooks are created in Azure Automation Account and work against Azure Resources such as VMs, Azure SQL, Web Apps etc to automate manual process.

Runbooks can also run on-premises where-in you can install one or more Hybrid Runbook Workers in your data center which run runbooks against local resources. Each Hybrid Runbook Worker requires Microsoft Management Agent to be installed and an Automation account. The agent must have a connection to an Azure Log Analytics workspace.

Example of Process Automation

You want your Azure VMs to run only during office hours only (8 AM – 5 PM). To save money an administrator shuts down VMs at 5 PM and Re-Starts at 8 AM. Using Azure Process Automation you can Automate shutdown and re-start activity. You can use Azure Process Automation to create Runbooks (containing Powershell scripts) to shutdown VMs and Re-start VMs which run against your Azure VMs at Schedule time daily.

Automate configuration management using Desired State Configuration

Desired State Configuration (DSC) is a configuration management platform in Windows PowerShell that deploys and enforces the configuration on Windows VMs and Physical Servers.

PowerShell DSC configurations are PowerShell scripts that apply Desired Configurations to Windows VMs and Physical Servers. You can apply DSC to Azure VMs in following 2 ways:

1. Azure Automation DSC Service.
2. Add DSC Extension on Azure VM.

Azure Automation DSC Service

Azure Automation provides a pull server in the cloud that manages DSC configurations which nodes can access to retrieve required configurations.

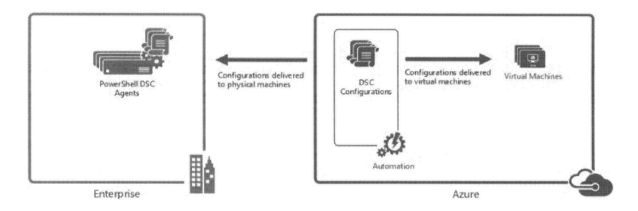

PowerShell DSC configurations are PowerShell scripts that apply Desired configurations to DSC Nodes from a DSC Pull Server in the Azure cloud. If DSC nodes deviate from there desired configuration then you can manually or automatically update desired machine configuration on DSC nodes.

Azure VMs require Desired State Configuration agent extension. It is automatically deployed to Azure VMs when you add them as DSC nodes in Automation Account Dashboard. Non Azure VMs & Servers require Powershell DSC agents.

DSC Extension on Azure VM

The extension uploads and applies a PowerShell DSC Configuration on an Azure VM.

In this case node (Azure VM) is *not* centrally managed. DSC extension involves a singular action that occurs during deployment.

The other disadvantage of this approach is that you have to apply DSC Extension to each VM separately.

Important Note: DSC extension differs from Azure Automation DSC Service in a sense that this involves a singular action that occurs during deployment. No ongoing reporting or configuration management is available, other than locally in the VM.

Advantages of Using Desired State Configuration (DSC) with Azure Automation

Advantage 1 of Using DSC with Azure Automation is that you can apply configuration to Multiple nodes simultaneously.
Advantage 2 of Using DSC with Azure Automation is that if nodes drift from their configuration it is reapplied by DSC Pull Server.

Exercise 164: Desired State Configuration using Azure Automation

In this exercise we will disable IIS Web Server role on VM wvmportal using Desired State Configuration (DSC). Recall that IIS role was enabled in VM wvmportal in Chapter 3, Exercise 26.

Step 1: Create a PS script which ensures either the presence or absence of the Web-Server Windows Feature (IIS).

I created below PS script in notepad and saved it as **TestConfig.ps1** on my desktop.

```
configuration TestConfig
{
  Node IsWebServer
  {
    WindowsFeature IIS
    {
      Ensure            = 'Present'
      Name              = 'Web-Server'
      IncludeAllSubFeature = $true
    }
  }

  Node NotWebServer
  {
    WindowsFeature IIS
    {
      Ensure            = 'Absent'
      Name              = 'Web-Server'
    }
  }
}
```

Step 2: Import the Configuration into Azure Automation

1. In Azure Automation **aaportal** Dashboard click **State Configuration (DSC)** in left pane> DSC pane opens.

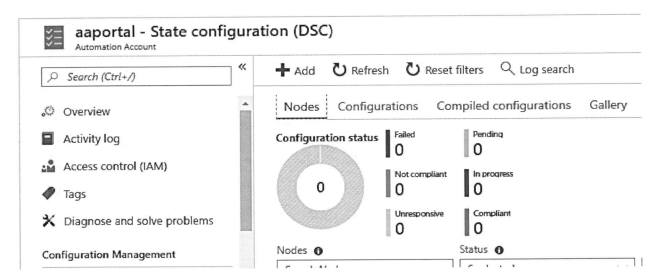

2. Click Configuration in right pane>Click + Add>Import Configuration blade opens>Upload TestConfig.ps1 from your desktop. This was created in step 1> Click Ok.

3. You can now see the Configuration which was imported. If required press Refresh tab.

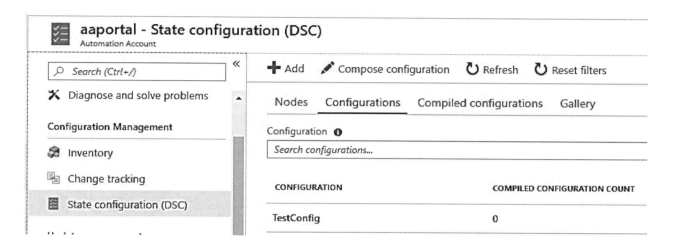

Step 3 Compile the Configuration

1. Click the Configuration TestConfig as shown in above screen>TestConfig Pane opens.

2. Click Compile>Compile DSC Configuration box pops up>Click Yes.

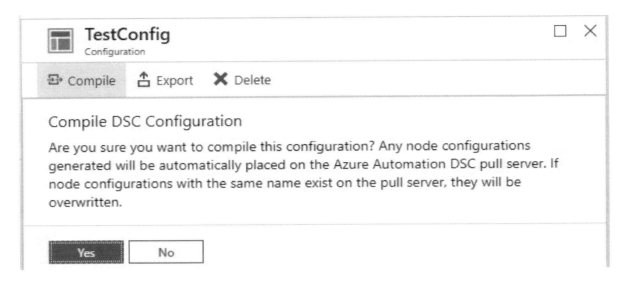

3. It will take 1-2 minutes to compile the job. You can see compiled configuration. If required press Refresh screen.

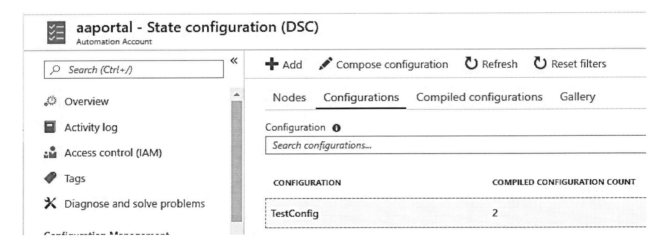

Step 4 View the Node Configurations which were compiled

In Azure Automation **aaportal** Dashboard click **State Configuration (DSC)** in left pane> DSC pane opens>Click Compiled Configurations in right pane> You can see the 2 configurations options. No Node is assigned.

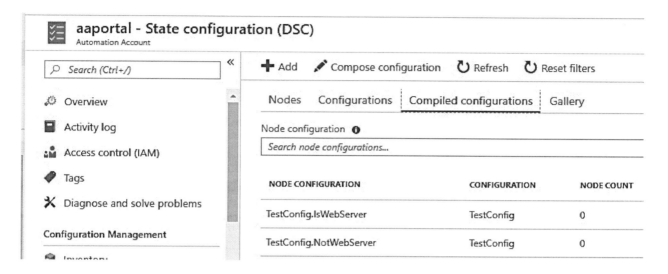

Step 5 Assign the Node VM wvmportal to DSC Pull Configuration Server

1. In Azure Automation **aaportal** Dashboard click **State Configuration (DSC)** in left pane> DSC pane opens>Click Nodes in right pane>Currently no node is assigned.

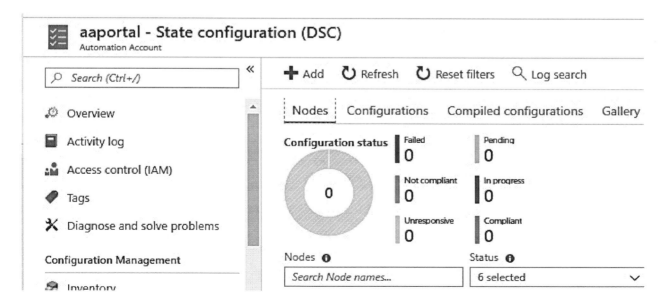

2. Click + Add>Select wvmportal>Connect pane opens>Click + Connect> Registration pane opens>Select your Configuration from Drop down box> I selected **TestConfig.NotWebServer**>Rest Select all default values>Click Ok.

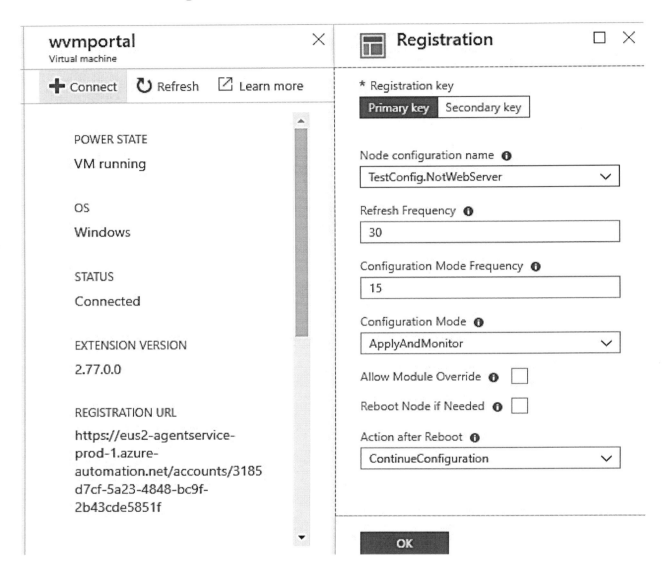

3. It will, take 2-5 minutes for Node to get connected.

4. In Nodes screen you can see 1 Node added and it is not compliant. It is showing in progress.

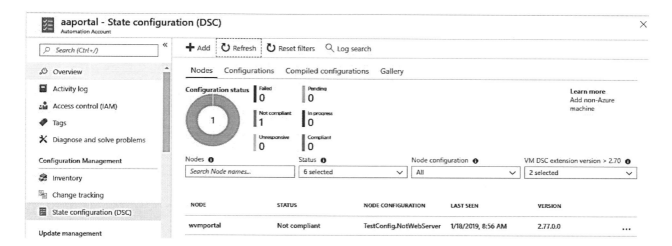

5. After 3-5 Minutes you can see node is compliant.

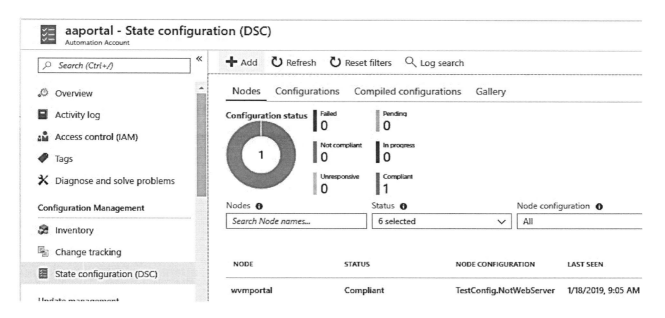

Step 6 Check that IIS Role has been removed from VM wvmportal

RDP to VM wvmportal>Open Server Manager>Click Add Roles and features>Click next>Select Role based or Feature based Installation and click next>Select VM wvmportal and click next>In Server Roles you can see IIS Role (4th from bottom) has been removed. Recall that IIS role was enabled in VM wvmportal in Chapter 3, Exercise 26.

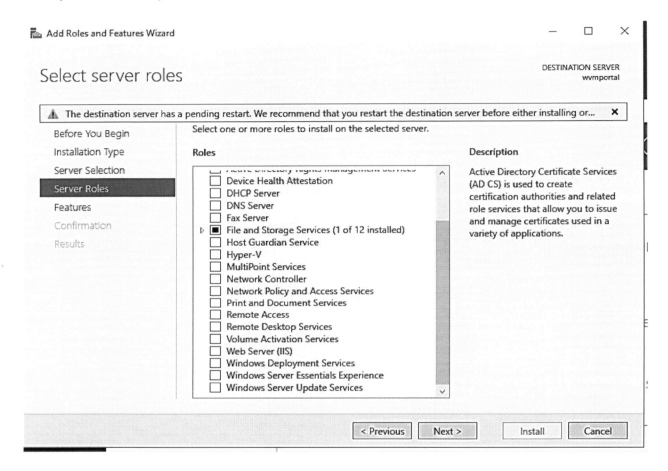

Note: For testing I am not using URL to access default IIS website on VM wvmportal as in CDN lab we had setup endpoint to cache the default website. It will be served from CDN endpoint despite being disabled in VM wvmportal.

Exercise 165: PowerShell DSC Extension

In this exercise we will just demonstrate on how to apply PowerShell DSC extension to Azure VM.

3. Go to VM wvmportal dashboard>Click Extension in left pane>In Right pane click + Add> Add Extension blade opens>Select PowerShell Desired State Configuration> PowerShell Desired State Configuration blade opens in right pane.

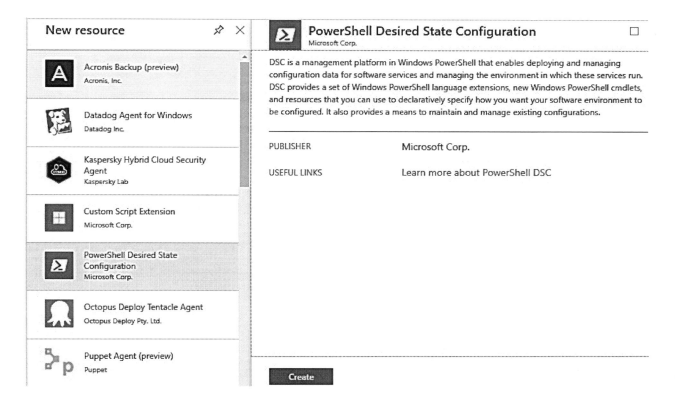

4. In right pane click create> Install Extension Blade opens>Click folder icon and upload file for executing on VM wvmportal.

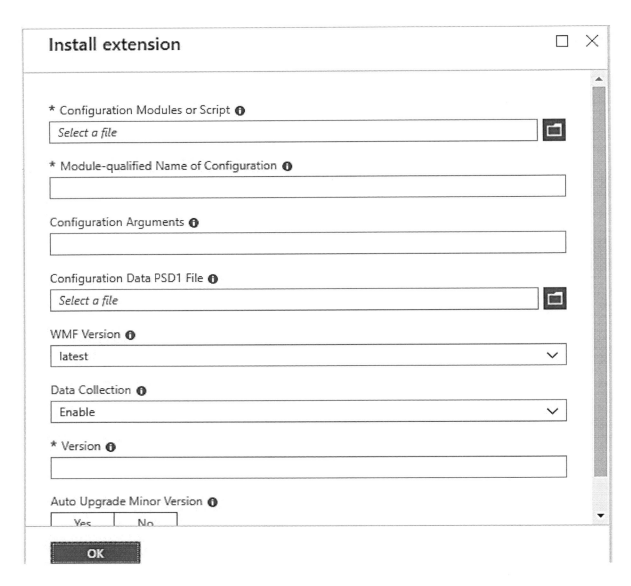

Disadvantage of this approach is that you have to apply PowerShell DSC extension to each Azure VM separately.

Update Management

The Update Management solution in Azure automation allows you to manage operating system security updates for your Windows and Linux computers deployed in Azure, on-premises environments, or other cloud providers.

Update Management Functionality requires Log analytics workspace.

With update management, you will always know the compliance status for Windows and Linux machines and you can create scheduled deployments to orchestrate the installation of updates within a defined maintenance window.

Exercise 166: Enabling Update Management and Add Azure VM

This exercise will enable Update Management and add Azure VM wvmportal for Assessment. After this is enabled you can see the missing updates. This step will not deploy the updates.

We will use Log Analytics workspace created in Chapter 15, Exercise 156. You can enable Update Management through Automation Account Dashboard or through Virtual Machine Dashboard. For this exercise we will use Automation Account Dashboard.

1. In Azure Automation Account aaportal Dashboard click Update Management in left pane>In right pane select Log Analytics workspace created in Exercise 156>Click enable.

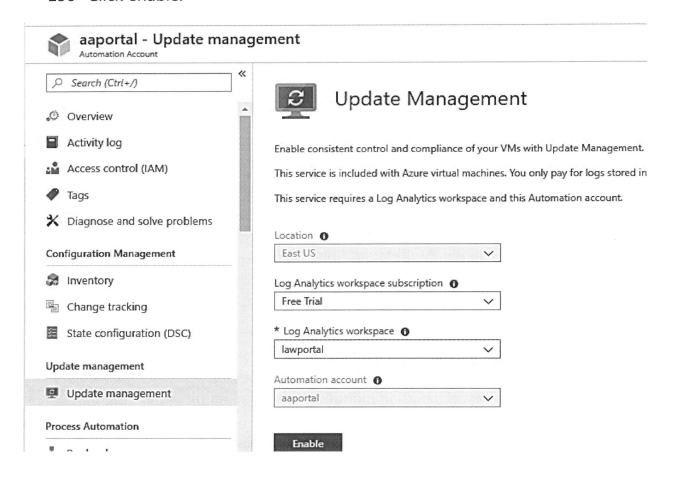

2. After Deployment is enabled refresh the screen with F5. Make sure Update Management is selected in left pane.

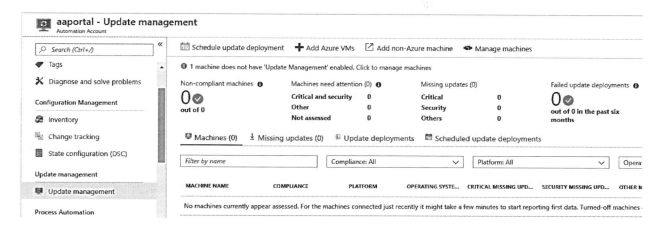

3. Click + Add Azure VMs in Right Pane> Enable Update Management pane opens>Select VM wvmportal> Click enable.

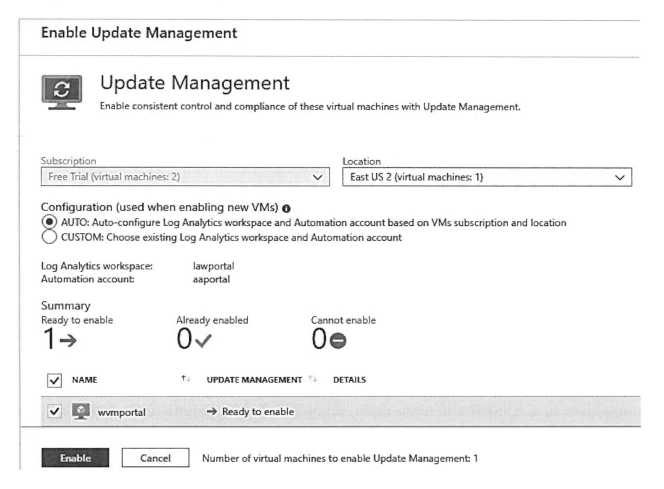

4. Wait 20-25 minutes for Virtual Machine to appear on Update Management pane. Just refresh the screen with F5 continously with update Managemnt selected in left pane.

In Figure below you can see one security update and one other update is missing.

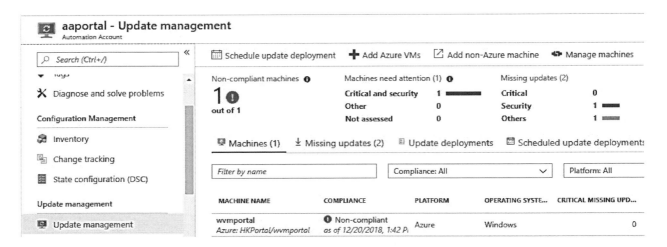

Click on missing updates> you can see the updates which are missing.

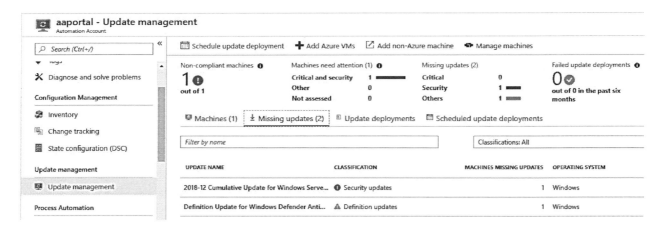

Exercise 167: Scheduling Update Deployment

1. In Update Management pane click schedule update deployment>New update Deployment pane opens>Enter a name> click Machine to update>In Right pane select Machines from dropdown box>Make sure VM wvmportal appears under Machines >Click VM wvmportal and it now also appears under selected items>Click Ok in right pane>In left pane in schedule settings select the start time and Recurrence as Once or Recurring>Click Create.

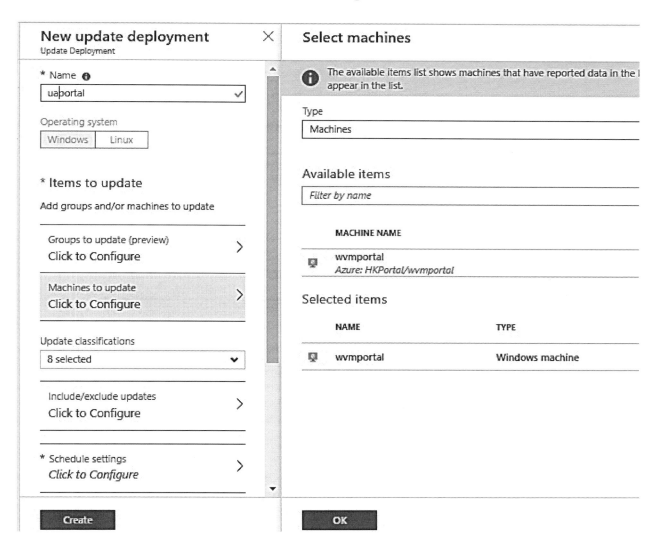

Note: Readers are advised to check options in update classification pane. Also scroll down to see all the options.

2. Click on Scheduled Update Deployments and you can see one deployment Job created in step 1 is scheduled for 2.28 PM.

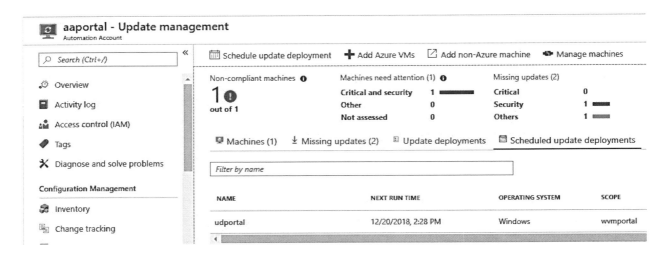

3. Click on Update deployments> It will start the deployment and will show you the progress of the updates being applied. In figure below shows 2 updates were applied and Machine is now compliant.

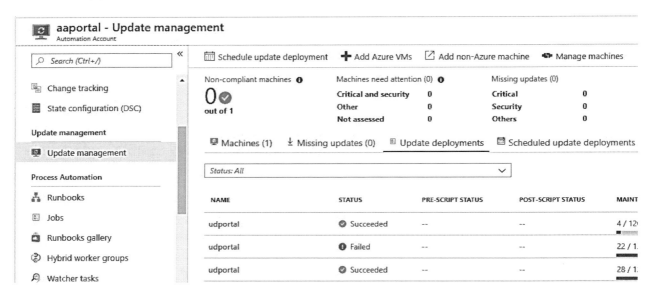

Inventory Management

Enabling inventory of your VMs in Azure Automation gives you visibility into installed applications as well as other configuration items you wish to track. Rich reporting and search is available to quickly find detailed information to help understand everything that is configured within the VM.

Change Tracking

Change tracking tracks changes across services, software, registry, daemons, and files to quickly identify what might be causing issues and to enable diagnostics and alerting when unwanted changes occur.

Note: When you enable Inventory for a VM then change tracking is also enabled automatically.

Exercise 168: Enabling Inventory Management and Add VM wvmportal

1. In Azure Automation Account **aaportal** Dashboard click **Inventory** in left pane> In Right pane select Log Analytics workspace lawportal created in Chapter 15, Exercise 156>Click enable

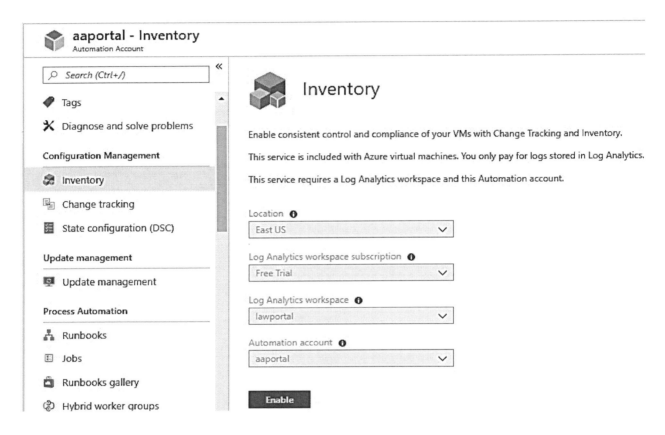

2. After Deployment is enabled refresh the screen with F5. Make sure Inventory is selected in left pane.

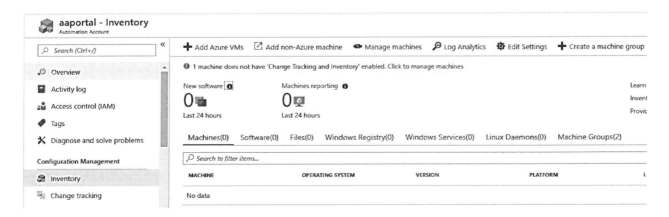

3. Click Add Azure VMs in Right pane>Enable Inventory Blade opens>Check the VM wvmportal>Click enable> Close the enable inventory pane.

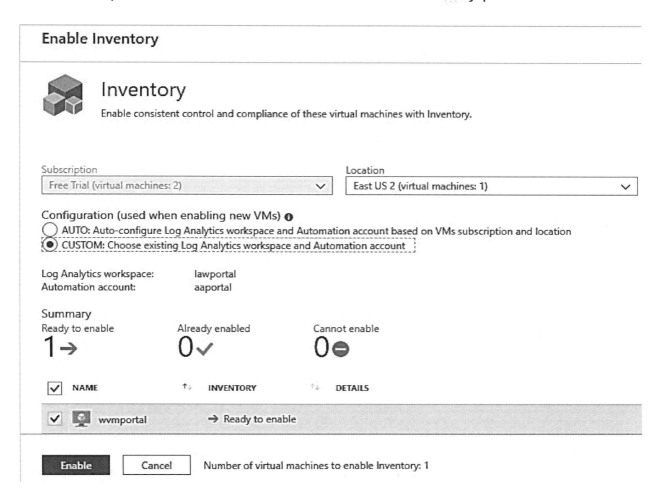

4. After 30-40 minutes VM wvportal appeared in inventory pane. Keep on refreshing Automation Account Dashboard with inventory selected.

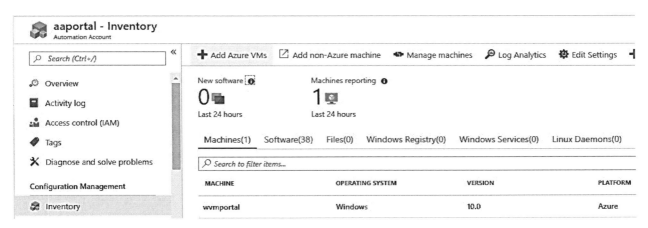

5. Click on the software tab in right pane> You can see software installed in last 24 hours.

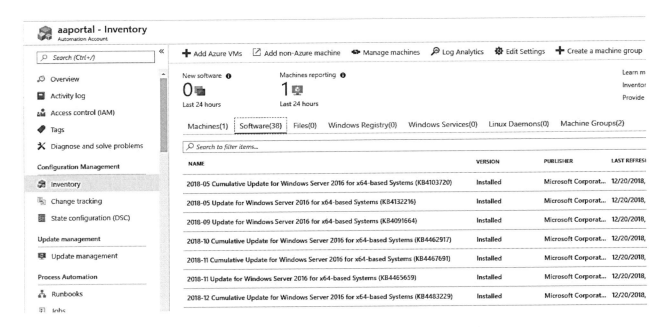

Exercise 169: Checking Change Tracking for VM wvmportal

In Azure Automation Account **aaportal** Dashboard click **Change tracking** in left pane> In Right pane you can see changes which have occurred in Azure VM wvmportal.

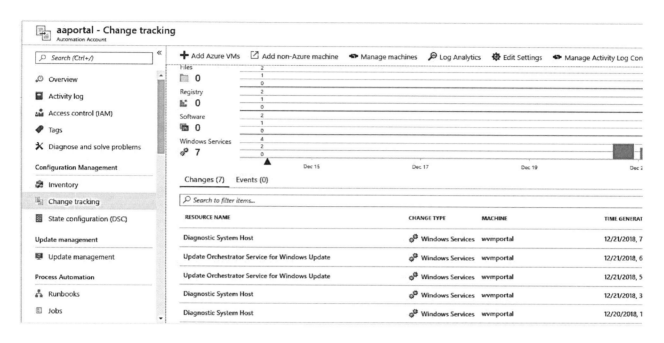

Chapter 17 Azure Resource Manager (ARM) Template

This Chapter covers following Topic Lessons

- Azure Resource Manager (ARM) Template
- Why we need ARM Template
- Advantages of ARM Template
- Creating ARM template options
- ARM Template Deployment Options
- Viewing ARM Template

This Chapter covers following Lab Exercises

- View ARM Template of an Existing Resource
- Save a Template in library
- Deploy or Edit Template

Azure Resource Manager (ARM) Template

ARM Templates are used to deploy resources using Infrastructure as a Code.

ARM Template is a text based JavaScript Object Notation (JSON) file that defines one or more resources to deploy to a resource group. It also defines the dependencies between the deployed resources. The template can be re-used to deploy the resources consistently and repeatedly.

Templates are also created by MS and 3rd parties. Figure below shows a sample ARM Template for Storage account creation.

```
 1  {
 2      "$schema":
        "https://schema.management.azure.com/schemas/2015-01-01/deploymen
        tTemplate.json#",
 3      "contentVersion": "1.0.0.0",
 4      "parameters": {
 5          "storageAccounts_arm4100201_name": {
 6              "defaultValue": "arm4100201",
 7              "type": "String"
 8          }
 9      },
10      "variables": {},
```

Why we need ARM Template

Take an Example that you need to deploy a 3 tier application (Web/App/DB) in a new Virtual network. Internet user will connect to Web Tier, Web Tier will connect to App and App will connect to DB tier.

Using Azure Portal or Powershell we can deploy these resources one by one. To deploy we first need to create Virtual network and 3 subnets. Deploy VMs to these 3 subnets. Configure NSG on Subnets and VM NICs. There are following disadvantages to this approach:

1. It is time consuming to deploy and configure the resources.
2. It is error prone
3. You require skilled resources for deployment.

Instead of above option of deploying resources individually we can create an ARM template once, specifying multiple resources and other configurations parameters for deployment. Using this ARM template you can now deploy multiple resources (VNET, Subnet, NSG & Virtual Machines) simultaneously. The ARM template can be re-used multiple times.

Advantages of ARM Template

1. We can deploy, manage, and monitor all the resources for our solution as a group, rather than handling these resources individually.
2. We can re-use the ARM template any number of times.
3. Saves time.
4. We can define the dependencies between resources so they are deployed in the correct order.

Creating ARM template options

1. Create an ARM Template from scratch using JSON.
2. Download a template of a resource from Azure Portal and Edit it as per your requirement and then deploy it.

ARM Template Deployment Options

1. Powershell
2. CLI
3. Azure Portal

Viewing ARM Template of an Existing Resource

You can view Template of a resource using **Automation Script** Tab in Resource Dashboard.

Exercise 170: View ARM Template of an Existing Resource

In this Exercise we will view Template of Storage Account sastdportal. Storage Account sastdportal was created in Chapter 6, Exercise 50.

1. In Azure Portal click Storage Accounts in left pane>All Storage Account Blade opens>Click sastdportal > sastdportal Dashboard opens>Click **Automation Script** in left pane>In right pane you can see ARM template of Storage Account sastdportal.

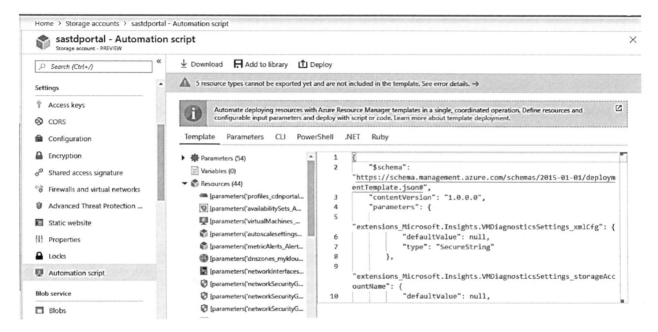

Note the 3 options in Top right – Download, Add to library and Deploy.

Download: With this option you can download Template to your desktop.

Add to Library: With this option you can save the template in Library in Azure.

Deploy: With this option you can deploy the template to create a Resource.

Exercise 171: Save a Template in library

In this lab we will save template of Storage Account sastdportal in Library in your Azure Account.

1. In Azure Portal go to Storage Account sastdportal Dashboard>Click Automation script in left pane> In right pane you can see template.

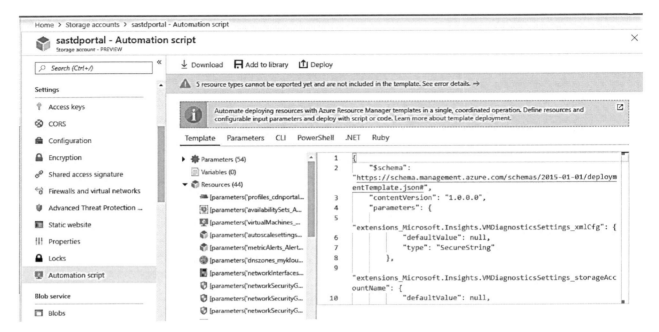

2. Click Add to Library in Right pane>Save template blade opens> Enter a name sa2 and Enter Description>Click Save (Not shown).

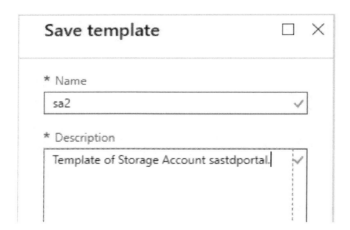

3. **Check the saved Template**. In Azure Portal click All Services in left pane>All Services Blade opens>Note Templates option under General.

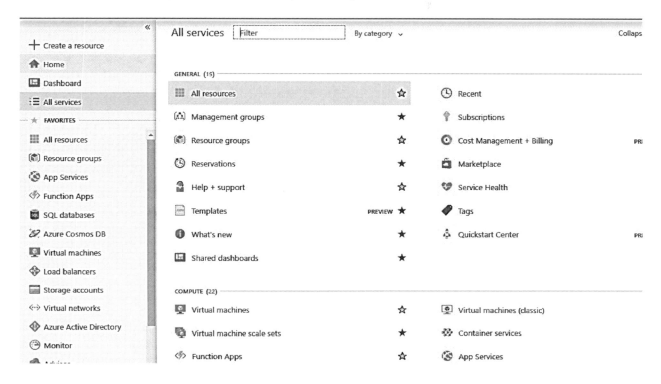

4. Click Templates under General>All Templates blade opens>You can see the sa2 template.

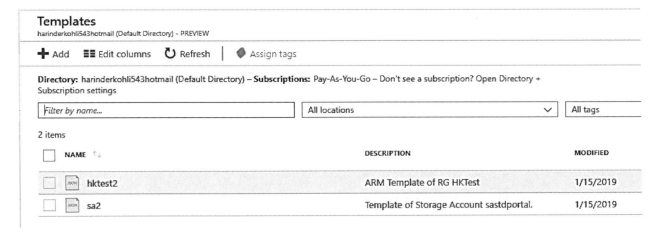

Exercise 172: Deploy or Edit Template

In this Exercise we will demonstrate deployment or Editing of Template. We will use the template sa2 which was saved in library in Previous Exercise.

1. In Azure Portal click All Services in left pane>All Services Blade opens>Click Templates under General>All Templates Blade opens>Click Template sa2 >sa2 Template blade opens.

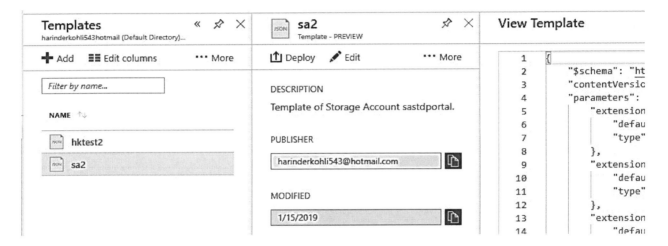

2. From here you can deploy or edit the template.

Chapter 18 Installing Azure PowerShell Module & Azure CLI

This Chapter covers following Topic Lessons

- Azure PowerShell Module
- Azure CLI

This Chapter covers following Lab Exercises

- Install latest Version of PowerShellGet
- Install & Import Azure PowerShell Module
- Connecting to Azure using Azure PowerShell Module

Azure PowerShell

Azure PowerShell provides a set of cmdlets that use the Azure Resource Manager model for managing your Azure resources. You can use it in your browser with Azure Cloud Shell, or you can install it on your local machine and use it in any PowerShell session.

Exercise 173: Install latest Version of PowerShellGet

1. Open PowerShell in your Windows 10 Desktop and run following command.
2. Install-Module PowerShellGet -Force

```
PS C:\WINDOWS\system32> Install-Module PowerShellGet -Force

NuGet provider is required to continue
PowerShellGet requires NuGet provider version '2.8.5.201' or newer to interact with NuGet-based repositories. The NuGet
provider must be available in 'C:\Program
Files\PackageManagement\ProviderAssemblies' or 'C:\Users\Harinder Kohli\AppData\Local\PackageManagement\ProviderAssembli
es'. You can also install the NuGet provider by running
'Install-PackageProvider -Name NuGet -MinimumVersion 2.8.5.201 -Force'. Do you want PowerShellGet to install and import
the NuGet provider now?
[Y] Yes  [N] No  [S] Suspend  [?] Help (default is "Y"): y
PS C:\WINDOWS\system32>
```

3. Set the PowerShell execution policy to RemoteSigned.

```
Administrator: Windows PowerShell                                              —    □    ×

Windows PowerShell
Copyright (C) Microsoft Corporation. All rights reserved.

PS C:\WINDOWS\system32> Set-ExecutionPolicy -ExecutionPolicy RemoteSigned

Execution Policy Change
The execution policy helps protect you from scripts that you do not trust. Changing the execution policy might expose
you to the security risks described in the about_Execution_Policies help topic at
https://go.microsoft.com/fwlink/?LinkID=135170. Do you want to change the execution policy?
[Y] Yes  [A] Yes to All  [N] No  [L] No to All  [S] Suspend  [?] Help (default is "N"): y
PS C:\WINDOWS\system32>
```

Exercise 174: Install & Import Azure PowerShell Module

1. Install-Module -Name AzureRM –AllowClobber
2. Import-Module -Name AzureRM

```
PS C:\WINDOWS\system32> Install-Module -Name AzureRM -AllowClobber

Untrusted repository
You are installing the modules from an untrusted repository. If you trust this repository, cha
nge its
InstallationPolicy value by running the Set-PSRepository cmdlet. Are you sure you want to inst
all the modules from
'PSGallery'?
[Y] Yes  [A] Yes to All  [N] No  [L] No to All  [S] Suspend  [?] Help (default is "N"): y
PS C:\WINDOWS\system32> Import-Module -Name AzureRM
PS C:\WINDOWS\system32>
```

Exercise 175: Connecting to Azure using Azure PowerShell Module

1. On your desktop open Windows PowerShell App. Just type Powershell in search box and you can see Windows PowerShell App.
2. Connect-AzureRmAccount
3. This will open a browser for connecting to Azure. Enter username and password for connecting to Azure.

4. After you have successfully authenticated to Azure through Browser, The Powershell window will now show Azure information as shown below.

```
PS C:\WINDOWS\system32> Connect-AzureRmAccount


Account            : harinderkohli@hotmail.com
SubscriptionName   : Pay-As-You-Go
SubscriptionId     : d293caf2-261c-4101-848a-c7e69524dc3a
TenantId           : 37f410dd-05ca-42c2-997a-24223270b9aa
Environment        : AzureCloud
```

5. You can also confirm above by running following command.
   Get-AzureRmSubscription

```
PS C:\WINDOWS\system32> Get-AzureRmSubscription


Name     : Pay-As-You-Go
Id       : d293caf2-261c-4101-848a-c7e69524dc3a
TenantId : 37f410dd-05ca-42c2-997a-24223270b9aa
State    : Enabled
```

Azure CLI

The Azure CLI is a command-line tool for managing Azure resources. The CLI is designed to make scripting easy, query data and support long-running operations. Azure CLI is installed via an MSI.

Note: You have the option of using Azure CLI Cloud Shell in Azure Portal instead of installing Azure CLI on Windows Machine.

Exercise 176: Install Azure CLI on Windows Machine

Download and Install Azure CLI MSI Installer
https://aka.ms/installazurecliwindows

Accessing Azure CLI
You can access Azure CLI through the Windows Command Prompt (CMD).

Exercise 177: Login to Azure with CLI

1. Open windows CMD> az login. This will open a browser. Enter your azure subscription credentials.

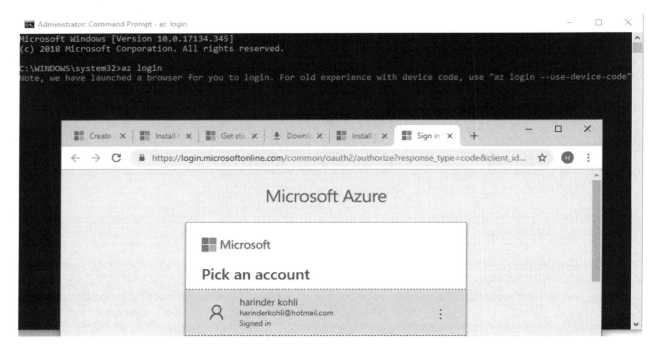

2. After you have successfully authenticated to Azure through Browser, The CMD window will now show Azure information as shown below.

```
Administrator: Command Prompt
Microsoft Windows [Version 10.0.17134.345]
(c) 2018 Microsoft Corporation. All rights reserved.

C:\WINDOWS\system32>az login
Note, we have launched a browser for you to login. For old experience with device code, use "az login --use-device-code"

You have logged in. Now let us find all the subscriptions to which you have access...
[
  {
    "cloudName": "AzureCloud",
    "id": "d293caf2-261c-4101-848a-c7e69524dc3a",
    "isDefault": true,
    "name": "Pay-As-You-Go",
    "state": "Enabled",
    "tenantId": "37f410dd-05ca-42c2-997a-24223270b9aa",
    "user": {
      "name": "harinderkohli@hotmail.com",
      "type": "user"
    }
  }
]

C:\WINDOWS\system32>
```

35333009R00308

Made in the USA
San Bernardino, CA
09 May 2019